Unscripted

ALSO BY JAMES B. STEWART

Deep State: Trump, the FBI, and the Rule of Law

*Tangled Webs: How False Statements Are Undermining
America: From Martha Stewart to Bernie Madoff*

Disney War: The Battle for the Magic Kingdom

*Heart of a Soldier: A Story of Love, Heroism, and
September 11th*

*Blind Eye: The Terrifying Story of a
Doctor Who Got Away with Murder*

Blood Sport: The President and His Adversaries

Den of Thieves

*The Prosecutors: Inside the Offices of the
Government's Most Powerful Lawyers*

*The Partners: Inside America's
Most Powerful Law Firms*

Unscripted

The Epic Battle for a Media Empire and
the Redstone Family Legacy

JAMES B. STEWART

and

RACHEL ABRAMS

PENGUIN PRESS ★ NEW YORK ★ 2023

PENGUIN PRESS
An imprint of Penguin Random House LLC
penguinrandomhouse.com

Image Credits

Insert page 1 (top): Jeff Kravitz/FilmMagic, Inc., (bottom): Reuters/
Fred Prouser/Alamy Stock Photo; page 2 (top): Kevin Winter/Getty Images,
(bottom): Jeffrey Mayer/WireImage; page 3 (top): Alberto E. Rodriguez/
Getty Images, (bottom): Stefanie Keenan/Getty Images for LACMA;
page 4 (top): David Crotty/Patrick McMullan via Getty Images, (middle):
© 1996 Lynn Goldsmith, (bottom): Lina Rueda; page 5 (top): Stefanie
Keenan/Getty Images for Hammer Museum, (bottom): Kevin Mazur/
WireImage; page 6 (top): Pat Greenhouse/The Boston Globe via Getty
Images, (bottom): Reuters/Kevork Djansezian/Alamy Stock Photo;
page 7 (top): Barry King/Alamy Stock Photo, (middle): Marcus Yam/
Los Angeles Times via Contour RA by Getty Images, (bottom): David
Livingston/Getty Images; page 8 (top): Antoine Antoniol/Getty Images,
(bottom): Todd Williamson/Invision for LA Friendly House/AP Images.

Library of Congress Cataloging-in-Publication Data

Names: Stewart, James B., author. | Abrams, Rachel (Journalist), author.
Title: Unscripted : the epic battle for a media empire and the Redstone
family legacy / James B. Stewart, Rachel Abrams.
Description: New York : Penguin Press, 2023. |
Includes bibliographical references and index.
Identifiers: LCCN 2022030865 |
ISBN 9781984879424 (hardcover) | ISBN 9781984879431 (ebook)
Subjects: LCSH: Viacom Inc. | CBS Corp. | Corporations—United States |
Mass media—United States—Management. | Redstone, Sumner |
Redstone, Shari | Moonves, Leslie | Executives—United States—Biography
Classification: LCC HD2796.P373 S73 2023 |
DDC 658.1/145—dc23/eng/20221104
LC record available at https://lccn.loc.gov/2022030865

Printed in the United States of America
1st Printing

Designed by Amanda Dewey

FROM JAMES:
For Benjamin Weil

FROM RACHEL:
For my parents, Alice and Ian

Contents

You are seeing a great company in a civil war and there are bodies all over the road.

—Leslie Moonves, former chairman and chief executive of CBS, in confidential testimony on September 9, 2018

Preface

I can say every report about CBS' toxic work environment is true," the October 2018 email to *The New York Times* tip line read. "This case enrages me so much, and it breaks my heart to look behind the curtain and see the ugliness and moral bankruptcy of institutions and people I admired since childhood."

The "case" was that of CBS chairman and chief executive Leslie Moonves. Moonves had resigned just a month earlier, the same day *The New Yorker* published the second of two articles detailing the accounts of twelve women accusing him of unwanted sexual advances. CBS had launched an internal investigation to determine, among other issues, whether Moonves should receive $120 million in severance pay.

In many ways Moonves's sudden departure had been only the beginning of the story. At the *Times*, the two of us—media reporter Rachel Abrams and business columnist James B. Stewart—were separately pursuing different angles. Rachel, who'd contributed to Jodi Kantor and Megan Twohey's Pulitzer Prize–winning coverage of movie executive Harvey Weinstein, was focusing on the CBS internal investigation. Was the company really trying to get to the bottom of what had happened, or—as with so many self-directed corporate investigations—was it trying to sweep the scandal under the rug and protect other powerful interests? James was exploring the inner workings of the CBS board and how it had handled the accusations against its chief executive.

After the email landed in the *Times*'s "tip jar," a screener forwarded it to Jim Windolf, the *Times*'s media editor. He in turn sent it to Rachel. She was heading out that day when she passed James at his desk in the *Times*'s third-floor newsroom. They barely knew each other, but Rachel paused because she'd heard he, too, was looking into Moonves and CBS. She described the email, and he was excited: the source sounded like someone who could both confirm and expand upon what he was hearing from other people, which was that the real reasons for Moonves's departure had been far more intriguing than reported and had even involved an attempt at extortion.

Rachel spoke to the source that evening. Her impression was that the source's motive for reaching out and putting a career at risk was altruistic: having closely followed the #MeToo movement, this person didn't want to see men get away with abusing their power by exploiting women and then covering it up. Rachel felt the source was equally interested in the structures that enabled such behavior—in this case a public corporation. She was confident the source had no allegiance to any of the warring factions at CBS.

This source became one of a number of people who turned over hundreds of pages of original material—emails, texts, interview notes, internal reports—documenting an astonishing saga of sex, lies, and betrayal at the highest levels of a major corporation.

At CBS, the #MeToo movement had collided explosively with the corporate boardroom. Moonves was the first chief executive of a major publicly traded company forced to resign for predatory sexual conduct. (The much smaller Weinstein Company was privately owned.)

And Moonves wasn't just any chief executive. As a leading media and entertainment company with a vaunted news division, CBS had an outsize influence on American politics and culture. Under Moonves's leadership, the CBS network had gone from last to first place in the ratings and stayed there for over ten years. CBS stock had more than doubled in price. *The Hollywood Reporter* named Moonves the most powerful person in entertainment. He had earned over $700 million during his tenure, making him one of the highest-paid chief executives in the country.

For all his power and influence, Moonves still reported to a board of directors with the power to hire, fire, or otherwise discipline or reward him. At CBS, members of the board included a former secretary of defense, a former head of the NAACP, the former dean of Harvard Law School, and an Academy Award–winning film producer. But they could be replaced by a controlling shareholder that exercised 80 percent of the shareholders' voting rights.

That controlling shareholder was National Amusements Incorporated, a movie theater chain and holding company for a media empire assembled by the ninety-five-year-old and increasingly infirm Sumner M. Redstone. Sumner owned Viacom (the entertainment company that included Paramount Pictures and cable channels MTV, Comedy Central, and Nickelodeon) and CBS. In recent years he had largely ceded control to his sixty-four-year-old daughter, Shari Redstone, who was vice chair of both the CBS and Viacom boards and might—or might not—be his heir apparent.

Shari Redstone was in many ways an unwilling participant, dragged into the drama because her father's increasingly erratic and bizarre behavior threatened his family's fortune and legacy—everything he'd spent decades building. She was largely unversed in the ways of Hollywood, unprepared for the all-male bastion and deep-seated gender stereotypes that greeted her, and repeatedly underestimated, especially by her own father.

Moonves and his allies found Shari's attempts to assert herself and play a role in running CBS to be intolerable. Just months before he was forced to resign, Moonves had declared war on the Redstone family by seeking to strip them of their voting power. One of the mysteries we confronted was why Moonves would have unleashed a corporate civil war knowing (as he did) that his predatory sexual past was at great and imminent risk of being publicly revealed.

Of course, the great media moguls—from Louis B. Mayer, Adolph Zukor, Ted Turner, John Malone, Rupert Murdoch, and Redstone himself—had never worried about such issues. They were all white men whose power and authority went unquestioned no matter how unbridled their outbursts of temper or insensitive or even bigoted their treatment of women and minorities.

Their boards of directors, charged with protecting all shareholders, were little more than window dressing for their autocratic control. Sumner boasted that the Viacom board had never defied his wishes.

In their world, sexual indiscretions were as routine as deals cut on the eighteenth tee at the Bel Air Country Club. Though hardly confined to the business of media and entertainment, the notion of the "casting couch"—sex in return for a job or a part—got its name in Hollywood. Rumors about Harvey Weinstein, the head of Miramax and then the Weinstein Company, had circulated for years without getting in the way of his many Academy Awards. If anything, it was the women who bore the brunt of the criticism—the "bimbos" using sex to extort something from powerful men. The veteran Hollywood producer and CBS board member Arnold Kopelson seemed baffled by concerns over Moonves's alleged sexual advances in the workplace. "We all did that," he said dismissively.

Hollywood's traditional business model had thrived for decades on cable fees and theatrical film rentals. That was the model Sumner Redstone had mastered and dominated. It had made him a billionaire. But at CBS—as well as every other major media and entertainment company—that world was crumbling under the combined assault of technological advances and changing cultural norms. Netflix, the entertainment streaming service that had already crushed Viacom's Blockbuster DVD-rental business, had nearly 210 million global subscribers.

It was creating its own content in direct competition with Viacom's Paramount Pictures and CBS television. The new world of direct-to-consumer streaming and cable cord-cutting called for a radical change in strategy at every traditional media company.

The workplace was also undergoing radical change—not just from #MeToo but from a reinvigorated Black Lives Matter movement and ongoing advances in lesbian, gay, bisexual, and transgender rights. The chief executive as autocrat was giving way to a more plural, democratic governance model that recognized the competing interests of diverse customers, employees, and communities as well as shareholders.

All these forces played out in Redstone's media empire. They unleashed a torrent of litigation among the warring factions fighting for dominance as Sumner's authoritarian grip weakened and his daughter tried to assert herself. While the clashes at Viacom and CBS may have been especially bitter and personal, the same forces are colliding to varying degrees at every public company confronted with generational turnover, fast-changing technology, and rapidly evolving social norms.

Many of the often-startling twists in the Redstone saga made headlines in the tabloids, Hollywood trade publications, the national media, even Sumner's own CBS News. But these stories only hinted at the drama inside Sumner's lavish Beverly Hills mansion, Paramount's Times Square headquarters, the CBS boardroom at Black Rock, and previously secret legal proceedings in courthouses from Los Angeles to Boston to Delaware.

Our reporting led us to a cast of characters that included not just top corporate executives, board members, and Redstone family members but glamorous paramours, a former soap opera and reality-TV star, a down-at-the-heels talent agent mounting a comeback, and a celebrity matchmaker, all drawn to the spoils of a multibillion-dollar fortune and the mythmaking allure of Hollywood.

As we dug deeper into the story over three years of reporting, we gained access to hundreds of pages of original material. We obtained additional information from court files, much of it sealed from public view. With litigation continuing—and the threat of more lawsuits hovering over every participant—many sources asked to remain confidential. The source who initially reached out to the *Times* declined to be identified or cooperate further for this book. Other sources are identified in the notes.

All of this material afforded a detailed and unprecedented look at the usually secret inner workings of two public companies, their boards of directors, and a wealthy family in the throes of seismic change. For many of these people, money, power—even love—was never enough.

The drama that unfolded may have occurred at Viacom and CBS, but the recent drumbeat of greed, backstabbing, plotting, and betrayal at the upper levels of American business and society has hardly been confined to one or two companies or one wealthy family and its hangers-on. It's no wonder there has been a growing backlash against what many Americans see as self-serving entertainment and business elites who, no matter how bad their behavior or serious the consequences, emerge with their fortunes intact or even enhanced, ready and able to step out onto the next red carpet that lands at their feet.

Unscripted

Trailer

Actor George Pilgrim wasn't getting many parts these days, but he still scanned the trades. On June 25, 2014, he noticed an item about the billionaire Sumner Redstone: "Sydney Holland, the 43-year-old girlfriend of the 91-year-old mogul, has been waging litigation for 10 months against Heather Naylor, a singer who starred on the short-lived MTV series *The Electric Barbarellas*," *The Hollywood Reporter* disclosed.

There was a photo of Holland next to a frail-looking Redstone, who controlled a media empire ranging from the CBS television network to Paramount Pictures and cable channels MTV, Comedy Central, and Nickelodeon.

Pilgrim thought Holland was gorgeous. And he detested Naylor. Pilgrim was developing a reality-TV series, *Search IV Truth*, about paranormal phenomena and had tangled with her after he tried to recruit one of her employees.

Pilgrim impulsively tapped out a message to Holland on Facebook: "So glad you're taking down Heather Naylor," Pilgrim wrote. "I have so much Shit on her!!! Call me anytime."

At age forty-nine Pilgrim still had the chiseled physique, high cheekbones, blue eyes, and dark-blond hair that had landed him a three-year contract on the long-running soap opera *Guiding Light*, a featured part in the 1994 camp horror classic *Tammy and the T-Rex*, and a role in the

Showtime erotic cable series *Red Shoe Diaries*, which aired in the mid-1990s. In 1996 he was featured in a photo spread, "Hunks in Trunks," in *Cosmopolitan* magazine's All About Men issue. More recently, he'd appeared in an episode of the reality series *Uncovering Aliens* as "one of the foremost experts on the wild, wild UFO West."

Pilgrim also had a prison record and a past that could have come from the pages of *The Talented Mr. Ripley*.

Pilgrim had starred in a VH1 reality-TV series, *Hopelessly Rich*, which chronicled his courtship of Louise Hay, a blond aspiring actress from Scotland. Pilgrim was having an affair with Hay, but little else about the program was true. Pilgrim was not, as he represented himself, George William Randolph Hearst III, the wealthy great-grandson of media tycoon William Randolph Hearst. And Hay did not, as she maintained, have a billionaire father. But on-screen, their romance blossomed. At show's end, a bikini-clad Hay chartered a yacht and popped a bottle of champagne to celebrate, even though "I still can't trust George as far as I can pick him up and lob him."

Pilgrim/Hearst did have the trappings of wealth—a new jet-black BMW 740i, a matching twin-turbo Porsche 911 Carrera, and a mansion in the Hollywood Hills with sweeping views of downtown Los Angeles. He'd even bought at auction Hearst's original desk from San Simeon. Pilgrim's real father had abandoned the family when he was nine, and it comforted and inspired him to think of the great newspaperman as a father figure and mentor. Posing as a Hearst heir also "got me entry to A-list parties, dates with hot women, and acceptance in the circles I'd always longed to travel in," he'd written in a first draft (subsequently deleted) of his autobiography. He was calling his book *Citizen Pilgrim*, the title a reference to Orson Welles's classic *Citizen Kane*.

But the reality show had proved his undoing. He knew appearing on the show was "an insane risk," but "my own stupidity, my own need to stoke my ego" caused him to do it anyway, he wrote.

After billboard ads for *Hopelessly Rich* showed pictures of Pilgrim interspersed with archival footage of William Randolph Hearst, the (real) Hearst family sued him. VH1 pulled the series from distribution. And the feds closed in. Pilgrim pleaded guilty to tax evasion for a scheme in which he sold millions of dollars in ads in nonexistent publications. He'd served two and a half years in Los Angeles's Metropolitan Detention Center. (Pilgrim's costar, Louise Hay—later Louise Linton—married Pilgrim's lawyer, Ronald Richards, divorced him, and eventually married Donald Trump's future treasury secretary Steven Mnuchin.)

Since his release from prison Pilgrim had been living with his mother and stepfather in Sedona, Arizona. While in Los Angeles he stayed with his current girlfriend, Amy Shpall, a former talent agent with an executive producer credit for the Bravo fitness reality show *Work Out*.

Pilgrim no longer partied with celebrity friends like the action director Michael Bay. His acting career had also withered, though he didn't understand why everyone focused on his criminal record rather than his acting talent. Wesley Snipes and Robert Downey Jr. had criminal records, too, but they landed leading roles.

Still, he thought he could join forces with Holland to get his reality show off the ground.

Holland hadn't answered his Facebook post, his tantalizing reference to her nemesis Heather Naylor notwithstanding. That didn't stop Pilgrim. Women had always found him irresistible, as long as he persisted.

"I know who has your laptop," he wrote next. In her lawsuit, Holland alleged Naylor had stolen it.

Still no answer.

"Congrats on your beautiful child!!!" he wrote, referring to Holland's new daughter, Alexandra Red, whom Pilgrim had seen in Holland's Facebook postings.

Then he tried something more sexually explicit: "I think your hot!!" and "Damn I'm hung."

Her continued silence prompted an outburst: "I could say Fuck u!! To not responding!!! But I can't you are a real class act. Call me."

The barrage finally worked.

"Who is this??" Holland wrote back. "Sorry I never read Facebook. I will call you tomorrow and thank you for reaching out to me!"

When Holland called Pilgrim, she told him she cared for a "high-profile individual" and suggested they meet in a very visible location: the rooftop pool at the Peninsula Beverly Hills hotel, an "A-List playground" according to travel website Oyster.

Pilgrim borrowed his girlfriend's BMW to get there. According to Pilgrim, when he got to the rooftop pool area, Holland was sitting at a small cocktail table. She was on one of her three cell phones and held up a manicured finger to acknowledge Pilgrim's arrival while continuing her conversation, which involved some kind of wire transfer of a large sum of money.

Pilgrim's practiced eye quickly took in her Birkin bag, the Rolex watch, the Jimmy Choo shoes. The phone conversation ended and Holland slowly removed her oversize sunglasses to gaze directly at Pilgrim.

All he saw was her blue-lavender eyes.

Holland revealed that the "high-profile individual" she had mentioned was Sumner Redstone. Did Pilgrim know who that was?

He'd heard the name, he said.

Sumner owned the Paramount movie studio, Holland explained. He owned book publisher Simon & Schuster. He was one of the most powerful men in Hollywood. He was a billionaire. Because of her relationship to Sumner, Holland could make things happen for Pilgrim: a book, a movie—anything he wanted.

Pilgrim reached out and touched her hand. He felt something like an electric current.

Pilgrim did tell Holland some of what he knew about Naylor and her relationship to Sumner. But the conversation soon shifted to how Holland could help Pilgrim. She proposed buying the movie rights to

Citizen Pilgrim for her production company. After two hours of intense conversation, they rose to leave.

They were alone as they waited for the elevator. Suddenly Holland grabbed Pilgrim and passionately kissed him.

Downstairs, they parted, and Pilgrim walked alone to his car, which he'd parked at a nearby Starbucks. His cell phone rang.

"Did you feel that?" Holland asked.

He did, but he pointed out he was living with another woman.

"Don't worry about her," Holland said. Holland would take care of him now. Her psychic had just predicted she'd meet someone like him.

Pilgrim contemplated Holland's offer as he drove back along the Pacific Coast Highway. Maybe it was time to stop hustling and just give in.

Season 1

"I'm Going to Hell Anyway"

Of course, Pilgrim knew more about Sumner Redstone than he let on. Everyone in Hollywood and on Wall Street knew who the billionaire mogul was.

And Holland was hardly just Sumner's caregiver. Even *The Hollywood Reporter*'s description of her as his "girlfriend" fell far short of the mark. Unknown beyond a few people in Sumner's family and inner circle, Holland—along with her ally Manuela Herzer—was well on her way to controlling two of America's leading media and entertainment companies.

As Holland had bragged to Pilgrim, she could get Sumner Redstone to do pretty much whatever she wanted, though she left out that she and Sumner were engaged and she had a rare nine-carat canary-yellow diamond ring to prove it. Being Sumner's fiancée, as opposed to wife, conferred certain advantages. There was no need for a prenuptial agreement, and it left Holland free to pursue other interests, both financial and romantic.

In these she was abetted by her alliance with Manuela Herzer, a striking blond who years earlier had dated Sumner after sitting next to him at a dinner party hosted by Sumner's close friend, the producer Robert Evans. Herzer had complained she couldn't get a dinner reservation at the celebrity-studded Hollywood restaurant Dan Tana's. Sumner was a regular—and said he'd take her there the next night.

Sumner was soon calling her "the love of his life." He bought her a $3.85 million house in Beverly Hills and made her a joint tenant of his apartment in New York's Carlyle Hotel. After two years, he'd proposed marriage but Herzer had declined. The affair turned platonic, but the two remained friends and confidants. While Herzer's house was undergoing renovations, she'd moved into the Beverly Park mansion with Sumner and Holland—and stayed.

As a billionaire, Sumner certainly had more than enough wealth to go around. Holland and Herzer hoped Sumner might replace his grandchildren with them in the supposedly irrevocable trust that on his death conveyed his ownership stakes in his media empire. Thanks to Sumner's generosity, the pair had already amassed a vast fortune, a war chest with which to pursue their larger ambitions. They had hired a prominent New York estates lawyer to explore their options. And Holland had already initiated efforts to have Sumner adopt her daughter, Alexandra, putting her in the line of succession.

There was only one major obstacle: Sumner's daughter, Shari Redstone.

At age sixty Shari was petite (five feet two inches tall) and, like her father, spoke with a Boston-area accent. She embraced the dress code of the professional businesswoman, favoring simple black skirts and jewel-toned blazers that set off the reddish-blond hair she had inherited from her father. She owned 20 percent of National Amusements—not enough to control anything, but enough to secure a seat in the boardroom. Shari's relationship with her father was, to put it mildly, complicated. Over the years, she had clashed bitterly with her father, sometimes publicly. At the same time she craved his affection and approval, which he dangled frequently before her (especially when he needed something) but then withdrew. Shari had nonetheless hung on as president of National Amusements and held the title of vice chair and board member at both CBS and Viacom.

Shari, naturally, followed her father's erratic late-life romantic entanglements with mounting dismay. She and Holland maintained, on the surface, a polite coexistence, even though they had little in common. Shari had graduated from law school, practiced law in Boston, raised a family, and held an executive position at National Amusements for years. Holland had skipped college and lurched from one unsuccessful business venture to another (including a dating service for high-net worth men). Before meeting, dating, and moving in with Sumner, she had been constantly pursued by creditors. She wore her glossy, raven hair long, owned an enormous collection of designer shoes, and favored provocative dresses—especially in faux animal prints—that flattered her figure. Above all, she wanted to appear "chic," to use one of her favorite words.

Holland felt she had gone to considerable lengths to reassure and cultivate Shari, insisting that she did her best "to bring the feuding family together." But in Shari's estimation, Holland had done everything she could to drive a wedge between her and her father. By and large, she accepted that her father had made his choice, and it was his life. As she wrote to her children in 2014, "I have come to the conclusion that there is absolutely nothing that I can do" about Holland and Herzer, whom she referred to as "S and M."

Privately, she was far more blunt: "I am not going to that home with Sydney's baby living there," she wrote to her sons after Alexandra was born. In another email to her children, she referred to Holland and Herzer as "whores."

———

Sumner Redstone was hardly the first or last aging single man to fall for a much younger woman. But he was surely one of the richest, with a fortune estimated at over $5 billion that year. And he was one of the most powerful: he would ultimately determine the fate of two major corporations with thousands of shareholders and employees and hold significant roles in the cultural and political life of the nation.

While Sumner maintained a lifelong fixation with the performance and value of his business empire—even into his nineties, he monitored every movement in Viacom's share price on multiple stock tickers mounted inside his home, even in his bedroom—as he grew older, he became increasingly indiscreet about his personal life.

Close colleagues watched in dismay as the once-brilliant, driven businessman developed a bizarre fixation on eternal life and indulged himself in long-suppressed sexual impulses. It would be difficult to pinpoint exactly when, but over the years his indiscretions began to affect his companies. His film and television executives grumbled about the women their boss suddenly wanted on a TV show, in a meeting, or working at Viacom. The luckiest women he dated wound up with millions of dollars in cash, expensive houses, Viacom stock, and other assets.

Perhaps Sumner was making up for lost time. He had come from modest circumstances. He was born in 1923 to Bella (later Belle) and Max (later Michael) Rothstein, known as Mickey, who anglicized the family name to Redstone. The family lived briefly in a Boston tenement with no bathroom, according to Sumner. His father "peddled linoleum," Sumner wrote, moved into the liquor business, and eventually owned two drive-in movie theaters through a company Sumner later christened National Amusements Incorporated, often abbreviated as NAI. Eventually the family, now flush, took up residence in Boston's stately Copley Plaza Hotel.

"My mother had one dedication in her life, which was my education," he wrote in his 2001 autobiography, the aptly titled *A Passion to Win*. He told colleagues that his mother punished him if he made a mistake in piano lessons or failed to earn a perfect grade at the prestigious Boston Latin School. At the same time, she doted on him while all but ignoring his brother.

Sumner graduated at the top of his class from Boston Latin, a feat that earned him guaranteed admission and a scholarship to Harvard College. "I had no social life. I had no friends," he wrote. "I knew that any girl I took out would not be good enough for my mother."

At Harvard he "studied all the time." In just two years he had enough credits to graduate. He excelled at languages, mastering formidably difficult Japanese, and in 1943, before graduating, he joined the military to help crack Japanese codes. Harvard eventually granted him his degree (although he hadn't completed the four-year residency requirement) and he went on to Harvard Law School. The next year, at twenty-four, he married Phyllis Raphael, the blond, vivacious daughter of a prosperous department store owner whom Sumner met at a temple dance (even though her wealthy family looked down on the Redstones). Their son, Brent, was born in 1951, and Shari in 1954. Sumner joined the family drive-in movie business and ruthlessly outmaneuvered his brother for control. Beginning in the 1960s, he converted the drive-ins into a chain of movie theaters, building multiscreen indoor cinemas on the drive-ins' suburban sites. Sumner coined the word *multiplex*. He developed a prodigious knowledge of the movie distribution business and was obsessed with his theaters' ticket sales. He knew every film playing on every screen and memorized the weekend box office.

He was a micromanager, and little escaped his attention. When *Jaws* opened at a National Amusements theater in Davenport, Iowa (population 100,000), he personally wrote to the editor of the *Quad-City Times* to compliment the newspaper's review of the blockbuster shark thriller as unusually "perceptive" and "brilliant film-making."

A formative experience of Sumner's adult life was a fire that occurred in March 1979 while he was staying at the Copley Plaza, the same hotel where he'd once lived with his parents. With the fire raging outside his room, Sumner escaped through a window and hung from a ledge as flames engulfed his hand and arm from inside the window frame. "The pain was excruciating but I refused to let go," he wrote in his autobiography. After being rescued from the ledge by a hook-and-ladder fire truck, Sumner required sixty hours of surgery at Massachusetts General Hospital. Even then, his right hand was permanently deformed, little more than a gnarled claw.

In his book, Sumner maintained that the near-death experience didn't change him in the least: he was always fiercely driven to succeed, and "the will to win is the will to survive." But others detected a growing sense of invincibility. After the fire his ambitions expanded. His little-known National Amusements chain began buying large stakes in major entertainment companies: Twentieth Century Fox, Warner Communications, MGM Films, Columbia Pictures, and Time, Inc. The 1980s saw the emergence of the Michael Milken–financed corporate raiders, and Sumner joined their ranks.

His opponents consistently underestimated his business acumen and fierce determination. Viacom management, who bid against him in 1987, belittled him as a provincial Boston theater operator, an impression reinforced when Sumner showed up at Viacom's New York headquarters wearing a sports jacket he'd just bought at the discount chain Filene's Basement—with the tags still on it.

In his contest with media titan Barry Diller to acquire Paramount Communications in 1994, he ignored his bankers' financial projections and told Viacom's chief financial officer, Tom Dooley, "I just want to beat Barry. Do what we have to do to win." In his biggest conquest ever, Viacom paid $40 billion for CBS in 2000. Buoyed by the surging popularity of cable, the value of Sumner's assets soared. In October 2000 *Forbes* estimated his net worth at an astonishing $14 billion.

At the ripe old age of seventy-seven, Sumner Redstone had arrived as a full-fledged Hollywood mogul. In 2012 he got a star on Hollywood's Walk of Fame. For the ever-driven Sumner, that wasn't enough. He repeatedly told Viacom's communications director, Carl Folta, he wanted to be on the cover of *Time* magazine.

U nmentioned in Sumner's dramatic account of his escape from the Copley Plaza was his longtime lover and companion Delsa Winer, who exited the hotel window ahead of him and emerged largely unharmed.

At least in those days Sumner was discreet. He extolled his devotion to family in *A Passion to Win*. Phyllis accompanied him to high-profile events like the Academy Awards even as he led a parallel life with Winer (she dropped the *e* after her divorce). He bought her a house and often stayed with her in suburban Lincoln, Massachusetts. Though he still found the time to take his daughter, Shari, out for ice cream, it could hardly have escaped Shari's notice that her father was frequently absent. Phyllis tolerated all this up to a point. Twice she'd sued Sumner for divorce, once in 1984 and again in 1993. Phyllis had a shrewd sense of timing, leveling her threats just as Sumner was focusing on new takeover targets. Both times he'd persuaded her to drop the suits out of fear she'd claim half his assets, thereby forcing him to break up his growing empire.

But when accounts of an affair with Christine Peters turned up in the tabloids in 1999, Phyllis was publicly humiliated. Peters, blond with prominent cheekbones, was a former model and the ex-wife of Hollywood producer and former hairdresser Jon Peters, though the couple had separated just two months after their wedding. Christine worked for Sumner's close friend producer Robert Evans, who first introduced her to Sumner. Evans, a notorious womanizer and sybarite, not only was Sumner's friend but also had a lucrative production deal with Viacom's Paramount Pictures. Soon after meeting, Sumner and Peters were spotted by paparazzi vacationing together in Sardinia. Phyllis hired a private detective, who produced photos of Sumner and Peters holding hands in Paris after dining at the famed La Tour d'Argent restaurant. After the Rupert Murdoch–owned *New York Post* plastered photos of the pair on its front page, Sumner flew into a towering rage witnessed by top Viacom executives. Using a string of expletives colorful even by Sumner's standards, he blamed his rival media mogul Murdoch, convinced that he was behind the embarrassing publicity. (The *Post* had actually bought the photos from the photographer working for Phyllis.)

Armed with evidence of Sumner's infidelity, Phyllis filed for divorce, citing both "adultery" and "cruel and unusual treatment." She demanded half of his fortune, a share to which she was entitled under Massachusetts law. This time Phyllis didn't back down, and her lawyers embarked on protracted negotiations. An exasperated Sumner told his daughter, Shari, that he'd never marry again.

The Peters affair also brought down the curtain on Sumner's long relationship with Winer, now in her early seventies. She, too, felt betrayed after reading the tabloid coverage. Still, Sumner sent her huge flower bouquets on her birthday for the rest of her life.

Despite his vow to never marry again, Sumner proposed marriage to Peters almost immediately after divorcing Phyllis. She declined. "I just didn't see myself married to him because he was so demanding and got his way in everything he did," she later wrote in a *Hollywood Reporter* essay. Her refusal infuriated him. He dictated and faxed her a letter saying he hated her, but as was typical with his outbursts, a week later he was pleading for her friendship. Peters disclosed that their ensuing platonic relationship continued for eighteen years despite his public "rudeness"—"he had been banned from every restaurant in L.A."—which included an incident in Hawaii during which Sumner summoned a chef to his table, then threw his steak at him, claiming it was overcooked.

"Why are you so mean to people?" Peters asked.

"I don't care," he replied. "I'm going to hell anyway."

Peters indulged him and continued to have lunch with him at his regular table at the Hotel Bel-Air.

With his $14 billion fortune and control of movie and television studios, there was no shortage of women willing, even eager, to be seen with Sumner, an unlikely lothario at any age, least of all pushing eighty. He was six feet tall and had once had thick, wavy reddish-blond hair, perhaps his best feature, though he now dyed it varying shades of pink. (One of his advisers witnessed Sumner applying the dye himself in a bathroom of his Carlyle Hotel apartment.) He had a weak chin and rounded cheekbones. Although he worked out with a trainer and was obsessed with antioxidants and vitamins, his physique was pear-shaped. He wore unfashionably wide, flamboyant ties, often set off by a black or dark-colored shirt.

That hadn't deterred Herzer from embarking on an affair with him. When she and Sumner met, she'd been taking tennis lessons at Evans's estate. Herzer was born in Argentina and was a naturalized American citizen. Her family must have been reasonably affluent: she'd been educated in France and was conversant in several languages. She'd already gone through a bitter divorce and at least one affair and had three children, two—Bryan and Christina—with her former husband, Eric Chamchoum, scion of a wealthy Lebanese family based in Nigeria; and the third—Kathrine—with her then-boyfriend Larry Hansel, founder of the Rampage teen clothing line. That relationship ended after Hansel went to court and got a restraining order against Herzer "based on allegations that she had physically attacked him in front of their daughter."

Despite a wealthy former husband and a romantic partner with whom she'd had a child, Herzer appears to have struggled to maintain an affluent Beverly Hills lifestyle. Judging from a series of lawsuits filed against her at the time by auto lease companies, a Century City condo association, and even her divorce lawyer, Herzer seems to have been dodging creditors. But she continued spending money on designer clothes, shoes, and jewelry, all to wear while mingling with Hollywood moguls.

So it's somewhat surprising that Herzer turned down Sumner's marriage proposal. Her only public explanation was that she wanted to devote herself to her children and wasn't interested in marrying again. Perhaps, like Holland, she'd realized that in twenty-first-century America marriage wasn't the only—or even the best—route to wealth and financial security.

After being rejected by Peters and Herzer, and still in negotiations over his divorce from Phyllis, Sumner found himself living alone in luxury hotels and searching for women to date. His mood swings and erratic romantic behavior became more pronounced. Steven Sweetwood, Sumner's stepnephew and a stockbroker who handled Viacom's stock buybacks, decided the answer might be a woman from an entirely different milieu than Hollywood. Sweetwood set Sumner up on a blind date with an elementary school teacher in Manhattan named Paula Fortunato, a friend of a colleague of his at Bear Stearns.

Fortunato, age thirty-eight, was living in a one-bedroom apartment on the Upper East Side. She'd never heard of Sumner Redstone or, for that matter, Viacom. Sumner was, by his own account, instantly smitten by the attractive brunette. After their first dinner, at Manhattan's Il Postino restaurant, he had a messenger deliver a packet of press clippings about him. He immediately asked her for another date.

Soon his limousine was routinely waiting to pick her up outside P.S. 158, where she taught third grade. They'd fly on the Viacom plane for weekends in Los Angeles, staying in suites at the luxurious Bel-Air or Beverly Hills hotels. They described themselves as inseparable. Sumner soon proposed marriage by offering her a choice from a tray filled with engagement rings. Fortunato picked one, although at first she was reluctant to wear it. But after Sumner prodded her, she showed off the ring at a restaurant dinner with talk show host Larry King.

After three years of intense negotiations, Sumner finally worked out a settlement with Phyllis that left him in full control of National Amusements and by extension Viacom and CBS. The divorce was finalized in 2002. Sumner would continue to vote all the shares. In return, the shares themselves would be placed in an irrevocable trust for the benefit of Sumner while he lived, and then, after he died or became incapacitated, into a trust for his and Phyllis's children and grandchildren. There were five nonfamily trustees in addition to Sumner and Phyllis: George Abrams, a courtly, Harvard-trained Boston lawyer who advised Sumner in his divorce; David Andelman, his estate planning attorney; Philippe Dauman, his longtime corporate lawyer and a Viacom executive; and two other lawyers. Sumner and his staunch allies controlled a solid majority, and should anyone's loyalty to Sumner falter, Sumner retained the power to replace them.

As part of the settlement, Sumner also gave Phyllis half of his large stake in a pinball machine and video games maker, Midway Games, best known for its *Mortal Kombat* franchise, the fantasy fighting game introduced in 1992. Sumner knew Midway's management, since its pinball games had long been a fixture in National Amusement theaters, and seemed to think Midway was on the brink of a new hit game and corporate turnaround.

———

Redstone and Fortunato were married the following April at Temple Emanu-El on Fifth Avenue. Tony Bennett, Sumner's favorite singer, sang at the reception at the New York Public Library.

Having gotten a taste of the Hollywood lifestyle while dating Peters and Herzer, Sumner took his new bride to Beverly Hills. He paid close to $16 million for a sprawling eight-bedroom house with sweeping views of downtown Los Angeles from its infinity pool and adjoining hot tub. The seller and next-door neighbor in the gated Beverly Park enclave was actor Sylvester Stallone.

Sumner cultivated exotic koi in a front-yard pond with a waterfall, installed an elaborate tropical fish tank (the world's largest, he maintained) inside the house, and surrounded himself with TV screens constantly tuned to CNBC and Viacom's stock price. He operated as though he were still on eastern time. He'd rise at 4:00 a.m., don a robe, and settle into a soft chair near his fish tank to begin making calls to his East Coast–based executives.

Chief among them was Philippe Dauman at Viacom. The two were so close that a Viacom executive told *New York Times* reporter Amy Chozick that Dauman was "the son Sumner wishes he had" (much to Shari's dismay). Their relationship had been forged over more than three decades, ever since Dauman as a young lawyer at Shearman & Sterling had shrewdly attached himself to his firm's biggest client by personally delivering documents to Sumner at his Carlyle apartment. Over the years, Dauman guided Sumner through the hostile takeover of Viacom and the acquisitions of Paramount and then CBS. "We shed a lot of blood, sweat and tears in a very long process," Dauman said, as reported in the *Times*, trench warfare that made Dauman one of Sumner's "closest advisors and colleagues," as Dauman put it.

Sumner admired Dauman's intelligence—he had scored a perfect 1600 on the SAT when he was just thirteen—and his Columbia Law School pedigree. Dauman's parents were French and he'd attended the Lycée Français growing up in Manhattan, where his father was a photographer for *Life* magazine (he shot portraits of Marilyn Monroe and Jacqueline Kennedy). As an adult, Dauman always insisted on the French pronunciation of his name.

But his most conspicuous quality was his unswerving loyalty to Sumner, a fealty that bordered on the obsequious. Sumner is "the smartest person I've ever met," Dauman once gushed to the *Times*.

Loyalty was a virtue that Sumner, like many media moguls of his generation, both prized and demanded in his subordinates. It was no coincidence that his favorite movie was Paramount's *The Godfather*, the 1972 blockbuster whose characters elevated loyalty, nepotism, and the Mafia code of omertà over the rule of law. The title consciously invoked the Sicilian primacy of blood ties and quasi-family relationships in a world where no one else could be trusted. Sumner, too, constantly extolled the importance of family, notwithstanding his sexual indiscretions. He rewarded his surrogate son Dauman by making him a trustee of the Sumner M. Redstone National Amusements Trust and a Viacom board member. Dauman became Viacom's chief executive in 2006.

Sumner's next call was usually to Les Moonves, the actor–turned–television executive whose competitive drive propelled him into the upper ranks of Hollywood. In contrast to the cerebral, balding Dauman, a rare and awkward presence at red carpet events, Moonves was gregarious, handsome, charismatic, and firmly ensconced on Hollywood's A-list. He'd grown up in Valley Stream, Long Island, a middle-class suburb where boys all seemed to have nicknames ending in *y* (Moonves was "Moony"). He started acting at age nine at Camp Tioga in the Catskills and played basketball on the Temple Gates of Zion team.

Moonves broke into television with roles in *The Six Million Dollar Man* and *Cannon* and moved to Los Angeles, where he met and married the actress Nancy Wiesenfeld. He soon realized his future lay in producing rather than acting. He rose rapidly through the ranks of Lorimar Television, the producer of the hits *Dallas* and *Falcon Crest*. After Lorimar merged with Warner Bros., he became president of Warner Bros. Television and secured his place in television history by producing the NBC megahits *Friends* and *E.R.* He joined CBS in 1995 and vaulted the network from last to first place in the ratings on the strength of hits like *Survivor, CSI, NCIS,* and *Cold Case.* His ratings success earned him the nickname "the man with the golden gut."

Still, the once-struggling actor in Moonves never seemed far from the surface. Friends in a men's support group he joined in the mid-1980s thought it was what gave him his palpable drive to succeed. Moonves was intensely competitive, whether on the basketball court in pickup games or in charades—a game at which he excelled. "This is too intense for me," the famously intense producer Brian Grazer (*A Beautiful Mind*) observed after one charades session.

Like Sumner, Moonves was an entertainment mogul from the old school: he, too, quoted from *The Godfather* and prized loyalty in his subordinates. Unlike the lawyerly Dauman, he had his hand in every creative aspect of the business but delegated financial and legal details.

Delighted by CBS's ratings success and accompanying profits, Sumner largely left Moonves alone to run CBS as he saw fit. As he told a *Times* interviewer in 2004, he let Moonves "run with the ball."

Dauman may well have aspired to similar autonomy. Shari, for one, blamed Dauman for encouraging her father's move to the West Coast, which she saw as an attempt to distance Sumner both from his daughter and from Viacom headquarters, thereby cementing Dauman's control.

———

I n 2006 Sumner agreed to cooperate with a *Vanity Fair* profile. Moonves was pressed into service to extol the virtues of Sumner's new wife: "There's no question, Paula brings out the better side of Sumner Redstone. Paula doesn't take any guff from him. She'll say, 'Sumner, behave yourself.' I don't know if it's true, but I hear she gives him demerits if he misbehaves. He's on a point system."

But the article garnered far more attention for its unsparing depiction of Sumner at the age of eighty-three: "He looks frail and has a senior moment or three, losing his train of thought, repeating stories, and asking that a question or two be repeated," wrote the reporter Bryan Burrough. Worse, as the interview ended, Sumner rose to shake the reporter's hand, tilted to one side, and collapsed.

Just months later, the Hollywood writer Nikki Finke reported on an angry outburst between Sumner and Paula in front of numerous onlookers at the premiere of the Paramount film *Stardust*, followed by a "meltdown" by Sumner at Dan Tana's—the celebrity hangout where he'd once courted Manuela Herzer. Soon Sumner was again squiring Christine Peters, who now had a production deal at CBS. And Herzer was back on the scene as well. Sumner confided in both women, telling Herzer that his relationship with Paula was "horrible" and Peters that "I'm so unhappy."

A media firestorm soon ensued over a different incident. After Tom Cruise appeared on *The Oprah Winfrey Show* and proclaimed his undying love for his pregnant girlfriend, the actress Katie Holmes, Paula voiced to Sumner her objections to Cruise's behavior. Sumner soon ejected the Hollywood megastar from Lucille Ball's former quarters on the Paramount lot and terminated the studio's fourteen-year relationship with him. Much of the publicity surrounding the news was unflattering to Sumner. "It's absurd for Redstone to make an issue of Cruise's conduct like he has," Finke wrote. "My god, Sumner himself was openly *shtupping* one of his producer girlfriends on the lot for years," referring to Peters. "And Redstone looked the other way when Les Moonves carried on a long adulterous affair with employee Julie Chen and then married her after dumping his wife in the process. Which are all violations of so many corporate codes of conduct that I don't think I can count that high."

But Paula was soon to vanish from Sumner's life. Citing the usual irreconcilable differences, Sumner filed for divorce from Paula in October 2008. He was gracious toward her in his public comments, noting that the financial terms of their divorce settlement went far beyond anything mandated in their prenuptial agreement, and he said the two would remain companions. He bought her a $4 million house in Beverly Hills and a $2.6 million condo in Florida.

"Sumner in a Skirt"

No one had been more surprised by Sumner's sudden marriage to Paula than Shari, given Sumner's vow to never marry again. But if that was what made her father happy, so be it, even if Paula was eight years younger than her new stepdaughter.

Both of Sumner's children had initially embarked on independent careers far removed from the family theater chain and their father's increasingly ambitious media and entertainment acquisitions. Like their father, both had earned law degrees: Brent at Syracuse University in 1976 after following in his father's undergraduate footsteps at Harvard; Shari at Boston University in 1978 after graduating from Tufts. Brent became a prosecutor in Boston; Shari joined a law firm where she practiced corporate, trusts and estates, and criminal law until she had a third child in 1987.

But this didn't mean that they could entirely extract themselves from their father's empire, given that each owned one sixth of National Amusements under the trust arrangement reached when their parents divorced. Also, Shari's husband, Ira A. Korff, who was both a lawyer and an Orthodox rabbi descended from a prominent line of Hasidic Jews, had joined National Amusements after they married in 1980. Sumner, increasingly preoccupied with Viacom, found it reassuring to have a family member involved in the running of National Amusements. Korff was subsequently named the company's president.

By all accounts Korff was an effective president of National Amusements. He oversaw the company's successful first international expansion into the United Kingdom. In contrast to the tempestuous Sumner, who swore, yelled at employees in meetings, and repeatedly fired them (only to relent the next day), Korff was calm and evenhanded. But by the late 1980s his distinguished Jewish lineage weighed heavily on him. He became increasingly spiritual and was less interested in movie grosses and lease deals. He grew a beard, dressed in black, and began to go by Yitzhak Aharon Korff, no longer Ira. He and Shari divorced in 1992, the same year Korff bought the weekly publication *The Jewish Advocate* and became its publisher. Still, Sumner said the divorce had no effect on his close relationship with Korff, who was, after all, still the father of his grandchildren. Sumner persuaded Korff to stay on at National Amusements in a more limited role, and though Korff resigned as president in 1994, he remained on the payroll as a consultant until 2009.

Sumner would periodically cajole his children to join the family business full-time, hinting that one or both would someday succeed him as chief executive and chair. Brent had finally agreed and joined the National Amusements board in 1992, but Shari seemed more determined to keep her distance. Even after leaving her law firm to focus on her growing family, she pursued a master's degree in social work, anticipating a career change.

But after her divorce, suddenly a single mother, Shari needed at least a part-time job. Her father stepped in, saying she could work at National Amusements two days a week. He also offered her board seats at Viacom and CBS. She declined but he persisted, "pushing her" to join, as she described it. She finally gave in in 1994, joining the boards and taking the job of vice president of corporate strategy at National Amusements. She expanded the chain in markets where it already dominated; helped push into new markets in Russia and South America; and confronted the growing challenge of home entertainment on the internet by upgrading theaters and introducing luxury touches like gourmet food, craft cocktails, and valet parking. This was a radical change, since for decades the focus in the theater business was getting patrons in and out as quickly and efficiently as possible. Now Shari wanted them to linger in the multiplexes—and spend more money.

Shari was convinced that change was inevitable, so better to get ahead of it. She also had little attachment to the status quo, perhaps because her father had never let her become comfortable with it.

Sumner seemed delighted, gushing in a 2002 *Forbes* interview, "Nobody in the entertainment industry is rising as fast as Shari," and going so far as to compare her to himself: "It's like father, like daughter: She has no major weakness. She is a great businesswoman."

Sumner made no mention of Brent. Earlier that year Sumner had tried to buy back Brent's and Shari's National Amusements stakes as part of his effort to retain control after his divorce from Phyllis. To gain Shari's support, he dangled the prospect of a much bigger role for her at his companies, even promising to name her as his successor. Shari had agreed in principle, but Brent refused to sell his stake and had sided with his mother in the divorce. Although Brent was still a director of both Viacom and National Amusements, his responsibilities at the companies dwindled. Brent maintained that his father never forgave him and retaliated by sidelining him.

Shari, not Brent, was named Sumner's successor as chair in the 2002 divorce settlement, and a year later Sumner removed Brent as a Viacom director. He threatened to eject him from the National Amusements board as well.

The last straw came at a Viacom board meeting where Brent made a presentation about his plans for Showtime, Viacom's premium cable network. Sumner erupted in a stream of profanity and criticism, belittling Brent as Shari and other directors watched in horrified silence. Brent walked out of the meeting and never came back. He and his family moved to a 625-acre ranch in Colorado. National Amusements nonetheless continued to pay him more than $1 million a year. (He needed the salary, since his minority stake in the business was illiquid and paid no dividends.)

That didn't mean Shari's position was all that secure. Armed with her new status as Sumner's heir apparent, Shari began expressing her opinions more openly, even purporting to speak to outsiders on behalf of Viacom. That prompted furious outbursts from Sumner, many witnessed by Viacom management, in which he railed against his daughter's presumption. While she might succeed him as chair, he declared he wasn't about to give her his other title—chief executive—and the real power that went with it. Two years after the divorce settlement, *New York Times* reporter Laura Rich asked Sumner if he planned to name Shari as his successor as chief executive.

"Absolutely, positively, irrevocably: no, no, no," Sumner answered. "She will not have an executive or an operational role at the company. I have said, and I mean it, that it's best for Viacom for her to learn and know as much as she can about the company through interaction with the actual managers because, someday, I hope in the far distant future, I will be gone. And she may then be the controlling stockholder. But she will not be in an executive role."

For her part, Shari was uninterested in titles that conferred no authority. After his comments to the *Times*, Sumner offered her the title of vice chair, which clearly positioned her as his heir apparent. "There has to be a succession plan," he stressed.

But she turned him down, arguing that she was already spending too much time in New York away from her children. She felt guilty when she wasn't there to make them a home-cooked meal even as she embraced her expanding management duties—a tension that, like many women with both children and careers, she never fully resolved.

Sumner didn't want to hear any of this and angrily raised his voice. "Then in that case, I'm throwing you off the board," he said.

"Fine, throw me off," she responded.

She suspected he was bluffing, which proved to be right, since he didn't seek to remove her.

In 2005 Sumner told the *Los Angeles Times* that "control of the company is likely to pass to Shari," and a year later Brent took the extraordinary step of suing to dissolve National Amusements so that he could extract the value of his one-sixth stake, which he assessed then at about $1.3 billion. Sumner was enraged by the lawsuit—as angry as his Viacom colleagues had ever seen him. Brent maintained that his father had stripped him of any meaningful responsibilities; that his position as a director of National Amusements was "nominal"; and that his father and sister had frozen him out of information. Sumner, needless to say, would never have allowed a dissolution of the empire he'd spent his lifetime building. He fought his son vigorously in court and, after losing several attempts to have the suit dismissed, agreed to buy Brent's stake for $240 million—a fortune by any standard but just a fraction of its value. The breach with his son seemed irreparable. Brent vowed never to speak to his father again.

The settlement terms increased Sumner's stake in National Amusements from two thirds to 80 percent, leaving Shari with the remaining 20 percent.

When Shari had joined the company in 1994, management of National Amusements as well as that of the companies it controlled—not to mention the entertainment industry as a whole—was the preserve of men, most of them, like her father, a generation older. Once, when she accompanied her father to Viacom's offices, its then-president, the silver-haired Mel Karmazin, asked sarcastically, "What is this, bring-your-daughter-to-work day?" Karmazin dismissively referred to her as "Sumner in a skirt," a nickname that stuck and circulated widely within the company. Fully aware of this, Shari had trod carefully. When meeting with others, she made a point of showing she was listening. This led to her asking the occasional question and, later, making suggestions.

Even though Shari was his daughter and designated successor as chair, Sumner was often dismissive of her ideas and belittled her in meetings. But after occasional outbursts of temper aimed at his daughter, he'd call Tad Jankowski, a National Amusements executive who had been Sumner's teaching assistant at Boston University decades earlier and had worked for Sumner ever since graduating. "Is Shari okay?" Sumner would ask, and then urge Jankowski to "take care of her."

Sumner may have loved Shari in his way, but as an executive, he held her to the same exacting standards as anyone else who worked for him, perhaps even higher ones. When it came to business, Sumner often treated her as a rival, another competitor to be vanquished. One Father's Day Shari beat him at tennis (Sumner played with a racket strapped to his right arm because of his hand injury). He wouldn't congratulate her. "Aren't you happy I won?" she asked.

"No," he replied.

Another time they played cards on the corporate jet for a penny a point. Dauman was along and joined in the game. After Sumner lost, he changed the rules so that he had won. Shari refused to pay up—but Dauman did. At some point Shari realized a fundamental difference between her and her father: he always had to win. She just didn't want to lose.

Sumner treated other executives much the same way he did his daughter, even Jankowski. Sometimes he went so far as to fire them. The next day he'd act as though nothing had happened.

On occasion, however, Sumner went too far. In 2004 he dictated a scathing memo, intended for Viacom board members, critiquing Karmazin's performance and intelligence. A secretary typed the profanity-laced missive and mistakenly sent it to Karmazin. Karmazin came storming into Sumner's office brandishing a copy and said he wouldn't stand for such treatment. He left the company and Sumner replaced him with copresidents, Tom Freston, the head of MTV, and Leslie

Moonves, who ran CBS, setting up a two-man contest to succeed Sumner as chief executive.

The same year he named Shari his successor as chair, Sumner proposed splitting Viacom into two publicly traded companies: Viacom, which would hold Paramount Pictures and the cable channels; and CBS, which would retain the broadcast network and publisher Simon & Schuster. Viacom's stock had fallen 18 percent that year, and the fact that the company had nonetheless paid Sumner and two other executives $160 million prompted a shareholder lawsuit demanding that they return the money and that Viacom revise its compensation policies. By splitting the company, Sumner reasoned, the value of its fast-growing cable and entertainment assets would no longer be dragged down by slower-growth broadcast and publishing businesses.

It also solved the vexing problem of who would be named chief executive of Viacom once Sumner was gone. Sumner wanted to keep both Freston and Moonves in the company, but neither would agree to work for the other. Now each could be a chief executive in his own right.

Another issue was voting control. Sumner had long chafed at the existence of what was called the "Redstone discount"—a lower share price because Sumner's National Amusements–owned shares had voting power while regular shareholders' shares didn't. To address this, the charters for both companies would specify that each would have a majority of "independent" directors—i.e., not employed by or related to Sumner. Sumner knew that this was little more than window dressing. He could still replace any director who defied him, "independent" or not.

Shari firmly opposed the move. She felt an inability to choose between two contenders for the top job was no reason to split the company. Viacom was a vertically integrated entertainment company: its studios produced and sold content to its cable and broadcast operations. Its rivals, like Disney and Fox, were moving in the opposite direction. And its greater size gave it more bargaining power with cable distributors. The idea that media companies could bypass cable operators and sell directly to consumers was just gaining traction. In a direct-to-consumer future, scale would be vital.

Sumner had never shown much tolerance for executives who disagreed with him on important issues. But he couldn't really fire his own daughter. Sumner tried to persuade her to support the split, and when that failed, he told her he was doing it anyway.

She told him he was wrong but she'd support him. He wanted to make her vice chair of both companies, but she still didn't want a title without any responsibilities. She finally agreed after Frederic Salerno, a longtime Viacom director and confidant of her father's, assured her she could help shape the new boards.

After the companies separated, and as part of a settlement of the shareholder suit, they agreed to name seven new directors, four to the CBS board and three at Viacom. Three of these new directors were women—the first women to serve on the board beyond Shari herself. Judith A. Spreiser, a former Sara Lee executive, was named chair of CBS's compensation committee.

Sumner issued a press release promising that CBS and Viacom executive pay would be more closely tied to the companies' performance, something he claimed to have long believed in. But the addition of new board members had little impact on how the companies actually operated. Sumner relied on a few confidants and expected other board members to go along with their decisions. Within a year, Spreiser had clashed with Moonves, who didn't consider her a "team player." She and the other two women had quit, telling Shari they felt marginalized and ineffective. They felt frozen out.

After their departure, CBS named five new board members, all men, and all handpicked by Sumner.

Despite splitting Viacom, nothing had really changed when it came to corporate governance.

―――

$\mathbb{S}$ hari's fundamental disagreement with him over Viacom, and her stubborn refusal to change her mind, remained a thorn in Sumner's side. In an October 2006 interview on CNBC with former Disney chief executive Michael Eisner, Sumner said flatly that he had no intention of naming Shari to the chief executive position. "You wanna give away what you have to your family, be my guest," he said. Referring to his then-wife Paula, he added, "My wife is closer to me these days than my daughter."

He also suggested he disagreed with Shari's strategy for reviving National Amusements' movie theater operations by investing in upgrades. (She oversaw the costly transition to so-called stadium seating, which soon became the industry norm.)

Father and daughter clashed again over Sumner's ever-larger investment in Midway Games, the video game company whose shares he'd given Phyllis as part of the divorce settlement. After the divorce Sumner kept buying more Midway shares, although the company failed to replicate the success of *Mortal Kombat* and the stock price declined. By 2007 Sumner and National Amusements owned nearly 90 percent of the shares of Midway, even as its stock dropped from $23 in 2005 to less than $5 a share. Apart from Viacom's disastrous Blockbuster acquisition in 1994, it was probably the worst investment decision Sumner ever made.

In 2005 Sumner had transferred 33 million Midway shares to a National Amusements subsidiary in return for National Amusements assuming a $425 million personal loan Sumner had taken out from Citibank. This obviously favored Sumner's personal interests over the other National Amusements shareholders, namely Shari, who owned 20 percent. Sumner promised her it would never happen again, and she was given sole authority for any further investments by National Amusements in Midway.

But two years later, Sumner brazenly ignored their agreement. He unloaded another 12.4 million Midway shares, selling them to the National Amusements subsidiary for $85 million, over Shari's vehement objection. She was outvoted by her father, Dauman, and the other National Amusements directors, demonstrating yet again that her 20 percent stake conferred no real power.

Shari was further infuriated when Sumner voted his Midway shares to make Shari chair of the Midway board, a position that conferred no authority whatsoever. Now she was publicly in charge of the floundering company while having no power to do anything about it.

Shari's anger was nonetheless mild compared with her father's fury over her defiance of his wishes. He disparaged his daughter to Viacom executives, board members—practically anyone who would listen. He pelted her with profanity-laced emails and faxes, copying Viacom executives, even on multiple occasions calling her the four-letter "*c*-word," as it was delicately described inside the company. When his longtime lawyer and confidant George Abrams, among those copied on the missives, begged Sumner not to use such hurtful language, he erupted, insisting he'd call his daughter whatever he pleased.

Real estate developer Donald J. Trump weighed in on the dispute. He wrote Sumner a letter saying he should listen to his daughter. Trump had shared a box with Shari at a New England Patriots game, and she evidently made a favorable impression. Trump had followed up with questions about the theater business, and Shari gave him and his daughter Ivanka a tour of one of National Amusements' new luxury theaters. With the National Amusements board firmly lined up behind Sumner, Trump was one of the few people willing to stand up for Shari—a gesture she never forgot.

Shari was eventually vindicated, not that Sumner or any other board member ever acknowledged it. Sumner's massive Midway investment ended up all but worthless. Shari resigned as chair. National Amusements sold its entire stake for a nominal $100,000 and Midway declared bankruptcy soon after.

Still furious over her father's use of National Amusements as his personal piggy bank, Shari objected when Sumner decided to make $105 million in charitable gifts in his name to several hospitals, using National Amusements assets to pay for them.

When Shari suggested that Sumner sell some of his shares in CBS and Viacom from his personal account, he erupted. He insisted he would never sell any of those shares, even if it meant National Amusements went bankrupt.

Shari argued that, at the least, the gifts should be in the name of the company that was paying for them—National Amusements—rather than purporting to be personal gifts from Sumner.

No one listened to her. When the issue came to a vote at a National Amusements board meeting, the vote was four to one. Her father and the ever-loyal Dauman supported the gift, and Shari was the lone dissent.

That may have been the last straw for Sumner. In April, when Shari was honored by the USO of Metropolitan New York as its Woman of the Year, her father didn't attend the ceremony (he said he had a conflict). They stopped speaking to and seeing each other, communicating only through faxes or lawyers.

Their disputes threatened Shari's status as Sumner's designated successor as chair. In a 2007 letter to trustees, Sumner stated bluntly that "Shari does not have the requisite business judgment and abilities to serve as chairman," and he took his disparaging views public in a letter to *Forbes* in July: "While my daughter talks of good governance, she apparently ignores the cardinal rule of good governance that the boards of the two public companies, Viacom and CBS, should select my successor." But in Sumner's view, good governance apparently did not include the exercise of any independent judgment by those directors. "If she insists on trying to succeed me, there's no question the boards will do what I ask them," Sumner continued. "They've never gone against my wishes."

In a final slap at his children, he asserted, "It must be remembered that I gave my children their stock" (although it was Shari's grandfather who had established the trust, not Sumner) and "it is I, with little or no contribution on their part, who built these great media companies with the help of the boards of both companies."

When Shari read her father's letter in the magazine she burst into tears. All her life she'd struggled to gain her father's respect, but in return she'd been publicly humiliated.

Dauman soon reached out to negotiate her exit from the family enterprise, or at least persuade her to accept a much-reduced role. Shari could barely bring herself to speak to him. She was convinced he'd orchestrated the *Forbes* attack, since a letter like that to a national publication would never have been issued without being vetted and approved by Dauman. And despite his combative reputation, Sumner did not like conflict with his daughter, let alone a public one. And once she and Dauman were in contact, it felt to her like Dauman could barely contain his satisfaction at the prospect of getting rid of his chief family rival.

(Dauman always maintained that he had nothing to do with the letter and was as surprised by it as anyone else. Sumner had his assistant type and fax the letter directly to *Forbes*, bypassing both Carl Folta, the head of public relations, and Dauman.)

Shari agreed to sell her stake but wanted $1.6 billion, a sum that valued the entire company at $8 billion. Instead Dauman offered her ownership of the national theater chain.

They were nowhere near agreement when, in October 2008, Lehman Brothers collapsed and the financial crisis began. Shares of Viacom and CBS plunged in value. With $1.6 billion in bank debt that had to be repaid, National Amusements teetered on insolvency. It was forced to sell $1 billion in CBS and Viacom stock and a large part of its theater chain, including Shari's upscale cinema in Los Angeles.

Forbes estimated that Sumner's net worth had plunged from

$6.8 billion in 2008 to just $1 billion in 2009—barely enough to keep him on the magazine's annual ranking of the world's billionaires. There was no further talk of buying out Shari's interest. She threw herself into efforts to repay debt and renegotiate loans. Shari also took advantage of Sumner's sudden financial vulnerability, demonstrating that she could be every bit as tough as her father. She had her lawyers draw up an eighty-page legal complaint that detailed, among other allegations, Sumner's self-dealing in the Midway fiasco, and threatened to file it the next day.

Viacom and CBS employees, well aware of the growing father-daughter tensions, joked that the Redstones would be giving each other "subpoenas for Christmas."

Sumner had to make concessions to stave off Shari's complaint: Shari got to keep her 20 percent stake and was granted a lifetime employment contract at National Amusements, ensuring she would remain involved in the company for the foreseeable future. She would continue to be a director, but while she retained the title of president, it was largely ceremonial and she gave up any day-to-day management of the theater chain. She also got full ownership of the Russian theater chain—which she later sold for $190 million—and received $5 million to start her own venture capital fund.

Father and daughter entered into an uneasy truce. Shari never discussed the *Forbes* letter with her father or told him how much it had hurt her.

EPISODE 3

Sumner Will Live Forever

In 2008 Malia Andelin, a twenty-six-year-old makeup artist living in Laguna Beach, was, like so many Americans at the time, supplementing her income by buying and flipping real estate using borrowed money. Then the financial crisis struck, credit abruptly evaporated, and that was the end of that. Andelin was looking for another source of income when a friend recommended she try working as a flight attendant on a private jet. Part of her training was a self-defense course, where she met two pilots who recommended she work with them at the aviation company that staffed the CBS and Viacom planes.

Slim and blond, Andelin had grown up in Utah, the youngest of eight children in a straitlaced Mormon family. She'd never flown professionally, but she was willing to give it a try. On her first outing one of her passengers was the movie star Robert Downey Jr.

Andelin liked the work and seemed to have an aptitude for it. Inevitably the day came when Sumner was on board. In late November, little more than a month after he filed for divorce from Paula, Sumner was flying from New York back to Van Nuys Airport outside Los Angeles with his friend Arnold Kopelson, a producer and CBS board member, and his wife, Anne. While waiting for takeoff, Andelin went into the passenger cabin and asked Sumner if she could help him with his seat belt.

"Who the fuck are you?" he asked.

"Sumner, stop," Anne Kopelson interjected.

Andelin hardly knew how to respond. "I'm Malia," she said. "I work on the plane." She reminded him she'd flown with him once before.

"I'd remember a pretty face like yours," he replied.

That angered her. "Who the fuck are you?" she said, and left the cabin.

That she could give as good as she got seemed to drive Sumner wild. He buzzed for her constantly once they were in the air.

"I hear women like to be spanked," Sumner told her at one point. "Do you like to be spanked?"

Anne Kopelson tried in vain to silence him. Arnold said nothing.

"Please don't sue me for sexual harassment," Sumner told Andelin, and then laughed.

Sumner pelted Andelin with inappropriate comments for the rest of the flight, and she grew increasingly upset. He asked repeatedly for her address and phone number. She refused.

The pilots were aghast but not surprised—Sumner had made a habit of harassing women on the corporate jets and then getting them fired. After the plane landed, one of the pilots pulled Andelin aside.

"I'm probably not going to see you again," he said. "I know how he is. We all know how he is."

Despite her refusal, Sumner had no trouble getting Andelin's phone number, presumably from the aviation company. He called incessantly—so often she turned off her phone. He left messages proposing they have dinner to discuss the menu on the corporate plane. She ignored him. Meanwhile, she wasn't getting any assignments despite her persistent requests for more work. Sumner seemed to be dangling the prospect of getting her job back if she'd join him for dinner.

"Some say I created *Mission: Impossible*, and some say that this mission is impossible," Sumner told her in one voice message. "But I made this mission possible. And I know that you're risk averse and you wouldn't talk to me on the plane, but I know that if you called me back and you were a risk-taker, this call could perhaps change your life."

The message infuriated Andelin. How dare he leave her suggestive voice mails after she'd refused to give him her number and he'd blacklisted her from working on the plane? She called him and left a message. "Who do you think you are? This is not okay. I just want to know when I can have my job back."

Sumner responded by sending her a gift—a Judith Leiber crystal-encrusted handbag in the shape of a panther (current versions retail for over $5,000). "I'm a panther and I'm going to pounce," the accompanying note read.

Sumner's driver finally showed up at her house. Would she have dinner with Sumner? Just once?

Nothing Andelin had done or said had deterred Sumner. She worried: given his enormous wealth and power, to what lengths might he go? Perhaps it would be easier to accept his invitation, at least once. Maybe she'd get her job back.

She eventually agreed to have dinner with Sumner. Something told her she'd come to regret it.

———

From the Zagat guide Sumner picked a restaurant in Newport Beach, not far from where Andelin lived. When the day arrived, Sumner picked Andelin up and had his driver take them there. She rarely drank alcohol, but that evening she sipped a glass of wine to calm her nerves.

After they left the restaurant, Andelin got in the back seat and Sumner slid in next to her. But instead of taking his seat in front, the driver lingered outside, leaving them alone in the car. Suddenly Sumner lunged at her and tried to get his hand under her blouse. Andelin pushed him away and managed to open the door and get out. She was in shock. She later didn't remember how she got home.

The next day Sumner called and sent Andelin an email, which she ignored. Then his driver showed up and told her Sumner wanted to apologize in person. Various thoughts crossed her mind. Her first reaction was that she never wanted to see him again. But as she wrote in her journal at the time, Sumner had so much money and power he'd crush her eventually. She didn't really feel she had a choice.

She reluctantly agreed to see him again.

Carlos Martinez, Sumner's house manager for over ten years, greeted her when she arrived at Sumner's mansion. He tried to reassure her. "There's nothing to be afraid of," he said. "I'm here. You're not alone. You're going to be okay. He just wants to give you the world." But while Sumner was showing her his fish tank, she felt sick and thought she might faint.

Somehow she got through the evening. The next time Sumner invited her, she accepted. After one of her subsequent visits, Martinez gave her a check for $20,000, the amount, he said, she would have been paid had she worked on the jet that month. "Sumner wants you to know that," he said.

She didn't get any more work as a flight attendant. After about a month, Sumner told her there was no need for her to work on the plane. Instead, she could accompany him to dinners and join him on the red carpet at the many Hollywood premieres, galas, and benefits he attended.

Soon Andelin was a fixture at Sumner's mansion, usually having dinner with him every week. As he did with others, Sumner often disparaged his children, Brent and Shari, when confiding in Andelin. Occasionally she had to sit through father-daughter visits, which she found awkward and tense. After a dinner with Sumner and Shari, Andelin shared a car with Shari, who cried during the trip.

One day Andelin was at the mansion when Shari brought Sumner some homemade biscotti. As Shari was leaving, she pulled Andelin aside. "You're so sweet," Shari told her. "I don't know what your relationship is with my dad, but one thing you need to know: always speak your mind to him. Never back down, and always say how you feel."

Andelin felt Shari was one of the few people around Sumner who was nice to her.

———

At its annual global conference in April 2009, the Milken Institute paired celebrity CNN host and interviewer Larry King with eighty-five-year-old (about to turn eighty-six) Sumner. King titled his "conversation" with Sumner "If You Could Live Forever . . ."

After all, Sumner had survived the hotel fire and a serious bout of prostate cancer in the mid-2000s (thanks in part to Milken, a prostate cancer survivor as well, who referred Sumner to a doctor at Cedars-Sinai Medical Center).

The room at the Beverly Hilton was packed; Moonves quietly took a seat in the back row. Clad in a navy suit and an open-necked blue shirt, Sumner began by asserting, "I have the vital statistics of a twenty-year-old," a claim somewhat belied by the substantial paunch visible at his waist. "Even twenty-year-old men get older. Not me. My doctor says I'm the only man who's reversed it. I eat and drink every antioxidant known to man. I exercise fifty minutes every day." (Sumner told Andelin that he inspired the 2008 Paramount film *The Curious Case of Benjamin Button*, in which Brad Pitt plays a man who ages in reverse.)

However amusing the audience may have found Sumner's claim to immortality, it reflected something more than just vanity. Even though he sometimes dismissed notions of an afterlife—quoting the passage from Genesis "From dust you are and to dust you will return"—Sumner had also confided in Andelin that the prospect of death terrified him because he'd face judgment and punishment for his many sins—a reckoning that thus far he'd escaped in life.

"How old are you?" King asked.

"Sixty-five," Sumner replied. The audience laughed.

"Realistically," King pressed him, "how old are you?"

"Sixty-five," he insisted.

Sumner said he felt better than he had at age twenty.

"You have not slowed down sexually?" King asked.

"No, I haven't."

If anything, that appeared to be an understatement. Even as he courted Andelin with money, gifts, and attention, he was dating Rohini Singh, who at age nineteen had been the subject of an embarrassingly detailed 2001 *Los Angeles Magazine* cover story: "Hooking Up: Sex, Status and the Tribal Rituals of Young Hollywood." ("A lot of guys say I have a reputation for sleeping around," she'd told the reporter.) At Sumner's insistence, CBS's Showtime hired Singh that summer despite a hiring freeze at the cable network. As a job candidate Singh rotated through several departments at Showtime before picking public relations, a field in which she had no professional experience. Sumner showered her with Viacom stock, as well as a reported $18 million in payments.

The same year Sumner also started seeing Terry Holbrook, a brunette former Ford model and Houston Oilers cheerleader. Sumner bought her a $2.5 million house and paid for her stable of show horses. He also gave substantial amounts to RainCatcher, a Malibu-based charity she supported that focused on clean drinking water. Herzer maintained that Sumner paid Holbrook $4,500 a month in cash and those and other payments eventually amounted to $7 million. He also made Holbrook a beneficiary of his trust.

Over the years Sumner amended his trust more than forty times to add and remove numerous beneficiaries, many of them women he dated. Dauman, who as a cotrustee of Sumner's trust was aware of many of the gifts, acknowledged that "several" women received over $20 million each, "a lot" of women received over $10 million, and "many, many" women received over $1 million.

In the spring of 2010 *The Daily Beast*'s Peter Lauria reported

Sumner was dining with Moonves and Chen at Dan Tana's with a "tall, tan, fembot-like blonde, young enough to be his granddaughter." The "fembot" was Heather Naylor, Sumner's latest fixation and the lead singer of a largely unknown girl group called the Electric Barbarellas. Sumner was pushing a reluctant Viacom-owned MTV to develop a reality series featuring the group's quest for stardom, and he also wanted CBS to promote them.

Moonves dreaded these requests, but Sumner was his boss. Clad in satin hot pants and singing wildly off pitch, the Barbarellas made their CBS network debut on *The Late Late Show with Craig Ferguson* on March 27, 2011. The operative word was *late*: their appearance came close to the end of the show at 1:30 a.m., when Moonves could only hope few people would be watching.

Lauria reported that Sumner spent half a million dollars flying the Barbarellas to New York for MTV auditions and had pushed the reality series into development over MTV executives' strident objections. They told Lauria the show was "unwatchable and the music just as bad."

Even Dauman tried to kill the project, but "I won't be defied," Sumner insisted.

The mildly embarrassing episode might have remained largely confined to Hollywood insiders, had Sumner not picked up the phone and called Lauria—not to deny the story but to try to unmask Lauria's Viacom source, who Sumner speculated was a "young, male executive" who worked for MTV.

"You will be thoroughly protected," Sumner assured Lauria in the call, which Lauria taped in its entirety and the *Beast* made available to the public. "We're not going to hurt this guy. We just want to sit him down and find out why he did what he did. You will not in any way be revealed. You will be well-rewarded and well-protected."

Lauria refused to disclose his source and instead turned the encounter into another story, which, thanks to Sumner's direct involvement, got even more media attention. *New York Times* media columnist

David Carr called the tape "a classic, a must-hear document of mogul prerogative in full cry."

When Viacom's Carl Folta saw the story, he told Dauman, "You're not going to believe this."

Folta asked Sumner about it, and Sumner denied making any such call.

"Sumner, they've got it on tape!" Folta exclaimed.

"Then fix it," Sumner said.

The Electric Barbarellas debuted in MTV's 2011 lineup and, thanks in part to the publicity surrounding Sumner, attracted nearly a million viewers. The "premiere was the #1 original cable series across all TV," according to an email from an MTV executive to Naylor. But the show attracted some scathing reviews—a "hypercontrived, superstaged, and hair-extensioned mess," as a *New York* magazine critic put it.

Ratings rapidly fell off, despite a classic reality show ending: a record executive calls and, to judge by the excited shrieks from the band members, a big recording contract seems imminent. But MTV canceled the show.

Redstone stayed in touch with Naylor, speaking with her by phone three to five times a week, according to Naylor. He encouraged her Hollywood aspirations and gave her career advice. Sumner also showered Naylor with Viacom stock and other payments that totaled over $20 million, according to Herzer.

After *The Hollywood Reporter* revealed that Naylor had on one occasion sold $157,000 in Viacom stock, questions arose about Sumner's increasingly unseemly behavior. "Some who have been close to Redstone said he has long since crossed into unconscious self-parody, making graphic sexual comments over social or business meals," the magazine reported. Said one Hollywood executive: "He acts like a 15-year-old kid at summer camp."

The Inner Circle VIP Social Club

In the fall of 2010, Brandon Korff, Sumner's twenty-five-year-old grandson, enlisted Patti Stanger, the "Millionaire Matchmaker" of the Bravo reality-TV hit, to find a suitable romantic match for his grandfather. Sumner's serial dating—not to mention the accompanying bonanza of lavish gifts—was driving him crazy. "I can't deal with him," Brandon confided in Stanger. With Paula out of the picture, perhaps what Sumner needed was a steady romantic companion to bring some stability to his personal life.

Brandon had witnessed his grandfather's antics firsthand. He'd recently moved to Los Angeles to work at MTV after graduating from George Washington University and had sometimes stayed with Sumner. He was boyishly handsome, sporting trendy stubble on his face, and was soon driving a Bentley around town and accompanying Sumner to numerous entertainment industry events. He often watched sports with his grandfather on TV and attended the weekly Sunday movie screenings Sumner held at his home.

Brandon was the second of Shari Redstone's three children from her marriage to Ira Korff, whom she'd divorced in 1992. Notwithstanding his troubled relationships with his children, Sumner doted on his grandchildren: Kimberlee, Brandon, and Tyler, Shari's three children; and Brent's daughters, Keryn and Lauren. Law ran in the family: Brent and Shari were both lawyers like their father, and so were Kimberlee, Keryn, and Tyler (who was also an ordained rabbi).

Brandon didn't share their scholarly bent. In Los Angeles he dated a series of models and actresses, some of whom in turn dated Sumner. Sumner was relentless in his insistence that Brandon socialize with him and introduce him to potential romantic companions, sometimes calling him at 3:00 or 4:00 a.m. It was Brandon who had introduced Sumner to Singh, the young woman who landed the job in PR at Showtime, a move that Brandon almost immediately regretted.

Sumner's constant demands on Brandon, not to mention his pursuit of some of the same women, contributed to a sometimes-awkward relationship between grandfather and grandson. Brandon brought his then-girlfriend, a willowy brunette with long, flowing hair, to the 2009 MTV Video Music Awards in Los Angeles, where they posed for photographers with Sumner. Throughout the evening Sumner brazenly flirted with Brandon's date, often putting his arm around her, a spectacle witnessed by senior Viacom executives sitting nearby.

A year later, Brandon invited another girlfriend and tried to enlist Malia Andelin as Sumner's date, perhaps in hopes of fending off a similar incident. He emailed Andelin in May: "Lets us 4 go I dont want him to humiliate himself and us at MTV and if u were not here he may bring a whore." But Andelin turned him down.

It eventually proved too much for Brandon. He felt he needed professional help finding his grandfather a companion. With the approval of other family members, he turned to Stanger.

———

Stanger had moved to Hollywood from Miami, where she ran a large dating service, hoping for a career as a producer. Her role model was Sherry Lansing, the former model and actress turned successful studio executive. Lansing ran Paramount for twelve years and was chair of the studio when Sumner acquired it. Stanger never worked in the executive rungs like Lansing, but now she was probably much more famous, thanks to the recent broadcast phenomenon of reality TV. Production companies now had their own "unscripted" departments to handle the burgeoning reality phenomenon.

Stanger's mother and grandmother had both been traditional matchmakers in the conservative Jewish community in which she grew up, and she drew on their experiences to launch a Hollywood dating service. Lansing introduced her to veteran producer Arthur Cohn, who encouraged her to pursue matchmaking full-time. "Someday you're going to have your own TV show," he predicted.

Which she did, starting in 2008 on the Bravo cable network. On *The Millionaire Matchmaker*, Stanger interviewed millionaires, screened potential dates, and then threw them together in a VIP "mixer," culminating in a date for the winner, all filmed, edited, and televised.

Brash, outspoken, earthy, and funny, Stanger seemed made for reality TV, even if her sweeping generalizations sometimes sparked controversy. However blunt her comments, she never strayed far from a traditional narrative of love and marriage. She limited contestants to two drinks at the VIP mixers and banned sex until a couple was in a "committed relationship." The show was a hit for Bravo.

Stanger was a celebrity by the time Brandon called. She'd never met Sumner Redstone, but knew he was a mogul and, more to the point, a billionaire. So Stanger drove to Beverly Park to meet Sumner in person, in order to, as she put it, "read his energy."

She walked past the koi pond and was ushered into the house, where Sumner was sitting in a chair in front of his fish tanks, watching his ticker tape mounted on a nearby wall. Her first impression was that he might have been good-looking in his youth, but he now looked very old. She knew he was eighty-six, but his appearance was startling nonetheless, especially his disfigured hand. She had plenty of available women interested in rich older men. Still, this might be a challenge.

Redstone seemed instantly smitten by Stanger, who checked all the boxes he told her he was looking for in both a date and a potential marriage partner—Jewish, with dark brown hair, and younger (though late forties or fifties would be fine). Sumner brazenly flirted with her, sprinkling his speech with profanities, to which she responded in kind. In the course of the interview he persuaded her to sit on his lap, which she did briefly before politely but firmly extricating herself. (Stanger had a strict rule against dating clients.)

That Sumner was willing to date middle-aged women opened up a world of possibilities. She had a long list of single, charming, and attractive older women most of her wealthy male clients wouldn't even consider.

"Let's do it," she said.

Stanger explained that Sumner would be enrolled at the VIP level, which guaranteed twenty-four-hour, seven-day-a-week access to the Millionaire Matchmaker herself. The fee was $120,000 a year, payable up front, which covered a year, although it rarely took her that long—on average, she maintained, just three dates.

Redstone offered to pay her $60,000 right away and the balance later. He seemed uncomfortable and told her he'd been placed on an allowance to curb his increasingly lavish spending on women.

Stanger was incredulous. "What? I don't believe your sob story," she said. "You can get $120,000. I'll trust you, but if you don't deliver the other $60,000 I'll cut you off."

Redstone seemed pleased. "No one ever trusts me," he said. (He eventually paid.)

One of Sumner's first dates was with Renee Suran, an actress, a model, and the ex-wife of the rock guitarist known as Slash. Suran was beautiful, tall, and brunette, and Sumner was crazy about her. But she didn't reciprocate his ardor and wasn't all that interested in his money. Sumner appeared hurt by the rejection and kept begging Stanger to arrange another date with her.

No one else seemed to measure up. Sumner often called Stanger the day after a date, screaming and berating her for an unsatisfactory match. "You don't talk to women like that," Stanger warned him. "I'm not fixing you up again unless you call and apologize," and then she hung up on him. When he inevitably called back, she told him to calm down. "Are we ready to focus on love?"

Over the course of the year Sumner and Stanger became close. She called him "old man" and "Nubby," referring to his injured hand, and sprinkled her remarks with profanity that matched his own. He seemed to like that she stood up to him and teased him, and he enjoyed her company. He told her repeatedly that she was his "dream girl" and that she was the one he wanted, a proposition she rebuffed. Still, other than the swearing and periodic outbursts when he'd lose his temper, she found him to be a gentleman of the old school. He sent a car for her when they went out to dinner and always wore a suit. He tried to coax her into moving her reality show from Bravo to a Viacom channel.

At the end of his contract Sumner was the rare Stanger millionaire (or, in his case, billionaire) who hadn't found a successful match. "What else do you have?" he kept asking, even after meeting someone he liked. Stanger offered him a 10 percent discount to renew for a second year, but he didn't want to pay. So she encouraged him to have a second date with someone he'd earlier said he liked but had nonetheless passed over—a woman named Sydney Holland. "If what you want is me, you should go out with Sydney," Stanger argued. "Sydney is the mini version of me."

Holland was a personal friend of Stanger's, not a client of the dating service. The two women did have a lot in common: similar physical attributes; age (Holland was thirty-nine years old); religion (they were both Jewish); and an interest in health, wellness, and New Age spirituality. Holland was a recovering alcoholic and didn't drink. She and Stanger were both into herbal medicine. They even shared a last name—Holland's maiden name was Stanger—though they didn't know of any common family ancestry.

Holland grew up in affluent La Jolla, California, a San Diego sub-urb, the daughter of a dentist who died when she was twenty. Holland had a history of dating (and marrying) older men. Cecil Holland, a building contractor and former model she'd married in 2000 when she was twenty-nine, was sixteen years older than she was. The marriage lasted three years.

Six years later, at an Alcoholics Anonymous meeting, Holland met Bruce Parker, the top sales executive for Callaway Golf, who'd made a fortune when the manufacturer of the popular Big Bertha driver went public in 1992. (His Callaway stock alone was worth over $21 million.) He was fifteen years older than Holland.

A month after they met, she moved into Parker's Wilshire Boulevard apartment and he leased her a Mercedes. But just months later, in October 2009, Parker had a heart attack and died while he and Holland were having sex. Despite their participation in AA meetings, an autopsy identified the cause as "acute cocaine toxicity." Parker was just fifty-three years old.

Apart from the trauma of a sudden death in such awkward circumstances (the police investigated Holland for murder, though no charges resulted), Holland was struggling financially. Many of her bills went unpaid, and she'd racked up court judgments and liens of $47,540. She described herself as an entrepreneur, but she'd moved from one failed business venture to the next: "eco-friendly" yoga apparel; a line of sportswear and lingerie; even her own matchmaking business, the Inner Circle VIP Social Club, modeled on Stanger's Millionaire's Club. (Stanger didn't appreciate Holland's attempts to poach her clients but didn't view Holland as serious competition.) Holland even hoped to launch her own matchmaking reality show but lacked Stanger's brash, made-for-television personality. Nothing had panned out.

Holland claimed Parker had promised her a $10,000-a-month allowance and the Mercedes. To the dismay of Parker's extended family and heirs, Holland consulted a lawyer and refused to move out of his

apartment. She kept the Mercedes and wanted to be named an execu-
tor of Parker's estate. She left—taking a set of Gucci luggage with
her—only after Parker's family paid her a $164,000 settlement.

So when Stanger approached her about Sumner, the prospect of
meeting a billionaire couldn't have been more timely from Holland's
perspective. Holland all but begged Stanger to arrange a date for her
with Sumner. Stanger obliged, but issued some stern warnings: "Do
not sleep with him on the first date. He's old-fashioned, like out of the
1940s. He could have anyone in Hollywood for sex. He's looking for
the real thing," meaning love and marriage.

Holland described their courtship as idyllic, "consisting of long
drives along the Malibu coast, listening to Tony Bennett and Frank
Sinatra." At restaurants they shared Sumner's favorite dessert, choco-
late mousse. Holland began appearing in public as his girlfriend, "at
his side at charity events, movie premieres, and parties." Sumner was
as instantly smitten with Holland as he'd been with Fortunato. Before
she knew it, they "were spending nearly every waking moment with
each other," Holland maintained.

Soon after they met, Holland and Sumner had dinner with Manuela Herzer and her son Bryan so Herzer could size up Holland. Holland passed muster, and Herzer bestowed her stamp of approval on
the relationship.

Less than a year later, in 2011, Sumner proposed marriage, and Holland "happily accepted," she recounted. He gave her a nine-carat diamond
ring, which she proudly showed off to Stanger. (Sumner sent Stanger
a diamond Cartier "Love" bracelet as a thank-you.) Sumner showered
Holland with cash, more jewelry, art, and flowers—specifically, red
roses and orchids. He bought her a house in West Hollywood, just
across the Beverly Hills line, and she commuted back and forth in a
new Porsche. Sumner paid for her membership at the Beverly Hills
Tennis Club and, after that was revoked, at the Riviera Country Club
in Pacific Palisades, where the initiation fee was $250,000. He wrote

her love notes, some on stationery from the Japanese restaurant Matsuhisa. "I will always love you. You can always depend on me. Love, Sumner," read one.

Holland reached out to her lawyer, Andrew Katzenstein, for tax advice about the ring and other gifts. Did she have to declare the "gorgeous diamond" as income? Yes, he replied (in an email leaked to the *New York Post*), but added that many people "ignore" the rule.

She also told Katzenstein that she was a named beneficiary in Sumner's will to the tune of $3 million. Katzenstein estimated that, thanks to Sumner's largesse, Holland was now worth $9 million or $10 million. "Starting to get some comfort?" he asked.

"20 would be best!!!" she replied. "Just saying."

The Porsche, house, club memberships, and cash made an impression on Tim Jensen, a Paramount employee hired in 2011 to be Sumner's full-time driver. When Jensen first met her, Holland had been driving a small red compact car so decrepit that its side mirror was held in place with duct tape, according to Jensen.

Jensen soon realized that even though he'd been hired by Paramount/Viacom as a driver for the studio head, Holland was his de facto employer. One of his primary duties was to take checks made out to "cash" to a Bank of America branch and return with the currency— thousands of dollars at a time—which he handed to Holland. Holland, in turn, used cash to pay seven different women who visited Sumner on a regular basis.

To keep track, Jensen kept a spreadsheet listing the various women and payments. In a year they totaled more than $1 million. Jensen complained to a Viacom security official in New York, in part because he didn't feel safe carrying so much cash, and also because he didn't consider paying these women to be within the scope of his employment. His complaint went nowhere, but Holland became "hostile," according to Jensen, and he was fired soon after.

Although Stanger was no longer on retainer to Sumner, she continued to dole out advice to Holland: Give Sumner whatever he wants. Do anything for him within reason. And do not, under any circumstances, cheat on Sumner with another man. Sumner—like many men of his generation—maintained a brazen double standard as far as women were concerned: he could have as many affairs and sexual encounters as he wanted, but anyone he dated, was engaged to, or married was held to a strict standard of monogamy. For Sumner, loyalty was as prized a quality in his wives and mistresses as it was in his business subordinates.

Stanger was convinced that despite their age difference and Holland's obvious financial motive, Holland was in love with Sumner. Stanger had known plenty of women who were romantically drawn to much older men. Holland took Stanger's advice to heart. She served at Sumner's beck and call. She'd interrupt lunch with friends (as she often did with Stanger) the instant Sumner called.

Soon Holland was indispensable. When Sumner asked Holland to move in with him, she did, taking on the roles of wife, secretary, business manager, and, increasingly, nurse. She redecorated the mansion. She arranged visits there with Sumner's longtime friends Charlie Rose, Michael Milken, and Sherry Lansing, not to mention the women she imported for his sexual gratification. She oversaw his dealings with CBS and Viacom, organized a CBS board meeting at the house, arranged his Sunday movie screenings, and got him to his dentist and doctor appointments.

Sumner made many demands on Holland, all of which she maintained she met: that she be present for every lunch and dinner with him; that she go to sleep when he did (even though this was much earlier than she preferred); that she not take overnight trips without him; that she stop seeing her friends. Sumner, however, "could do whatever he wanted."

EPISODE 5

"What's Mine Is Yours"

In June 2012, Paramount celebrated its hundredth anniversary at its studio lot, the only one still located in Hollywood. About a hundred guests and employees entered through its historic arched gateway and, with flutes of champagne in hand, strolled past the sound stages and film lots that had launched the careers of Gloria Swanson, Rudolph Valentino, Cary Grant, and Mae West and cinema classics from *Wings* (1927) to *Breakfast at Tiffany's* (1961) to *Chinatown* (1974).

Despite her still-contentious relationship with her father, Shari Redstone was there to mark the occasion, but she had no speaking role. As the theme music from *The Godfather* played from speakers mounted in trees, Sumner entered wearing a dark suit and flamboyant tie. He was helped along by Dauman. Holland, in a revealing dress and Lucite stiletto heels, followed just behind. Her appearance prompted curiosity.

"Who's that?" a reporter asked Viacom's head of public relations, Carl Folta.

"That's his home health care aide," Folta answered.

Dauman helped his eighty-nine-year-old boss into a chair in front of the lot's central administration building, known as building 217, where studio founder Adolph Zukor had presided over the golden age of Hollywood.

"It was your fondest dream to own this place," Dauman reminded Sumner. He offered a toast: "Here's to us who won"—the same words

Sumner had used in 1994 after beating out rival Barry Diller in a two-year bidding war for the studio.

Then Dauman and Paramount studio head Brad Grey pulled back a red velvet curtain to unveil the building's new signage: SUMNER RED-STONE BUILDING.

Redstone remained seated but took the microphone. "Usually buildings are named for people who are dead," he said. "But that will never apply to me because I will never die."

Dauman's prominent role at the ceremony didn't go unnoticed in Hollywood, nor the fact that the $84.5 million he was paid in 2010 made him the country's highest-paid chief executive. That also piqued media interest, and Sumner agreed to talk to a *New York Times* reporter. Sumner was given specific talking points but, during the interview with journalist Amy Chozick, blurted out, "Everyone understands, I think, that Philippe will be my successor." That was not in the script.

Chozick quoted Sumner and understandably played up the news given the constant speculation about who would succeed Sumner. When the story appeared in *The New York Times Magazine* in September, the title was "The Man Who Would Be Redstone." The story went on to say that Dauman and Sumner each "gushe[d] with admiration and hyperbole typically reserved for familial relationships or personal publicists." It quoted Sumner: "I've called Philippe my mentor, and he says 'No, Sumner, you're my mentor.' . . . I would never think of overruling Philippe."

Dauman was pleased that Sumner was so publicly supportive of him. Folta knew there would be trouble—"World War 3," as he put it.

Shari was hurt and upset by her father's designation of Dauman. She was also angry with Dauman and suspected he had orchestrated the remark.

Folta was pressed into service to issue a "clarification" stressing that Sumner's successor had yet to be determined and would be chosen in due course by the CBS and Viacom boards.

Still, no one claimed Sumner had been misquoted, and Dauman's status seemed secure. Despite grumbling by Hollywood insiders about his lack of creative talent and heavy-handed treatment of stars, Dauman had delivered the results Sumner really cared about: Viacom's stock price, which was up more than 50 percent since Dauman became chief executive in 2006.

———

Despite her prominence at the Paramount anniversary celebration, Holland was hardly the only woman in Sumner's life. He was still courting Malia Andelin. And he had continued seeing and confiding in his old flame Manuela Herzer. Holland may have been first among equals, but she and Herzer had forged an alliance. While Herzer's house was being renovated in 2013 at Sumner's expense, Sumner invited Herzer and her daughter Kathrine to live with him and Holland. Herzer began sharing the duties of overseeing the staff at the house and Sumner's medical care. Staff members viewed Herzer as the enforcer and thought Holland rarely made any significant decisions without Herzer's approval. She stayed on, more or less, and her house renovations seemed to go on indefinitely—two years later they were still underway and the costs had topped $9 million.

At Sumner's, Herzer had her own room, but she infrequently stayed the night there. But Sumner seemed pleased with the added attention.

In fact, neither woman really spent all that much time with Sumner. Holland would reluctantly go to bed with Sumner much earlier than she wanted, but get up as soon as he fell asleep. One of his nurses, Jeremy Jagiello, who worked twelve-hour shifts at the mansion starting in May 2013, observed that Holland, whom he considered to be Sumner's "live-in girlfriend," typically joined Sumner for lunch and dinner and sat in on some of his physical- and speech-therapy sessions but was otherwise absent. Herzer was often traveling and even when at the house spent only "a few minutes" with him. Herzer nonetheless complained that she had to limit her travel and spend far more time at home with Sumner than she wanted.

Even so, by now Sumner routinely referred to both Holland and Herzer as members of his extended "family," explicitly using the term in amending his will and trust documents. He attended Bryan Herzer's graduation from the University of Southern California, and when Kathrine Herzer got her first job in New York, Sumner escorted her to work.

Christina Chamchoum, Herzer's other daughter (who later used the name Christy Cham), was hired as a costume production assistant on the 2012 CBS series *NYC 22* and became an assistant costume designer for Paramount's *Teenage Mutant Ninja Turtles*.

When Kathrine was a junior in high school (and had already interned for Al Gore's Climate Reality Project, a Redstone grant recipient), her mother started pushing Sumner to cast her in the new CBS drama *Madam Secretary*, starring Téa Leoni as Secretary of State Elizabeth McCord. Moonves was summoned to the mansion, and with Holland and Herzer at his side, Sumner all but ordered him to cast Kathrine in a role on the show. Moonves felt he had no choice but to do it.

In the series pilot, Kathrine played Alison, the only daughter in the fictional McCord family. Later, for the series, the producers added a second, older daughter, Stephanie, and cast a talented young Juilliard graduate, Wallis Currie-Wood, in the role. Herzer was predictably furious that her daughter's character was being diluted. She made Sumner read aloud to Moonves from a handwritten script on a yellow pad: "Les, I asked you to put Kathrine on the show, then you added a daughter. Why would you do that?"

It was too late to undo the casting, but Herzer showed up on the set and monitored the lines and airtime Kathrine was getting. She frequently called Moonves to demand that her daughter's role be expanded. Moonves finally extricated himself by handing Herzer over to one of the producers.

Herzer constantly sought smaller favors from CBS and Viacom executives, including backstage passes, tickets, and VIP treatment at various awards shows and events for herself and her children. If Herzer didn't get what she wanted, she'd scream at Viacom and CBS employees and complain to Sumner. Then Sumner would call and complain. It fell to Folta to keep Herzer happy. Even so, Folta warned Sumner that it was unacceptable for Herzer to verbally abuse Viacom employees. But Sumner didn't seem to care.

———

With Herzer's arrival, the atmosphere changed dramatically inside Sumner's mansion. Surveillance cameras were installed throughout the Redstone property, and nurses and staff were subjected to lie detector tests. She ordered them to speak only in English and threatened to fire a nurse who used his native Tagalog. Anyone deemed disloyal to Holland or Herzer was fired. As the women consolidated their control over the mansion, its staff, and Sumner himself, the number of people with unrestricted access to him dwindled.

This included his immediate family—Shari and the grandchildren he so doted upon. Holland or Herzer sat in on all their visits or had staff members present who would report on their conversations. According to Giovanni Paz, who joined the staff as a caretaker and personal assistant to Sumner, "When family members came to visit, Sydney instructed me to remain in the room, eavesdrop on the conversations, and report back to her. Sydney was especially insistent that I monitor Mr. Redstone's visits with his daughter, Shari."

Most of the family's calls to Sumner were also blocked, though Holland and Herzer then told Sumner his family never called. According to Jagiello, "Sydney and Manuela reacted angrily when they learned that a nurse or member of the household staff had put those calls through and made clear that it was a fireable offense."

In what Jagiello described as a "constant bombardment," Holland and Herzer "regularly disparaged Shari to Mr. Redstone, telling him that she was a liar, was only after his money, and was defying his wishes in both personal and business matters."

There was a prominent exception carved out for Keryn Redstone, Brent's daughter, now in her early thirties and a graduate of the University of Denver law school. Keryn had stayed close to Sumner even after the breach with her father, and she was a frequent overnight visitor to the mansion. She'd met Herzer soon after Herzer had met Sumner, and over the years they'd stayed in touch. At the same time, Keryn was bitterly hostile toward Shari, her aunt, who she said "consistently expressed hostility to me, my father, and Grumpy in sometimes dark, threatening ways." (All the grandchildren referred to Sumner as "Grumpy.") Her opinion of Shari made Keryn a valuable potential ally for Herzer and Holland.

Holland and Herzer also seemed to tolerate Sumner's continuing infatuation with Malia Andelin, who still showed up at the mansion nearly every week notwithstanding Sumner's purported engagement to Holland. Sumner called her constantly, sometimes multiple times a day, leaving long messages saying he loved her. "I am thinking of you all the time—like how much I love you, miss you," he told her. "If you ever need anything, call me," he said in another message. "You promise, if you need anything at all you call me, baby—remember that. I am sorry I am crying. Every time I think of you I cry. I can't help it. And remember, if you ever need anything at all—money, advice, whatever—you call me. I will always be there for you." He called her "my one and only."

Andelin tolerated this, but she had no romantic feelings for Sumner. Although Sumner often made lewd and inappropriate sexual comments, Andelin doubted he was even physically capable of sex in any conventional sense. Andelin felt it was more that he wanted his cronies, like Bob Evans and Larry King, to think he was sleeping with attractive young women.

Sumner liked showing off Andelin in public. She was on the red carpet with him at the 2009 Tony Awards and 2010 Academy Awards. He often brought her to dinners he hosted for friends and entertainment executives and their spouses at expensive Beverly Hills restaurants, where he regularly insisted everyone order the Dover sole, even if they said they hated fish.

Sometimes Sumner sounded a more paternalistic than romantic note. After Andelin met and started dating a sporting goods entrepreneur at the end of 2010, Sumner seemed to accept that she had a boyfriend and had fallen in love, even saying he looked forward to walking her down the aisle. "You are doing the right thing," he said in one voice message. "You'll marry him and you will have children and a family, which is what you always wanted, and I want you to have everything you want. As I told you, all I ever wanted was for you to be happy."

Andelin felt Holland and Herzer were jealous of Sumner's affection for her but knew there was little they could do about it. Her presence also gave them what may have been some welcome evenings off from catering to Sumner's whims. The two women even helped Sumner pick out expensive gifts for Andelin, like diamond earrings and a Rolex watch, sometimes inflating the tab by adding purchases of clothing and jewelry for themselves.

Herzer counseled Andelin that she could be asking Sumner for much more. Turning down his marriage proposal years earlier was the biggest mistake of her life, Herzer confided.

Andelin had never asked Sumner for money and initially resisted when Sumner said he wanted to help buy her a house. But she gave in after he said he'd choose one for her if she didn't. She ended up with a $2.65 million cottage in exclusive Corona del Mar, not far from her home in Laguna Beach. When Sumner saw it, he professed disappointment that it lacked a pool and wasn't on the beach.

Sumner even lavished gifts on Andelin's sister, Vanessa, who was going through a messy custody battle. Andelin suspected something was going on between her sister and Sumner when she heard that Vanessa had suddenly come into a significant amount of money. When Andelin asked for an explanation, Vanessa said, "I don't need to tell you," which prompted a rupture in the sisters' previously close relationship. Martinez, the house manager, told Andelin that he didn't know what was going on but that Sumner was calling Vanessa a lot. Herzer later maintained that Sumner gave Vanessa a total of $6 million.*

As time went on, Sumner's gifts to Andelin grew more extravagant. Six- and even seven-figure deposits of cash and CBS and Viacom stock started showing up in her account. As Sumner said in one voice mail, "Remember, honey, I will always love you and I will always do whatever I can do to make you happy." He continued, "Even though we don't sleep in the same room, my house will always be your house." He added, "Just remember, if you ever need anything, let me know. It gives me pleasure to do things for you. Never say you want to give me anything back. That would hurt me terrible. I gave you those things because I love you. I still do."

Sumner also urged her to buy CBS and Viacom stock. On the morning of April 16, 2012, he had his executive assistant, Gloria Mazzeo, send her an email directing her to purchase eight thousand shares of Viacom and four thousand shares of CBS. Andelin knew enough about insider trading rules to be wary. "I cannot talk to you or Sumner about Viacom or CBS," she replied.

Undeterred, Sumner sent a letter, purporting to be from Andelin, to her financial adviser at U.S. Trust directing the adviser to buy the

---

* The description of Vanessa Andelin and Sumner's relationship was confirmed by multiple sources, but Andelin said that the account of her conversation with her sister Malia is "untrue and hearsay."

Viacom and CBS shares "at the opening or as close to the opening as possible. There is no limit on price."

Andelin was angry when she found out. She wrote to her financial adviser that she had no intention of buying any shares, adding, "SR should not be asking about my account or whether you've bought stock or not."

Sumner never told Andelin why he was so insistent she buy stock that day, and she didn't want to ask. There were no obvious catalysts. Viacom had released its latest earnings the day before. They were lackluster and had little impact on the stock. Viacom announced an exchange offer to retire some debt on November 16, but the stock rose only modestly.

As chairman and chief executive, Sumner may well have known about other impending positive developments, like progress in big cable renewal deals—which is why there are strict rules for the purchase and sale of company stock by chief executives and other insiders. Legendary investor Warren Buffett had disclosed a large position in Viacom in a public filing the previous week and later disclosed more purchases. Securities and Exchange Commission filings show that top Viacom executives Dauman, Dooley, and the general counsel were also exercising options and buying stock that month.

Whatever his reasons, Sumner's market timing was uncanny. Over the next three months both Viacom and CBS shares roughly doubled, while the S&P 500 index rose only about 10 percent.

———

Andelin never added up how much money Sumner gave her in total, but it was at least millions of dollars. She was well aware of what other people thought of her and their relationship. She didn't like it. She hated the idea that people thought of her as another Holland or Herzer. Still, she accepted the money and gifts. The more she did, the lower her self-esteem sank. Sometimes she wondered: Was she experiencing a version of Stockholm syndrome, in which a victim of abuse develops an attachment to the perpetrator? For all Sumner's faults, over their years together Andelin developed some compassion for him. She felt he was fundamentally lonely and deeply insecure.

She also rationalized the arrangement by thinking of it as her job. However "foul-mouthed and crude" he could be, as she put it, she considered Sumner a mentor, a brilliant businessman from whom she could learn a great deal. And perhaps she could change Sumner for the better.

In this she had her work cut out for her. At a dinner at e. baldi restaurant in Beverly Hills, Sumner complained that the director Steven Spielberg had been pushing him to be nicer about Barack Obama. Obama was wildly popular with the Hollywood elite, but Sumner was no fan of the president. "Obama is a . . . ," Sumner loudly said, using the *N*-word.

Andelin was horrified. "You can't say that word!" she exclaimed.

"It's a joke," he insisted.

"You still can't say it, especially where people might hear you."

At one point Sumner asked Andelin if she thought he was a "horrible person." "If I was your age and we met, would you be friends with me?" he asked. "Is there a chance you would even like me if I were your age?"

Andelin didn't want to hurt his feelings, but, following Shari's advice, she was honest. "I don't know," she said. "You're not very nice."

Sumner started to cry.

———

Sumner turned ninety in May 2013, an event celebrated with a lavish birthday dinner hosted by Holland and Herzer at Sumner's Beverly Park mansion. The pair installed a red carpet leading to the front door, over which was a canopy that looked like a theater marquee—a nod to Sumner's beginnings in the movie theater business. A large tent filled the backyard, where Tony Bennett again serenaded guests and thanked Sumner "for putting me on MTV" and reviving his career.

The guest list was a who's who of current and former Hollywood moguls, although virtually everyone had some direct financial interest in being there: Philippe Dauman and Leslie Moonves, of course; Sumner's old pal Robert Evans; Sherry Lansing; the producer Brian Grazer; Michael Eisner, the Disney ex-chair; and Jeffrey Katzenberg, the DreamWorks cofounder Eisner had forced out at Disney. (Viacom had bought DreamWorks' live-action studio for $1.6 billion in 2006.)

The former junk-bond king Michael Milken, who had advised Sumner about his prostate cancer, was there, too. Sumner had given $30 million to George Washington University, home to the Milken Institute School of Public Health. Al Gore showed up; the former vice president's Climate Reality Project was the recipient of $10 million from Sumner.

And there were celebrities connected in one way or another to Paramount: actors Mark Wahlberg, Danny DeVito, Sidney Poitier—even Tom Cruise, who, after being ejected by Sumner in 2006, had been coaxed back into the Paramount fold with another installment in the *Mission: Impossible* franchise.

Sumner's first wife, Phyllis, and Bob Evans occupied the seats of honor on either side of Sumner. Also at the head table were Shari and Malia Andelin. After years of railing against Phyllis, Sumner told Andelin that divorcing her had been the biggest mistake of his life. Completing the family contingent were his grandchildren Brandon, Kimberlee, and Tyler.

"Celebrating with you has always been memorable," Shari said in a tribute video organized by Holland and Herzer, which, under the circumstances, might be deemed an understatement.

Andelin appeared on camera professing her "love" for Sumner, "my favorite person in the whole world."

Dauman took the prize for sheer fawning, calling Sumner "my inspiration, my guiding light, my mentor."

But the real stars of the video were the cohosts. For Holland and Herzer, Sumner's birthday was their coming-out party as the women in Sumner's life, the real powers inside the mogul's mansion. The pair figured prominently in the video, "created with love by Sydney and Manuela," as the credits put it. Holland posed in a black sequined gown holding Sumner's miniature poodle Sugar in her lap. "I'm so blessed to spend every day of my life with you," she said. "You complete me, Sumner. I love you."

Herzer wore a flesh-toned lace-and-chiffon gown that set off her long blond hair. She studded her remarks with the word *family*: "They say you don't pick your family, but they must not have had you in mind when they coined that phrase." She continued, "There are not enough words to express how grateful and blessed we are to be a part of your family yesterday, today, and tomorrow, and for the rest of our lives."

At one point Robert Evans sat next to Andelin and urged her to call Sumner more often. "Please save him from these women," Evans implored.

———

Given Sumner's impulsive behavior and potential infatuation with other women, Holland and Herzer had to be constantly vigilant. Malia Andelin was emerging as a serious threat. She'd secured a prime seat at his birthday dinner—not even Holland and Herzer were at his table. Since then Sumner was leaving her as many as twenty messages a day (since he was no longer physically capable of operating his phone, Holland had to place the calls and listen to him leaving the messages). In the evenings, Sumner played music and sang to Andelin, mostly Frank Sinatra and Bing Crosby standards.

That was going too far. A private detective—hired, she assumed, by Holland and Herzer but paid for by Sumner—followed Andelin.

Strange cars were parked outside her house. One followed her so tenaciously it nearly ran her off the road.

Panicked, she called Sumner. "Tell your girlfriends to stop following me," she said. "I'm going to tell the authorities that Paramount, Viacom, and CBS money is being used to harass and follow me."

"What are you talking about?" Sumner answered. Then she heard Sumner yell to a person in the background, "Is someone following her?"

Although Sumner had seemingly embraced the reality of Andelin's boyfriend and eventual marriage, he had evidently come to believe that Andelin loved him and him alone. Andelin was convinced that Holland and Herzer fostered this romantic delusion, then turned it against him, encouraging Sumner to believe that his "one and only" had betrayed him.

In June, Sumner called and left a message inviting Andelin to his mansion "right away. I can't wait to see you," sounding like all was forgiven. Despite the sudden about-face, Andelin was prepared to go. Then Martinez, Sumner's house manager, called.

"Don't come," he warned. "It's a setup." Martinez told her a lawyer was waiting there with a lie detector test. Andelin had already confided in Martinez that she was troubled by her relationship with Sumner. He told her now was the time to get out.

As Stanger had warned, one thing Sumner would not tolerate was infidelity. He removed Andelin from his will and trust documents. He hired Martin Singer, the aggressive fixer to the stars and longtime lawyer for Bill Cosby, to consider suing Andelin for having "seduced and influenced [him] to give her tens of millions of dollars, stocks, valuable property, financial backing for an alleged non-profit business, and other benefits by representing to him that she was in love with him, and loyal and honest with him," as Sumner later alleged in a court filing.

Increasingly fearful for her safety, on June 12, less than a month after Sumner's birthday party, Andelin sent him an email saying she couldn't see him again under the circumstances. "I don't know what's going on with you, Sydney and Manuela, but I am in fear for my life," she wrote. "I am still being followed and harassed and I'm fearful to even be on my own without protection. I don't know what to do, who to turn to, or how to protect my life. I do not feel safe. This is very serious. Please put a stop to all this because I fear my life will be taken from me. This has to be the end until I know I am safe."

Sumner didn't respond, but she did get threatening voice mails from Singer, saying she'd lose her house unless she spoke to him. She didn't respond.

Over the next few months Sumner dictated a stream of angry messages intended for Andelin in which he railed against her alleged betrayal, saying he wished he'd never met her.

Holland dutifully transcribed and sent the messages—to Herzer.

On June 12, 2014, exactly one year after Andelin cut off contact with Sumner, a surrogate gave birth to Holland's daughter. Holland named the child Alexandra Red Holland and appointed Herzer as the child's godmother.

Alexandra had Sumner's distinctive red hair and bore enough resemblance to him to prompt speculation that she was Sumner's biological daughter, the product of artificial insemination. The child's middle name, "Red," was interpreted by some as a not-so-subtle reference to Redstone.

Holland acknowledged, somewhat ambiguously, that Sumner helped her "conceive her daughter." If Alexandra were Sumner's biological child, it would have certainly cemented Holland's claims to Sumner's fortune. But when Holland's matchmaker friend Patti Stanger asked her point-blank if Alexandra was Sumner's, Holland denied it and added she'd used a surrogate. Regardless, Sumner doted on the child and seemed to enjoy having Alexandra around the house. Holland showed photos of the baby bouncing in Sumner's lap. He added Alexandra as a beneficiary in his will and said he planned to formally adopt her. His long-time tax and estate planning lawyer in Boston, David Andelman, began looking into the tax implications of his marrying Holland and adopting Alexandra.

———

The same day Holland picked up her baby in San Diego, Heather Naylor took advantage of Holland's absence to have lunch with Sumner at his mansion. Naylor had been hearing disturbing reports for over a year that Holland was bad-mouthing her—specifically, telling people that she had no talent, that Sumner was wasting his time with her, and that her new reality show was a flop. Naylor had gotten back on MTV at Sumner's insistence, this time with *The Alectrix*, a show with exactly the same premise and even some of the same band members as *The Electric Barbarellas*. Naylor attributed Holland's campaign against her to jealousy over her relationship with Sumner.

Despite Holland's efforts, Sumner seemed as enthusiastic as ever about Naylor's talent and potential. At their lunch Sumner assured Naylor that *The Alectrix* would be renewed for another season and, if not, Naylor would be given another MTV show, according to Naylor. He said he'd help her get a record contract and volunteered to attend a music showcase for her, urging her to invite major record producers.

Naylor then took her opportunity, with Holland out of the house, to mount a counterattack: She showed Sumner emails from Holland to her lawyer discussing her financial prospects and status in Sumner's will. She also showed him nude photographs of Holland that, she maintained, Holland was sharing with men on the internet.

They were interrupted by Herzer's unexpected return. Herzer breezily made light of the incriminating evidence and quickly steered Naylor to the door. Naylor had inflicted little, if any, lasting damage on Holland, who was nonetheless furious when Herzer gave her a detailed briefing on what she had witnessed. Holland's laptop had vanished several years earlier, and she now suspected it was the source of the nude photos. Naylor must have stolen the laptop, Holland reasoned.

Holland called Naylor and ordered her not to call Sumner or have any further contact with him, a directive Naylor ignored. She went ahead and scheduled the music showcase for July 8, assuring representatives from major recording studios that Sumner was backing her and would be present. But to her increasing frustration and dismay, Sumner no longer answered when she called, nor did he respond to any of her messages. When the date for the showcase arrived, Sumner was a no-show. No recording contract materialized.

On July 24 Naylor and her assistant pulled up to the Redstone mansion hoping to see Sumner in person. They were blocked at the door by Carlos Martinez, who said Naylor had been barred from seeing Sumner or having any contact with him. Sumner's phone number had been changed on Holland's orders, and Naylor wasn't allowed access to it. Naylor's number had been deleted from Sumner's phone so he couldn't call her. Naylor left empty-handed.

Not long after, Holland fired both Martinez and his wife, who also helped manage the household, on suspicions they were in league with Naylor. Sumner and Martinez had become so close over the years that Martinez was a beneficiary in Sumner's will. But now Sumner excised him.

The decision alarmed Sumner's longtime lawyer, David Andelman, who worried that Holland and Herzer were behind it. Andelman pressed Sumner on the issue, questioning whether he really wanted to take such a drastic step. But the questions only seemed to anger Sumner, and he ordered Andelman to implement the change "literally and immediately" and said he "didn't want any second-guessing from his lawyer." Andelman duly complied.

Without Sumner's support, Naylor's nascent television and recording career hit a wall. MTV aired six episodes of *The Alectrix* rather than the promised eight, in what Naylor deemed an undesirable time slot (11:00 p.m.) and with minimal advertising or promotion. After weak ratings (less than 200,000 viewers a week) the show was canceled. Naylor wasn't offered any new series.

That might have been the end of Naylor's involvement with Sumner, but later that summer Holland sued Naylor, claiming Naylor had stolen her laptop containing "private and confidential" photos from the Redstone mansion. She sued Martinez, too, alleging that Sumner's long-time house manager had abetted the theft. Martinez hired Bryan Freedman, a prominent entertainment litigator with a long list of celebrity clients.

"Sydney Holland's decision to sue Mr. Martinez is the biggest mistake she has ever made," Freedman said.

———

Having survived the financial crisis without losing control of either Viacom or CBS, Sumner saw his fortunes quickly rebound along with his companies' share prices. Other than his female lovers and companions, nothing interested Sumner more than the value of his stock and options. Jagiello observed that Sumner "obsessively" tracked the value of his Viacom and CBS options. He even had an electronic ticker installed in his bedroom. He often asked Jagiello and other nurses to run calculations for him. He "was very engaged and appeared to derive great pleasure from tracking his holdings," as Jagiello put it. That year *Forbes* placed Redstone's net worth at $4.7 billion.

Since consulting her lawyer about the diamond ring, Holland had easily reached her stated $20 million goal and then some. Sumner assured Herzer that she and Holland "would be cared for during the rest of their lives," according to Herzer. "What's mine is yours," he said, and "you will never have to worry or want for anything."

Sumner amended his estate plan to give Holland and Herzer the $40 million he had previously bestowed on Shari's charitable foundation.

In an amendment to his trust dated September 26, 2013, Sumner gave Holland a minimum of $20 million when he died, and up to $45 million; Herzer would receive the same amount, and each of her three children would receive $1.5 million. This was on top of the already constant gifts of cash. (Holland and Herzer received combined cash gifts of $9.1 million in 2013.) Holland and Herzer would inherit the Beverly Park mansion and run the Sumner Redstone Foundation. Holland would get custody of Sugar and Butterfly, Sumner's miniature poodles.

Sumner also spent millions funding charitable foundations in Holland's and Herzer's names.

With Sumner's financial backing, Holland launched a movie production company called Rich Hippie Productions and dabbled in high-end real estate. She redecorated a Beverly Hills property she bought from Jessica Simpson and flipped it just a year later to actress Jennifer Lawrence.

Sumner deleted Shari as a beneficiary in his will, though there was nothing he could do about her 20 percent stake in National Amusements (short of buying her out), nor could he excise her from the trust.

"You Know How He Is about Women"

By March of 2014, Holland and Herzer were planning their most brazen gambit by far—a plan to get their hands on the over $200 million in Viacom and CBS stock and stock options Sumner had earned while serving as chairman of the companies. Unlike the billions in stock held by National Amusements and locked up in the irrevocable trust, these securities were in an unrestricted account. The women wanted Sumner to sell the assets—and give the proceeds to them immediately, rather than having to wait until he died.

Holland and Herzer hired a prominent trusts and estates lawyer—Richard B. Covey at Carter Ledyard & Milburn in New York—to advise them on how to go about it. On March 21, in anticipation of meeting with him, Holland sent Herzer an email with "a list of things I think we should cover." On the list were "changing the trust to add both our names to it"; "changing the Sumner Redstone Foundation so we can run it now and after Sumner's demise"; and "get the monies now rather than waiting until Sumner dies."

Getting Sumner to go along with the plan required a sustained campaign, much of it overheard by Giovanni Paz and other staff at the Redstone mansion. His nurses, ordered out of the fish room and told to wait in the kitchen in one instance, reported hearing Holland and Herzer cajoling him for money. They told him that Shari hated him and only cared about money and would likely sue to contest any bequests to them. She might litigate even sooner. They might get nothing. The only way to ensure they got the money was to give it to them now.

Sumner resisted.

They kept at it, at one point saying they "were the only ones who loved and would protect him. If he loved them back he would cash out. If he did not, he would die alone."

Another obstacle was David Andelman, the Boston estate planning lawyer who had represented Sumner for over thirty years. He was a trustee of the trust controlling National Amusements and on the boards of National Amusements, Viacom, and CBS. Andelman watched closely over Sumner's assets, and Sumner always consulted him about tax consequences. Like many billionaires, Sumner was obsessed with minimizing his tax bill.

To Holland's frustration, Andelman kept raising tax objections to any sale of stock and options. (As well he might have, since the sale would trigger capital gains taxes and gift tax on any transfer to Holland and Herzer.) "David keeps using that gift tax excuse," Holland complained in the March 21 email to Herzer.

A few weeks later, in April, Sumner hired a new tax and estate planning lawyer: Leah Bishop of the Los Angeles firm Loeb & Loeb, a lawyer who was later suspected to have been recommended by Holland and Herzer. Andelman, who found out only when Bishop asked for copies of the National Amusements trust documents, worried that Sumner might be trying to change the terms to marginalize Shari and her children.

With Andelman sidelined, Sumner gave in. On May 16 Holland instructed Paz, whose duties included answering the phones, to block all calls to Sumner, even those from his doctor. That day he sold $236 million in stock and stock options, according to regulatory filings he was required to record. The proceeds went into his checking account at City National Bank in Los Angeles.

The next day Holland had the stock ticker removed from Sumner's bedroom so he couldn't follow his share prices. His nurse, Jagiello, observed that Sumner "fell into a depression almost immediately."

Two days later, Andelman called Elvira Bartoli, Sumner's account manager at City National Bank, to check on Sumner's balance. It was $90 million less than he expected. He was even more surprised when Bartoli told him she wasn't allowed to disclose where the money had gone, something that had never happened in his many years of working with Sumner and the bank. Sumner had always discussed such large financial transactions in advance with Andelman, in part to go over the tax consequences. Andelman usually handled the mechanics of any transfers.

Andelman pressed for an explanation, and finally Bartoli capitulated: the $90 million had passed by wire transfer to Holland and Herzer, $45 million to each, on the same day Sumner sold his stock and options.

Andelman was alarmed. The sale had generated about $100 million in after-tax proceeds. Gift and other taxes would now come to more than $90 million. Holland and Herzer had virtually drained Sumner's account. (He would eventually have to borrow $100 million from National Amusements to pay the taxes.)

Andelman confronted Sumner the same day and said he was concerned he was being "pressured" by the two women. Sumner became "visibly angry" at the suggestion, going so far as to call Andelman an "asshole." He "insisted the decision to transfer those funds had been his alone," Andelman recalled.

Andelman told George Abrams much the same thing when Sumner's longtime lawyer expressed his dismay. Abrams tried to raise the issue directly with Sumner, but he flatly refused to discuss it, saying his personal life was none of Abrams's business (though the lawyer had advised him on both his divorces).

Sumner wondered aloud how he could give the two women even more, asking, "If I sell my unvested options sometime in the future, can I receive any money from them?" and "Will there ever be a time when I can withdraw money from National?"

Moonves found out about the two $45 million transfers when the CBS general counsel told him Sumner was struggling to find ways to pay the gift tax. Moonves didn't want to touch the issue; he thought the situation was a mess and wanted to stay as far from it as possible.

Sumner didn't act in isolation. Besides his lawyers Bishop and Andelman, other trustees, including Dauman, were aware of the changes to the trust and the massive gifts. "Sometimes I would be surprised by the amounts involved," Dauman acknowledged. "So I would discuss with David. And he says 'this is what he wants to do.'" Andelman added, "You know how he is about women and, you know, these women take good care of him," and "obviously he didn't have a good relationship with his daughter."

In the midst of this, Bishop asked Sumner to meet with Dr. James E. Spar, a noted geriatric specialist and professor of psychiatry at the David Geffen School of Medicine at UCLA, on May 21. Prior to the meeting Holland and Herzer allegedly spent "hours" with Sumner "telling him exactly what he was supposed to say."

The effort worked. Dr. Spar reported that Sumner "demonstrated impressive knowledge of his estate, knew the people named in his estate plan and how they are related to him, and revealed no hint of delusional thinking in the discussion of his estate plan." In his opinion, "the testamentary decisions [Sumner] discussed in this evaluation struck me as reflecting his own authentic wishes, and not the influence of Manuela, Sydney, or anyone else."

Dr. Spar's report would now help insulate Holland and Herzer from any future claims they had exerted undue influence on Sumner. With such large sums involved, that was more than just a possibility. These latest developments understandably caused renewed concern on the part of Shari and her children.

When she first heard about the giant transfers, Shari was dumbfounded. When she'd raised the issue of selling some of his CBS shares after the Midway incident, Sumner had said he'd never sell them under any circumstances. Now he had sold them all. And Sumner hated paying taxes. Yet he'd just gone and needlessly triggered enormous gift and capital gains taxes.

Shari believed that either was inconceivable, unless Sumner had succumbed to the undue influence of Holland and Herzer, no matter what he told his lawyers and Spar.

"There needs to be a plan where they don't control access to my father," Shari wrote in an email to Andelman that month. And on May 26, 2014, the day before Sumner's ninety-first birthday, when Shari and her three children would be in Los Angeles for his party, they agreed to meet at the Peninsula Hotel to discuss the situation. Shari vowed to "go after them regardless of the strength of the case."

The stage was now set for an exceedingly awkward celebration of Sumner's ninety-first birthday on May 27. Given his declining health and difficulty with both speech and eating, Holland and Herzer had planned a much smaller and low-key affair in a private room at Nobu, the Malibu outpost of celebrity chef Nobu Matsuhisa. No gossip columnists or photographers were tipped off, and the guest list was private.

When Shari and her children arrived, Brent's daughter Keryn Redstone was occupying the seat next to her grandfather. According to witnesses, a heated argument broke out between Shari and Keryn over the seating arrangement. Keryn maintained in a sworn declaration that her grandfather had recently injured his hand and asked her to sit next to him to help him eat. But then "Shari demanded that I change seats with her, so she could sit next to Grumpy. I declined because Grumpy specifically asked me to be next to him to help him eat. Shari erupted and threatened to kill me." (Shari has denied that any such exchange took place.)

That summer Shari also hired lawyers, who retained an ex–FBI agent, Jim Elroy, to investigate Holland and Herzer, a prospect which so unsettled Sumner (not to mention Holland and Herzer) that he hired four sets of legal counsel to counter the effort. "It's upsetting that this is happening," wrote Leah Bishop, Redstone's personal estate lawyer at Loeb & Loeb, in a November 2014 email to Holland and Herzer, "but Sumner cannot stop Shari from doing this."

Bishop also reached out on their behalf to the famed trial lawyer David Boies, who earlier in his career had represented Sumner. Now she asked him if he'd represent Holland and Herzer in an anticipated lawsuit by Shari. Bishop insisted that Sumner wanted to make the gifts and didn't want any interference from his daughter or other family members. Boies thought it odd that Bishop, Sumner's lawyer, was the one arranging a lawyer for the two women. He said he'd need to speak to Sumner directly to confirm that these were indeed his wishes. Bishop said that wouldn't be possible because Sumner's speech was unintelligible.

Boies nonetheless agreed to interview Holland and Herzer in New York, before deciding he wanted no part of it. No representation ensued.

The intrafamily feud did nothing to deter Sumner from continuing to shift assets away from his daughter and grandchildren to Holland and Herzer, whom he seemed to consider his real family. Bishop had him meet again with Dr. Spar. Sumner was "quite concerned that the documents made sure that Manuela and Sydney would inherit the house and its contents," Dr. Spar reported. He quoted the following exchange:

"In your relationship with Manuela and Sydney, who's in charge?" Spar asked.

"I am," Sumner said.

"Some might say they have you wrapped around their finger and can manipulate you."

"That could never happen."

"What if they threatened to leave you if you did not give them something they want?"

"They wouldn't do that."

"But what if they did?"

The question angered Sumner, according to Spar. "I would tell them to go fuck themselves!" Sumner replied.

Once Bishop was out of the room, Sumner "said to me something like, 'Make sure Manuela and Sydney get everything,'" Spar added in his report.

Meanwhile, Shari's pleas to her father for financial assistance went unheeded. In a June 2014 email to her son Tyler, she lamented, "My father delivered a message to me thru his attorney that he understands my children are struggling and he doesn't give a shit and he doesn't care that everyone in Sidney and Manuela's family including their parents and children are treated better and have an easier lifestyle than my children."

And to all of her children she wrote, "If my father wants me to drop dead he doesn't need to do anything else. He has made how he feels about me perfectly clear."

"I Want My $45 Million Back"

Holland's million-dollar lawsuit against Naylor and Martinez had languished since she filed it the previous August. It had been ignored by the press, perhaps because Holland and Naylor were relative unknowns. But on June 25 the case burst into the headlines: Naylor filed court papers that not only denied stealing Holland's laptop but also contained the far more explosive counterclaim that "Holland has effectively taken over Redstone's life and does not allow anyone independent access to him." With the link to Sumner, the story was suddenly newsworthy.

The lawsuit instantly became fodder for tabloid speculation and gossip that spread far beyond the confines of Hollywood. In New York, *Vanity Fair* editor Graydon Carter smelled a good story—an aging Hollywood billionaire with two live-in companions was a delectable mix of serious business and tabloid sex, the perfect recipe for a *Vanity Fair* feature. Carter asked the investigative business journalist William Cohan to look into it.

Naylor's counterclaim had also triggered the *Hollywood Reporter* article that captured the reality-TV star George Pilgrim's attention and prompted his string of Facebook messages to Holland—"I think your hot"—culminating in their passionate kiss at the Peninsula Hotel and Holland's promise that she'd "take care" of him.

Notwithstanding her psychic's prediction that she'd meet someone like Pilgrim, Holland surely knew only too well the perils of infidelity. She'd wielded the charge against the flight attendant Malia Andelin and had witnessed Sumner's explosive reaction. Patti Stanger had warned her explicitly about cheating on Sumner, and even beyond that, Holland had reason to believe she was under surveillance by Jim Elroy, Shari's private detective.

Nonetheless, the day after their first encounter, Pilgrim and Holland met at another entertainment industry watering hole, the Polo Lounge at the Beverly Hills Hotel.

Nestled in a curved, velvet-upholstered booth, they couldn't keep their hands off each other. Holland suggested they get a room at the hotel so they could have sex, but Pilgrim declined. That only seemed to heighten his allure. Afterward Holland pelted him with suggestive texts and emails. When he told her he had to visit his mother in the New Age spiritual mecca of Sedona, Arizona, she proposed she meet him there.

Holland arrived by private jet and looked askance when Pilgrim picked her up in the aging Ford LTD he'd inherited from his grandmother. They went for lunch at the secluded Enchantment Resort, nestled in the red rocks of Boynton Canyon, then booked a room there.

Pilgrim felt "a lot of pressure," he recalled, but "we made love," and "it was beautiful."

Afterward Holland told Pilgrim she thought she had already fallen in love with him. She promised to give him everything he could possibly want. "I'm in charge of a lot of power and a lot of things Sumner Redstone relies on," Holland told him.

Holland booked the ($1,500) room for two nights but couldn't stay—she needed to get back to Sumner. She told Pilgrim she was protecting Sumner from his daughter, Shari, who "hated" her and was trying to eject her. She warned him that Shari had hired a private detective to investigate her.

At one point Pilgrim asked Holland if she and Sumner were romantically involved.

"Are you crazy?" she responded. "He's ninety years old."

———

Closely allied though she and Herzer were, Holland made it clear to Pilgrim that she didn't trust Herzer with the potentially explosive information about their love affair. Holland described Herzer as very aggressive about getting what she wanted, prompting Pilgrim to nickname her "Pitbull." From Pilgrim's perspective, the two women were constantly jockeying for power within the mansion and picking petty fights, like the time Herzer angrily blamed Holland after Sumner's chauffeur failed to pick up her daughter on time. At one point Holland texted Pilgrim: "I am afraid to use the phone because I heard pitbull just walk by my room to go downstairs." To avoid being overheard, Holland often communicated with Pilgrim via text.

Pilgrim knew of her plans to inherit Sumner's estate but worried that Sumner's family might supplant her. "I really don't trust [Sumner]," Pilgrim warned her.

"I agree too but [Sumner's family] won't be able to do much I will be there the whole time so will pitbull," Holland texted.

"I definitely wouldn't leave [Sumner] alone with any of [Sumner's family] now!!!" Pilgrim wrote.

"No way!!"

"Fuck them," Pilgrim added.

"Exactly."

"They're going to try to play the Jewish family card watch!!!"

"Totally!!!" Holland agreed.

"But we're family grandpa."

"We love u."

"BS!!!"

"Exactly they love his money," Holland asserted.

"Yes," Pilgrim agreed. "And to get all of it."

———

Holland made good on her promise to take care of Pilgrim. They went house shopping in Sedona, looking for something in the range of $1 million to $5 million. To establish her financial bona fides, Holland showed the real estate agent, who happened to be Pilgrim's stepfather, a trust account in her name with a balance of over $50 million.

After admiring the expansive decks and sweeping views of the surrounding cliffs, they settled on a 6,500-square-foot, five-bedroom house with a pool and hot tub for which Holland paid $3.5 million.

Pilgrim moved in that fall. Holland paid for their membership in the Seven Canyons club, with its championship golf course, spa and fitness center, and "privileged" access to the nearby Enchantment Resort. She paid for his health insurance. She bought him a new Jeep Cherokee and an iPhone. She dressed him in Ralph Lauren. She sent him gift coupons to Whole Foods.

She also bought him thousands of dollars' worth of healing crystals, including black tourmalines, said to enhance sexual potency in men, which she positioned under their bed. Holland boasted she had Sumner's signature and other paperwork on file and could use it to get Pilgrim a book deal for *Citizen Pilgrim* with Viacom-owned Simon & Schuster.

Holland showered Pilgrim's parents with gifts, too. On her first visit she gave his mother an expensive bracelet, which the older woman considered odd, given that Holland had just met Pilgrim.

When not paying in cash—sacks of hundred-dollar bills were arriving weekly at Sumner's mansion—Holland and Herzer charged virtually everything to Visa and American Express credit cards paid for by Sumner. In 2014 alone, the year Holland met Pilgrim, she and

Herzer ran up over $3.5 million in charges. Holland charged $752,737 that year to her interior designer, Tracie Butler. For her part, Herzer splurged on expensive clothes: $128,780 at Barney's, $82,624 at Hermès, $54,212 at Miu Miu, and $34,147 at Chanel.

Holland made the hour-and-twenty-five-minute flight from the Van Nuys Airport by private jet whenever she could (at a round-trip cost of $7,900 per flight, receipts show), spending the day with Pilgrim and having sex but leaving in time to be home for dinner with Sumner—her "curfew," as Pilgrim described it. ("I can barely leave the house," she complained in one text.) Sometimes she sent the private jet to pick Pilgrim up and meet her in Los Angeles. But Holland promised to move in with him in Arizona as soon as Sumner died—presumably soon.

On days Holland couldn't travel she often sent him sexually provocative videos of herself in the mansion along with explicit text messages. Pilgrim saved them all.

"Need my cock sucked," he wrote.

"I love you."

"And I would love to do that soon."

When she was away, Sumner called Holland constantly. She'd often put him on speaker, and Pilgrim heard him asking where she was and when she'd be back. Moments later he'd call again with the same questions. "Where is she? Somebody's sick and Manuela's not here and the dogs are running around. This was what her life was like," Pilgrim recalled.

Much of what Pilgrim heard from Sumner was incomprehensible mumbling. But suddenly he'd articulate several relatively clear and coherent sentences.

Sumner's constant calls got on Pilgrim's nerves. At one point he suggested he meet Sumner, thinking it would allay the old man's worries if he met and liked Holland's new boyfriend. Holland firmly rebuffed the idea, saying Sumner was "old-fashioned" and wouldn't understand. Pilgrim didn't get it. Why would Sumner care? "What do you mean if you're his fucking nurse?" he asked her.

The two fought often over Sumner's constant demands, but Holland assured him it would all be worth it.

Pilgrim grudgingly agreed, but he pressed Holland to make sure her financial agreements with Sumner were "iron clad."

"We need to be a family healthy working and having fun, this old man is draining u!!! He better come through," he texted her.

"I agree."

"U need now iron clad guarantee. No lip service. Cover us." Pilgrim added, "You're dropdead gorgeous beautiful woman, the situation [with Sumner] is temporary just cover all bases get everything ironclad. . . ."

"It is iron clad but can be changed while he is alive and of course hard to challenge," she responded.

———

Sumner's health continued to deteriorate that summer. In late June Holland and Herzer insisted that Sumner accompany them to New York over the objections of his nurses. "Sydney and Manuela nagged, cajoled, and pressured Mr. Redstone until he finally agreed to go," Jagiello reported. The trip "took a real toll on Mr. Redstone. He was physically much weaker."

One of his nurses, Joseph Octaviano, grew increasingly concerned about the care Sumner was receiving from Holland and Herzer. Sumner was frequently dehydrated, but Holland didn't answer Octaviano's text messages alerting her to the problem. He felt they were careless about Sumner's feeding, cutting food into pieces too large for him to swallow comfortably. In August Octaviano had to perform the Heimlich maneuver after food blocked Sumner's windpipe and he turned blue. Holland and Herzer "ran from the room," Octaviano reported.

Pilgrim was also a witness to Holland's often-dismissive treatment of Sumner, listening in when she'd put Pilgrim on speakerphone while she tended to Sumner. "I'm not your fucking nurse," he heard her say on one call, and she told Pilgrim she was annoyed that Sumner had urinated in bed. Another time, he heard her say, "Why are you slobbering all over yourself?"

In early September Herzer was feeding Sumner fried rice and seemed oblivious that he was struggling to swallow and breathe. Octaviano and another nurse intervened and administered oxygen, which succeeded in reviving him.

Two days later Holland was with Sumner when he started choking and gasping. She called Pilgrim and put her phone on speaker so he could hear Sumner's plight. From the strangled sounds he heard, he couldn't tell whether Sumner was having a heart attack or a stroke or just choking. But it sounded serious. He overheard Holland say she was going to call 911 and Sumner repeatedly shouted "no."

"Call 911 immediately!" Pilgrim yelled.

———

Sumner was rushed to Cedars-Sinai Medical Center and spent the night in intensive care, at which point his family was summoned. He was diagnosed with aspiration pneumonia, an infection often caused by inhaling food into the lungs.

Holland seemed more concerned about what to wear at the hospital than about Sumner's condition. She sent Pilgrim a video of herself in what she called her "Star Wars" bathroom. "This is what I'm wearing today," she says on camera. She pans over her diaphanous top and tight jeans while saying, "Gotta go to the hospital today." She dons oversize sunglasses. "This is my casual chic outfit, with my big sunglasses so I don't have to talk to people." She takes off the sunglasses and shakes her dark hair. "Sending you a big kiss," she mouths and then blows him a kiss. "Love you."

Sumner was transferred to a private room that morning, and his nurse Giovanni Paz came to help with his care. As he was helping move Sumner from his bed to a reclining chair, Paz heard Sumner tell Holland, "I want my $45 million back."

Holland did her best to change the subject, but Sumner persisted.

"I will give you your money back, but let's not talk about this now, let's talk about this another time," Holland replied, according to Paz. But Sumner kept insisting that he wanted his money back.

"Your family is coming, please don't do this to me," Holland pleaded. Even as she spoke, Brandon was on his way to the hospital and Shari was flying in from Boston.

Holland spoke to someone on her cell phone—Paz assumed it was Herzer—then turned back to Paz and another nurse. "We have to put him to sleep," she said. "You have to help me with this."

Holland and the other nurse left the room, leaving Paz with Sumner. Five or ten minutes later a hospital nurse arrived and gave Sumner some medication. He was soon asleep, or close to it.

Brandon had called the hospital that morning to find out if it was a good time to visit, and was reassured that it was. His grandfather was awake and alert.

But when Brandon arrived and passed Paz in the hallway soon after the exchange with Holland, Paz tried unsuccessfully to get his attention. He followed Brandon into Sumner's room, and Brandon was stunned by what he encountered—at first he thought his grandfather was dead.

But he was breathing shallowly. Brandon asked Paz why his grandfather's eyes looked so "strange." Brandon asked him to lower the shades so Sumner could sleep undisturbed.

Paz was deeply troubled by what he'd just witnessed. He strongly suspected the sleep-inducing medication was meant to prevent Sumner from raising the issue of the $45 million with Brandon, Shari, or anyone else.

When Paz left the hospital about a half hour later, he texted Brandon and asked him to call him when his visit was over, even though he knew that, if discovered, he could be fired for reaching out to Sumner's grandson. When Brandon called, Paz told him what had happened. Brandon agreed with his assessment that Holland had asked for the sleep medication to keep Sumner from talking to his family. Brandon assured Paz he'd done the right thing and said he was going to call Shari.

"I think they might be trying to kill him," he told his mother.

Shari arrived later that day. She was alone at her father's bedside, holding his hand, when Octaviano came into the room. Like Paz, he mustered the courage to say something.

"Ma'am, could you lead your father's care?" he asked.

Shari seemed startled and asked who he was.

He explained he was a nurse who spent six days a week with her father. He asked her to step outside the room and briefed her on what he described as Holland's and Herzer's "constant abuse" of her father.

Shari was upset. She gave him her email address and phone number and asked him to keep her informed.

Worried that he might be discovered and fired, Octaviano had his wife create a new email account solely for the purpose of communicating with Shari. "I am at your side and . . . will be willing to testify against Manuela and Sydney," he wrote.

Sumner had evidently suffered some degree of brain damage—Herzer described it as a brain ischemia, a condition caused by insufficient blood flow to the brain. Symptoms include difficulty speaking and swallowing, slurred speech, and loss of coordination. In Sumner's case, he could no longer chew and swallow food; a feeding tube had to be installed through his abdomen.

Sumner was discharged from Cedars-Sinai on September 9 at 3:00 p.m. and returned home to Beverly Park. Octaviano started filing detailed reports of the day's events with Shari. In his first missive, he recounted a conversation between Holland and Sumner while he was watching television in the fish room:

"Will you still marry me?" Holland asked.

"Yes, tomorrow we will call a rabbi," Sumner answered.

"Why don't we wait for Friday?" Holland replied. "I will invite my lawyer and Manuela is here."

But Holland could hardly marry Sumner and stay engaged to Pilgrim. By Friday talk of marriage had evaporated. So had talk of returning the $45 million.

———

The perils of communicating with Sumner's family soon became apparent. Once Sumner was home, Holland told Paz he should have no further contact with him, leaving Paz little to do. "Don't touch him," she ordered when he tried to assist another nurse.

Two days later, a lawyer told Paz he was being "let go" but offered him a check for a month's salary if he signed a declaration. When Paz declined, saying he wanted his own lawyer to read it first, Holland came over and stood "inches away from me," he recalled, and said: "Get out of my house."

Sumner was now more dependent than ever on Holland, Herzer, and the nursing staff at the mansion. In addition to the feeding tube, he needed a catheter. He couldn't walk unassisted. His speech was seriously impaired, all but unintelligible to those unused to interpreting him. Still, he managed to communicate, usually through his nurse Jagiello. Jagiello spent so much time with Sumner and became so skilled an interpreter that his nickname was "the Sumner whisperer."

Sumner still watched sports on television. No one had been a more avid sports fan than him, especially when it came to his favorite hometown teams, the Patriots and the Red Sox (at least when they were winning), but now he rarely seemed to know what team was playing.

Nor did he seem aware that most of the games he watched were prerecorded rather than live. He had ongoing, substantial bets on the outcomes with his nephew Steven Sweetwood, the broker who had set him up with his second wife, Paula. Sumner always won the bet, because Sweetwood already knew the outcome and arranged for Sumner to bet on the winning team.

Shari was planning a follow-up visit for September 15, and the day before, she spoke to her father on the phone. Despite her earlier vow to take legal action against Holland and Herzer, she now had second thoughts. As she wrote in an email to her three children: "We would not win a lawsuit to get rid of S and M," again referring to Sydney and Manuela. "And that would not necessarily be the right thing to do." After all, Sumner himself had made the decisions he did. "I just called to tell him that I love him and I would be there tomorrow, and all he kept saying was leave Sydney and Manuela alone. He said it one hundred times. He was not interested in the fact that I loved him or that Tyler and I were coming out.

"We all have amazing lives surrounded by people we love and who love us," Shari continued. "This should not be taking over our lives and destroying our days . . . and nights!!!! Agonizing everyday accomplishes nothing. I do not deny that this is an awful situation, but it is an awful situation that he created and that we cannot undo. This is a very hard decision but after much agony and many tears, I really believe that we cannot let this destroy our lives any longer. . . . Rosh Hashana is next week and I think we all need to commit to a new beginning."

The next day Shari and Tyler arrived at Sumner's mansion at about noon. Fortunately for them, Holland and Herzer were both out shopping. Mother and son's main goal was to reassure their father and grandfather they loved him and to counter Holland's and Herzer's claims to the contrary. But a staff member quickly alerted Holland that Shari and Tyler were at the house. They'd been there about twenty minutes and thought they were having a good conversation, given the constraints of Sumner's speech, when Holland phoned and was put through to Sumner.

Shari and Tyler could hear Holland's end of the conversation.

"Are they upsetting you?" she asked. "Are they making you cry? You have got to get them out."

Sumner turned to his daughter and grandson. "You have to go," he said, and then started crying. Shari knelt by his chair and held his hand.

"Do you really want us to leave?"

Sumner nodded yes. "I love you so much," he managed to articulate. "But you have to go."

Shari, too, was now in tears. She thought it likely this was the last time she'd see her father alive.

"At least you heard what you needed to hear," Tyler said as they walked out.

After witnessing the exchange, Octaviano sent Shari an email: "Today's incident is so unforgiving. I'm so sorry. It is not the end of the rope ma'am Shari. I am at your side and 99% of the staff will be willing to testify against [the] brutality of Manuela and Sydney to your Dad. From the day I worked there, I witnessed verbal abuse almost every day. Nagging, threatening and back stabbing to win your Dad's sympathy and a lot of document signing. One time Manuela told your Dad that none of his family loves him except them. Yesterday, Sydney ask your Dad if he still loves her and he replied, 'NO, I'm so tired, leave me alone, I want to die.'"

Octaviano continued that Sumner sometimes cried out for help, but there was little or nothing the staff could do: "Every move in that house is controlled by Manuela and Sydney."

Octaviano's email concluded: "Your Dad always looks so sad and helpless. My heart really falls apart every time these happen."

This was too painful for Shari to read. She thanked Octaviano for the information but asked him to send all future correspondence to Tyler.

Shari felt there was nothing more she could do. Maybe it was time to follow her brother out of the family business and sell her stake in National Amusements. She could invest the proceeds in Advancit Capital, her venture capital enterprise, and continue her philanthropic efforts, free from the drama of her father and his consorts. She and Bishop started negotiating for her father to buy out her stake.

"This Is Your Family"

Although Holland was still officially engaged to Sumner and had again proposed marrying him, she never mentioned this to Pilgrim. In the fall of 2014, just after Sumner got out of the hospital, Pilgrim texted Holland emojis of a family and then a bride and wedding band. He called her and proposed. She didn't answer for fear of being overheard by Herzer.

"Is that yes?" he texted.

"Yes, yes," Holland answered.

"Omg. I'm so happy," Pilgrim replied.

"Me too," Holland typed, followed by a long string of heart emojis.

Pilgrim impulsively suggested they drop everything and "run away."

"Let's get married and run away and hide in Sedona."

"Our World," Holland answered.

"And we travel all over run away," Pilgrim wrote in successive texts.

"Yes please."

"Perfect to me."

"I'll save u let's run away," Pilgrim suggested again.

"Done."

"There's a whole Universe."

"Fuck those losers."

"Agreed," Holland wrote.

"Waiting for a man to die!!! Fuck that we can be explorers travel the world Indiana jones stuff," Pilgrim elaborated.

"I know," Holland responded.

"It sucks for both of us I am sorry."

"Sorry."

In their text messages, Holland and Pilgrim began referring to each other as "husband" and "wife."

"God I need you inside of me. I miss your smell and taste," Holland texted him.

"Love u more my wife."

"Love you more Husband xoxoxoxoxo."

"I'm your soulmate."

"Husband."

"Your my soulmate . . ."

"I hope we die at the same time."

"Wouldn't want to be without you."

On October 8 Holland brought her parents to Sedona to meet Pilgrim and his family. The future in-laws had lunch together at the Enchantment Resort, which seemed to be going well until Holland's mother told Pilgrim's mother that she should consider losing weight. Afterward Holland and Pilgrim had sex while her parents went shopping for crystals.

As soon as Holland accepted his marriage proposal, Holland and Pilgrim started planning for a baby of their own, with Holland again using artificial insemination, an egg donor, and a surrogate. Pilgrim signed a formal sperm donor agreement relinquishing any paternity rights. They went to the same fertility doctor in Beverly Hills whom Holland had used to conceive Alexandra, where Pilgrim complained to the doctor about having to masturbate into a cup while people walked by in the adjacent hallway. The doctor said it wasn't necessary—he could "stick a needle" into Pilgrim's testicles, just as he'd done for "the old man." But at that point Holland signaled the doctor to say no more.

Pilgrim dutifully used the cup, even though his mind was racing: Who did he mean by "old man"? Had Sumner and Holland also planned to have children? Who was Alexandra's father? Once they were in Holland's chauffeur-driven car outside, Pilgrim demanded an explanation. "If we're going to have kids together, I have to know the truth," he said. "What the fuck is going on?"

Holland looked at him, and Pilgrim thought she was finally going to give him an honest answer. But then the driver asked for directions, and the spell was broken. "Just let it go," Holland said. "We'll talk about it later."

On October 28, Pilgrim and Holland exchanged another round of text messages:

"I gave you my blood today . . . my sperm," Pilgrim wrote.

"I know. Thanks," Holland replied. "I give you my heart and soul. . . . Thanks for doing all of this I know it is so different to do things this way."

"It's my honor my wife. Anything for u. Anything!!"

"Thank you Husband."

"Love u my wife."

"Love you my Husband."

"We are so lucky to have each other," Pilgrim reminded her.

"We sure are," she answered. "Very. I waited my whole life for you."

Holland's devotion didn't extend to spending Christmas Day with Pilgrim in Sedona. Instead, she and Herzer and their children gathered at Sumner's mansion. While they celebrated in the living room, Sumner languished in another room, alone except for Octaviano and other nurses. At about 3:00 p.m., Sumner asked to see the Christmas tree. When Octaviano wheeled him into the living room, Herzer seemed surprised but exclaimed, "Sumner, this is your family."

Sumner "immediately began sobbing," Octaviano recalled.

———

After nearly a year's effort, by November Sumner and Shari had reached the framework of an agreement for him to buy out his daughter's 20 percent stake in National Amusements. Shari would receive $1 billion in cash and stock, tax-free. In return, she would no longer succeed Sumner as chair of either CBS or Viacom.

Shari was ready to sign.

But Holland and Herzer, apparently, were not ready for Sumner to sign.

Octaviano's daily missives to Tyler described a stream of visits from Andelman, Bishop, and other lawyers, meetings that often left Sumner in tears. In one meeting with Bishop, Octaviano recalled hearing Sumner cry out, "No, no, no," and then start to sob.

As Tyler told Andelman in an earlier email, "Manuela and Sydney dictate to SMR everything he MUST say in conversation with Leah and verbally abuse him if he deviates. I'm told they verbally abuse him, threaten him and nag him on a daily basis."

Suddenly, Bishop injected a new condition into the buyout: Sumner insisted that Shari had to agree not to contest any of the enormous gifts he'd made (and was continuing to make) to Holland and Herzer.

Octaviano was on duty January 8 and reported that Sumner was "exceedingly groggy and disoriented that morning." In Octaviano's account, a befuddled Sumner asked his nurse Jagiello, "What's happening, where am I?"

Bishop arrived at 11:30 a.m. and spent twenty minutes with Sumner, with Holland present. Octaviano heard Sumner cry throughout the meeting and then off and on throughout the day. Holland instructed

Octaviano to block all calls to Sumner and specifically banned any from Shari or Kimberlee. When Kimberlee called, she was rebuffed.

Later that afternoon, Octaviano overheard a conversation between Sumner and Holland, with Herzer connected by speakerphone. Holland told Sumner that "his family did not love him" and "never even called," Octaviano reported. Holland said Shari was suing her, which further upset Sumner (and wasn't true). Herzer added that Shari was "mentally unstable."

In this instance Sumner pushed back: "I know Shari cares," Sumner insisted; Shari and her children were his family.

But Holland and Herzer prevailed. A letter sent that day to Shari and his grandchildren, signed by Sumner, read: "I want to be able to spend the rest of my life, however long that is, knowing that Sydney and Manuela will not be faced with litigation from my family at a time when they are grieving my passing."

The letter continued. "I want to enjoy the rest of my time on earth with peace of mind. If you decline to sign a release agreement, I will be compelled, albeit with deep regret, to direct Sydney and Manuela not to allow you, Phyllis or your children to attend the funeral or in any way be involved in the burial arrangements."

Shari was stunned. That was asking too much. She refused to sign the release. Negotiations to sell her stake in National Amusements came to an abrupt halt.

The next day Octaviano reported that Sumner was "very unstable" and "cries most of the time."

That evening Sumner's executive assistant in New York, Gloria Mazzeo, dispatched an email from Sumner to Brandon, Kimberlee, and Tyler: "Your mother has no respect for me. The letter I wrote to all three of you and your mother are my wishes, and they apply to all three of you, including you, Tyler. I want there to be no misunderstanding."

Tyler couldn't believe this really reflected his grandfather's wishes, given Octaviano's report of what happened that day: "Sydney wrote a note and made SMR [Sumner] approved it and Jeremy read it to Gloria and that Gloria needed to send it to Ma'am Shari, Brandon, Kim and you. I did not hear the whole thing but what I catches was that, 'your Mom has no respect on me.'"

This was obviously a description of the email Mazzeo had transmitted. On January 12, 2015, Tyler wrote to Bishop:

Now that the spin-off negotiations between National Amusements and my mother have concluded, it is apparent that Sydney and Manuela are prepared to ban the family from attending my grandfather's funeral unless we sign releases.

Please be advised that my grandfather expressed his explicit wishes recently that his family must not be prevented from attending his funeral. Additionally, Sydney and Manuela have now blocked my siblings' and my own telephone calls to my grandfather and have effectively prevented us from speaking with him. Instead, they lie to my grandfather that we do not call him or love him.

For thirty years, my siblings and I have had a wonderful, loving, and caring relationship with my grandfather, and we continue to love him dearly. Both the January 8th letter and the January 10th email, however, make it abundantly clear that Sydney and Manuela will continue to drive a wedge into that relationship and to abuse my grandfather until we agree to immunize them for their past and continuing misconduct.

Because I am prevented from calling my grandfather directly, please relay to him how much I love and care for him, and how I welcome the opportunity to speak and visit with him soon.

Almost immediately Holland had a copy of Tyler's letter. She came out to the patio where Sumner was sitting with Octaviano brandishing it. She ordered him and the other nurses into the kitchen, but Octaviano heard her angrily read parts of the letter aloud to Sumner and call Tyler a liar. She complained his family was "ruining her life."

For her part, Bishop wrote Tyler that "this letter did not come from Sydney and Manuela. I prepared it at Sumner's direction. I met with him and went over it multiple times to confirm it was exactly what he wanted and he signed it. My only goal here is to carry out Sumner's wishes."

———

That same day, January 12, one of the nurses put through a call to Sumner from his granddaughter Kimberlee. Octaviano reported that it made Sumner "very happy and he told Kim repeatedly that she and her family can come visit him anytime soon."

Holland, predictably, was furious when she found out. Of the Redstone grandchildren, Kimberlee seemed to annoy Holland the most. In texts to Pilgrim she called her "such a little spy," a "manipulator," and "her mother's daughter."

Holland told Sumner that Kimberlee was a liar.

"I love Kim," Sumner responded.

Her whole family were liars, Holland insisted.

"No, they are not!" Sumner argued.

This back-and-forth went on for an hour, punctuated by yelling and crying episodes.

———

Octaviano duly reported these events to Tyler, who had been willing to at least discuss the possibility of litigation releases with Holland and Herzer. But he was disturbed by their demands for control over the funeral, their threats to exclude family members, and now these latest attempts to turn Sumner against his family. When he again complained to Bishop, she responded, "Sydney and Manuela are not banning anyone from Sumner's funeral. Sumner has given this direction."

If Sumner (or Holland and Herzer) thought threatening to exclude his daughter from his funeral would be persuasive, they were mistaken. It seemed to have the opposite effect. Shari told her children she'd refuse to "sign releases against the whores who will be grieving his loss" and that "there is absolutely nothing more to be said . . . EVER!!!!"

———

The ongoing pattern of abuse was too much for Octaviano. On January 29 he and several other staff members lodged the first of two complaints against Holland and Herzer with Los Angeles County Adult Protective Services. They also filed a separate complaint against Bishop, whom Octaviano deemed complicit in the abusive conduct.

Sumner's nurse Jagiello joined in the complaints. "From my personal observations during my frequent 12-hour shifts, I was firmly convinced that Sydney and Manuela were emotionally and financially abusing Mr. Redstone," he stated. "I further believed, and still believe today, that both Sydney and Manuela extorted Mr. Redstone by leading him to believe that if he did not keep them financially satisfied he would die alone because they were the only people who loved him."

Like Octaviano, Jagiello also lodged a complaint against Bishop: "Based on the interactions I observed her having with Sydney and Manuela, I was concerned that she might be advancing their agenda rather than the interests of her client, Mr. Redstone."

———

Through all of this turmoil, Sumner was not just a controlling shareholder—he was also the executive chairman of two major publicly traded companies. His base pay was $1.75 million at CBS and $2 million at Viacom.

Even though Sumner named the directors by virtue of his controlling shares, they owed all shareholders a fiduciary duty of care. On January 28 the CBS compensation committee met to consider what CBS should pay Sumner for the prior year, 2014. The committee had clearly spelled out Sumner's duties as executive chairman: serving as "a sounding-board/counselor to [the] CEO on issues of strategic importance," ensuring that "strategic plans are up-to-date" and "being executed on," providing "effective communications with the Board," and assisting "the Board in maintaining best governance practices."

At the CBS annual meeting in May 2014, Sumner had had to be carried into the room in a chair, and at subsequent board meetings he attended by phone and usually said nothing other than "Hello, everyone."

Yet the minutes of the compensation committee's meeting reflect no discussion of Sumner's condition or whether he in fact performed any of his specified duties. The committee recommended, and the full CBS board approved, a $9 million bonus, bringing Sumner's pay that year to $10.75 million.

At Viacom, Dauman was presumably well aware of Sumner's mental and physical limitations from his frequent visits. Yet Viacom paid Sumner even more—over $13 million for fiscal year 2014.

A few days after Jagiello and Octaviano lodged their complaints, two investigators from Adult Protective Services showed up at the Beverly Park entrance gate seeking access to Sumner. The entrance guard called the house, and a staff member there promptly informed Holland, who was out. She ordered the staff not to admit the investigators and insisted they make an appointment for a later day.

Once they were back in Los Angeles, Holland and Herzer met with Sumner. He was "upset," in Jagiello's recollection.

"I'm in trouble," Sumner said. "Sydney and Manuela got me in trouble."

Minutes later Robert Shapiro, the celebrity lawyer best known for his defense of O. J. Simpson, showed up at the mansion, evidently retained by Holland or Herzer or both. Bishop arrived soon after and all of them met with Sumner to rehearse him for an encounter with the investigators, who arrived later that day. All were present for Sumner's interview, such as it was, in which Herzer maintained that Sumner denied being abused or pressured. Jagiello reported that the investigators stayed only briefly and spoke to none of the nurses or anyone on the household staff—even though the multiple complaints had been lodged by nurses. Nor did they reach out to anyone in Sumner's family.

That was the end of any investigation.

By now Herzer and Holland must have been aware, or at least suspicious, that someone on the household or nursing staff was leaking information, despite the strict confidentiality agreements they'd signed. Octaviano warned Tyler in April that they were out to "catch the person that gives you guys informations. CAREFUL is the name of the game this time."

"Yes, careful is key!" Tyler responded. "I don't tell anybody anything about you or Jeremy. Thanks for the update and the warning."

Jagiello kept reporting the latest developments to Tyler. Though his effort to enlist Adult Protective Services had gone nowhere, he was more determined than ever. "These women and their fucking cronies are going down!" he texted Tyler on May 14. "Can't stand them and who they are and what they do. I want to vomit!"

"You Want to Go to War?"

When *Vanity Fair* reporter William Cohan first called Carl Folta, Viacom's head of public relations did his best to prevent any article from happening. He wouldn't allow Cohan to meet or speak to Sumner and urged Holland and Herzer not to participate.

The women hired their own public relations consultant, but defying her advice as well, each sat for on-the-record interviews and posed for full-length portraits by celebrity photographer Douglas Friedman.

The June 2015 issue of *Vanity Fair* appeared that May. As Folta had feared and predicted, Cohan's article—"Endless Sumner"—was hardly flattering to Sumner, describing the ninety-one-year-old mogul as "clearly ailing."

"I think he's pretty out of it," one (unnamed) source told Cohan. "He can't speak, and I don't know how much he knows what's going on."

Sumner's old friend Robert Evans "can't get off the phone fast enough" when asked about Sumner's health, Cohan reported. "I really don't want to talk about him," Evans said.

The article went on, "A person who was visiting with Bob Evans recently broached the topic of Redstone's health. 'He looks like he's dead,' he told Evans, who is said to have replied, 'Well, you should see him in person—he looks even worse.'"

By contrast, Holland and Herzer got the full star treatment. Herzer posed in the warmly lit Bemelmans Bar in Manhattan's Carlyle Hotel (where Sumner had "gifted" her the apartment); Holland was photographed on a green velvet cushion in a manicured Pasadena garden. Herzer wore a clinging, shimmering sheath that barely concealed her breasts. Holland wore a more demure, all-white, full-length gown with one leg peeking through a slit.

In what the magazine billed as a "wide-ranging interview, her first ever about Redstone," Holland stayed dutifully on message, implying without ever quite saying explicitly that she loved Sumner and theirs was a deeply romantic relationship. "Sumner is a very different and unusual person," Holland told Cohan. "I've never noticed his age. Let me just start by saying that. If you ever saw the way he looked, he's got this beautiful hair and has the most beautiful skin I've ever seen in my life, not one wrinkle on his face."

Over breakfast with Cohan at the Carlyle, Herzer was far more revealing. "It's such a fine line when you talk about money," she told Cohan. Sumner "considers me family and my children family. I mean, that's his whole thing. He's like, 'You're my family.' You don't pick your family in life, but Sumner Redstone does. He just does. He wants who he wants in his life."

Asked about her endorsement of Holland when she and Sumner started dating, Herzer seemed to distance herself: "I was like, 'You know, this girl can't be so bad,'" she said. "Do I know anything about her background? Nothing, and I don't care, because why do I need to judge her? I'm not dating her."

Cohan asked Herzer if Sumner was going to take care of Holland in his will.

"It would be almost disgusting if he didn't do what everyone says he's doing and going to do," she answered. "I mean, five years of your life with a man every single day like that. I have to tell you, would she be there if he wasn't doing something for her? Probably not. But does she love him? Absolutely. I don't have a doubt in my mind." But then she went on, "For her it's a job almost, it's a job."

After the story ran, Sumner told Folta that everybody loved it.

Folta thought it was an embarrassment for all concerned, but all he said was, "It will be fine," and "we'll move on."

———

Officially, Shari Redstone and her children had no comment on the *Vanity Fair* story. All Shari said for publication was "There is nothing more important to me than my family," and added, "I'm not going to publicly comment on my father's two current female companions or their impact on our family."

The story could have been worse. Shari had earlier written in an email that the women and their allies "were all out to do a major trashing of me," and Octaviano reported that Holland was rehearsing Sumner to say he "kicked Shari out of the house." But lawyers persuaded Holland and Herzer not to needlessly provoke Shari, and the story didn't include any quotes from Sumner about his daughter. (The allegation that he had kicked Shari out of the house "100 times" did appear but was attributed to an unnamed source "close to Holland and Herzer.")

But Herzer's attempts to establish herself and her children as Sumner's "family" were infuriating to Shari. And Herzer's comments that Holland saw her relationship with Sumner as a "job" underscored the family's concern that both women were exploiting Shari's father for monetary gain.

That concern was only heightened on June 22, when Sumner transferred an additional $10 million to Holland and Herzer and afterward seemed confused, repeatedly asking his nurse Octaviano what he'd just done and to whom he'd spoken at the bank.

In July he further upset Shari. In an email to Tyler, she reported, "Your grandfather says I will be chair over his dead body."

———

In Arizona, Pilgrim was stunned by the *Vanity Fair* article. Holland had told him a "fluff piece" in the magazine was coming, but the public depiction of the extent and nature of Holland's relationship with Sumner came as a shock. He read Holland's fawning description of Sumner's "beautiful hair" and "the most beautiful skin I've ever seen in my life" and felt jealous and betrayed.

His friends saw the story and needled him about it. It made him look like a "kept man," he thought.

An angry Pilgrim called Holland. "What the fuck is this? I don't understand, Sydney. I'm flying back and forth on private jets, you're flying out here, buying me houses, you're giving me the world. We're supposed to have a fucking life and all Sedona, Arizona, knows about us. You got a country-club membership." He went on, "My family and everybody wants to know what's going on. Sydney, you're posing in a fucking magazine taking pictures in Pasadena, that shows me a lot. The both of you look like high-class call girls. What's going on?"

Holland insisted she'd only participated because if she didn't, Shari would seize the narrative, characterizing her and Herzer as gold diggers or worse. It was all an effort to protect the inheritance she'd be sharing with Pilgrim. As for her relationship with Sumner, she sent Pilgrim videos of other women with Sumner at the mansion. How could she be in a romantic relationship with someone having sex with other women?

Pilgrim was mollified, up to a point. But he wondered: Was Holland "playing" him, manipulating him for sex the way she did Sumner for money? She always had a story.

———

With the *Vanity Fair* article still reverberating, Holland and Herzer hosted another birthday party for Sumner, incongruously dubbing this one a "passion to party." There was little passion in evidence at the subdued affair on May 27. Originally slated for the Paramount studio lot, the venue had been abruptly shifted to the Vibrato Grill Jazz, a club owned by jazz trumpeter Herb Alpert and located in a Bel Air strip mall closer to Sumner's home. It was hard for family members to imagine that Sumner wanted a party, let alone a dinner, given his feeding tube. But Holland and Herzer had insisted.

Guests included the usual suspects—Moonves and Dauman, of course, as well as Milken, Evans, and Lansing—but not celebrities like Tom Cruise or Al Gore. Keryn Redstone represented the family; Shari and her children weren't invited. Tyler had made plans to show up anyway, when suddenly a last-minute invitation arrived via fax.

"I'm so glad we could arrange for you to come," Bishop said when they met at the event.

"I was going to come anyway," Korff replied. He managed to sit next to his grandfather at least part of the time but was never alone with him.

Holland and Herzer went to considerable lengths to conceal the existence of Sumner's feeding tube. The ninety-two-year-old made his entrance from behind a black curtain and was helped to his seat by several aides. But his frail appearance couldn't be hidden by his dark suit and light blue tie. He'd lost weight; his once-rosy hair was snow-white; the beautiful skin extolled by Holland was marred by red blotches. He made no public remarks. Tony Bennett reprised his performance of "Happy Birthday," but Sumner was disappointed. He'd been listening obsessively to *Cheek to Cheek*, Bennett's 2014 collaboration with Lady Gaga, and he'd hoped the pop diva would be there.

When the lights came up, aides helped Sumner out and the party ended. It was only 8:00 p.m.

———

The next month Holland and Herzer consolidated their hold on the most intimate aspect of Sumner's life, taking control of his funeral and burial instructions. In June Sumner revised his instructions to direct that his funeral would be a private service and that Holland and Herzer would draw up the guest list, decide who would officiate, choose a grave marker, and arrange for a reception after the service. Sumner asked that Herzer's son, Bryan, be a pallbearer and that her two daughters recite prayers or poems. On July 7, Sumner executed instructions that if Shari or anyone else contested his estate plan, ownership of the family's burial plots would be conveyed to Holland and Herzer to do with as they pleased.

Later that summer Holland and Herzer flew to Boston and met with the Redstone family's longtime undertaker in suburban Newton to discuss their funeral plans. When they returned to Los Angeles, they consulted Bishop about how to transfer ownership of the burial plots.

Alarmed, the funeral director called Tyler and filled him in. It had been one thing for Holland and Herzer to divide Sumner's estate. But for a deeply religious family like the Redstones, the idea of Holland and Herzer supplanting them in Sumner's funeral service and burial— and, even worse, resting for all eternity in Sharon Memorial Park, the Jewish cemetery where Sumner's parents were buried—was unthinkable.

———

Even before the *Vanity Fair* article inflamed his suspicions about Holland and Sumner, Pilgrim had heard gossip in Sedona to the effect that his girlfriend was "banging some old man," as he put it. He didn't like having to keep their engagement a secret. And even though Holland was at the beck and call of Sumner, if another woman even looked at Pilgrim, Holland was jealous and possessive. She'd even had surveillance cameras installed in their Sedona house.

There were days when Pilgrim didn't feel any better off than the aging Sumner Redstone: they were both lonely men imprisoned in gilded cages.

In the weeks after the *Vanity Fair* article, Pilgrim and Holland fought more often than usual over Sumner and his incessant demands. Pilgrim was drinking heavily, and Holland, an enthusiastic participant in and proponent of Alcoholics Anonymous, pressed him to check into an alcohol rehab program. Her friend Eloise Broady DeJoria, a former *Playboy* centerfold model who married the billionaire founder of Paul Mitchell hair care products and Patrón tequila, had launched a residential substance abuse treatment center outside Austin, Texas. Holland had lined up her mother to serve as Pilgrim's AA sponsor and offered to pay the center's $25,000-per-month fee and his first-class airfare to Austin. She promised Pilgrim a "huge party" once he completed the thirty-day, twelve-step alcohol-addiction recovery program.

Pilgrim didn't concede that he might be an alcoholic or needed professional help, but he still loved Holland and wanted their relationship to work. He figured his willingness to embrace sobriety, as Holland herself had done, would be a measure of his commitment.

So Pilgrim flew to Austin and checked into the Arbor.

With Pilgrim now safely ensconced in Texas, Holland called Lina Rueda, a former Sedona girlfriend of Pilgrim's whom Holland had hired to oversee renovations and keep an eye on the house when Holland wasn't there. Although Rueda now worked for Holland, she'd stayed close to Pilgrim after they broke up. She and Pilgrim were like brother and sister, and she often stayed at the house.

By now, Holland must have been aware that the private detective working on Shari's behalf, Jim Elroy, was monitoring her movements, hoping to find ammunition Shari could use against her. Elroy had already called Pilgrim at the house in Sedona; Pilgrim had answered but then pretended he spoke only Spanish to put Elroy off.

Holland told Rueda her lawyers had insisted she dump Pilgrim and get him out of the house. She would be coming to Sedona with her assistant and "two Navy SEALs" to change the locks and remove Pilgrim's belongings.

Rueda called Pilgrim at the Arbor. She was upset and in tears by the time she reached him, and took Holland's reference to Navy SEALs as a veiled threat to Pilgrim's safety.

Pilgrim sprang into action. The Arbor had taken his wallet and cell phone when he checked in, so he had no money, no identification, and no means of communication. He nonetheless shoved his way past two clinical staff and jumped a fence. He flagged down a passing truck, which took him as far as a nearby curio shop. A taxi was idling outside the shop. Pilgrim promised the driver $5,000 to make the thousand-plus-mile trip across the desert Southwest to Sedona. Pilgrim acknowledged that the proposition seemed crazy, given that he had no cash and no identification—nothing except the clothes he was wearing. To convince the driver, Pilgrim borrowed a cell phone from the shop clerk and called Rueda. She in turn texted the cab driver to vouch for the fact that Pilgrim had cash in a safe at his parents' house.

Pilgrim got in the cab. As the miles rolled by, he and the driver chatted, bonding over the fact the driver was a recovered alcoholic. The sixteen-hour trip also gave Pilgrim time to reflect on his recent past and his many frustrations with Holland. He used the driver's phone and called his former girlfriend Amy Shpall to confess he was romantically involved with Holland.

When they arrived in Sedona, Pilgrim went to his safe and produced the promised $5,000 in cash. The Arbor had already reported Pilgrim's premature departure. The next day Holland called him, furious that he'd broken out and made it back to Sedona.

Pilgrim, in his telling, "snapped."

"You want to go to war?" he yelled at her. "I'll go to war, motherfucker!"

Season 2

"I'd Better Not Tell Manuela"

After he calmed down, Pilgrim realized he still loved Holland, even though she'd tried to lock him out of their house. On Friday, June 26, 2015, just days after their blowup, they spent a romantic weekend at the Loews Santa Monica Beach Hotel. Loews had firepits on the beach and views of the ocean, and they were much less likely to encounter anyone they knew there than at the Peninsula or Beverly Hills hotels.

On a long walk along the beach, Pilgrim apologized and told Holland he still loved her. She in turn professed her love for Pilgrim. How could he doubt her? She was risking everything—her relationship with Sumner and all the financial security and power that came with it—to be with him. If that didn't prove how much she loved him, she couldn't imagine what would.

Pilgrim had to agree. He got down on one knee on the sand and proposed to her all over again. Holland accepted.

A week later Pilgrim was back with his parents in Sedona and took his grandmother to a July 4 party at Seven Canyons. Holland was spending the holiday with Sumner but urged Pilgrim to have a good time and charge anything he wanted to their club account.

Pilgrim drove past his old house, from which he was still locked out, on his way to the club. There, people kept asking him about the

Vanity Fair article and why Holland wasn't with him at the party. Pilgrim started feeling agitated.

He called Holland from the club and asked if he could take his grandmother to see their house. Holland flatly refused. He couldn't get her to explain why. They could talk about it later, she said. (Holland didn't tell him she believed the house was now under constant surveillance by Elroy, Shari's detective.)

After Pilgrim dropped off his grandmother and got back to his parents' house, he called Holland again and, by his own admission, boiled over. He wasn't going to let her "control" him the way Sumner controlled her. Soon they were shouting at each other. It was their worst fight ever. Pilgrim told her the engagement was off and he never wanted to see or speak to her again.

————

Days later, on July 8, Holland's lawsuit against Naylor and Martinez came to a quiet end. Holland withdrew her complaint, having failed to produce any evidence Naylor had stolen her laptop. Judge Ernest Hiroshige seemed puzzled by the outcome, since Holland didn't say whether the case had been settled or she was just dropping it. He noted the dearth of any evidence and how Holland had evaded Naylor's attempts to question her about, among other things, love affairs she might have had behind Sumner's back. The judge ruled that Holland had to pay Naylor's $190,000 legal bill.

The case settled on terms subject to a strict nondisclosure agreement. But Holland had to pay Martinez as much as $8 million to get his signature.

Of course, Holland didn't actually pay the multimillion-dollar settlement—like nearly all her expenses, no matter how large, Sumner picked up the tab.

After the stormy breakup with Holland, Pilgrim commuted between Sedona and Los Angeles, where he stayed with Amy Shpall. The reconciliation that had begun with his phone call from the taxi cab had proceeded over more calls, texts, and emails, and Shpall had agreed to take him back, putting most of the blame for the affair on Holland. She knew Holland—in the small world of Hollywood, one of Shpall's best friends worked for Holland's Rich Hippie Productions. She told her friend and his wife all about Holland's affair with Pilgrim and her ties to Sumner.

Those friends pointed out what was surely obvious: Pilgrim's secret affair with Holland gave him enormous leverage. Now that they'd broken up, Holland needed Pilgrim's continued silence and cooperation to prevent Sumner from learning of her infidelity.

Pilgrim reached out to Bryan Freedman, the lawyer who'd represented Martinez. Holland had complained bitterly about Freedman and his tactics, which impressed Pilgrim now that he was thinking about suing her. He and Shpall met Freedman at his office in a Century City tower, where Freedman was taking calls while walking on a treadmill.

Pilgrim laid out the full story, which got Freedman's attention. Both Freedman and Shpall, also seeing and hearing the details for the first time, acknowledged it was quite a saga. And it wasn't just his word—Pilgrim had saved virtually everything, including a bevy of photos, explicit texts, and emails between him and Holland.

Pilgrim wasn't sure he wanted to make any legal demands on Holland—though hurt and angry, on some level he still loved her.

"Rest assured," Freedman said, "you don't know Sydney."

What did he mean? Pilgrim asked.

After representing Martinez, Freedman had a pretty good idea of what had gone on at the Redstone mansion. He told Pilgrim he'd seen explicit photos of Holland with other men, not just Sumner. "I know this may be hard for you," he told Pilgrim.

Perhaps he'd been naive, but Pilgrim had believed Holland had been faithful. What Freedman told him erased any reservations he had about confronting his former fiancée. Pilgrim signed on with Freedman, agreeing to pay a 25 percent contingency fee.

Freedman was baffled by Holland's willingness to put so much at risk for an affair with someone who had a criminal record. Pilgrim might be handsome and charming, but so were plenty of other men in Hollywood. Freedman wondered aloud: What had Holland seen in him?

On some level Shpall got it. "He's George Pilgrim. He's one of a kind," she said.

Holland soon got wind of the fact that Pilgrim had consulted a lawyer.

"I suggest you back down and disappear Quietly from my life," she texted Pilgrim's confidante Rueda. "Three facts: I am smarter than you, I am richer than you, and I do not have a criminal past."

———

W ith the explosive evidence about Holland's affair with Pilgrim, Freedman thought there was little chance any case would ever go to trial, just as the Naylor and Martinez case had settled. So confident was Pilgrim of a favorable outcome that he agreed to raise Freedman's fee to 40 percent of any settlement.

On July 17, Freedman drafted a letter laying out the grounds for Pilgrim's claims against Holland for breach of contract, express or implied. There was no mention of any threat to go public with Pilgrim's account, but there didn't need to be.

"I am writing this letter as a result of Sydney's . . . fraudulent and deceptive campaign to lure George into signing his life rights to Sydney's production company and donating semen for her benefit, only to manipulate him into a rehabilitation center so she could abruptly end the relationship and lock him out of his home," the letter began. "Sydney's conduct is nothing short of abhorrent, and George intends to pursue all available legal remedies to ensure this conduct does not go unanswered."

The letter mentioned various "witnesses" who could attest that Holland bought the Sedona house for Pilgrim and "will testify that Sydney agreed to financially take care of George for the rest of his life, which is consistent with her having paid for his private jets to see her, his country club membership and his health insurance."

As for Sumner, "Sydney repeatedly assured George that her relationship with Mr. Redstone is not based upon emotion, is strictly financial, and is meant for no purpose other than cashing in on Mr. Redstone's wealth upon his death. Sydney repeatedly conveyed to George that she has simply been manipulating Mr. Redstone from the outset, and we have several witnesses to affirm these statements. Sydney repeatedly assured George that he was the real love of her life and future husband, and that her relationship with Mr. Redstone would be short-lived."

The letter concluded with a stern warning: "Given the severity of these claims, we require an immediate response to this letter. We are very familiar with Sydney's dilatory tactics, and will not allow her any opportunity to engage in that type of gamesmanship under these circumstances. Be advised that if (i) you do not respond to this letter within 24 hours with substantive settlement offers that are commensurate with the severity of the claims, and (ii) the parties are unable to reach a settlement within 48 hours thereafter, we will file litigation. While the settlement terms are obviously negotiable, the timing parameters outlined herein are not."

Freedman never sent the letter. Simply summarizing its contents was enough. Freedman negotiated with Brad Rose at Pryor Cashman in New York, who was handling the matter for Holland. He responded quickly with an offer for Holland to pay Pilgrim $15,000 a month for ten years, plus half the proceeds from the sale of the Sedona house up to $2 million.

It wasn't bad for an opening offer.

Freedman said Pilgrim wanted $10 million.

Negotiations continued. Rose eventually offered Pilgrim more than $10 million, paid over a ten-year period, including a percentage of the proceeds from the sale of the house in Sedona and some of what Holland eventually inherited from Sumner. In return, he'd sign a strict nondisclosure agreement and make no mention of Holland or the affair in his proposed autobiography or in any other context.

At this point Pilgrim had everything he'd said he wanted—and then some. There were still a few details to work out, and as the deal was coming together, Pilgrim was in Los Angeles with Shpall. On Friday, August 28, they went to a party at Wally's, a restaurant and wine bar in Beverly Hills co-owned by two founders of Guess jeans, Maurice and Paul Marciano. Their nephew Matt Marciano, who also worked at Wally's, was there with his girlfriend Christy Cham, Manuela Herzer's older daughter.

A week earlier, Pilgrim and Shpall had ended up sitting next to Marciano and Cham at a communal table at Wally's. Pilgrim's ears had perked up as soon as he overheard disparaging references to Holland and Sumner. He quickly realized Cham was Herzer's daughter, from both her comments and her striking physical resemblance to her mother. To Pilgrim it felt like fate had brought them together.

As he pondered the situation over the next week, it dawned on him that he could blow up everything and inflict his revenge on Holland. Sumner "had turned her into his whore," Pilgrim thought bitterly, and now, with her offer of $10 million–plus on the table, she was doing the same thing to him. With the money paid out in installments over years, Holland would remain in control. He'd still be a kept man.

At Wally's that Friday night, Pilgrim had way too much to drink.

He went to the bathroom and splashed cold water on his face to try to clear his head. As he gazed at himself in the mirror, he heard a voice: "Don't take the money." The voice added, "It's blood money."

Pilgrim walked back into the party and pulled Matt Marciano aside. They went outside for a cigarette. Pilgrim blurted out an account of his love affair with Holland and told Marciano about their plans to marry and have children. He showed him pictures on his cell phone to back up his account.

When Shpall joined them, Marciano asked her if Pilgrim and his story were for real. They were, she affirmed.

"I'd better not tell Manuela," Marciano said.

———

Marciano went straight to Herzer with the explosive information, as Pilgrim knew he would. Herzer was stunned and furious, and no wonder: Holland had put everything they'd worked so hard for at risk. At the same time, what might be a catastrophe for Holland promised a huge windfall for her. After all, why should she share the anticipated inheritance from Sumner with Holland?

According to household staff members, Herzer ordered Holland to confess the affair to Sumner—and if she didn't, Herzer would tell him.

News of Pilgrim's startling disclosure reached Freedman late on Saturday morning when a hungover Pilgrim called to tell him he might have "made a mistake" the night before. He said he'd talked about Holland to Marciano at Wally's, but was vague and evasive. He claimed, unconvincingly, that he hadn't really told him anything. Freedman thought Pilgrim sounded like a child caught misbehaving by a parent. When he spoke to Shpall, she confirmed that Pilgrim had told Marciano all about his affair with Holland.

Freedman called Holland's lawyers. It was a bad sign that no one returned his call.

Settlement talks collapsed. Freedman was incredulous. On what seemed a drunken impulse, Pilgrim had forfeited what promised to be a lifetime of financial security. And he'd cost Freedman a potential $4 million contingency fee.

———

The next day, Sunday, August 30, Holland, with the lawyer Patty Glaser at her side, confessed to Sumner. Though Holland asked for privacy, nurses and household staff witnessed the entire exchange. Holland described the affair as an "indiscretion" and told Sumner she "hoped for the same forgiveness and understanding that she had shown him during all his affairs."

Holland apologized profusely and was in the process of begging Sumner's forgiveness when Herzer could apparently no longer contain herself. She burst into the room and unleashed an onslaught of increasingly wild-eyed allegations: Holland was a prostitute and Pilgrim an ex-con. Pilgrim was the father of Holland's baby. Holland and Pilgrim were plotting to kill Sumner.

Herzer demanded that Sumner throw Holland out immediately.

Faced with this barrage and presumably overwhelmed by feelings of betrayal, Sumner told Holland to leave but gave her two weeks to get out. Herzer cut the grace period to two days.

Forty-eight hours later, Holland and her daughter, Alexandra, were gone, decamping for the time being to the luxurious Montage Hotel in Beverly Hills.

EPISODE 2

"Operation Freedom"

On September 2 estate lawyer Leah Bishop met with Sumner to revise his legal documents. He eradicated Holland from his will. Herzer was now slated to get everything, which was more than twice as much as before—$50 million—plus the Beverly Park mansion, then valued at $20 million, for a total of $70 million. Herzer was designated Sumner's sole health care proxy. (Sumner named Viacom chief Dauman as a backup.)

With Holland vanquished and Herzer in sole command of the Redstone household, the last thing Herzer wanted was any interference from Shari or her family. Just two days after Holland's unceremonious exit, on September 3, Herzer walked into the room while Sumner was on the phone. After Octaviano told her he was talking to his granddaughter Kimberlee, Herzer angrily grabbed the receiver and hung up. Sumner started crying.

A week later Shari was scheduled to visit, but Herzer told Sumner he was too busy to see her and canceled the visit. Herzer asked Sumner's doctor to write a letter advising him that contact with his family was a threat to his health. Octaviano overheard Herzer on the phone with Dauman, insisting that Shari not be allowed to discuss business matters with her father.

Herzer quickly consolidated her newfound power. She installed hidden cameras throughout the house, including in Sumner's bedroom. She tightened her grip on the staff, banned any contact with Holland, and threatened to send one housekeeper to jail for suspected leaking. The staff was barred from reading the newspaper to Sumner or transmitting any information to him.

Herzer asked Keryn to move into the mansion full-time to help with Sumner's care and gave Keryn access to her grandfather's credit card to pay moving expenses and other charges. She also had Sumner create a $1 million trust fund for Keryn that allowed her to spend the income from the principal.

Then, her mission apparently accomplished, Herzer took off for Paris and the premiere of *Knock Knock*, an erotic thriller starring Keanu Reeves, Herzer's latest "infatuation." The film made its debut at the American Film Festival in Deauville, France, on September 5 to mixed reviews (a "giddily sadistic black comedy," per *The New York Times*). While Herzer was away, her brother Carlos moved in and stood guard.

One week, while the Beverly Park mansion was being fumigated, Herzer took Sumner to a Malibu beach house she'd rented on his behalf, even though, according to Jagiello, it was being used as a "party house" by Herzer's children. (Sumner, of course, paid the rent.) Once they arrived, Herzer occupied the master bedroom suite with a sweeping view of the ocean. Sumner was relegated to a small guest room at the back of the house, within earshot of the busy Pacific Coast Highway. A nurse complained that the room's small dimensions made it difficult for Sumner to maneuver in his wheelchair.

However close they may once have been, Sumner didn't love Herzer the way he had Holland. "He appeared to care far less for Manuela," Octaviano observed.

Nor did Herzer participate in any sex with him. Herzer complained that Sumner was "fixated on sex on a daily basis." He asked repeatedly to see Terry Holbrook, the former Oilers cheerleader whom he'd been dating in 2010 before meeting Holland and who later got monthly cash retainers for providing sexual services, Herzer later alleged. With her long brunette hair, Holbrook bore a striking resemblance to Holland and thus must have posed an especially potent threat to replace Holland in Sumner's affections and even in his estate plans.

That was not about to happen. Herzer gave the staff strict orders to prevent any contact between Sumner and Holbrook. When Sumner asked for Holbrook, Octaviano and other staff members told him she was sick, she was out of town, or that she couldn't be located when, in fact, she was nearby and willing to visit him. After Sumner asked Jagiello to send Holbrook flowers, Herzer countermanded the order but told him to tell Sumner that the flowers had been sent. When Sumner asked his nurses to dial Holbrook in his presence so he could get on the phone and speak to her, Herzer instead dialed her own number, handed the phone to Sumner, and had him leave a message when no one answered.

"Manuela told me and the other nurses that she did not want Mr. Redstone seeing Terry," Jagiello stated. As a result, "I was lying to Mr. Redstone on an almost daily basis at Manuela's direction."

In place of Holbrook, Herzer arranged for visits by Heidi MacKinney, a brunette who also bore some resemblance to Holland. Unlike Holbrook, MacKinney posed no threat to Herzer; though she had gone on a few dates with Sumner before he met Holland, she now worked for Herzer as a personal assistant while caring for her special-needs child. She'd been a character witness for Herzer years earlier when Herzer was in a bitter custody battle with her ex-husband.

Still, it must have come as something of a shock that her job as Herzer's personal assistant included ministering to the sexual appetites of a ninety-two-year-old man. In a sworn affidavit, MacKinney said she visited Sumner five times after Holland left, or about once a week, and tried to "engage" sexually with him. Jagiello, his nurse, was always present and orchestrated the encounters, "directing me and telling me what sex acts to perform," she said. But during her visit on October 2, Sumner was "completely unresponsive," she asserted, and she vowed not to return.

And Holland was by no means entirely out of the picture. Sumner was clearly still enamored of her—he talked about her constantly and seemed obsessed by her relationship with Pilgrim. Holland herself had every intention of returning to her rightful place at the mansion, and likely in his estate plan as well. As she put it, she "tried her best to show Redstone her remorse." She sent him letters, cards, flowers, and notes, but she never got a response. When she tried to phone, his line had been disconnected and the number changed. Holland explored the possibility of suing Herzer, but her lawyer talked her out of it.

Finally Holland tried an end run by having her lawyer send a letter intended for Sumner to Leah Bishop, with a request to hand-deliver it to Sumner. "I am beyond sorry that I hurt you," the letter began. "I am so sad that I was not allowed to say goodbye and I want nothing from you, but to see you. . . . I beg of you to consider letting Alexandra and I visit. She is such a beautiful little girl. . . . She reminds me of you and how resilient you are and how you never give up."

Holland continued. "Sumner, just know that I will love you forever and always, not a day goes by without me thinking of what we shared. Please Sumner, have Leah arrange for us to see each other. Love Always, Sydney."

Bishop brought the letter to the mansion in early October. Jagiello was there when she arrived, and he recalled that Herzer "grabbed" the letter from Bishop and started to read it to Sumner.

But after just a few words of this seemingly heartfelt apology, Herzer abruptly broke off, folded the letter, and told Sumner she'd finish reading it to him later.

Later that day Herzer rejoined Sumner with what purported to be Holland's letter and read it aloud in its entirety.

"I did not lie to you everyone else is lying," the letter began. "I never had an affair with that man. . . . It's not true people are just trying to break us up. . . . You have to believe me I never lied to you. I don't know who he is. . . . Don't understand why you don't believe me and you believe everyone else."

It was readily apparent to Jagiello, who was at Sumner's side for both readings, that this missive bore no resemblance to the one Herzer had earlier started to read, which was never seen or heard again. Nothing about this letter sounded like Holland. It also strained credulity that Holland would now assert she "never had an affair with that man" and "I don't know who he is" when Holland, with her lawyer present, had already confessed the affair with Pilgrim and begged Sumner's forgiveness. Herzer turned the contradiction to her advantage, telling Sumner, "You can't believe her."

Sumner asked Herzer to read the letter aloud again. Herzer handed it to Jagiello to read and walked out.

The next day Sumner told Jagiello he wanted to hear the letter a third time. The nurse couldn't find it, so he went upstairs to Herzer's room to get a copy. When he entered, Herzer, one of her daughters, and Keryn were huddled over a laptop computer, apparently composing yet another letter. "I waited about 10 minutes while Manuela finished the letter," Jagiello recalled. Herzer "then handed it to me and told me to go read it to Mr. Redstone, which I reluctantly did."

The constant deception took a toll on the nurses and staff. While Holland could be temperamental and demanding, she was also often considerate and understanding. By contrast, Herzer was "exceptionally domineering," as Jagiello put it. Pilgrim's nickname for her—"Pitbull"—had stuck for good reason. Octaviano acknowledged that "it would be fair to say" that he hated Herzer.

Within weeks of Holland's departure, Jagiello, Octaviano, and Sumner's driver, Isileli Tuanaki, with the tacit encouragement of Tyler, began planning a palace coup. On September 18 Jagiello texted Tyler:

"Thanks for talking last night. Seal team commence operation freedom today! FYI! I will keep you posted." He added, "Let's hope this goes well."

As for Sumner, "Once he knows the truth, he is going to be livid!" Jagiello texted Tyler.

"I Never Thought I'd See You Again"

It was probably just as well that Herzer had removed the stock screens from Sumner's view, for by October 2015 Viacom stock had plunged roughly 40 percent from its peak the prior year. In part this reflected a decline in the stock of most media companies, especially those owning cable channels, as *cord-cutting* and *streaming* entered Americans' vocabulary. The cable companies' long stranglehold on viewers began to give way to competition from the internet and streaming companies like Netflix and Amazon. Hit series like *House of Cards*, *The Crown*, and *Transparent* racked up Emmy nominations and put them in direct competition with traditional content creators.

That year, Netflix spent nearly $5 billion on original programming, launching an arms race that few competitors could match. But Viacom had fared much worse than other entertainment companies, and increasingly, Hollywood, Wall Street—and Shari Redstone—blamed Dauman.

Dauman, the consummate deal lawyer, had ascended to the top of Viacom promising more of the transformative acquisitions that had made the company what it was under Sumner. Instead, he spent $15 billion buying back stock, standing passively by while rival Disney bought Marvel and Lucasfilm, owners of the *Avengers* and *Star Wars* franchises, before paying $1 billion for a minority stake in a streaming service.

Confronted with an industry in upheaval, Dauman played defense, clinging to what Viacom already had. As a lawyer, his first instinct seemed to be to go to court. Years prior, Viacom had sued Google in a self-destructive and ultimately failed effort to keep Viacom content off YouTube, which Google had recently acquired. When Shari asked Thomas Dooley, Dauman's chief operating officer, for an explanation, he predicted YouTube would be out of business in a year. (YouTube revenue hit $7 billion in the second quarter of 2021, more than that of CBS and Viacom combined.)

Working primarily out of Viacom headquarters in New York's Times Square, Dauman never seemed to fit comfortably in the entertainment business, where personal relationships are crucial. Early in his tenure he gratuitously alienated Hollywood royalty Steven Spielberg, Jeffrey Katzenberg, and David Geffen—the troika that founded DreamWorks, which Paramount had acquired in 2005 and then run into the ground. He had gotten rid of Judy McGrath, the popular longtime head of MTV. MTV's ratings had since plunged due to a lack of new hits and a youth exodus to the internet. He didn't cultivate talent and seemed to have little interest in celebrities. His tone-deaf comments were blamed for the departures of Comedy Central stars Jon Stewart, John Oliver, and Stephen Colbert, all of whom went on to spectacular careers elsewhere.

When Shari asked Dauman for an explanation for the loss of Stewart, Dauman seemed unconcerned. He asserted Stewart was too much of a "prima donna." But "that's our job," Shari countered. "At CBS we deal with prima donnas all the time." (A spokesman for Dauman denied he made any such remark. But accounts of the exchange circulated widely inside Viacom.)

Dauman's relations with cable operators—Viacom's biggest customers—were, if anything, worse. Dauman prided himself on his dealmaking skills, and he'd aggressively squeezed the cable operators for higher fees to carry Viacom programming. He'd succeeded up to a point, and higher affiliate fees were the main driver of Viacom's stock price, apart from buybacks. But Dauman still acted like the hard-nosed mergers and acquisitions lawyer he'd once been.

Successful M&A deals are, by definition, one-time negotiations. If Dauman alienated his opponents, it hardly mattered. But Viacom had to deal with the cable operators repeatedly. In October 2014, when Viacom demanded a 50 percent increase despite declining viewership, internet service provider Suddenlink dropped Viacom's channels rather than meet the demands. Sixty small cable companies did the same.

Worse, Charter Communications, the country's second-largest cable operator (where Sumner's archrival John Malone was a board member), was threatening to follow suit. The loss of Charter, some top executives feared, might send Viacom into a death spiral.

Morale sank at Viacom. As former MTV executive Jason Hirschhorn told *Vanity Fair* in 2016, "When you don't like your C.E.O., when you don't hear from him, when you read all these terrible things, when your friends get fired, when you don't get the bonuses, when the stock has dropped . . . and you have a guy that doesn't even talk about the programming . . ."

Nor did Dauman do anything to court Shari or even treat her with much respect. As potential heirs to her father's empire, they were, of course, rivals. It was galling to her that her father would name Dauman his health care proxy rather than his own daughter. Worse, in order to maintain his access to Sumner, Dauman had aligned himself with Holland and Herzer in what Shari deemed no less than an attempt to destroy her family. Her animosity toward him had roots that went far deeper than just business.

Exasperated, Shari finally asked Dauman alone to her recently renovated apartment at the Pierre. She gave him a tour and ordered drinks and canapés before settling in the study overlooking Central Park. She'd been such a gracious host, he was unprepared for what came next: "You and I both know you're completely unsuited to be chief executive of Viacom," Shari said, laying her cards on the table.

"I respectfully disagree," Dauman answered.

He realized she was asking him to resign as chief executive. Someday he'd step aside, he told her, but now wasn't the right time. The company was at an "inflection point" and needed continuity of leadership.

Sumner was blind to criticism of Dauman, even when it came from his daughter. To counter the drumbeat of bad publicity and speculation about Dauman's future, Sumner issued a statement on October 6: "Philippe is my long-time friend and partner. He continues to have my unequivocal support and trust, which he has earned over our many years together." The statement continued, "We are both long-term thinkers and I am more confident than ever that he is on the right track."

Sumner was quoted in *The Wall Street Journal* the next day saying Dauman "is out in front navigating an unprecedented level of change in the industry and he has articulated a smart, innovative and sustainable path to success."

No one actually heard Sumner say any of these things. The statement for *The Wall Street Journal* came via email and was crafted by Folta. But Sumner made a few changes to the text and signed off on it before sending it to the *Journal*.

Moreover, just what that "path to success" might be remained a mystery, even to top Viacom executives. Dauman kept assuring them he had a strategy but never revealed just what it was. Some of them began to suspect there was none—that Dauman was just running out the clock, waiting for Sumner to die so he could sell the company and cash in.

At one point Robert Bakish, who'd come up through the ranks at MTV and now ran Viacom's international division, confronted Dooley, the chief operating officer. "Maybe you and Philippe think we're idiots," Bakish said, "in which case you should fire us. But if not, put us all in a room and let's figure things out."

"Philippe will never do that," Dooley responded.

The day after the *Wall Street Journal* article Dauman met with Sumner at his mansion to discuss the recent publicity and other "personal matters," as Dauman described the encounter. He insisted Sumner was "engaged and attentive."

But Herzer, who was, as usual, at Sumner's side throughout the meeting, said it lasted no more than twenty or thirty minutes, and Sumner spent the entire meeting "gazing somewhat vacantly" at a baseball game on television. She said there "was no two-way conversation or discussion" between Dauman and Sumner and characterized the encounter as "a monologue" by Dauman.

As for the press statements supporting Dauman, "Sumner did not say or articulate the flattering words," Herzer said.

Two CBS directors—Sumner's friends Arnold Kopelson and Leonard Goldberg—met with Sumner that October and found him anything but "engaged and attentive." They reported that he was "especially vacant and absent" and "appeared out of touch, remote and non-responsive to the people around him."

Sumner was no longer even saying "Hello, everyone" on board calls. CBS didn't pay him a bonus that year but still paid his $1.75 million base salary. Viacom similarly paid his $2 million salary. Both companies again nominated him to their respective boards.

———

Though Herzer still ruled the mansion with an iron fist, revolt was brewing. Jagiello had hinted to Sumner that there was more to Holbrook's unavailability than he'd been told, but he didn't say much out of fear that Sumner would reveal something to Herzer and he'd be fired. With the incident involving the fake letter from Holland, he and his allies now had more ammunition. Still, they hesitated to act.

But something seems to have aroused Sumner's suspicions. He had "become irate," as Herzer put it, when he discovered his granddaughter Keryn had been using his credit card (even though Herzer insisted he was the one who approved the arrangement). And perhaps even Sumner, notwithstanding his diminished state, saw through Herzer's clumsy subterfuge involving the purported letter from Holland.

On October 10 Herzer persuaded a reluctant MacKinney to make another attempt to engage in sexual activity with Sumner. This time proved a fiasco. "He appeared even more disoriented, distant, and non-communicative," MacKinney asserted. "I cut the visit short and left after spending only about 20 minutes with Sumner." He was "barely a shadow of the man whom I had once known," she concluded.

Jagiello observed that Sumner was "especially cold and aloof" toward Herzer throughout the weekend.

That same day (October 10), Sumner complained to Jagiello, with Tuanaki listening nearby, that Herzer "made him" give her $50 million, evidently a reference to the change in his estate plan, which clearly troubled him. Sumner asked Jagiello to contact Gloria Mazzeo so that she could arrange a meeting with Sumner's lawyers, Bishop and Andelman. Ordinarily Herzer met with Sumner before any meeting with his lawyers to rehearse what he would say, and she almost always stayed with him to make sure he stayed on message. But Sumner was insistent that Jagiello keep this appointment a secret and not say anything to Herzer. Though Jagiello was still apprehensive that Herzer would fire him if she found out, he followed through and called Mazzeo.

Mazzeo told him Bishop was out of town that weekend but would be back on Monday, October 12. They agreed Bishop would come to the mansion that morning, when Herzer was typically out of the house shopping and doing errands.

It was time to strike. As Jagiello put it, "Since Mr. Redstone had articulated such a serious concern about Manuela and called a meeting with his lawyers, I thought it would be a good time to let him know about the constant lies, isolating behavior, surveillance, and deception that Manuela had been instructing the nursing staff to engage in."

It was just as well, because someone else in the household had already warned Herzer that Jagiello was plotting against her. In the couple of months since Holland departed, Herzer had run up over $365,000 in credit card charges paid by Sumner. Just over a week earlier, she'd gotten him to sign for a delivery of $40,000 in cash and agree to a $5 million donation to her personal foundation. That weekend Herzer was spotted in a room at the mansion shredding financial records.

Despite the growing tensions and suspicions, Sunday's movie (now a matinee) proceeded on schedule, with guests including Sumner's old friend and CBS board member Arnold Kopelson and his wife. On tap was the new Universal Pictures release *Steve Jobs*. Before the movie began, Sumner started choking, and Herzer called a nurse to suction his throat. Sumner fell asleep soon after and was wheeled away.

Later, after the guests left, Sumner woke up and started watching a baseball playoff game. But when Herzer checked on him at about 6:30 p.m., he was again asleep. This was "very troubling," Herzer said, because Sumner had always been "extremely passionate" about baseball.

The next morning, October 12, Herzer told Jagiello to summon Sumner's doctor. She left to do errands.

With Herzer out of the house, the moment the "seal team" had been planning had arrived: Jagiello, Octaviano, Tuanaki, and two other nurses met with Sumner to confront him with the deceptions they'd been compelled to participate in. As Jagiello put it, "I did not know whether Mr. Redstone would believe us, and I knew that we would be fired if he did not. However, because I could not in good conscience continue to conduct myself as Manuela demanded, I was prepared to accept that outcome."

The group told Sumner that Herzer had made them lie to him about Holbrook's availability; that Herzer had concealed Holland's letter to him and fabricated another one; that she'd installed a hidden camera in his bedroom; and that her brother Carlos was living in the house. They said they'd been afraid to tell him the truth because Herzer would fire them. Jagiello described Sumner as "shocked" by the disclosures.

Bishop and another Loeb & Loeb lawyer, probate litigator Gabrielle Vidal, arrived soon after and met with Sumner. His other lawyer, Andelman, was connected by speakerphone. With Jagiello translating, Sumner told the lawyers "he wanted Manuela out of his will and he wanted all of his money back."

While this meeting was underway, Herzer returned to the Beverly Park front gate. She was denied entry on Bishop's orders, acting on Sumner's behalf. Herzer nonetheless proceeded to an unmanned back entrance, used her pass code to get in, and then "stormed" into the house, in Jagiello's recollection. Tuanaki intercepted her in the hallway. "Mr. Redstone doesn't want you here," he said, but she brushed past him.

Bishop looked startled when Herzer burst into the room. "You're not supposed to be here," she said. Then, speaking to Andelman on the phone, "Manuela is here but she is not supposed to be here. I don't know how she came in." In Herzer's description, "A frenzy ensued."

Herzer went up to Sumner and asked him if he was okay. "Are you mad at me? Do you want me to leave?" Sumner responded with what Herzer called a "grunting noise," but Jagiello interpreted as "Get out of my house."

"He wants you to leave," Jagiello told Herzer.

"But where will I live?" she asked.

"You have a house," Sumner replied, as translated by Jagiello, referring to the house he'd bought for her and she had been renovating for years. Then he began to cry.

Herzer turned to Bishop, her longtime ally. "What do I do?"

But Bishop had turned cold. She said she needed to consult with

Sumner without Herzer there, though that had never seemed necessary before. She said Herzer could return later to collect her belongings. As Herzer left the room, she turned to look back. Sumner was still sobbing.

When Herzer left, the nurses and staff exchanged high fives.

Herzer went to her daughter's house to calm down. She was summoned by Tuanaki a few hours later. A guard followed her to her room. "Get away from me," she demanded. She asked to see Sumner, but the guard told her if she didn't leave, he'd call the police.

Herzer tried frantically to get some explanation for her abrupt exile. She called Bishop repeatedly, but all Bishop would say was that Herzer had "lied" to Sumner, without being more specific.

In a measure of their close relationship, Herzer next called Dauman, who elaborated that the lies involved Keryn's use of Sumner's credit card and the hidden cameras she'd had installed without telling him (both of which Herzer maintained Sumner had known about but evidently forgotten). Dauman apparently made no mention of the far more significant lies involving Holbrook's availability, the fake letter from Holland, or attempts by Sumner's immediate family members to speak to him and visit.

"Manuela, now you have so much money. You have a beautiful family. You're a nice person. You have everything. If you ever need anything, you can always call me," Dauman told her, according to Herzer. "You know there's nothing more you can do for him. These are his words. He loves you. He loves your family. Don't worry, I've got your back."

(Dauman disputed nearly every aspect of Herzer's version of their conversations. While he acknowledged speaking to her, he said he was only being polite and maintained he'd never said anything about the reasons for her exile or having her "back.")

Tyler was in Napa Valley that weekend to attend a wedding when Jagiello told him the news that Herzer was out.

"Manuela evicted . . . her family no longer welcome either," Tyler excitedly texted Brandon.

"I wonder what the info he got was," Brandon responded.

"Long story . . . this is what we've been working towards," Tyler replied.

Tyler flew to Los Angeles and went to Beverly Park to make sure his grandfather was okay. Sumner didn't say much, but he seemed relieved that the crisis had passed and Herzer was gone. He was adamant that he wanted his money back. And he wanted to see other people again, especially members of his family, Keryn excepted.

Shari got there as soon as she could. She rushed in to see her father and threw her arms around him. "I never thought I'd see you again," she said.

Four days after the nurses' intervention and Herzer's exile, on October 16, Sumner met again with Bishop. He excised Herzer as his health care proxy and replaced her with Dauman. He removed Herzer and her children from his will, leaving them nothing. The $50 million and the proceeds of the mansion Herzer was to receive were now directed to charity.

Dr. Spar was again on hand to assess Sumner's mental acuity and understanding of his actions. With Bishop out of the room, he asked Sumner what had prompted the changes to his estate plan and health care directive.

"I threw Sydney out," Sumner answered. "Then I threw Manuela out. Manuela lied to me. Everybody knows that."

What did she lie about? Spar asked.

"She lied about Terry," Sumner said, referring to Holbrook.

And Sumner mentioned the purported letter from Holland: "The letter was all bullshit."

"I'm Not Going to Fire Him"

Shari quickly filled the void in Sumner's Beverly Park mansion. She all but moved to Los Angeles, spending nearly half the next year there. When father and daughter weren't together, they communicated regularly via FaceTime. Still, Sumner counted the days between her visits. His nurses installed a large clock so he could track the hours and minutes until Shari's arrival.

Shari became adept at interpreting Sumner's speech. She hired professionals to oversee his medical care. She and her father watched sports and movies together. But most of all they talked business, once again Sumner's favorite subject. She kept him informed about everything she knew as a board member and vice chair of both Viacom and CBS.

In trying to sort through her father's affairs, Bishop proved to be little help. Although she had collaborated closely with Holland and Herzer, and then with just Herzer once Holland was expelled, it infuriated Shari that Bishop now refused to meet alone with her unless Bishop had her lawyer present.

And Dauman had by no means retreated. He was often at Sumner's mansion, too, watching sports on TV with him and discussing the movie business. Dauman seemed to feel his position was secure. His second-in-command, Tom Dooley, warned him that Herzer's eviction and Shari's ascendance put their status in jeopardy, but Dauman just shrugged. "We'll see," he said.

Dauman had always filtered everything he told Sumner about Viacom through his point of view, which had typically omitted Shari's. She now had the opportunity to point out their many areas of tension and disagreement and explain that she was only trying to do what she thought Sumner would have wanted.

But Dauman's loyalty was still paramount. "I'm not going to fire him," Sumner insisted.

———

On November 24, just six weeks after she was ejected from Sumner's mansion, Herzer filed a lawsuit to reclaim her position as Sumner's health care proxy. Describing Sumner as "a tragic figure in the waning days of an accomplished life," she claimed that Sumner now lacked the mental capacity to revoke his earlier health care proxy, signed when Sumner "was lucid and in full possession of his faculties." And she took a slap at Shari: "His choice was based on a close bond formed over many years that he repeatedly described as a loving familial relationship. Though Mr. Redstone has two adult children and five adult grandchildren," he had nonetheless chosen Herzer "to care for him in his last years, knowing that he could always trust her to honor his wishes and look out for his best interests."

Herzer was the first to say publicly what many suspected: ninety-two-year-old Sumner Redstone, still the highly compensated executive chairman of two publicly traded companies, was in fact incapacitated—"a living ghost," the suit maintained. "Those who know him now describe him as vacant, unable to reliably communicate, unaware of his surroundings, and without interest in things that used to excite and engage him."

It fell to Shari to break the news of the lawsuit to Sumner. His immediate fear was that Herzer might be reinstated as his health care proxy. He hated Herzer, he reiterated, and became agitated at the prospect she might be coming back into his life. Shari reassured him that would never happen.

Litigation was nothing new for Herzer. In keeping with her pit-bull reputation, she may well have concluded that the best defense was to launch a preemptive strike before Shari could sue her for the return of the lavish gifts. Thanks to Sumner's generosity, she had the war chest to assemble a formidable legal team and launch a scorched-earth litigation campaign.

After her visit to David Boies with Holland had gone nowhere, Herzer had hired Pierce O'Donnell, one of Los Angeles's highest-profile lawyers. O'Donnell had gained a national reputation by successfully representing columnist Art Buchwald in a suit claiming that Paramount had stolen his idea for the Eddie Murphy comedy *Coming to America*. O'Donnell had also handled some high-profile divorce cases, including a recent successful effort to recoup lavish gifts to a mistress.

Sumner had paid O'Donnell's $250,000 retainer. After Holland was ejected and she and Herzer were at odds, O'Donnell represented only Herzer. Since Sumner was no longer paying her expenses, O'Donnell agreed to represent her on a contingency fee basis, in which he and his firm would take a percentage of any settlement or verdict.

In focusing solely on Herzer's status as Sumner's health care proxy rather than on her aborted inheritance, the lawsuit suggested Herzer was on a purely humanitarian mission. Herzer maintained her motive was "to accomplish one single objective: to see that she is able to honor her sacred promise to Mr. Redstone to care for him for the rest of his life."

But the wording of the lawsuit suggested something less benign than a single-minded devotion to Sumner's well-being. The petition was merciless in its detail and unsparing of Sumner's privacy or decorum. It described Sumner as "obsessed with eating steak" despite the feeding tube and said he "does not seem to recall or understand why he cannot do so. Similarly, Mr. Redstone demands, to the extent he can be understood, to engage in sexual activity every day."

The petition was all but guaranteed to generate sensational media coverage, and it did: "SEX-OBSESSED" SUMNER REDSTONE KEPT BEAUTIFUL WOMEN ON RETAINER, trumpeted the *New York Post*. *The New York Times* described the lurid personal details included in the petition as "excruciating."

Herzer's former ally Holland wanted no part of it. Holland "is absolutely disgusted with what's going on in court with Manuela," her lawyer Brad Rose told *Fortune* magazine.

To succeed, Herzer's lawsuit also had to thread a factual needle: that Sumner had been fully alert and mentally competent just months earlier, when he made Herzer his sole health care proxy (not to mention the many times he gave her vast sums of money and made her the beneficiary of his trust), but not when he removed her. So Herzer alleged that after Holland was ejected for having the affair with Pilgrim, "it was like a switch had been flipped, and his mental presence and acuity were faint shadows of what they had once been for the once vital, towering figure."

Herzer offered several declarations in support of the petition, which might have been more persuasive if made by less self-interested and obviously conflicted witnesses: one was from her paid medical expert, and the others were from her brother Carlos and Heidi MacKinney—Herzer's employee and Sumner's sometime sex partner.

Redstone's lawyers issued a press statement portraying Herzer as a ruthless gold digger. Her "claim that she filed this lawsuit out of concern for Mr. Redstone is preposterous," said Loeb & Loeb partner Vidal, who had witnessed Herzer's expulsion. "It is a meritless action, riddled with lies, and a despicable invasion of his privacy. It proves only that Ms. Herzer will stop at nothing to pursue her personal financial agenda."

A spokesperson for Shari said only, "Sumner's family members now have unfettered access to him. Shari is, and has been, actively involved in Sumner's care."

A few weeks later, on December 11, Sumner sent a letter to Shari, in care of Bishop, that repudiated his former relationship with Herzer and sought to erase her recent presence: "I wish to put our family back as we were before Sydney and Manuela, and restore our family relationship to what it was then," the letter read. "This is very important to me. I love and trust you and your family. You are all invited to stay with me and visit me any time. I am very sorry to hear that others have excluded you and your family from my house. That will never happen again."

For good measure, he stressed that previous documents and statements that criticized Shari or members of her family "should be considered withdrawn, terminated, voided, cancelled, inaccurate and of no effect whatsoever." And he asserted that he was under no duress or coercion while composing and signing the letter, an event witnessed by Jagiello. By now Sumner's signature was little more than a sloping line.

———

With Herzer banished and Shari and her family back in her father's good graces, the 2015 Christmas holidays bore little resemblance to the previous year's, when Herzer's and Holland's extended families had taken over the house. Shari, her children, and two great-grandchildren spent the holidays with him, playing games and, in Shari's case, discussing the media business.

Dauman soon turned against Herzer and tried to placate Shari by agreeing to testify against her. In a pretrial deposition he said he'd met with Sumner "several times a week by telephone regarding both business and personal matters" and had found Sumner "to be engaged and attentive" when he visited him as recently as November 3. "Sumner asked me to send regards to various people, and I updated him on the regards others have asked me to pass along to him," Dauman testified. "We talked about the conference at which I would be speaking the following morning, and we reminisced about corporate history and personal matters." Dauman also said that when he met with Sumner on October 8, the same meeting Herzer had characterized as "a monologue," he and Sumner "had an extensive business discussion regarding articles that appeared recently." On both occasions, Sumner "was engaged, attentive and opinionated as ever."

Dauman added that he cared "deeply for Sumner and will do whatever is necessary to ensure that he continues to receive superior care."

Still, the implications of Herzer's departure and Shari's return weren't lost on Dauman. In January he quietly hired lawyers at the prominent firm of Paul, Weiss, Rifkind, Wharton & Garrison to explore his options.

———

Herzer's lawsuit, with its devastating assertions about Sumner's physical and mental decline, coupled with his conspicuous absences at recent shareholder meetings and presentations—not to mention the millions CBS and Viacom were still paying Sumner—caught the attention of Wall Street. With a controlling shareholder like Sumner, activist investors had shown little interest in Viacom. In the wake of the lawsuit, that changed. Even Sumner's handpicked directors had a fiduciary duty to all shareholders.

At an investor conference in December hosted by Reuters, the influential media investor and major Viacom shareholder Mario Gabelli asked about Sumner, "Is he or isn't he in the position where he should be chairman emeritus or something?" Salvatore Muoio, another major Viacom shareholder, echoed the sentiment: "If Sumner is no longer fit to lead the board, then he should give up that role."

Eric Jackson, managing director of SpringOwl Asset Management, an activist investor with a stake in Viacom, attracted widespread publicity in January after he posted on the internet a slideshow with a devastating critique of Viacom's leadership. Jackson called Viacom "creatively bankrupt." He compared the situation with Sumner to *Weekend at Bernie's*, a comedy in which two young executives prop up their dead boss so they can enjoy a weekend at his Hamptons estate.

The numbers alone were devastating: Viacom stock had lost 46.9 percent in the previous year, compared with a decline of just 1.2 percent in the S&P 500 stock index. Over the past three years Viacom had lost 21.4 percent, compared with a gain of 47.1 percent by the S&P 500. CBS had gained 34.5 percent over the same period, and Disney had more than doubled. It seemed inconceivable that the once-stock-obsessed Sumner would have tolerated such dismal performance, had he been cognizant of it.

Jackson criticized Sumner as an "absent chair," faulted the lack of succession planning, and bluntly called for "a new chair, CEO, COO and board." He noted that despite Viacom's abysmal performance, Dauman and his chief operating officer, Dooley, had been paid a total of $432 million over the previous five years, "far ahead of any other media company" (with the exception of Moonves at CBS, who was paid even more, but CBS stock had soared). Jackson concluded: "Viacom management has underperformed for years with no accountability."

A shareholder lawsuit in Delaware soon followed, accusing Viacom directors of breaching their duties to shareholders.

Viacom directors dug in. "Mr. Redstone's physicians have publicly attested that he is mentally capable, and this information is consistent with other medical and other information available to me," William Schwartz, a lawyer and chair of Viacom's governance and nominating committee and a longtime friend of Sumner's, said in a statement. But there was no mention of any actual meeting or interaction between Sumner and Schwartz, and the odd wording—"consistent with"—only fueled more speculation about Sumner's condition.

All of this was followed with intense interest at CBS, where it was perfectly obvious that Sumner was in no mental or physical condition to serve as board chair or, more fundamentally, as a controlling shareholder. He hadn't appeared at either Viacom's annual meeting of shareholders in March or CBS's in May. Thanks to Moonves's leadership, CBS shares had fared far better than Viacom's, and CBS had escaped the scrutiny and scathing criticism heaped on Dauman at Viacom. (With Herzer banished, Sumner had also stopped meddling in CBS casting decisions. *Madam Secretary* was canceled in 2019 after six seasons, and Kathrine Herzer didn't get another role at CBS.)

Nonetheless, CBS could as easily find itself at the whim of whoever managed to gain sway over an incapacitated Sumner, which at the moment seemed to be Shari.

Moonves had no intention of letting that happen. In December, the independent directors on the CBS board, without telling Shari or Sumner, formed a special committee to investigate eliminating Sumner's controlling interest. Options included having CBS buy National Amusements' controlling shares at a premium, and a more drastic route: to issue a dividend consisting of a fraction of supervoting shares to all shareholders, which would have the effect of diluting National Amusements' voting power.

Moonves's second-in-command, CBS chief operating officer Joseph Ianniello, warned Moonves in an email that such a drastic step would "take away Ms. Redstone's whole life." But there was no doubt where Ianniello's loyalty lay. If Moonves ever went to war with the Redstones, "I will have your back to the end," Ianniello told him.

"This Is Your Battle, Not Mine"

Very few people were actually meeting Sumner these days. Herzer complained that Shari was cutting her father off from the outside world (much as Shari had complained about Herzer) and insisted she and her lawyers had the right to interview Sumner and evaluate his mental state.

In January Los Angeles Superior Court judge David Cowan rejected Herzer's attempts to conduct a deposition of Sumner but ruled that Herzer's geriatric psychiatric expert, Dr. Stephen Read, a respected member of UCLA's medical faculty, could examine Sumner for an hour at Sumner's home without Herzer or any lawyers being present (his nurses and an interpreter were allowed to be there).

Read administered a version of what's known as the Mini-Mental State Exam, a commonly used test for cognitive function in the elderly. In some respects Sumner performed well. Read felt Sumner was "fully alert and attentive" during their meeting. Sumner knew the date (January 29) though not the year (2016). He understood that if his feeding tube were removed he might choke. He was able to repeat three words from memory. He knew how many children (two), grandchildren (five), and great-grandchildren (two) he had, and he remembered the names of his great-grandchildren, though Read had to accept the interpreter's word for that, since he couldn't understand what Sumner was saying.

But Sumner failed other tests. Asked to identify a picture of a blue star, he pointed to a green square. Read asked him to perform three simple tasks in order, a test known as sequencing. But as soon as Read mentioned the first task—touch your nose—Sumner did, without waiting to hear the other tasks, which Read described as an impulsive or "disinhibited" response. Read tried again, asking Sumner to touch his nose, stick out his tongue, and touch his ear, in that order. Sumner touched his nose and stuck out his tongue. But then he kept moving it from side to side, an exercise he'd performed in speech therapy. He never touched his ear.

Sumner couldn't perform simple arithmetic. Asked to subtract seven from one hundred, he struggled and then said ninety-six (as best the interpreter could tell). Asked to spell *world* backward, he began correctly with the letter *d* but then faltered.

Read asked Sumner about his sports bets with his nephew Steven Sweetwood, and Sumner boasted that he always won, apparently oblivious to the fact that the betting was rigged or that such a perfect record was all but mathematically impossible.

Sumner also insisted that Herzer had stolen the sum of $40 million from him. To be certain, Read wrote the figure "$40 million" on a whiteboard. Sumner nodded to confirm that it was accurate. But Sumner also nodded "yes" when Read asked if "responsible people" managed his money. Read found it improbable that Herzer had "stolen" $40 million, given that Sumner had the benefit of professional money management and, as Read put it, "$40 million would not have slipped out undetected." But Sumner reiterated without further explanation that Herzer had stolen it. "Everybody knows that," Sumner insisted.

When frustrated, Sumner often experienced an "uncontrollable outburst of anger," which Read found to be "very severe" and a "very serious problem."

Read concluded that "Redstone manifests features of dementia, toward the severe end of moderate." He "believed Redstone suffered cortical brain damage, likely from a shortage of blood flow and oxygen to his brain over a period of time, which caused Redstone's language impairment."

In a thirty-seven-page written report he submitted to the court, Read concluded that when Sumner replaced Herzer as his health care proxy, "his mental capacity was severely compromised to such a degree that he did not have the requisite mental capacity to understand and appreciate the consequence of his actions in changing his health care directive." He added that this made Sumner "extremely vulnerable to undue influence."

It was a shocking diagnosis for a man who had sped through Harvard College in three years and quickly mastered Japanese. As Read described his interview and evaluation of Sumner, "It was a very sad event," and "very painful to see." He continued, "Mr. Redstone was a phenomenal figure in his day, lauded appropriately for very high intelligence, served his country admirably in World War II. But the Mr. Redstone that we have today is a very, very thin shadow of what he was."

Putting aside the legal question of whether Sumner understood the consequences of removing Herzer, it was obvious that Sumner had no business serving as executive chairman of two major public companies and should have stepped down long before. The trust holding his National Amusements shares provided for his removal if he were found to be incapacitated, but the trust agreement said a court had to find Sumner incompetent, and three doctors also had to attest in writing that he was incapacitated—a highly unlikely scenario. But Sumner's public absence from board meetings and overall lack of participation was attracting criticism, and directors at both companies, supported by Shari, agreed it was time for him to step down.

Just a few days after Read's damning assessment, on February 2, Sumner sent a letter to the boards of both CBS and Viacom announcing that he was resigning as executive chairman and a director of each company.

Even then, the companies couldn't bring themselves to simply let him go. Both boards named him chairman emeritus, with a base salary of $1 million at CBS and $1.75 million at Viacom. Whatever his physical and mental state, Sumner was still the controlling shareholder.

The CBS board met the next day and first offered the chair position to Shari, as mandated by the National Amusements Trust. She declined and instead nominated Moonves. The board voted unanimously to approve him.

———

At Viacom, Shari didn't believe the transition would go as smoothly. "It is my firm belief that whoever may succeed my father as chair at each company should be someone who is not a trustee of my father's trust or otherwise intertwined in Redstone family matters, but rather a leader with an independent voice," she said in a press statement that same day.

A spokesperson added, "Shari is going to continue to advocate for what she believes to be in the best interests of Viacom shareholders."

These were clear references to Dauman, who served as a trustee of the National Amusements trust. Shari lobbied her father to oppose Dauman's elevation, but her influence had its limits. She made what she thought was a compelling case against Dauman, starting with Viacom's slumping stock price. But over their decades together, Sumner had never wavered. Even in his impaired state, his support for Dauman seemed unshakable.

Viacom directors met by phone the next day, with Dauman calling in from vacation and Sumner on the line from his home. As the roll call proceeded, all the directors, including Sumner, voted to elevate Dauman to chair, with one prominent exception. Shari voted no.

Schwartz, the nominating committee chair, made no public mention of the dissenting vote. "In choosing a successor to Sumner, the board considered the need for seasoned leadership in this time of unprecedented change, Philippe's business experience and unparalleled knowledge of Viacom, and his long-term vision for the company," he said.

But just five days later, Viacom shocked Wall Street with earnings that fell far short of projections. Cable ratings and revenues fell as news spread that Paramount had ended 2015 in last place at the box office for the fourth consecutive year, despite releasing another installment in the *Mission: Impossible* franchise. Viacom's stock plunged 21 percent, hitting a five-year low.

On the earnings call, with Sumner purportedly listening by phone, Dauman, the newly appointed chair, was testy and obviously in a bad mood. He lashed out at an analyst who asked about the company's "exceedingly poor performance," responding, "Our outlook and the facts have been distorted and obscured by the naysayers, self-interested critics and publicity seekers." He attributed the stock's decline to "noise" about the company and, in what was perceived as a criticism of Shari and her public remarks, said, "I think it's obvious to everybody what the noise is."

Dauman was sounding increasingly desperate. His strategy, such as it was, had been to buy back stock, cut costs, and shrink the studio's output, hoping to reduce risk. The studio would focus on making sequels in its franchise series, like *Mission: Impossible—Rogue Nation*. But two sequels that year—*Terminator Genisys* and *Paranormal Activity: The Ghost Dimension*—were embarrassing flops. And even *Rogue Nation* had faltered compared with earlier installments.

Paramount had lost over $100 million in the quarter ending December 31. And Ben Stiller's *Zoolander 2*, a much-anticipated sequel to his 2001 cult favorite, had just opened to tepid box office and scathing reviews, which didn't bode well for 2016 results, either. Dauman told analysts he was confident Paramount had hits in the pipeline: *Star Trek Beyond*, a *Teenage Mutant Ninja Turtles* sequel, and a Brad Pitt spy vehicle, *Allied*, among them.

Then an opportunity emerged that might rescue both Dauman and Viacom's plummeting stock price. Investment banker Alan Schwartz, former chief executive of Bear Stearns, approached Dauman about selling a stake in Paramount to the Chinese property conglomerate Dalian Wanda, which also owned movie theaters in China and a stake in the AMC chain in the United States. Selling all or part of Paramount wasn't exactly an original idea: several Wall Street analysts, including SpringOwl's Jackson, had been pushing Dauman to unlock value by selling a stake. Viacom was being valued on Wall Street as a multiple of cash flow, and since Paramount was losing money, its value was minimal.

But Dauman thought he could extract a premium price. Schwartz had said he thought Paramount might be worth $5 billion; he could possibly get his Chinese bidder to $7 billion, maybe even $8 billion. Dauman wanted to hold out for an even higher number: he told directors he could get $10 billion for the studio.

But some Viacom executives were skeptical. Ten billion dollars was astronomical. And co-ownership of a major Hollywood studio had a terrible track record—Comcast had had to buy out General Electric's stake in NBC/Universal, and Rupert Murdoch had done the same with oilman Marvin Davis's stake in Twentieth Century Fox. Moreover, shrinking Viacom flew in the face of an increasing need for larger scale to remain competitive in the fast-changing industry. But it was still a potentially career-making move for the embattled Dauman.

It would also mean the undoing of Sumner's legacy. Beating Barry Diller to acquire the legendary film studio had been the crowning achievement of Sumner's long dealmaking career. George Abrams warned Dauman that Sumner would never sell Paramount, not even a minority stake, unless the price was exorbitant, and Abrams would support Sumner in that regard. As long as Sumner was alive and legally competent, even if impaired, it would be all but unthinkable to proceed without his support—especially with Shari back in the picture.

Just days after succeeding Sumner as chair, Dauman showed up at Sumner's mansion without an appointment. He didn't want Shari to know he was coming and risk having her there when he arrived. Dauman asked Jagiello and other nurses if he and Sumner could have some privacy, and Jagiello left the room but positioned himself in an adjoining doorway (he never let Sumner out of his sight), where he was a witness to the ensuing conversation.

Sumner was sitting in his chair near the living room window with the television on. Dauman leaned in and deliberately turned his back toward Jagiello, whom he considered a spy for Shari. Dauman whispered into Sumner's ear so Jagiello couldn't hear what he said.

In Dauman's account of the conversation, he told Sumner he had received significant interest from parties who wanted to buy a minority stake in Paramount at a price that would amount to an extraordinary valuation for the studio. He asked for Sumner's permission to convene a board meeting to discuss the possibility.

Sumner nodded in what appeared to be agreement. In any event, that's what Jagiello subsequently reported to Shari.

Dauman repeated the request to make sure Sumner understood, and he nodded again.

In a telephone meeting on February 22, Dauman briefed the Viacom board on the substance of his plan for Paramount and his interaction with Sumner. Both Shari and Sumner were on the call, though as usual Sumner said nothing. In Dauman's telling, he'd explained his plans for Paramount and asked Sumner if he understood, which is what prompted the nod witnessed by Jagiello. Shari didn't hear anything in Dauman's presentation about selling a large stake in Paramount. The board—including Sumner—voted unanimously to pursue the negotiations, with one exception: Shari voted no.

The next day Viacom announced that it had been approached by several unidentified strategic investors interested in buying a stake in the studio. In a company-wide memo, Dauman talked up the added capital, which would help expand production and unspecified "creative opportunities" for Viacom employees, but didn't say anything about the size of the stake he planned to sell. Battered Viacom shares jumped 5 percent on the news.

Despite the clash with Shari, Dauman remained on good terms with Sumner, as best he could tell. Dauman met again with Sumner the first week of March. This time, Sumner was "almost totally nonresponsive, and could not meaningfully communicate at all," Dauman maintained.

In later discussions with some board members, Dauman said he wanted to sell not a small stake but as much as 49 percent, or nearly half. When word reached Shari, she was stunned. Given the high price Dauman was negotiating, his argument was that Viacom should raise as much capital as possible while still retaining control of the studio. But Shari felt misled. She'd assumed he was selling a small stake in Paramount, perhaps 10 percent. Selling such a large stake flew in the face of everything she knew about her father. He loved content. He loved making movies. He loved the business. He even wanted to control it from the grave. And now, after a whispered briefing from Dauman, he wanted to sell nearly half his crown jewel and share decision making with another investor?

Shari met with her father to review Dauman's plans. In her account, he was as shocked by the proposed sale of such a large stake as she had been, perhaps more so. For Dauman to negotiate secretly to sell such a large stake in Paramount was a betrayal every bit as unforgivable as Holland's affair with Pilgrim, especially coming from someone he'd considered a son. And he felt the same way about the directors who seemed to be going along with Dauman, even old friends like George Abrams and Bill Schwartz.

Given Sumner's mental state and communication issues, it's hard to know how much of the intricacies of the proposed Paramount deal he knew or understood. But there's no doubt that, as quickly as he'd turned against Holland and Herzer, Sumner turned bitterly against both Dauman and Abrams, his lawyer and confidant of fifty-three years. Sumner, in a typically profane assessment, said Dauman was now a "fucking asshole."

"How can he do this?" Sumner asked his daughter. "I control the board. What do I do?"

"This is your battle, not mine," Shari replied. She was busy raising a family and running her venture capital operation. "I have a new life."

Sumner must have had some idea that the upcoming battle would require more physical stamina and mental determination than he could now muster.

"Shari, you have to do this," he insisted. "You need to stop this."

For Shari, that was the moment he finally said: "Shari, I trust you."

"I'll do it for you," she said.

EPISODE 6

"A Public Spectacle"

On March 11, 2016, Loeb & Loeb lawyers Gabrielle Vidal and Amy Koch took litigation attorney Rob Klieger to meet Sumner at his Beverly Park mansion. Southern California was uncharacteristically lashed with winds and heavy rain that afternoon, so they pulled up to the garage after navigating the entrance gates. Sumner was waiting in his favorite recliner in the living room while watching CNBC on his large-screen television.

Klieger had never met Sumner, and his physical appearance came as a shock. He looked extremely frail. Vidal did most of the talking, and when Sumner responded he did little more than grunt. Fortunately, Jagiello was on hand to translate.

Up to that point, Vidal had been leading Sumner's legal defense in the Herzer suit. But Judge Cowan, after digesting Read's report on Sumner's mental acuity and calling its details painful to read, had denied Sumner's motion to dismiss the case. He noted that both sides had agreed that Sumner was suffering from a "subcortical neurological disorder" causing "cognitive impairment" and decided that his mental competency was enough of an issue to warrant a trial. He also found it odd that Sumner would replace Herzer as his health care agent with Dauman, who didn't live in Los Angeles, rather than with a family member like Shari. He set a trial date for the first week in May.

Because Vidal herself was a potential witness, given her presence the day Herzer was ejected, not to mention her law partner Bishop's pivotal role in the events at issue, Sumner needed a lawyer who didn't face any potential conflicts. Hence the choice of Klieger, a partner at the litigation firm Hueston Hennigan who'd represented Paramount, MTV, and other Viacom entities from time to time but brought a fresh eye to the recent melodrama in Beverly Park. He'd never met Sumner or Shari.

Klieger's close-cropped hair was tinged with gray, but he still looked younger than his age, forty-four, which belied his intensity and determination. He'd grown up in Pittsburgh, the son of a hospital pathologist, living in the same modest family house until he went to Hamilton College and then Stanford Law School, where he graduated second in his class in 1997. He'd always been driven to excel as a student, and as a lawyer he was a self-described workaholic, typically billing three thousand hours a year, first at the prominent firm Irell & Manella, where he'd been named a partner at age thirty-three, and then at Hueston Hennigan.

"Could you understand a word he said?" Klieger asked as he and the other lawyers drove away from the estate. Because he hadn't.

It wasn't a promising start to a new lawyer-client relationship, but Klieger persisted. He came to see Sumner nearly every day the next week. On his third visit, he arrived before Vidal, and someone on the household staff told him Sumner wanted to get started. So Klieger met with Sumner without the other lawyers.

Sumner spoke with much more passion and conviction than on either of his previous visits. Jagiello was again on hand, which helped, but Klieger was beginning to understand Sumner's words without him. The message Sumner conveyed was perfectly clear: he did not want to sell Paramount or any part of it. He was angry that Viacom directors, handpicked by him for their supposed loyalty, had supported Dauman behind his back. He asked Klieger to call Viacom board members and tell them he adamantly opposed the proposed sale.

Klieger tried to beg off, since he'd been hired for the Herzer case, and this task was unrelated. But Sumner insisted. So Klieger called Viacom's longtime general counsel, Michael Fricklas, and told him Sumner was opposed to any sale.

The next day one of Sumner's nurses called Klieger and put Sumner on the line. Had Klieger reached any directors? When Klieger told him he'd spoken with Fricklas, Sumner became agitated and insisted he reach out directly to board members, not to someone who worked for Viacom.

The next day Klieger called two directors, both longtime friends and confidants of Sumner's: Frederic Salerno, the former chief financial officer of Verizon and Viacom's lead independent director, and George Abrams, the Boston lawyer who had long represented Sumner and was a trustee of his trust.

Salerno returned the call but was wary, never having dealt with Klieger. He also felt frustrated that none of the Viacom directors besides Shari, not even his oldest and closest friends, had heard directly from Sumner. Was this really Sumner speaking—or was it Shari? Salerno had growing doubts about Sumner's mental state. And he was suspicious of Shari's growing influence. Salerno had been seated next to Sumner at a 2014 Viacom board dinner at Sumner's mansion, the last time Salerno could say for sure that Sumner had his wits about him, and heard him insist then (as he had before) that Shari should not succeed him.

Salerno said he'd have to verify what Klieger said and later asked to meet in person with Sumner, a request neither Klieger nor Shari was inclined to grant given the pending litigation. In any event it was pointless, because Sumner refused to meet with anyone he considered a traitor.

Abrams didn't respond.

Hoping to defuse the tension and further explain the board's reasoning, Dauman scheduled a meeting with Sumner and in April flew to Los Angeles. An hour before the meeting, Sumner's office called him and canceled it.

On Klieger's next visit, Sumner wanted to know if he'd spoken to any directors and what they'd said. He seemed pleased that Klieger had reached Salerno and left word for Abrams.

Such exchanges gave Klieger more confidence that Sumner understood what was happening and could communicate his wishes. He asked him variations of the same question, some calling for a "yes" answer, others a "no," to be sure Sumner understood the questions. Sumner's answers were always consistent. And Klieger found he was getting better at engaging Sumner in conversation without having to rely on a nurse to translate. Still, when it came to important decisions, Klieger confirmed Sumner's wishes on more than one visit before acting on them.

Sumner was also keenly interested in his money and how it was being spent. He remained intent on getting his millions back from Holland and Herzer, asking Klieger about it repeatedly and demanding that he take legal action against the women.

Klieger managed to deflect him, explaining that it would needlessly complicate the Herzer case to argue that Sumner had been the victim of undue influence when he transferred millions to the women—in the presence of his estate lawyer and a psychiatrist, no less—and then argue in Herzer's lawsuit that he was not unduly influenced by Shari when he removed Herzer from his health care directive months later. Sumner relented, at least for the time being, but nevertheless kept saying he wanted his money back.

At one point Paula, Sumner's second wife, contacted Klieger and said Sumner had agreed as a birthday present to pay for up to $150,000 in renovations to her condominium in Florida. Where should she send the invoices?

Klieger confirmed with Sumner that he had indeed made such a promise, so Klieger told her to send the invoices to Sumner's accountant. But now Paula said the $150,000 was just the first of six install-ments.

Klieger went back to Sumner. Had he agreed to pay a total of $900,000? Sumner was adamant: he'd pay $150,000 but not a penny more.

———

Judge Cowan's ruling allowing Herzer's suit to go forward un-leashed a flurry of subpoenas from the Herzer camp, including one demanding testimony from Shari. Her deposition, in which Herzer's lawyers intended to explore Herzer's claims that Shari had organized a spy ring within the household staff and bribed and cajoled them to oust Herzer from her position, was scheduled for the second week of April. And Herzer's lawyers continued to push for a videotaped depo-sition of Sumner himself—a tape they expected to be exhibit A in the upcoming trial.

The litigation onslaught gave Herzer considerable leverage, since Shari and her legal team were eager to avoid sworn testimony, espe-cially from Sumner. The lawsuit and the possibility that Herzer might be reinstated were already making him anxious, and he was having trouble sleeping.

Nor did Shari look forward to being dragged through the mud by a lawyer like Pierce O'Donnell, Herzer's aggressive counsel. Though she thought Herzer's behavior had been despicable, Shari had already achieved her primary goal, which was to regain access to her father. She and her family were back in his life more than ever before. Galling though it was, she was willing to let Herzer keep the millions she had extracted from her father, including the $45 million transfer, and even pay her more, if she could get Herzer out of her life once and for all.

Herzer, too, had reasons to compromise, with an array of nurses and household employees lined up to testify against her. Shortly after Klieger was hired, the Herzer camp suggested a mediation proceeding to resolve the issues out of court. Sumner resisted, but his family all but begged him to try it. They worried that more litigation would take a further toll on his health and wanted him to focus on something positive for whatever time he had left. Anything it would cost him to be rid of Herzer was money well spent, they believed. Shari's and other depositions were postponed while the parties negotiated.

The mediator met separately with Herzer and Sumner, and it went well considering Sumner's hostility to his ex-lover and companion. At the end of the day, a framework was agreed upon: Herzer would get another windfall—$30 million plus the Carlyle apartment (then valued at $5 million), all tax free. She could keep everything Sumner had already given her. In return Herzer would relinquish her claim to be Sumner's health care agent and she and her children would stay away from him for good. They would waive any claim to his estate.

Herzer's lawyer, O'Donnell, considered it one of the best settlements he'd ever negotiated. It would be a windfall for his firm as well: a nearly $13 million contingency fee.

But just as the settlement seemed in hand, Herzer made more demands. She and her three children wanted to see Sumner in person at least once again. She wanted her legal fees paid if any member of the extended Redstone family ever sued her. And she wanted a guarantee that she and her children could attend Sumner's funeral.

O'Donnell was dumbfounded. He all but begged Herzer to accept the settlement he'd negotiated. The mediator also weighed in, warning Herzer that the Redstones had made their final offer and she risked losing everything by holding out for more. But Herzer wouldn't budge.

Her new demands were duly conveyed to the Redstones. As the mediator had foreseen, this was a bridge too far: there was no way the family would allow Herzer and her children to attend Sumner's funeral. Sumner himself was furious. He hadn't really wanted to settle anyway.

Little more than twenty-four hours later, with no word from the

Redstone camp and the clock ticking, Herzer changed her mind. She agreed to accept the earlier offer.

But it was too late. The $35 million offer was gone.

———

Sumner also made clear he wanted Shari to replace Dauman as his health care agent. But some of his lawyers worried that replacing Dauman with Shari would only reinforce Herzer's claim that Shari was taking over Sumner's life.

Klieger saw the point but argued that some things are more important than litigation. In what might be his waning days, Sumner was entitled to having anyone he wanted make life-and-death decisions for him. In early April, Sumner duly modified his health care directive and installed his daughter. In an ominous sign for Dauman, he was no longer named an alternate.

With the trial date looming, Judge Cowan ruled on May 2 that Herzer's lawyer could depose Sumner, on the condition that the session be videotaped at Sumner's home and last no more than fifteen minutes. The tape could be played at the trial, but only behind closed doors, so the public would not witness Sumner's debilitating decline.

"Nobody deserves to have a career tarnished by having been taken to a courthouse and made a public spectacle of when he would not allow that to happen had he the strength himself to stop it," Cowan stated.

On May 7, the day before the scheduled videotaping, Klieger and Vidal met with Sumner to practice. Sumner seemed to recognize the seriousness of the proceeding but was relaxed and in good spirits. He performed well and his speech was easier to understand than usual.

Klieger played the role of O'Donnell, Herzer's lawyer.

What was his favorite movie? Klieger began.

"The Godfather."

"Why?"

"My friend Robert Evans produced it."

What was his favorite team?

"The Yankees."

And his least favorite team?

"Any team playing the Yankees."

The lawyers thought the flash of humor was a healthy sign.

(Sumner's choice of the Yankees as his favorite team nonetheless caused some consternation in the family because Sumner had been a lifelong Red Sox fan. But Sumner could be fickle. If the Red Sox fell hopelessly behind in the pennant race, Sumner switched his allegiance to the Yankees. One year he even cast his lot with Tampa Bay. When push came to shove, winning trumped loyalty.)

The next morning Sumner's living room looked like a scaled-down set for a Paramount film, with a video crew, an interpreter, and the opposing lawyers. To keep the crowd to a minimum, only one lawyer attended from each side, Vidal for Sumner and O'Donnell for Herzer. In contrast to his appearance at the previous day's rehearsal, Sumner looked tired, pale, and gaunt.

A worried Vidal called Klieger from the house to report that Sumner hadn't slept at all the night before. He was having trouble focusing. But it was too late to postpone the deposition.

O'Donnell's questioning began at 11:55 a.m.

"Good morning, sir. I'm Pierce O'Donnell, attorney for Manuela Herzer. It's a privilege to meet you. How are you today?"

"Fine. I'm fine," Sumner responded.

"I want to ask you some questions. Who is Manuela Herzer?"

Sumner didn't answer.

The interpreter suggested he ask again and speak more slowly.

"Who is Manuela Herzer?" O'Donnell repeated.

"She is . . . ," Sumner began, then paused. "Manuela is a fucking bitch."

It was downhill from there. The much-anticipated deposition was over in eighteen minutes.

EPISODE 7

"A Modern-Day Love Story"

The trial of In re: Advance Health Care Directive of Sumner M. Redstone opened on May 6 in the concrete monolith of the Los Angeles Superior Court, just off Interstate 10 in downtown Los Angeles. The proceeding brought the bitter combatants into the same room: Herzer in a conservative black jacket, matching dress, and high heels; Shari in a gray suit over a pink blouse. By her side was her son Brandon, dressed casually in a black sweater.

The opening statements were filled with lofty rhetoric and literary allusions. Pierce O'Donnell began by "imploring" the court to "protect Sumner Redstone in the twilight of a storied life filled with challenge, triumph and tragedy, generosity and Olympian achievement." He continued, "This is a modern-day love story" between Sumner and Herzer. "That bond between these two human beings was cemented in the best of times and the worst of times in both their lives. Yet, your honor, you will see in a blink of an eye, literally in a 48-hour period, 17 years of friendship evaporated, the bond was severed, their love was sabotaged, and Manuela was banned from Sumner's life," leaving her "devastated and inconsolable." Her "soulmate had been ripped out of her life." O'Donnell concluded, "Sumner asked Manuela to care for him. He asked her to protect him and to stay by his side until the end. Manuela made him a promise that she would honor his wish and that, sir, is the only reason why she is in court."

Rob Klieger suggested there might well have been less noble reasons why Herzer was in court: "The only individuals who were monetarily impacted by what happened that day were Ms. Herzer" and her live-in ally, Keryn Redstone.

"Ms. Herzer and Ms. Holland were emotionally abusing Mr. Redstone, they were telling him his family didn't love him, they were telling him his family never called or came to see him while at the same time blocking calls from the family, blocking the family from visiting," Klieger continued. "They told him they were the only ones that loved him and if he didn't give them what they wanted, he would die alone. Classic emotional abuse."

Now that Herzer was gone, "his family is back in his life. He's going on outings outside of the house. You'll hear from the doctors he is doing well." While Sumner concededly suffered from serious speech impairments, he was "someone who does not have trouble comprehending, someone who knows what's happening, knows what he wants, the Sumner Redstone that has always been there," Klieger asserted.

Judge Cowan cleared the courtroom for the playing of Sumner's videotaped deposition. O'Donnell, Klieger, and the other lawyers, of course, knew what was coming. Still, it was another thing to see and hear his labored testimony. There was an audible intake of breath in the room at Sumner's first description of Herzer as a "fucking bitch."

"How long have you known Manuela Herzer?" O'Donnell continued on the videotape, ignoring Sumner's outburst.

"Years. Many years."

"Did Manuela ever reside here at your home?"

"Yes."

"How long did she reside at your home?"

"About a year."

After Sumner was unable to say what years those were, O'Donnell asked why she left.

"I kicked her out."

Again Sumner struggled to say when that had occurred, and O'Donnell gave up and pressed ahead.

"When Manuela was here, did she help with your health care?"

"Yes."

"What did she do to help you?"

Sumner was silent. Then he repeated: "Manuela is a fucking bitch."

O'Donnell asked the question again, but Sumner couldn't answer, even after the interpreter tried to help. Nor did he respond when O'Donnell asked him for his birth name before he changed it to Redstone.

Sumner was more communicative when shown a photo of himself and Herzer together at a Paramount opening.

"When was the photo taken, approximately?"

"Who cares?"

"Were you dating Manuela when the photo was taken?"

"Yes."

"Did you fall in love with Manuela at some point?"

"Yes."

"How long did you and Manuela date?"

"I don't know."

O'Donnell changed subjects.

"Mr. Redstone, did Manuela steal money from you?"

"Yes."

"How much money did Manuela steal from you?"

Sumner didn't answer, even when asked to point to a number on a chart.

"Did—did you ever say that Manuela was the love of your life?"

"Yes."

"Do you still love her?"

"No."

"When Manuela was leaving your house, did you ever confront her to tell her why you were making her leave your house?"

"No."

"Why not?"

"Because she's a fucking bitch."

O'Donnell had no further questions. He was confident he'd made his case that Sumner wasn't competent. He couldn't even remember his birth name.

No doubt thanks to his practice sessions, Sumner seemed more articulate and relaxed, if no less profane, when Vidal did the deposition questioning.

"Mr. Redstone, why did you kick Manuela out of your house?"

"She lied to me."

"What did she lie to you about?"

"About Terry's availability and Sydney's letter."

"Mr. Redstone, how do you feel about Manuela now?"

"I hate her. Fucking bitch."

"Do you want Manuela to make health care decisions for you?"

"No."

"If you are unable to, Mr. Redstone, who would you like to make your health care decisions?"

"Shar—Shari."

"Is that correct? I understood you to say Shari."

"Yeah."

"Mr. Redstone, have you been seeing your family lately? How do you feel about that?"

"I feel good about it."

"Mr. Redstone, are you satisfied—are you happy with the nursing care that you're receiving?"

"Yeah."

"Mr. Redstone, I want you to tell me what you want at the end of this trial."

"I want Manuela out of my life."

Sumner's testimony made an immediate impression on Judge Cowan.

"I told everybody Mr. Redstone may be his own best witness," the judge said after the tape was played. "He's given some strong testimony. I want to know why that testimony should not be respected at the end of the day."

Judge Cowan warned O'Donnell that he faced an uphill struggle, but O'Donnell pushed ahead with his next witness, Stephen Read, the geriatric expert who'd examined Sumner. Read conceded there was no way that Herzer could be reinstated as Sumner's health care agent given Sumner's intense hostility toward her.

Judge Cowan asked both sides for written briefs and pondered the case over the weekend. On Monday he brought the trial to an abrupt halt and issued a seventeen-page opinion.

"The court has heard from the one key witness Herzer herself insisted from the outset of this case that the court hear from: Redstone," he wrote. And "Redstone's testimony has ultimately defeated her case. Though Herzer may have believed that Redstone would not be able to say anything, or be able to understand the questions, Redstone did both."

He continued. "Even if Redstone and Shari have had disagreements about money or business over the years, as have many families, and even if they were estranged for periods for whatever reason, it is without controversy that the bond of love between a parent and a child is a hard one to break completely. Particularly when vulnerable, as it is agreed Redstone now is, it is natural that he would reach out to his daughter, particularly in the absence of a spouse."

Shari burst into tears and hugged Klieger as the implications of the sweeping victory sank in.

Outside the courtroom, she spoke to say, "I am grateful to the court for putting an end to this long ordeal. I am so happy for my father that he can now live his life in peace, surrounded by his friends and family."

For her part, Herzer told *The New York Times*, "I was thinking back at the video that I saw of Sumner and how vulnerable and confused and alone he was, his blank stare, his mumbling. It is sad and makes me want to protect him even more."

O'Donnell was taken aback by the ruling but was nonetheless prepared: that same day he filed a new $70 million lawsuit to reinstate Herzer as a beneficiary in Sumner's will, opening a new front in Herzer's campaign against the Redstone family. Herzer's complaint accused Shari of orchestrating a "coup" and enlisting the household staff to carry out her "insidious plan," resorting to "espionage, bribery, an illegal eviction and deceit to get her way. And she succeeded grandly." Herzer was evicted, and "literally, within 48 hours, a 17-year friendship had gone up in smoke."

Herzer later added that Shari, working closely with her son Tyler, had offered "secret financial inducements" to the nurses and staff to turn them into Redstone family spies. Herzer quoted emails from Shari discussing paying Paz a month's salary as severance after he was fired, and one from Octaviano asking for financial help for him and his wife to open a laundromat.

But Herzer's narrative ignored the fact that it was the nurses who approached the Redstones about reporting the goings-on at Beverly Park, not vice versa. And Tyler, as a lawyer, had been careful not to appear to interfere with Herzer's relationship with Sumner. As Tyler put it in one email to Shari, "I'd be careful about giving any of them money at this time as it could be interpreted as a bribe or tortious interference."

In any event, Herzer produced no evidence that any money had actually been paid. (The Redstone family made only one modest payment, which was a month's salary to Paz in lieu of a severance payout.)

A spokesperson for Shari called the lawsuit a "baseless attack" against the Redstone family and a "total fiction" that "continues to speak volumes about Herzer's motivation and character."

Still, Herzer's lawsuit achieved one public relations goal: the press coverage overshadowed the fact that she had just lost the health care suit.

———

With Herzer on the defensive, at least for the time being, Dauman loomed as the more potent threat to Shari's quest to protect her father's legacy and secure family control of his media empire. Dauman was both chief executive of Viacom and a trustee of the National Amusements trust that controlled Viacom and CBS. After years of what appeared to be slavish devotion to Sumner, Dauman had defiantly continued negotiating a sale of a Paramount stake, going so far as to predict the announcement of a deal by the end of June.

Dauman must have recognized that this all but guaranteed a showdown with the Redstones. But he told colleagues on the board and in management that he thought he could get such an extraordinary price for a Paramount stake that it would quell all opposition, even from the Redstones. And in any event, he believed he had gained Sumner's consent, both in his whispered conversation and in the subsequent board meeting. He still hoped and expected that he or another board member would be allowed to meet with Sumner, who would then confirm his true intention, which was to support Dauman. He also had little to lose: if Shari was indeed in control, the hostility between them ran so deep that his days were numbered whether he promoted a Paramount sale or not.

Dauman appeared to have the solid support of Viacom's independent directors, even though they had never before opposed the company's controlling shareholder on any issue of significance. Their reasoning, as Sumner's longtime friend and ally George Abrams told Klieger when he finally got back to him, appeared to be that they didn't believe that Sumner was of sound mind, and thus Abrams said he'd vote the way he believed Sumner would have wished if he had his faculties. But Abrams stressed that he understood the importance of Paramount to Sumner and would support a sale only at a price so high that even Sumner would embrace it.

Like other longtime employees, Tad Jankowski was torn. Sumner was his lifelong mentor. He was close to Shari, too, having watched her mature as a business executive over the years. But he also knew how loyal Sumner had been to Dauman and how close he'd been to Abrams. He flew to California himself to visit Sumner and assess the situation. Despite the usual communications issues, Sumner denounced Dauman and was as profane as he'd been with Klieger. Jankowski came away convinced that Sumner was adamantly opposed to any sale of Paramount and felt his long-standing allies Dauman and Abrams had double-crossed him.

At times Shari wondered how the board would have responded had she been Sumner's son. To the extent she threatened a comfortable status quo, she didn't think gender was an issue. Board members would have resisted change in any event. But they couldn't seem to accept that a woman could speak for her father and emerge as his heir, as opposed to Dauman, whom they seemed to view as Sumner's surrogate son and legitimate successor.

Just a week after Judge Cowan's ruling, the Redstone camp stepped up the pressure on Dauman. At Klieger's behest, Sumner had hired Michael Tu, a lawyer Klieger knew from prior cases, who had no conflicts with Viacom, Paramount, or any of its other subsidiaries. On Sumner's behalf Tu sent letters to Viacom board members Dauman, Salerno, and Abrams asking that Sumner receive a "comprehensive briefing" on the merits of a Paramount deal before any further steps were taken as well as an explanation of Viacom's turnaround strategy. Sumner "remains keenly interested in the business of Viacom, and as its controlling stockholder, and as a director, he is currently considering his next steps," Tu ominously stated.

Salerno's lawyers called Tu and insinuated Sumner wasn't competent to be making such decisions. They wanted to know if and when Tu had met with his new client. Tu bristled at the requests and said it was none of their business. (Tu had in fact met and conversed with Sumner.) Tu encouraged them to have Salerno and the other directors meet with Sumner and judge his state of mind for themselves. But Tu never got a response. Salerno maintained he couldn't be sure Tu was acting on Sumner's behalf.

The next day the Viacom board began a two-day meeting by phone. As had become routine, Sumner listened but said nothing, even as the board voted to eliminate his pay as executive chairman. Dauman led a discussion of the ongoing Paramount sales effort, and Sumner again said nothing. Nor did Shari raise any objections. She thought it would be pointless given the board's staunch support for Dauman. In any event, she'd already decided on a far more drastic course: getting rid of Dauman and his allies, using her father's power as the controlling shareholder.

Sumner had the power to remove any or all of the trustees—unless he was incapacitated, as he now seemed to be. In that case control passed to the five nonfamily trustees. Dauman's position seemed secure because he and his allies George Abrams and David Andelman were a majority of the nonfamily trustees and by sticking together could block any attempt to remove any of them. Andelman had long clashed with Shari over the money transfers to the women and just days earlier had confirmed his support for Dauman.

So Dauman and Abrams were blindsided when Tu emailed them on May 20 with the news they'd been replaced as trustees and also as directors of National Amusements, stripping them of their remaining sources of power over Viacom. Tad Jankowski, Sumner's longtime employee, and Jill Krutick, a close friend of Shari's, took their places as trustees, and Kimberlee, Shari's daughter, was named a director of National Amusements. Dauman and Abrams hadn't even known a meeting or vote was taking place. Shari and Sumner—and their former ally Andelman—had joined forces against them.

Stunned, Dauman picked up the phone. Andelman answered.

"What's going on, David?" Dauman asked.

Andelman seemed taken aback that it was Dauman calling. As several people in the room listened, Andelman stammered that he was sorry and confirmed he'd sided with Shari. He said he had no choice. He didn't want any trouble from her.

Those listening in the room took that to mean he was afraid Shari would sue him. Perhaps they should have realized Andelman was vulnerable to a lawsuit given his role in the lavish payments to Holland and Herzer. Even if he ended up winning such a case, the cost of defending it and the bad publicity could prove ruinous.

Dauman said he was disappointed. Andelman seemed eager to end the call. They never spoke again.

———

Dropping any pretense of cooperation, Dauman counterattacked. In a press statement, he called the move "a shameful effort by Shari Redstone to seize control by unlawfully using her ailing father Sumner Redstone's name and signature. As she knows, and as court proceedings and other facts have demonstrated, Sumner Redstone now lacks the capacity to have taken these steps. Sumner Redstone would never have summarily dismissed Philippe Dauman and George Abrams, his trusted friends and advisers for decades."

The timing of the ouster might have come as a surprise, but having already lined up a team of lawyers, Dauman was ready. On Monday, May 23, he and Abrams filed suit in Massachusetts, where Redstone's trust had been created and administered, asking that his and Abrams's termination be nullified and that they be allowed to continue as trustees and directors.

Dauman and Herzer were suddenly, once again, allies. Herzer's lawyer O'Donnell submitted a declaration supporting Dauman's complaint that said Sumner was little more than a "wax figure at Madame

Tussauds." Dauman was now in the awkward position of claiming that Sumner was mentally incompetent just weeks after he had described him as engaged and attentive during the Herzer proceeding.

Dauman attempted to argue that he'd "made no observations about Mr. Redstone's capacity to make significant business decisions," and that since the meetings on which he based his opinion, which took place the previous October and November, "Mr. Redstone's health has rapidly declined." Dauman now said he'd visited Sumner during the first week of March, and he "appeared almost totally non-responsive, and could not meaningfully communicate at all."

In total, Sumner "is being manipulated by his daughter, Shari. After years of estrangement, she has inserted herself into his home, taken over his life, isolated him from contact with others, and purports to speak for him. In doing so, she is attempting to use his control to dismantle his estate plan to serve her own interests and to assume control of his businesses which he long refused her."

Sumner's erstwhile surrogate son and actual daughter were now engaged in open warfare.

EPISODE 8

"No One Likes Drama"

Needless to say, Dauman wasn't invited to Sumner's ninety-third birthday party on May 27, 2016, just four days after filing his lawsuit. Nor, for that matter, was Moonves. With Holland and Herzer banished, the party was mostly a family reunion, at least for Shari's side of the family. She, her mother, Phyllis, Brandon, Kimberlee, and Tyler were all there. Sumner's two great-grandchildren bounced on a trampoline set up for the occasion. Only Robert Evans came from Sumner's Hollywood orbit.

Now that the Herzer trial was over and professional health care installed in Sumner's mansion, he seemed to have rallied somewhat. "Mr. Redstone seems much happier since Sydney and Manuela moved out," his nurse Jagiello reported. "He is more relaxed and seldom cries. He leaves the house on a regular basis and appears to enjoy spending time with his daughter Shari and grandson Brandon and talking regularly with his other grandchildren back east."

On Friday, June 10, Sumner and his nurses traveled by minivan to the Paramount lot in Hollywood, where they pulled up to the Redstone building. Brad Grey, the longtime head of Paramount Pictures, emerged and joined them for about fifteen minutes. Afterward he described Sumner as unresponsive.

The following Tuesday they drove over the Hollywood Hills to CBS

Studio Center, where Moonves joined them in the van for a visit lasting less than ten minutes. Sumner didn't seem to know who Moonves was.

Reports of the Paramount visit prompted a letter from Viacom's lead director, Salerno, addressed to Sumner.

"You and I have worked together for decades to create shareholder value and develop shareholder trust," Salerno wrote. But "strangely, in the last few months, a host of new advisors and spokespeople say they work for you. They claim that strongly held views you have expressed for decades have, in the past few months, completely reversed. They say you no longer trust your friends, your advisors, or your board. They tell us to believe that you have put your daughter Shari in charge of your trust and your board at National Amusements despite your clearly stated wishes and planning over many years that are to the contrary."

The letter continued. "Sumner, we sincerely hope you are doing well. But it is alarming that your representatives refuse us the opportunity to talk with you, express our perspectives, share our friendship, or understand directly from you what your wishes might be and why. Bill Schwartz and I have not been permitted to see you, despite repeated requests. Philippe hasn't been allowed to meet with you since early March. And we are quite concerned that your voice—and views—are not being heard. When your phone is dialed into our board calls from your home, no one says a word. When we ask for your vote, all we hear is silence.

"Statements from these people suggest you think we intend to sell Paramount lock, stock, and barrel, or that we would do it in the middle of the night and hide it from you. Nothing could be further from the truth. You may remember that in February, Philippe spoke to you at your home about new opportunities that could strengthen Paramount. He reported that you didn't react, other than to nod when he asked you if you heard him and understood what he said to you."

Salerno pleaded again for a meeting with Sumner. "They tell us they won't make you available for fear that such a meeting would become the source of more litigation. In reality, putting up a wall around you ensures more litigation—and that is not what we want. We want to understand what is happening with you. And I can assure you that you can count on us to stick up for you and for the many other Viacom shareholders you have served so well for so many years."

The Redstone camp was skeptical—when Tu had offered the chance for Viacom directors to meet with Sumner, they hadn't even responded. Now, with litigation raging, there was no way such a meeting would take place. In response to the letter, the new National Amusements board, which no longer included Dauman and Abrams and was reliably loyal to Sumner and Shari, simply amended Viacom's bylaws to require a unanimous vote to sell a stake in Paramount. (As the controlling shareholder of Viacom, National Amusements had the power to change Viacom's and CBS's bylaws at any time.) The rule change gave both Shari and Sumner veto power over any transaction.

Viacom management was now up against its controlling shareholder. Folta denounced the move as "illegitimate" and "completely at odds with good corporate governance."

The bylaw change pretty much ended whatever chance Dauman had of selling a Paramount stake, for who would negotiate such a deal knowing that a Redstone would veto it? The likelihood of a deal had already cooled anyway, as the Chinese balked at Dauman's $10 billion valuation and grew skeptical that Dauman had the authority to enter into a binding transaction. Wanda's investment bankers had put out feelers on Wall Street and were well aware that the Redstone camp opposed any sale, even a minority stake. No other bidders, assuming they existed, had ever been publicly identified.

Dauman had to disclose that the planned sale announcement by the end of June would be delayed and blamed it on Shari's machinations. Nonetheless *The Wall Street Journal* reported Wanda was still "in talks" to buy 49 percent of the studio despite opposition from the Redstone camp.

On June 16 the long-expected axe fell: National Amusements announced that it was exercising its power to replace five Viacom directors including Dauman and Salerno. The five proposed new directors brought a variety of entertainment expertise to the board and were younger and more attuned to the Viacom audience.

Dauman was still chief executive. But in a statement addressing his fate, National Amusements said, "It will be the responsibility of the newly constituted Board to evaluate the current management team and take whatever steps it deems appropriate to ensure that Viacom has in place strong, independent and effective leadership." Dauman's days running Viacom were obviously numbered. Investors celebrated the prospect of getting rid of him, driving up Viacom shares 7 percent on the news.

That same day Shari asked chief operating officer Tom Dooley to act as interim chief executive once Dauman was gone. When Dooley broke the news to Dauman, it couldn't have been much of a surprise. "If that's her plan, that's her plan" was all Dauman said.

The next day Dauman defended himself and his record in an interview with *Fortune* editor Alan Murray. Murray was blunt: Apart from the issues over Sumner's mental state, given the company's poor performance in recent years, why should shareholders want Dauman to stay?

Dauman gave a typically vague answer: "A stock price at any given moment is a snapshot. The stock goes up and down. No one likes drama, nor do I." Viacom had done well until two years ago, he stressed, and "a good investor invests for the long run and sees what's unfolding." He continued, "The press loves drama. People are missing the business story. This is a great place to work. We have great values. Creativity is at the center of it. We want to do good while we do well."

Lofty rhetoric aside, Dauman again articulated no turnaround strategy, long or short term. His only real hope was his Massachusetts court case. But the court hadn't set a trial date until October—far too late to offer Dauman any immediate protection.

———

Shari was nervous about the prospect of that year's Allen & Company media summit, which was held every year in Sun Valley, Idaho, and informally known as the "billionaires' summer camp." With participants Justin Trudeau, Mark Zuckerberg, Tim Cook, and Warren Buffett on the guest list, it would have been intimidating under any circumstances, especially since she was one of just a handful of women who weren't attending as "significant others." As usual, she'd be traveling alone. Adding to her anxiety: both Moonves and Dauman were supposed to be there.

It came as something of a relief that Dauman canceled at the last minute. Moonves made the most of his rival's absence. He turned on his legendary charm, shepherded Shari around the conference, made introductions, and took her to dinner. At a time when she felt she was being shunned by just about everyone, starting with the Viacom board, she was grateful to Moonves for taking her under his wing.

Shari was especially pleased when Moonves gave the *Los Angeles Times* a statement praising her as "a terrific board member and a strong voice for good corporate governance throughout her tenure here at CBS." *Vanity Fair* reported Shari had "taken center stage" at the conference and was "soaking up the spotlight."

———

While his mother was in Sun Valley, Tyler was deep in negotiations with Dauman. Without initially telling Shari, Tyler had opened a back channel to Dauman in early June. Dauman, too, kept the talks a secret and told no one on the Viacom board. They and their lawyers met alone in a Viacom conference room in New York, where

Tyler argued, persuasively, that it was in no one's interest for Dauman's lawsuit to go to trial.

Few people emerge unscathed from the kind of scorched-earth litigation shaping up in Massachusetts, which promised a far more probing excavation of the lurid goings-on in Beverly Park than had occurred in the brief Herzer trial.

Tyler also had some sympathy for Dauman's plight. They'd served together for years as National Amusements board members, and Tyler understood that the bond between his grandfather and Dauman went much deeper than the usual ties between chairman and chief executive.

With surprising speed, settlement terms were agreed to by the lawyers. Dauman would withdraw his lawsuit challenging Sumner's competency and step down as Viacom's chief executive. Dooley would replace him on an interim basis. In return, Dauman would get a payout of about $72 million—an enormous sum, to be sure, but pretty much what he was already entitled to under his contract. Tyler reached out to Klieger with word of the proposed settlement, and he and other lawyers started drafting the details.

It fell to Dauman to break the news to the Viacom board, which he did on July 27. It came as an unwelcome shock to other directors that Dauman had secretly undertaken settlement talks that lined his own pocket while they were publicly defending him. Salerno, the lead director, was furious and felt betrayed. The board declined to approve the deal, which effectively killed it, since Viacom, not the Redstones, would be making the payments to Dauman.

Dauman hadn't even told his coplaintiff, George Abrams, about the impending settlement. But without Dauman the suit was doomed. Although Abrams had been shocked and hurt by his replacement as a trustee, in some ways it was a relief to put the dysfunctional Redstone clan behind him and focus on his other clients and his extensive art collection. He never heard from Sumner again.

Dauman gave no hint of the board turmoil when he announced Viacom's third-quarter earnings a week later. They were another disaster, with profit falling close to 30 percent. The Paramount hits Dauman had promised had all flopped, starting with the *Teenage Mutant Ninja Turtles* sequel in June. *Zoolander 2* and *Allied* quickly followed, the latter tarnished by Brad Pitt's much-publicized divorce from Angelina Jolie. Even the latest *Star Trek* was a disappointment. It brought in $100 million less than the previous installment.

Those were just the most visible failures. Revenue for its media networks, including MTV, Nickelodeon, and Comedy Central, plunged 22 percent.

Wall Street's reaction was swift. The stock had dropped 50 percent in just a year. In June, Tom Freston, the Viacom chief executive Dauman replaced, had gone on CNBC to blast Dauman's performance. "Dauman is focused on stocks, lawsuits and leveraging nickels from customers," Freston said in a withering assessment. What Viacom needed, he said, was someone who was "turned on, attracted to and somewhat knowledgeable about the popular culture and what's going on there." In short, everything Dauman was not.

The grim results and growing distrust of Dauman drove Salerno and his fellow Viacom directors back to the bargaining table, this time without Dauman or Tyler present. After a weekend meeting on Long Island with Salerno, one of the proposed new board members, and an investment banker advising Shari, a new agreement was reached. It wasn't much different from the one Tyler had negotiated: in addition to Dauman's $72 million payment, Viacom would pay all his legal fees over the preceding three months and provide an office and executive assistant for another three years. One face-saving provision gave Dauman the right to present his plans to sell the Paramount stake in person to the new Viacom board.

Dooley, the newly minted interim chief executive, announced the agreement on August 18, and by then Dauman had retreated to his

East Hampton estate. He proceeded to buy a $24 million waterfront mansion in Palm Beach, as well as a private jet. Dauman was never seen at Viacom headquarters again. After negotiating so tenaciously for the opportunity, he never met with the new Viacom board to promote his Paramount sale (he sent a written memo instead), nor did he name the buyer he'd supposedly lined up to purchase the Paramount stake. Despite all the speculation about Dalian Wanda, Shari suspected that such a buyer didn't exist.

After Sumner canceled their meeting the previous April, Dauman never again saw or spoke to his longtime mentor.

———

By ousting Dauman and his allies, Shari had saved Paramount, as she'd promised her father she would. His empire remained intact and under family control. To do so she'd had to change the trustees of his trust, reconfigure the National Amusements board, replace most of the Viacom directors, and get rid of Dauman, all while fending off Herzer and caring for her father. She kept up appearances, but she was emotionally drained and physically exhausted.

"I can't say it was a great year, or the most fun year I've ever had, but if I look back from last year, the battles are over," Shari said at a *New York Times* DealBook conference in November. "It's been a tough year, but a year ago, to be sitting here today and talk about all we have accomplished, I don't think I would have believed it."

"An Overwhelming Stench of Greed"

With Dauman gone and the stresses of constant litigation at least temporarily at an end, Sumner seemed more relaxed. Shari continued to spend two weeks a month with him in California. She held her father's hand, read aloud to him, and watched TV and movies, even when he was at times unresponsive, which was often the case.

At the suggestion of his nurses, Sumner got a Microsoft Surface Pro laptop to help him communicate. It was programmed with his voice. All he had to do was tap, and the computer would respond "yes," "no," or—for use specifically with Shari—"I love you," "I'm proud of you," or "Would you like some fruit salad?" But Sumner's favorite was "Fuck you." It was the option he pressed repeatedly whenever anyone mentioned Donald Trump.

Every few months Shari took her father to the Montage Hotel in Laguna Beach, the resort community south of Los Angeles. They had ocean-view rooms close to each other and watched baseball on TV while wearing Red Sox baseball caps (with the team on a winning streak, Sumner was again a Red Sox fan). Even then, Shari worried she wasn't spending enough time in California and should be doing more to care for her father. Her friends were incredulous, given how badly Sumner had treated her for most of her life. But by now Shari had come to terms with the way her father had compartmentalized his life and emotions—loving her as a daughter but criticizing her as a business executive.

Shari had been thrust into running her father's media empire, and with the court battles at least temporarily over or on hold, Viacom still needed a permanent chief executive. Its business seemed to be in free-fall. One solution offered an answer to both problems: recombine Viacom and CBS with Moonves as the chief executive—as long as the Redstones retained voting control. Shari had always opposed separating the two companies, and recombining them would realize her long-held ambition to correct the mistake. A merger would also give the companies greater scale to compete with Netflix and Amazon. And she had complete confidence in Moonves, especially after he'd supported her in the Dauman fight.

This, of course, required getting her father to reverse his earlier decision to split the companies. Sumner was never going to admit he'd made a mistake, let alone that his daughter had been right all along. But he did respond—reluctantly—to arguments that they needed to recombine to remain competitive.

On September 29, Sumner and Shari issued a letter to the boards of both companies advocating a merger that cited the "challenges of the changing entertainment and media landscape." But their holding company, National Amusements, wouldn't accept any sale of either or both companies to someone else, nor would it give up control of the merged company.

Both Sumner and Shari signed the letter and, in the interest of fairness to other shareholders, promised to stay out of the boards' negotiations or deliberations.

The next day the boards of both Viacom and CBS named independent committees to evaluate a merger and discuss the terms of any deal.

That trying to combine the companies might trigger an unwanted offer for either Viacom or the more likely target, CBS, was more than a remote possibility. The upheaval in media caused by streaming and cord-cutting was prompting a wave of consolidation. After cable and broadband giant Comcast completed its acquisition of NBC Universal in 2013, other big distributors were rumored to be eyeing content companies, especially Comcast rivals AT&T and Verizon. In 2016 Shari met with Randall Stephenson, AT&T's chief executive, but over the course of the meeting she made it clear that CBS wasn't for sale.

After AT&T announced in October that it was buying Time Warner instead, speculation about CBS as a target only intensified. Verizon chief executive Lowell McAdam and Shari explored possibilities for their respective companies to work together, but Shari was focused primarily on bringing CBS and Viacom together before taking on any other big initiatives.

A potential merger of Viacom and CBS, with Moonves as the chief executive, complicated Viacom's search for a new chief executive, since no one from outside the company was likely to consider accepting the post only to be merged out of a job. As Dauman's longtime ally, Dooley wasn't the answer, and he announced his departure in mid-September after less than a month as chief executive, his exit sweetened by a $4.4 million "retention payment" to get him to stay another two months. That left a handful of Viacom division heads, including Robert Bakish, whose international division had been a relative success within the beleaguered company.

Bakish was nothing like Moonves, the former actor and charismatic CBS chief, but neither was he a cerebral lawyer like Dauman. Bakish was trained as an engineer before earning an MBA at Columbia. He came into the entertainment business via management consulting. He hadn't acquired any of the trappings or attitudes of Hollywood royalty. He didn't have any talent relationships to speak of and wasn't a fixture on red carpets. And yet when each division head was asked to make a presentation to the newly reconstituted board, Bakish was the only one with a detailed, long-term strategic plan. Shari was impressed and asked aloud where Bakish had been "hiding all these years."

There was no time to lose. As Shari emailed Klieger in October, "Viacom is tanking."

Bakish was happy to take the job, even on what he expected would be an interim basis (he was promised the job of global entertainment head once the companies were joined). He was fully aware of the challenges ahead: before Dooley left, he told Bakish, "Now you'll realize I've been underpaid." In his first memo to employees, Bakish pledged to dismantle the rigid "silos" erected by Dauman and "to take more chances, to be more experimental, more unexpected."

His first priority was to woo back the cable operators and internet providers. Hulu had just declined to offer Viacom channels. Charter renewal negotiations were imminent. When they met in Bakish's Times Square office, the chief negotiator for one of country's largest cable companies told him, "I'd made a vow never to walk into this building again." But now that Dauman was gone, he was willing to give Bakish a chance.

Shari was delighted with the early results. As she told the DealBook audience in November, "We have a great CEO at Viacom who I'm super excited about. He does a great job of our international business, embraces change and innovation, understands it's all about the brand."

Shari moved into her father's office on the fifty-second floor of Viacom's Times Square headquarters after removing her father's dark wood paneling, his leather furniture, and the Bloomberg terminal on which Sumner obsessively tracked Viacom and CBS stock prices. She redecorated the office in soothing grays and pastels. But she kept on display all of Sumner's family photos and the New England Patriots memorabilia he'd collected over the years. Though he never again crossed its threshold, she told her father that it was now "our" office.

Viacom executives saw the move as more than symbolic. Despite her protests over the years that she didn't want to run her father's media empire or aspire to be a mogul herself, Shari seemed delighted with her new role in a company with a board and chief executive who treated her ideas with respect.

———

With an impending merger and search for a permanent Viacom chief executive, the last thing Shari needed or wanted was the distraction of more litigation with Holland and Herzer. It was widely assumed that she and not Sumner now made all significant decisions regarding the Redstone family businesses, but on one issue Sumner was adamant: he still wanted his money back from Holland and Herzer. The two women had lied to and cheated him, Sumner repeated incessantly. He was obsessed, and when Sumner was obsessed, he wouldn't let a subject drop.

Klieger did his best to talk Sumner out of a lawsuit. He warned that the litigation could go on for years, extracting a physical and emotional toll. Holland and Herzer were likely to distract attention from their own behavior by publicizing Sumner's unorthodox sexual conduct. Sumner said he didn't care. Shari, too, was hardly looking forward to even more public accounts of her father's lurid behavior and willingness to bestow millions on various mistresses and companions. But she resigned herself to the prospect: her father had led the life he wanted, and it wasn't for her to judge.

Like Dauman's and Herzer's lawyers in the earlier proceedings, Klieger faced the seemingly contradictory task of arguing that Sumner had been mentally competent and alert when he ejected Herzer and replaced Dauman but was nonetheless subject to elder abuse and undue influence when he gave vast sums of money to the women—which had happened before Sumner got rid of Herzer and Dauman and presumably was both mentally and physically healthier.

Not only that, but Sumner's own lawyers—both Andelman and Bishop—as well as a doctor, Spar, had made explicit findings at the time of the gifts that Sumner was competent and understood what he was doing.

But Klieger was prepared to argue that mental capacity and undue influence can be quite different issues, even if related. The Redstones hired Bennett Blum, a psychiatrist and widely published expert on elder abuse. Blum acknowledged that Sumner suffered from "some degree of cognitive impairment." But due to the long duration and secretive nature of sustained elder abuse, Andelman and Bishop "could not have known" that Sumner was being unduly influenced by the two women, as he put it in a sworn declaration.

Blum stressed that even "strong-willed" and "decisive" people such as Sumner could be subject to undue influence and abuse. Sometimes they were even more vulnerable to manipulation. As Blum explained in his written declaration, a victim like Sumner may state emphatically that he desires a particular transaction, often because he's been persuaded the perpetrator "loves him" and that others have "malevolent intentions," or he may fear retaliation if he doesn't go along. Both Holland and Herzer "engaged in multiple behaviors that are commonly associated with undue influence," Blum concluded. They disparaged Sumner's family as caring only about money; repeatedly described themselves as the only people who loved him; and threatened to abandon him, leaving him to die alone if he denied their requests.

Sumner hired a retired FBI agent to gather evidence. He interviewed nearly every current and former nurse and member of the Beverly Park household staff. Little had escaped their notice, though some were more forthcoming than others. Martinez, the house manager and codefendant with Naylor, would talk only if subpoenaed—perhaps to protect his lucrative settlement agreement.

On October 25, Klieger filed the lawsuit Sumner had pleaded for. Citing Sumner's "near complete dependence" on them during the more than five years they occupied his home, the suit contended Holland

and Herzer "manipulated and emotionally abused Redstone to get what they wanted—jewelry, designer clothing, real estate in Beverly Hills, New York, and Paris, and money, lots of it. By the time Redstone threw Herzer and Holland out of his home, and out of his life, last fall, they had taken him for more than $150 million and left him in debt on account of the immense tax obligations triggered by those 'gifts.'"

For good measure, Sumner also sued in New York to have Herzer's name removed from the title to his Carlyle apartment.

Unlike the litigious Herzer, Holland had tried to stay out of court since settling the ill-fated Naylor lawsuit. But faced with the elder abuse complaint, which sought the return of all the money she'd gotten from Sumner, she filed a countersuit of her own against Shari, claiming she'd induced her father to breach his promise to take care of Holland and her daughter for life and had paid spies to gather damaging information about her.

As Klieger had warned, it was going to get ugly. Holland made a thinly veiled threat to further tar Sumner's reputation by alluding to his affairs with other women and the numerous lavish gifts to them. While she didn't name the women involved, her lawyer warned, "Sydney may be forced to disclose their identities and call Redstone's celebrity friends and call Viacom and CBS executives as witnesses," among them Moonves at CBS, who "knew about Redstone's largest monetary gift to Sydney, on May 20, 2014." And the reference to Viacom clearly meant calling Dauman as a witness.

Klieger responded that Holland's response was "punctuated by not-so-subtle threats of extortion and an overwhelming stench of greed."

Holland had witnesses of her own to worry about, starting with George Pilgrim. Pilgrim's stormy relationship with Holland had hardly ended with their incendiary breakup. Pilgrim almost immediately regretted his impulsive behavior and launched a phone, a text, and an email barrage to win her back. As his efforts failed to yield any hoped-for results, his messages, often transmitted in the middle of the night, turned increasingly angry, profane, and threatening: "I'm coming back to get you," "I will send you straight to hell," and "play this to your cops at LAPD; I don't give a fuck" among them. Holland had to change her cell phone number.

In 2016 she took the evidence to Los Angeles County Superior Court and obtained a restraining order against him. Months later, Pilgrim pleaded no contest to a misdemeanor violation of a California penal code banning obscene messages and threats to inflict injury and was sentenced to three years' probation. The court issued a criminal protective order barring Pilgrim from any contact with Holland.

That didn't stop Pilgrim from threatening to sue her, claiming that he was entitled to some of the proceeds from the sale of the Sedona property, the return of the rights to "Citizen Pilgrim," and other remedies. But his most serious threat to Holland was as a hostile witness who might cooperate with the Redstones.

Armed with this leverage, Pilgrim's lawyer reached a confidential settlement with Holland in December 2016, in which she agreed to pay him $330,000 in three installments and grant him other relief. In return, Pilgrim agreed to drop his legal claims, return all copies of emails, texts, and other communications between them, and identify under penalty of perjury all communications he'd had "with Shari Redstone and any person related to her, affiliated with her or employed by her." He also had to notify Holland if Shari or her lawyers reached out to him.

In addition, the settlement required Pilgrim to recognize that his sperm donation to Holland had been destroyed, that he'd received written confirmation from the sperm bank, and that the sperm bank had certified that no embryos were created from his sperm. "Accordingly, Pilgrim understands that he has no standing to make any claim for paternity of any of Holland's children and covenants and agrees that he shall not take any action or bring any legal claim with respect to Holland's children," the agreement stated.

This provision was more than an abstraction, since Holland was expecting the birth of twin boys, again using a surrogate. Despite the language in the agreement, when Liam and Harrison Holland were born in 2017, Pilgrim was convinced he was their biological father. He didn't believe that the declarations from the sperm bank were truthful and thought they might even be fabrications, given the absence of any signatures on the documents.

Predictably, Holland refused to allow Pilgrim any contact with the boys. In any event, he'd relinquished all parental rights under the contract he signed when he donated his sperm.

But in other respects the settlement appears to have had the intended result. When Klieger and other lawyers representing Sumner and Shari reached out to Pilgrim in 2016 as a potential witness in the elder abuse case against Holland and Herzer, his lawyer indicated Pilgrim was willing to cooperate. But then Holland went to court in an unsuccessful attempt to bar Pilgrim's testimony. By the time that was resolved, she and Pilgrim had signed their agreement. When the Redstone lawyers tried to schedule Pilgrim's deposition, he had become evasive and uncooperative. He kept finding excuses to postpone any testimony.

For her part, Herzer filed yet another lawsuit against the Redstones—this one accusing Shari of racketeering. "Knowing that her father's remaining life was limited, she instead methodically hatched a criminal scheme to take over her father's life and to then use that dominion to take over CBS and Viacom," Herzer's complaint alleged. This time she wanted $100 million in damages—a sum that under the racketeering statute could be tripled. (By now Herzer had fired Pierce O'Donnell and assembled a new team of lawyers.)

The lawsuits reunited Holland and Herzer, with the Redstones now their common foe. Herzer was still furious with Holland for having so recklessly upended their carefully laid plans. And Holland was angry with Herzer for betraying her to Sumner, presiding over her expulsion, and seizing control. But their fortunes and reputations were inextricably linked—perhaps forever.

"Don't Go Near This"

There was a distinct chill in the air at the CBS board meeting held in Los Angeles in February 2017. The night before, Shari had dinner with Sumner, then returned to the Four Seasons Hotel in Beverly Hills. She ran into fellow board members Charles (Chad) Gifford and Bruce Gordon in the lobby. Exactly what happened next became the subject of some dispute. In Shari's accounting, Gifford, who towered over his five-foot-two-inch fellow director, took her firmly by the arm and steered her off to a side room, where he badgered her about her plans to recombine CBS and Viacom. She was uncomfortable with his questions—her lawyers had told her not to discuss the issue. But Gifford demanded answers, becoming more insistent the more she resisted. What was she going to say at the board meeting? he demanded to know. She gave in, then felt bad about sharing the information. She felt talked down to and pushed around. It seemed all too typical of the disrespect she encountered from the old-guard CBS board members, despite her status as the de facto controlling shareholder.

(Gifford denied applying any inappropriate pressure, and Gordon said he didn't witness Gifford grab Shari's arm or otherwise behave inappropriately. What's not in dispute is that Shari came away shaken and upset by the encounter.)

Though Shari thought she'd gotten Moonves's consent to recombine Viacom and CBS, the reality was far more complicated. For all his power and authority at CBS, Moonves was by nature averse to conflict. He knew Shari wanted the merger; she and her father were the controlling shareholders, and he bowed to that reality by giving her the impression he supported her plan.

But with CBS board members, especially those on the independent committee evaluating the merger, he gave an entirely different view. With CBS the most-watched network for nine years and after eight consecutive years of earnings growth, Moonves was at the pinnacle of his career. Why would he—or CBS shareholders—want the burden of turning around a struggling Viacom? In his view, Shari's merger plan was a desperate effort to salvage a floundering Viacom by attaching it to CBS. It might be great for Viacom's shareholders, but not for CBS's.

Moreover, however logical in the abstract, merging the two companies posed a host of obstacles, starting with how to value them, especially since CBS was doing so well and Viacom so poorly. The outcome didn't matter to Shari or Sumner, since they'd own the same stake in both companies and would end up with the same assets. But CBS shareholders and the directors acting on their behalf would surely need to secure a significant premium—one that Viacom directors might be reluctant to grant. In ongoing talks valuation posed a significant obstacle.

More fundamentally, Moonves was willing to run the combined companies only if he had the autonomy he had long enjoyed at CBS. But the combined companies would have a new board—one chosen by and presumably stocked with allies of Shari, not Moonves. That had already happened at Viacom, now populated with board members chosen by Shari and with a new chief executive effectively chosen by Shari— a stark example of what could befall CBS.

The upshot was that the CBS committee insisted that negotiations continue only if Shari and Sumner agreed that the merged companies would be managed for at least five years as though it were not a controlled company—essentially requiring the Redstones to relinquish their control. By then Moonves would be seventy-four and ready to retire and make his exit. And it demanded that there be no bylaws requiring unanimous board consent, like the one the Redstones had used at Viacom to block the Paramount sale.

This proposal was a nonstarter from Shari's perspective. The Redstones' initial letter proposing a merger had stated explicitly they would not relinquish family control of the combined companies.

By now Shari had figured out that Moonves didn't really want a merger. On December 12, the companies announced that the proposed combination was off. Viacom said Bakish would become its permanent chief executive.

"We know Viacom has tremendous assets that are currently undervalued, and we are confident that with this new strong management team, the value of these assets can be unleashed," the Redstones said in a press statement. "At the same time, CBS continues to perform exceptionally well under Les Moonves, and we have every reason to believe that momentum will continue on a stand-alone basis."

But for Shari, the plan's collapse was a huge disappointment, and a measure of how little control she actually wielded. And, as she had long said, she hated to lose.

———

Frederic Salerno's exit from both the Viacom and CBS boards created an opening for Shari at CBS—the first new director there in ten years. It was high time—the only Fortune 500 company with an older board of directors was Warren Buffett's Berkshire Hathaway. CBS's sixteen-member board had three members of management (Moonves, Ianniello, and Anthony Ambrosio, head of human relations); three nonindependent National Amusements–affiliated members (Sumner, his lawyer David Andelman, and Shari); and two veteran Hollywood producers (Arnold Kopelson of *Platoon* and Leonard Goldberg of *Charlie's Angels*), both close friends of Sumner, as was veteran record producer Doug Morris. The former defense secretary William S. Cohen added gravitas. Linda Griego, a Los Angeles restaurateur, was the lone woman other than Shari.

But the real power resided with the committee chairs: Bruce S. Gordon, the lead independent director, a longtime Verizon executive, and former head of the NAACP; Gary L. Countryman, the retired chief executive of Liberty Mutual Insurance; and Chad Gifford, a former chair of Bank of America and the director who'd upset Shari at the Four Seasons. All were staunch supporters of Moonves.

Shari wanted to breach the wall of aging, mostly white males. "I need another you," she emailed her friend and new Viacom director Nicole Seligman, "but obviously it can't be you." She proposed meeting for coffee the following Friday. Soon after, in January, Shari called Harvard Law School dean Martha Minow. Seligman and Shari knew Minow from the John F. Kennedy Library, where they'd served on committees together. Seligman was also a graduate of Harvard Law School.

Minow seemed an ideal choice for the CBS board. As the Harvard Law School dean and a professor there, she had an impeccable résumé and was often rumored to be a nominee for the Supreme Court. She taught First Amendment courses. Media and broadcast were in her DNA—her father, Newton Minow, had been chair of the Federal Communications Commission, best known for his 1961 description of commercial television as a "vast wasteland." Her sister Nell was a film critic, a lawyer, and an expert on corporate governance.

Minow and Shari weren't personally close, and politically they were poles apart—Minow was a liberal Democrat who focused on social justice issues, while Shari had maintained a warm relationship with Donald Trump ever since their meeting at the Patriots game. She'd visited him in the White House, and while she didn't agree with many of his political views, she prized his loyalty and publicly described him as a "tremendous supporter of me personally." Differences aside,

Minow was impressed that Shari admired people who stood up for what they believed in, whatever their politics. They'd served together on a committee to choose the winners of the Kennedy Library's annual Profiles in Courage Award.

As for Sumner himself, Minow knew him only slightly. She'd made the pilgrimage to Beverly Park in 2014 to secure a $10 million donation to Harvard Law School. It hadn't been easy. Although Sumner had graduated near the top of his class, all he wanted to talk about with Minow was the D he'd received in Constitutional Law ("It galls me to this day," he griped in his autobiography). Otherwise he had seemed distracted, more interested in what was on television than in Minow or the public service fellowships he was funding at Harvard. But he had his photo taken with Minow to memorialize the occasion. He looked like a character from his favorite movie, *The Godfather,* in his black shirt and wide silver tie.

Joining the board of a public corporation wasn't what Minow was looking for as she neared the end of her term as dean, but CBS seemed a special case, especially given the importance of CBS News in the aftermath of the 2016 presidential election. The dual classes of shares didn't especially worry her: many of the great media companies had been family controlled, and that structure had long protected money-losing news divisions. But Minow made one thing clear when Shari called: "I can only do this as an independent person," she told Shari. "There will be times we'll disagree."

"That's why I want you there," Shari responded. "You'll have fun."

But Minow's sister Nell thought otherwise. "Don't go near this," she warned.

———

Soon after reaching out to Minow, Shari was at Super Bowl LI in Houston to watch her beloved New England Patriots take on the Atlanta Falcons when she spotted her fellow CBS director Chad Gifford on the field near the fifty-yard line. When she went over to say hello, Gifford grabbed her chin and tilted her head up. "Listen, young lady, we need to talk," he said.

For Shari, this demeaning treatment was all too reminiscent of their encounter at the Four Seasons. "We're at the Super Bowl," Shari protested, not wanting to discuss business, and tried to pull away. Gifford relaxed his grip, but the incident nearly spoiled an otherwise thrilling game, in which the Patriots overcame a 28–3 deficit to win in overtime.

The next day Gifford called her. "I hear you're upset with me," he said.

"Yes," she replied. "That was inappropriate."

"That's just how I'd treat my daughter," Gifford explained.

"I'm not your daughter!" Shari exclaimed. "I'm the vice chair of the board you serve on."

(Gifford insisted to fellow directors that he never touched her chin or face, pointing out that he was on crutches that day following surgery and wouldn't have had a free hand.)

Shari related the incident to Minow; as chair of the nominating and governance committee, Gifford and other committee members were interviewing her for the open board seat. In those interviews it was clear to Minow that to varying degrees they all distrusted Shari and seemed suspicious that Minow was a Shari plant. Some were balking at the idea that Minow qualified as an "independent" director, which was more than academic, since the CBS bylaws required that there be a majority of independent directors.

No one said anything explicitly, but the directors conveyed the message that Minow shouldn't expect CBS to conform to standard corporate governance rules. Sumner had been a tyrant in many ways, especially when it came to Shari. At board meetings he'd responded to her comments with thinly disguised contempt that bordered on cruelty, some directors told Minow. Now Shari appeared to be in charge, even though Sumner was still alive and the controlling shareholder. Board members were still figuring out how to adjust to that.

Minow also had to pass muster with Moonves. The two had lunch at the Regency Hotel in Manhattan, and, like so many people, Minow found him charming. He talked about the creative process, which he emphasized was his focus at CBS—his chief operating officer, Joseph Ianniello, handled the financial details. "I couldn't do what I do without Joe," Moonves said.

Minow asked Moonves how he came up with hit shows. Was it the script? The casting? Both, Moonves replied. And more. He warmed to the subject, describing a process that was more art than science. Ultimately it all came down to him and his unique sensibility.

Moonves laid out his vision for the future, which focused heavily on a direct-to-consumer streaming strategy he called CBS All Access. He was well aware that the old broadcast and cable distribution models were doomed. CBS could be a "big player with a small footprint" in the new streaming era, he maintained.

Afterward Minow got an email from Gifford, the head of the nominating committee, summoning her to CBS's annual meeting and election of directors on May 19 at the Museum of Modern Art in New York. She had evidently survived the gauntlet. Despite her sister's warning, she said she'd be there. At the very least, she reasoned, it would be an education.

These annual meetings of shareholders alternated between New York and Los Angeles and always featured a lavish dinner for board members to which spouses, dates, and a sprinkling of CBS celebrities were invited. Board meetings themselves were scripted, highly produced presentations orchestrated by Moonves. Board members rarely spoke. The producer Arnold Kopelson invariably thanked Moonves for choosing such a fine venue for the board dinner.

At Minow's first meeting, Moonves announced that Sumner was listening on the phone and would become chairman emeritus. He'd no longer be a voting board member. "Everyone at CBS owes his thanks to Sumner for everything he has done for this company," Moonves said, while also being sure to thank Shari.

The board approved lavish new employment contracts for Moonves and Ianniello. Moonves got a $120 million golden parachute if he had "good reasons" for leaving the company, which included too much meddling with the makeup of the board. Ianniello also got a $60 million bonus, which would be triggered if he did not succeed Moonves as CEO.

Then came the election of directors. As in nearly all shareholder votes, there were only as many candidates as openings. All the nominees were elected or reelected with over 36 million votes. Minow was the top vote getter, with 36.4 million votes in her favor, perhaps because she had no track record to oppose.

After the election Minow asked Moonves if there was an orientation for new directors. It had been so long since CBS had appointed a new director that the question took Moonves by surprise. "No, we don't do that," he said.

———

Despite Minow's pledges of independence, Shari felt she got no credit from her fellow CBS directors for picking someone of Minow's caliber and integrity. Most of them viewed both women with suspicion. Even though she had the title of vice chair, as a nonindependent director Shari wasn't a member of any committees and wasn't allowed to participate in their discussions. But under the bylaws she did have the power to call committee meetings.

Shari asked Minow if she could serve as her "eyes and ears" with respect to committee meetings, but Minow demurred, saying that made her uncomfortable. But she thought Shari should at least be able to sit in on meetings.

So after the board meeting in May, Shari called Klieger, who was on a rare vacation in Hawaii. "Would you be comfortable if I nominated you to the board?" Sumner's resignation and move to emeritus status had opened up another nonindependent board seat, but it was pretty much the last thing Klieger expected. He was not just close to Shari—he was her and her father's lawyer. Shari said that was the point. She'd gotten no credit for recruiting Minow, who truly was independent, so why not drop the pretense? It would be good to have an outspoken ally on the board.

Like Minow, Klieger made the rounds of breakfasts and lunches with other board members, culminating in lunch with Moonves at the Grill on the Alley, the power-lunch hangout in Beverly Hills. In some ways it was easier for Klieger than for Minow, since there was no need to assert his independence.

In late June he had lunch with Minow in Cambridge. They didn't know each other but had some things in common: Klieger had gone to Stanford Law School with Minow's sister Mary, and of course they were both lawyers. Minow said her board reception had been anything but warm. She couldn't understand why her independence was being questioned. She had no personal relationship with Shari.

The other board members he met with acted like Shari was about to launch a board coup like the one at Viacom. Klieger could feel the mutual tensions and suspicions. For her part, Shari interpreted almost every board action as an attempt to exclude and marginalize her. It was obviously a dysfunctional board rife with paranoia and misunderstandings.

One thing Klieger knew was that Shari did not want to replace Moonves or go to war with the rest of the CBS board. Viacom had been bad enough, but it was in crisis. CBS, by contrast, appeared to be thriving. Even if he was Shari's handpicked nominee, Klieger thought he might be able to bridge the gulf between the Les and Shari factions by talking to both sides.

Klieger assumed Sumner's vacant board seat on July 28.

The first public inkling of serious trouble for the prolific Hollywood producer Harvey Weinstein came on October 4 in *The Hollywood Reporter*: "Is *The New York Times* about to expose damaging information on Harvey Weinstein?" And it wasn't just the *Times*: reporter Ronan Farrow "is now said to be working with *The New Yorker* magazine on a 'lengthy' piece," the magazine added.

For most readers of *The Hollywood Reporter*, Weinstein needed no introduction. At age sixty-five, with over three hundred Oscar nominations under his belt, the Miramax cofounder and producer of *Sex, Lies, and Videotape*, *The Crying Game*, *Pulp Fiction*, *Shakespeare in Love*, and *The English Patient* was loved, feared, and lionized—and long rumored to be an inveterate practitioner of the proverbial casting couch. Despite his bullying personality, hot temper, and off-putting physical appearance—not to mention being married to the glamorous fashion designer Georgina Chapman—he often had beautiful young starlets on his arm.

Still, until the lengthy, in-depth bombshell articles foretold by *The Hollywood Reporter* appeared in *The New York Times* on October 5 and in *The New Yorker* on October 10, few members of the public knew the magnitude and the horror of Weinstein's serial assaults on women.

The *Times* article, by reporters Jodi Kantor and Megan Twohey (with a reporting credit to Rachel Abrams), described sexual misconduct that resulted in eight confidential legal settlements and occurred over three decades. Weinstein conceded he had "caused a lot of pain" and immediately took a leave of absence from the Weinstein Company, which he and his brother, Bob, had launched in 2005 after leaving Disney-owned Miramax. But he denied the charges of harassment. The Weinstein Company board fired him three days later.

The *New Yorker* article by Ronan Farrow contained allegations from thirteen women and even more serious examples, including three claims of rape. Weinstein again denied engaging in any nonconsensual sex.

The *Times* and *New Yorker* articles were hardly the first to expose the sexual misconduct of powerful men in media and entertainment. They arrived just a year after the airing of Donald Trump's *Access Hollywood* tape, in which he boasted that, as a celebrity, he could pretty much do whatever he wanted with women. As he'd said on the tape, "You can do anything . . . grab 'em by the pussy."

Bill O'Reilly, the star Fox News talk show host, had to resign in April 2017 after Fox paid five women millions of dollars to settle sexual harassment charges. Roger Ailes, the head of Fox News, resigned in July 2016 after he was accused by multiple women of sexual harassment. A slew of civil and criminal lawsuits were lodged against comedian Bill Cosby, and he was eventually convicted of aggravated indecent assault (the conviction was later overturned on technical issues).

But the *Times* and *New Yorker* articles triggered a national, even global, movement. The stories came from women who, breaking a decades-long code of silence, spoke voluntarily, mostly on the record, risking their careers and reputations, which rendered their stories both riveting and inspiring to others.

Five days after the *New Yorker* story appeared, the actress Alyssa Milano started using a hashtag coined by sexual abuse awareness activist Tarana Burke a decade earlier: #MeToo.

Milano posted a message on Twitter: "If you've been sexually harassed or assaulted write 'me too' as a reply to this."

———

The day after the Weinstein story appeared in *The New Yorker*, the actress Illeana Douglas texted Ronan Farrow: "We've got to talk about Les Moonves." His *New Yorker* article, Douglas said, had made Farrow "the patron saint of actresses." She went on, "There was just a collective moment for women. We threw down the doors and said we're not going to take this anymore."

For Farrow, the boyishly handsome son of actress Mia Farrow and filmmaker and comedian Woody Allen, sexual misconduct and Hollywood were in his DNA. Allen had famously married Farrow's adopted sister Soon-Yi (making Farrow, in his own words, both Allen's "son and his brother-in-law"). And Farrow had backed his sister Dylan after she accused Allen of having sexually abused her when she was seven. (Allen has repeatedly denied the claim and several investigations failed to corroborate it.)

Farrow had graduated from Bard College when he was just fifteen, won a Rhodes Scholarship, and graduated from Yale Law School. As a journalist, he'd looked into the Bill Cosby case and sexual abuse on campus, and had initially been researching Weinstein for NBC News, which in Farrow's view was trying to suppress the story before Farrow took it to *The New Yorker*.

Douglas also came from Hollywood royalty: her grandfather was the Academy Award–winning stage and screen actor Melvyn Douglas. Douglas met Moonves in 1996, when she was just emerging from a long-term romantic relationship with the director Martin Scorsese. After appearing in his films *Goodfellas* and *Cape Fear*, she was hoping to launch a television career.

But before she told her story, she told Farrow she'd go on the record only if he found other examples of sexual harassment involving Moonves. She didn't want to be the only woman named in the article. Moonves was still far too powerful for that.

Farrow didn't blame her. After dealing with Weinstein, he knew much better than Douglas the lengths to which a powerful man backed by a corporate organization would go, and CBS was far bigger and richer than the Weinstein Company.

Douglas went ahead with her story. In 1997 CBS had cast her in a new sitcom, *Queens*, set in the New York City borough. When she and Moonves met alone in his office, ostensibly to discuss the script, he asked if he could kiss her.

"In a millisecond," she told Farrow, "he's got one arm over me, pinning me." Moonves was "violently kissing" her, holding her down on his couch with her arms above her head. "What it feels like to have someone hold you down—you can't breathe, you can't move,"

Douglas emerged from Moonves's office disheveled and crying.

In the ensuing weeks CBS fired Douglas from *Queens* and withheld her pay. Her manager dropped her. Her agent—Patrick Whitesell, then at CAA, who became tabloid fodder much later, after his wife took up with Jeff Bezos—kissed her off by calling to "wish her well."

Farrow was amazed at Douglas's pinpoint recollection, even though it had happened twenty years ago. But could he corroborate it? It couldn't just be Douglas's word against Moonves's.

Douglas said she'd told Craig Chester, an actor she was staying with at the time, that same day. After she was fired by CBS and dropped by her manager and agent, she'd turned to Scorsese for advice; he referred her to his law firm. She'd consulted a lawyer there—who'd taken notes. And CBS had eventually settled to avoid litigation.

Farrow had all the leads he needed. After the two-hour call with Douglas, he rushed off to tell David Remnick, *The New Yorker*'s editor.

———

Given the popularity of Weinstein's movies and the many celebrities involved, the Weinstein news made front-page headlines all over the world. In London the American playwright and screenwriter Janet Dulin Jones was watching the coverage of Harvey Weinstein with a friend.

"I can't believe no one is talking about Les Moonves," Jones told her friend. "I know I'm not the only one. I know it."

Season 3

EPISODE 1

"We All Did That"

Virtually nothing of significance happened at CBS that didn't reach the ears of Gil Schwartz, CBS's head of corporate communications. The charming, garrulous Schwartz was unique among corporate public relations executives. For years, first at *Esquire* and then at *Fortune*, he'd written an acid-tongued column critiquing big business and lampooning boardroom follies under the pseudonym Stanley Bing. As Bing he'd published thirteen books, including three novels and the nonfiction *Crazy Bosses*. He'd become more famous as Bing than as Schwartz.

At CBS for over two decades, Schwartz was a throwback to old-school publicists, who gossiped with reporters and doled out the occasional scoop. Once a struggling actor, he loved doing spot-on impersonations at CBS affiliates meetings. And he never forgot the cardinal rule of public relations: "The ability to feel deep, stupid loyalty is a must," as he put it in one of his Bing columns for *Esquire*. When Moonves was named chief executive in 2003, Schwartz bestowed that loyalty on him.

Moonves responded with a high degree of trust in Schwartz. Within CBS Schwartz was known as the "Leslie whisperer," and when other employees had difficult issues to raise with Moonves, they often brought them first to Schwartz. From his years of writing the Bing column, he was a master at corporate politics and survival.

Schwartz knew little about Moonves's personal life. Moonves was often in Los Angeles and Schwartz was based in New York, so they didn't see each other all that much. Still, Schwartz knew Moonves wasn't exactly a boy scout. He'd had to bat down rumors of Moonves's intraoffice affair with Julie Chen, which began in 2003, while Moonves was still married to his wife Nancy and Chen was the host of CBS's *The Early Show*. (The two married in Acapulco in late 2004, two weeks after Moonves's divorce.) Had Moonves been a faithful husband to Nancy? Probably not, he assumed. But Schwartz didn't consider Moonves's romantic and sexual affairs any of his business unless they posed issues for CBS.

Which now might be the case. Just after the Weinstein story broke, Schwartz rather awkwardly asked Moonves whether CBS had anything to worry about. Moonves said he'd had a "long life" and had been "an active guy," but "I can't imagine any problems."

That was all Schwartz needed—or wanted—to hear.

———

A month after the Weinstein bombshells, Phyllis Golden-Gottlieb was watching late-night TV at her home in the Miracle Mile neighborhood of Los Angeles. Now retired, Golden-Gottlieb was a surprisingly youthful-looking eighty-two years old, a veteran television producer who'd given up her entertainment career years earlier to teach special-needs children.

"For those of you tuning in to see my interview with Louis C.K. tonight, I have some bad news," Stephen Colbert said that night on CBS's *The Late Show with Stephen Colbert*. C.K. had canceled after *The New York Times* reported he'd pulled his pants down and masturbated in front of women he lured to his hotel room.

For Golden-Gottlieb, the revelation was the latest painful reminder of her time at Lorimar in the 1980s, when she was in charge of sitcom development. She had her own stories to tell, and as she sat on her sofa

Sumner Redstone at the 1993 MTV Music Video Awards with his wife, Phyllis; his daughter, Shari; Shari's children, Tyler, Brandon, and Kimberlee; and, to Sumner's right, singer-songwriter Michael Stipe, of R.E.M. Absent was Sumner's increasingly estranged son, Brent. Phyllis's appearances at Sumner's side were largely ceremonial; she threatened to divorce him for infidelity that same year and followed through in 2002.

Talk show host Larry King interviewed Sumner at the 2009 Milken Institute in Los Angeles. Sumner claimed to have reversed the aging process and told the audience he had the vital statistics—and sex life—of a twenty-year-old.

Malia Andelin with Sumner and CBS chief executive Les Moonves at the premiere of a CBS film in 2010. Andelin was working as a flight attendant on the company jet when Sumner became obsessed with her. He sent her a jewel-encrusted handbag with a note: "I'm a panther and I'm going to pounce." Andelin later accused him of using Viacom and CBS resources to follow and spy on her.

After Sumner became infatuated with singer Heather Naylor (center, surrounded by other members of the Electric Barbarellas), he pressured CBS chief executive Les Moonves in 2011 to put the rock group on the network and got MTV executives to launch a reality-TV series about them. A subsequent lawsuit involving Naylor upended Sumner's estate planning and succession plans.

Shari's growing family surrounded Sumner at his induction into the Hollywood Walk of Fame in 2012, a measure of his status as a still-potent Hollywood mogul. (Shari's daughter, Kimberlee, is on Shari's right; her son-in-law, Jason Ostheimer, and her sons, Brandon and Tyler, are on her left.) By now Sumner was openly at war with Shari, totally estranged from his son, Brent, and bestowing millions of dollars on a succession of young mistresses and female companions.

Sumner and his live-in companion Sydney Holland attended a 2013 gala honoring famed director Martin Scorsese with Les Moonves and his wife, the CBS host Julie Chen. After Sumner and Holland were introduced by Patti Stanger, on reality-TV's *The Millionaire Matchmaker*, and after what Holland said was an idyllic courtship that culminated in a nine-carat diamond ring, Holland moved into Sumner's mansion. She was soon in his estate plan as well.

Holland and Sumner's former flame Manuela Herzer flanked Sumner at a 2013 gala given by UCLA to honor Al Gore, a recipient of Sumner's charitable largesse. While the house staff considered Holland to be Sumner's "live-in girlfriend," Herzer, too, moved into the mansion. She and Holland were soon plotting to gain control over Sumner's fortune and media empire.

George Pilgrim was photographed for "Hunks in Trunks," a *Cosmopolitan* magazine All About Men feature, in 1996. When Sydney Holland met Pilgrim at the pool deck of the Peninsula Beverly Hills years later, he still had the dark blond hair and chiseled abs of the soap opera star he'd once been.

Pilgrim and Holland outside the private jet Holland used to commute between Sumner's mansion and the lavish house in Sedona, Arizona, that she bought to share with Pilgrim. Despite Stanger's warnings that Sumner would never tolerate infidelity, Pilgrim and Holland traded passionate text messages, were soon engaged, and began calling themselves husband and wife. Pilgrim donated sperm so they could conceive a child.

Holland and Herzer at a Hammer Museum gala in 2013, as they cemented their hold over Sumner and emerged into the celebrity spotlight. "The both of you look like high-class call girls," an angry Pilgrim told Holland after provocative photos of the pair appeared in *Vanity Fair*. Herzer later joined the Hammer Museum's board as she and Holland restyled themselves as "renowned" philanthropists.

Viacom chief executive Philippe Dauman, at right, and his eventual successor, Bob Bakish, left, flank the singer/songwriter legend Bono backstage at a 2008 MTV awards ceremony. At the time Dauman was so close to Sumner that he was considered his surrogate son, much to Shari's dismay. But that changed abruptly after Dauman tried to sell a stake in Sumner's cherished but underperforming Paramount studio. By contrast, Bakish proved a master at relationship management, forging a close bond with Shari.

Redstone lawyer Rob Klieger speaks at a 2016 hearing in a packed Boston courtroom, where he defended the Redstones' efforts to oust Dauman and his allies and addressed an ailing Sumner's mental capacity.

Shari Redstone and her son Brandon Korff arrive with her attorney, Elizabeth Burnett, at Los Angeles Superior Court in 2016. Manuela Herzer launched the suit in an effort to regain her influence and inheritance after Sumner ejected both her and Holland from his mansion. Herzer's suit went off the rails when Sumner testified using colorful profanity: "I hate her."

The actress Bobbie Phillips at the People's Choice awards in 1996, a year after she experienced a traumatic encounter with Les Moonves, then the powerful president of Warner Bros. Television. Phillips told her manager, Marv Dauer, that she never wanted to see or work with Moonves again.

Marv Dauer at his Los Angeles home in 2018. As the #MeToo movement gained traction, Dauer used his newfound leverage with Moonves to resuscitate his flagging career. But, Moonves warned him, "If Bobbie talks, I'm finished."

Les Moonves with *CBS This Morning* cohost and talk show star Charlie Rose. When Rose was fired in November 2017 after he admitted he had "behaved insensitively" around women, Moonves assured the CBS board that the company had procedures in place, and said publicly, "It's important that a company's culture will not allow for this."

Les Moonves in 2018. Moonves agonized over the decision to go to war with Shari and the Redstone family, especially given the secrets in his past. "She will come after me big time," he texted his chief operating officer. "She will be enraged."

Shari and her father pictured in 2012, Shari's public smile masking their often tense relationship. After Sumner died in 2020, Shari asked Sumner's longtime confidant and protégé Tad Jankowski if her father had really loved her. Jankowski reassured her that she'd never given up the fight and she'd proven her mettle. Her father would have "loved and respected that."

in front of the television, she decided to do it that very night—not by calling a reporter but by filing a police complaint.

At first she didn't know where to go, but she quickly found the address for the Hollywood police station and drove there the next day.

Golden-Gottlieb told the officer on duty that she'd worked with Les Moonves while she was at Lorimar and he was the younger, fast-rising head of movies for television. One day in 1986 Moonves invited her to lunch. They got in his car and he drove her not to a restaurant, as she was expecting, but to a secluded area. There he parked, unzipped his pants, grabbed her head, and forced it onto his erect penis until he ejaculated.

Nonetheless they'd kept working together. Two years later she was in his office when Moonves excused himself to get a glass of wine. When he returned, his pants were down. She ran from the room.

The next day he berated her, then threw her against a wall. She fell to the floor and couldn't get up. She lay there crying.

That, in any event, was her story.

As the 1997 film *L.A. Confidential* should have made obvious, there are no secrets in Hollywood. Cory Palka, the veteran police captain for that Hollywood precinct, moonlighted as a security officer for CBS. He'd worked for CBS at the Grammy Awards show from 2008 to 2014. Palka called Ian Metrose, the head of special events for CBS and left a message: "Somebody walked in the station about a couple hours ago and made allegations against your boss regarding a sexual assault. It's confidential, as you know, but call me, and I can give you some of the details and let you know what the allegation is before it goes to the media or gets out." Metrose immediately called Gil Schwartz.

Schwartz was shocked. Since Moonves had assured him CBS had nothing to worry about, reporters from *The New York Times* and *The Washington Post* had called Schwartz about Moonves rumors. In early November Schwartz had heard from another reporter that Ronan Farrow was making calls about Moonves.

Now this. A police report was more than a rumor. It was a reportable fact. Schwartz told Metrose to get a copy of the police report, and Palka obliged, even though the report was marked "confidential" in three places and Golden-Gottlieb had expressly requested confidential treatment.

The allegations were graphic. If the contents of a formal police complaint became public, it could be a public relations nightmare for CBS, given the ongoing frenzy ignited by the #MeToo movement. Schwartz and CBS had to be prepared. So he took a deep breath and called Moonves, who was at his eight-year-old son Charlie's soccer game.

Schwartz outlined the allegations.

"That's preposterous," Moonves responded. He hadn't thought about his time at Lorimar in years.

"Do you know the woman?" Schwartz asked.

It wasn't hard for Moonves to figure out who she must be. He told Schwartz he'd had consensual sex a few times with a coexecutive—Golden-Gottlieb—and they'd been "friendly before, during and after."

Schwartz assured Moonves he didn't see any immediate threat. The incidents were so old the case would never be prosecuted. None of it had happened while Moonves was at CBS. Still, there was always the risk of a leak, or the woman herself might go public. Schwartz told Moonves he'd better notify a CBS board member. Should something become public, Moonves wouldn't want it to come as a surprise to board members.

Moonves promised he would. But he stressed that there was nothing to be concerned about. Nonetheless, "it was something that was upsetting to me over Thanksgiving. It was primarily all I could think about," Moonves later acknowledged.

Schwartz mentioned the police complaint to Moonves several more times over the next few weeks. Moonves seemed annoyed and finally told him to stop bringing it up. He said he'd already told two board members.

Based on Moonves's assurance, Schwartz drafted a press response just in case. If asked about it, he would confirm that CBS was aware of a Los Angeles police investigation of Moonves, say that the CBS board had been notified, and say nothing more. Schwartz alerted his press team over the weekend, sending a text message to one: "Stay close to your phone today" and we "have a situation."

But time passed and no one brought it up.

Moonves himself wasn't taking any chances. He hired Blair Berk, a criminal-defense lawyer. Berk preferred to work under the radar, a lawyer who, as CNN put it, "makes stars' legal scrapes disappear." Berk got in touch with Palka. On November 15, Palka texted Metrose and Berk to say he'd "make contact & admonish the accuser tomorrow about refraining from going to the media and maintaining 'her' confidentiality." He continued, "You will be the first and only point of contact regarding the Investigaton."

Ten days later, Moonves himself arranged to meet with Palka and Metrose at a Westlake Village restaurant and vineyard. Moonves stressed that he wanted the investigation closed and they discussed contacting other public officials.

But that proved unnecessary. On November 30, 2017, Metrose told Moonves he'd heard from Palka that they could stop worrying: "it's a definite REJECT—no witnesses and/or corroborative Evidence."

In the police referral to the Los Angeles County district attorney, Golden-Gottlieb was identified only as Jane Doe. Moonves was designated as a "VIP." The assistant district attorney reviewing the matter noted, "The applicable statutes of limitation have expired as to all three incidents."

Schwartz continued to hear from a trickle of reporters. Cynthia Littleton, business editor of the Hollywood trade journal *Variety*, had emailed him (on December 8) about "a rumor out there re Les being the focus of a sex harass story (not sure who)."

That was the end of it, or so it seemed.

———

The Weinstein articles had also dredged up painful memories for Dr. Anne Peters, the director of the clinical diabetes program at the University of Southern California, where she was also a professor. Since finishing her medical residency at Stanford and moving to Los Angeles, she had developed a reputation as the go-to doctor for diabetes and related issues. Among her prominent clients was Arnold Kopelson, still at the peak of his fame after winning an Oscar for *Platoon*. Kopelson was also a friend of Peters's, and at Kopelson's urging, in 1999 she had agreed to see a new patient who, like Kopelson, was diabetic: Les Moonves.

The appointment was early, at 7:00 a.m., before most of the medical staff had arrived, and she recalled "the early-morning light filtering through the blinds," as she described the scene. She and Moonves were alone in the room and sat on either side of a small table while she did her usual initial interview. As they stood and started to move toward an examination table, Moonves grabbed her, pulled her against him, and made grinding motions. His penis was erect. She couldn't forget the look on his face: that of a "monster," she recalled. Peters pushed him away, but he tried to remove her shirt and get into her pants. Peters managed to push him off.

"Oh, you're going to be like that," Moonves said. Moonves went to the corner of the room and masturbated. He left the room without saying anything more.

When Peters reported the incident at the hospital, she was warned that Moonves had "more money for lawyers" than the hospital and was told "to refrain from reporting this incident formally to the police because I would lose in court," she recalled.

But Peters had given Kopelson a detailed account of what happened. In 2007, when Kopelson was nominated for the CBS board, she had urged him to reject the position because of Moonves's behavior.

Kopelson had brushed aside her concerns as "trivial." He said the encounter had happened years ago and, in any event, "we all did that."

In the intervening years, Peters had been afraid to be alone again in a room with a male patient. She'd discussed the Moonves incident several more times with Kopelson, sometimes with others present. Now that the #MeToo movement was gaining momentum, the incident had taken on new urgency and relevance. Unlike other victims, Peters was prevented by the doctor-patient privilege from publicly naming Moonves. But she urged Kopelson to come forward, or at least warn his fellow CBS board members. Peters even enlisted a mutual friend to plead their case.

Kopelson did nothing.

———

On November 14, the #MeToo wave reached CBS rival NBC News when the network announced it had fired Matt Zimmerman, a producer and top talent booker for NBC's popular *Today* show, for "inappropriate conduct" involving multiple women. The little-known Zimmerman might have remained a footnote but for his close ties to *Today* star Matt Lauer, who, married with children, was known as "America's Dad." Zimmerman was widely seen as Lauer's protégé and the two often traveled together, including to the Tokyo Olympics.

With rumors swirling about Lauer, the CBS board compensation committee met on November 18. Longtime director Linda Griego— other than Shari, the only woman on the board until Minow arrived— veered from the agenda and asked if CBS was at risk of any similar situations to NBC. Moonves was quick to reassure her that CBS was "managing the situation" and "has the right processes in place."

Just two days later, *The Washington Post* published accounts of eight women who said they'd been sexually harassed by Charlie Rose while working for him on his public broadcasting interview program, *The Charlie Rose Show*. Rose was also a star for CBS News, helping to reinvigorate

CBS This Morning as a cohost, as well as a *60 Minutes* correspondent. The behavior identified by the *Post* included "lewd phone calls, walking around naked in their presence, or groping their breasts, buttocks or genital areas."

Rose conceded he "had behaved insensitively at times," and both CBS and PBS fired him within hours of the story's publication.

At CBS Rose's cohost Gayle King had the awkward task of opening the next morning's show without him. "I've enjoyed a friendship and a partnership with Charlie for the past five years," she said. "I have held him in such high regard. And I am really struggling. Because how do you—what do you say when someone that you deeply care about has done something that is so horrible? How do you wrap your brain around that?"

But at the next CBS board meeting, Rose was barely acknowledged. Moonves said CBS would be investigating his behavior at the network but stressed that no one at CBS knew anything about it and that it all had happened on his PBS show.

Moonves was the keynote speaker at *Variety*'s Innovate Summit on November 29 (the same day NBC finally fired Matt Lauer after weeks of rumors), where discussion of the #MeToo movement swamped the agenda. Moonves said there was "no question" CBS had been affected by the Weinstein scandal and ensuing revelations. He called it a "watershed moment." He added, "There's a lot we're learning. There's a lot we didn't know." But, "It's important that a company's culture will not allow for this."

A few weeks later, Moonves joined Hollywood heavyweights Kathleen Kennedy of Lucasfilm, Bob Iger of Disney, and Ted Sarandos of Netflix to form a "Commission on Sexual Harassment and Advancing Equality in the Workplace" headed by Anita Hill, whose testimony against Supreme Court justice Clarence Thomas made her a worldwide symbol of sexual harassment.

EPISODE 2

"If Bobbie Talks"

With a perpetual tan and blow-dried silver hair, Marv Dauer looked the part of the Hollywood talent manager. He knew just about everyone in casting at the networks, especially those in daytime, a genre in which he handled some bona fide stars: Eva LaRue (*All My Children*, *CSI: Miami*) and Joshua Morrow (*The Young and the Restless*).

For someone who'd made his way to Hollywood from his hometown of Austin, Minnesota, near the Iowa border, population 25,000 and best known as the birthplace of the canned meat Spam, Dauer had done well. He lived in a West Los Angeles neighborhood close to celebrity-studded Bel-Air and Brentwood, a stone's throw from the MountainGate Country Club, where he pursued two of his life's passions: golf (he'd scored four holes in one) and bridge (he'd amassed over three thousand masters points). He drove a Mercedes convertible. He was divorced, was surrounded by beautiful women, and, despite a few serial relationships, had no intention of remarrying.

But lately his personal finances had been strained. Casting directors seemed to be ignoring him. His income—a percentage of what he earned for his clients—had plunged. Only thanks to a winning hand in Vegas had he been able to make his last mortgage payment.

Dauer couldn't figure out what was going on, until a casting director asked him why he wasn't making any submissions. She said she hadn't heard from him since 2015. Dauer was incredulous. He'd been steadily making submissions, or at least he thought he had. He called in the Los Angeles police and the FBI and changed his email password. His submissions started going through. It turned out a disgruntled former client had stolen his computer password and for the last several years had been regularly deleting his submissions.

It was going to take time for Dauer to rebuild his client list and replenish his bank account. For someone in his seventies it was a daunting prospect.

Unlike many talent managers eager to get publicity for their clients, Dauer didn't cultivate reporters and didn't put much stock in the press. On November 28, 2017, when he got a call from Ellen Gabler, an investigative reporter at *The New York Times*, he was instantly wary. He was even more so when she told him why she was calling: a story about sexual assault involving Les Moonves. She didn't get much further because Dauer, flustered, said he'd have to call her back and hung up.

Dauer wasn't surprised that more names were being scooped up in the #MeToo net. The Weinstein exposés hadn't shocked him: in his view sexual misadventures were rampant and it had always been a man's world, at least until now, and not just in the entertainment industry. But why were reporters calling him? Moonves had just been named the fourth-most-powerful person in entertainment (two notches above Shari Redstone) by *The Hollywood Reporter*. By comparison, Dauer was a nobody. He'd never made anybody's power list. He barely knew Moonves. Thanks to his client Eva LaRue, a star for CBS, he'd been to two crowded CBS parties with him, one after the Rose Bowl and one at Moonves's house in Beverly Hills, but those were years ago. He and Moonves hadn't been in touch since.

Gabler from the *Times* wasn't the first, or only, reporter who had tried to reach him. Someone from *Deadline Hollywood* had sent him an email on November 10 asking about Moonves and another one of his clients, the actress Bobbie Phillips. Dauer's client LaRue had told *Deadline* that actor Steven Seagal had assaulted her at an audition, luring her into a room on the pretense of getting a script and then opening his kimono ("He had underwear on, thank God," LaRue told reporter David Robb). During the interview LaRue told Robb something bad had happened between Moonves and Phillips. She suggested he talk to Phillips's manager, who was Dauer. Dauer hadn't answered the email.

But the press inquiries got Dauer thinking.

Dauer had first met Bobbie Phillips in 1993, when she was twenty-five, with dyed blond hair and a striking physique that had already landed her on the cover of *Muscle & Fitness* magazine four times. Still, Dauer met beautiful women all the time. He'd gotten his start in talent management in 1984, and over the years Dauer's friends marveled at his uncanny knack for spotting and cultivating younger women. His refrigerator was virtually empty because he never ate at home. He went to every party to which he was invited or could get into. One casting director recalled the many times Dauer excused himself to get a drink and somehow reappeared with an attractive woman on each arm. He referred to Dauer as "the great white shark."

There didn't seem to be anything sexual about Dauer's allure. Rather, he came across as a reassuring father figure who happened to know casting directors all over town. When on the prowl, his opening line was straightforward: "You're attractive. Are you an actress?" Which was what he said to a young blond who turned out to be Reese Witherspoon long before she was famous (she didn't hire him). At a party in Beverly Hills attended by a dearth of celebrities, he walked up to a beautiful brunette. "What are you doing at a party like this?" he asked. She said she was a former Miss Teenage America and wanted to break into acting. Bingo, he thought. "I'm a manager."

The young woman was Eva LaRue, who became one of his earliest and most enduring clients, the first to break out of the backwater of daytime soaps into prime time.

When he met Phillips, Dauer had the same reaction as with LaRue: she had star potential. She had a smile that could light up a room—or a screen, Dauer thought. Born and raised in Charleston, South Carolina, she radiated a girl-next-door wholesomeness along with undeniable sex appeal. She'd just started breaking into television: a brief appearance on NBCUniversal's *They Came from Outer Space* and then two episodes of *Married . . . with Children*. But she kept getting offered what she considered "bimbo" roles—like a topless turn in the controversial R-rated movie *Showgirls* and the seductress "Luscious Lola" in an episode of the *Red Shoe Diaries* (by coincidence, the same Showtime series that George Pilgrim had acted in).

Dauer signed Phillips after just one meeting. A casting director suggested she'd be taken more seriously as an actress if she gave up the blond hair and became a brunette, which she did. Eight months later she landed her best role yet, the model/drug addict Julie Costello in fifteen episodes of *Murder One* on ABC.

It was what had happened next, Dauer surmised, that had prompted the questions from reporters.

On the strength of Phillips's clips, in February 1995 Dauer had set up a meeting for her with Moonves. By then Lorimar and Warner had combined their television operations, and Moonves was the powerful president of Warner Bros. Television, where he'd developed the megahits *Friends* and *E.R.* He was a hands-on executive when it came to casting, insisting on personally signing off on major roles and often sitting in on auditions.

Phillips didn't even know who Moonves was, but Dauer stressed that this could be her big break into prime time—even a part on the megahit *E.R.*

Phillips met Moonves at his Warner Bros. office. Afterward, her agent, Lara Smolef, called Dauer. Something bad had happened, Smolef told Dauer. Phillips had come straight to her office after the meeting and started sobbing.

Dauer called Phillips. "How did the Moonves meeting go?" he asked, not saying he'd just heard from her agent.

"Not very well," she answered tersely. "I don't want to talk about it."

But apparently it had gone well, at least from Moonves's perspective. Moonves called Dauer the next day and said he'd really liked Phillips and wanted to put her on some shows. Moonves called Phillips with the good news, expecting she'd be thrilled.

But Phillips was angry. "Absolutely not. Keep him away from me," she responded. She told Dauer she never wanted to see or work with Moonves again. Whatever had happened at that meeting must have been pretty bad, Dauer thought.

Before the meeting with Moonves, Phillips had loved going to auditions. Now the prospect gave her anxiety attacks. She refused to attend meetings alone with studio executives. Once, before a movie screening, she was so afraid she'd encounter Moonves that she vomited in an alley outside the theater.

Moonves left Warner Bros. to become president of CBS Entertainment a few months after meeting Phillips. True to her vow, she never spoke to Moonves again. But she did see him once more. She was one of three finalists for a role on *Martial Law*, a surprise hit for CBS in 1998. When she arrived for the audition, Moonves was there. He greeted her, sat in the front row during her reading, and stared at her with a fixed gaze. She found it unnerving. She didn't get the part.

Over the next few years, Phillips had roles in several prime-time series. Besides *Murder One*, she appeared in seventeen episodes of the syndicated drama *The Cape* as an astronaut trainee who, she complained, spent more time in a bathing suit than a space suit. Despite the change in hair color, she was never offered the more serious roles to which she aspired. She announced her retirement from acting in 2001.

Phillips focused on raising her son. She remarried and moved with her husband, a Canadian who worked in Hollywood as a hair stylist, to Toronto. She took up the cause of animal rights and cultivated an interest in religion and spirituality. She tried to put the past behind her and live in the present. And recently she'd put a toe back into acting, appearing in the independent political thriller *The Gandhi Murder*.

Dauer noticed her part in *The Gandhi Murder* mentioned in the Hollywood trade press. Maybe she could use a manager again. And then the calls about Moonves had come. Dauer sensed opportunity.

Dauer wondered how to approach someone as important as Moonves, someone he hadn't seen in years. He hesitated for several days. Then, on December 4, he called Moonves and left a voice message. He also sent him a cryptic email: "Leslie—it's very important you call me. Marv Dauer." He left his phone number. Would Moonves even respond?

Moments later, Moonves was on the phone.

"Remember Bobbie Phillips?" Dauer asked. "She came in many years ago and you had a thing?" Dauer somewhat delicately put it.

Dauer told Moonves he'd gotten a call from a *Times* reporter and also that Eva LaRue had mentioned Phillips and Moonves to *Deadline*.

Moonves knew very well what Dauer was talking about. He acknowledged he'd had a sexual encounter with Phillips at the time. But he insisted it was consensual.

Dauer said no one would believe it was consensual, not after Weinstein and the #MeToo movement. "Look, she's become very religious, but she wouldn't mind getting some work," Dauer added.

Moonves said he'd heard a #MeToo article about him might be published soon. "I think I'll be okay," he said. "But if Bobbie talks, I'm finished."

EPISODE 3

"I Was a Good Guy"

Dauer said he'd talk to Phillips and get back to Moonves, but before ending the call, Dauer reminded him again that Bobbie Phillips was an actress who was "always looking for work." And he mentioned two of his other clients who should be on CBS prime time: Joshua Morrow and Eva LaRue. He didn't need to be any more explicit: a quid pro quo was obvious.

Moonves gave Dauer two private cell phone numbers to use.

Two days later Moonves texted Dauer: "All quiet?"

"I'm sorta trapped because of the fires," Dauer responded. (California governor Jerry Brown had declared a state of emergency for Los Angeles County the day before because of widespread wildfires in the area.) "I live at MountainGate and they close at 4:05 and we can't go anywhere. I have quite a bit of stuff I could tell you but I'm uncomfortable unless we do it in person." He added, "I have not heard from anyone."

Moonves replied: "Sorry about your house. Stay safe. Can we talk by phone?"

"We can. I don't trust the media. I was going to be able to tell you everything that I heard and then you can figure out how to deal with it if it ever comes to the press."

"Needless to say I appreciate you," Moonves responded.

"I can't imagine what this is like for you," Dauer replied.

When Dauer answered his phone the next day, it was again the reporter from the *Times*, Ellen Gabler. He hung up again. "They caught me off guard," Dauer promptly texted Moonves. "I said I will call them back. I will leave the next step up to you."

"No need to talk to them," Moonves said.

"I won't," Dauer promised.

Shortly after, Phillips returned a call from her long-ago manager. Dauer told her the *Times* was calling him. Phillips said she'd gotten media calls, too. She hadn't responded, but some of her friends who knew what happened with Moonves all those years ago were urging her to speak out.

Dauer pressed the case for Moonves, pointing out he had a young son. "Please don't ruin his life," Dauer said.

The reference to Moonves's son struck a chord—Phillips's own son had committed suicide. She assured Dauer she had no intention of going to the press. Her mantra was to try to move forward and forgive. That was the only way she'd gotten past the loss of her son. She didn't want to relive the past and dredge up bad memories.

Dauer jumped on her mention of forgiveness. Moonves, he told her, felt terrible about what had happened. He was haunted by it. He didn't feel he could move forward unless he found a way to make amends.

Phillips said she didn't want anything from Moonves. Still, the reference to making amends got her attention. She wondered what he had in mind.

Dauer said Moonves might want to put her on CBS. Phillips rejected the idea, saying she wasn't looking for work. But Dauer persisted. "How about, if an offer comes in, I send it along?" Dauer said. "You don't have to decide anything now."

That seemed reasonable. She could always deal with it later. Phillips agreed to relist Dauer as her manager on her IMDb profile page.

Still, part of her thought it all seemed strange. And her husband was wary. He didn't see why Moonves couldn't come to terms with his past behavior on his own. Why did Bobbie have to be involved?

As soon as Dauer got off the phone he texted Moonves: "I just was on the phone 30 [minutes] with Bobbie and I think you are going to be very very happy," he wrote. He was hurrying off to see his friend, the actor James Woods, but would "Call u in an hour or so. Get a notepad."

———

Dauer and Moonves had gone overnight from being barely acquainted to constant pen pals. Dauer was quick to press his advantage by piling up favors, a time-honored currency in Hollywood. A former Los Angeles Dodgers baseball player, Reggie Smith, was among his friends, and Dauer arranged for Smith to give Moonves's young son baseball lessons and an autographed ball—gifts Moonves felt obliged to accept, whether he wanted them or not. ("Charlie is very excited to meet Reggie," Moonves texted.) Dauer found some old commemorative stamps depicting baseball greats Babe Ruth, Lou Gehrig, and Jackie Robinson, and he mailed them to Moonves. He sent Moonves a photo of his collection of sports jerseys from the greats—"George Brett Pete Rose Gretzky Jordan Carl Eller Marcel Dionne"—and invited him and Charlie to come see them over the holidays.

Dauer further ingratiated himself by scoffing at the #MeToo movement. *Time* magazine had just named "The Silence Breakers—the Voices That Launched a Movement" as the magazine's 2017 persons of the year. "Don't tell me the world's not fucked up," Dauer texted Moonves about the choice. "There must be some doctors or peacemakers or military that have contributed more to the planet than these women," he griped.

At the same time Dauer kept up the pressure by reporting every press inquiry he got, a drumbeat guaranteed to keep Moonves in a constant state of anxiety.

"NY Times just called again," Dauer texted on December 13. "Obviously I did not answer the phone. She left a 30 second message saying she's working on an article—& would like to speak on or off the record. Leslie—At this point you just have to have faith—They cannot reach myself or anyone else—consequently there cannot be any story—You have to be believe that—"

"Thanks. Praying," Moonves responded.

Later the same day Dauer reported: "Deadline Hollywood just called me and I hung up."

"Same guy?" Moonves wanted to know.

"There's going to be a way to beat these bastards," Dauer answered. "Even I'm not sleeping too well—Next week if your in town—maybe lunch. Till then—will keep you updated—and I hope I don't hear anything."

A few days later he reported another call from the *Times*.

"Same lady. I wonder when they will realize I'm not speaking to them." He added, "Within five minutes I received two other calls from numbers I did not know so I did not answer."

"This sucks," Moonves responded.

"I couldn't agree more," Dauer wrote. "They are even becoming a nuisance to me."

"They are clearly fishing."

"They won't catch anything here," Dauer assured him.

"So far your defense of not talking is good," Moonves told him.

Dauer's efforts to secure work for his clients soon started to bear fruit. On December 12, Peter Golden, head of casting for CBS, emailed Moonves that "per our conversation" he was considering LaRue for a part. (Golden didn't recall the conversation but said it was possible Moonves "called me and threw Eva LaRue in the mix.")

Two days later LaRue's name showed up on a casting list for a lead role on *History of Them*, a pilot for a multiracial comedy.

As the year neared an end and the holidays approached, Shari was busy trying to spend more time with her family on the East Coast while shuttling to California to tend to Sumner. But recent events had also forced her to consider renewing her effort to merge CBS and Viacom. When she'd abandoned the effort a year earlier, there didn't seem to be any rush to combine them. But now the need for greater scale in the entertainment industry appeared acute. Netflix and Amazon were throwing billions at new programming. The media industry was undergoing rapid transformation, and the traditional broadcast and cable business models on which CBS and Viacom depended were collapsing.

Even Rupert Murdoch had gotten the message. In November, CNBC had reported that Sumner's archrival was in talks to sell most of Twenty-First Century Fox's entertainment assets to Disney.

News of a potential Fox-Disney deal sent shock waves through the industry, including the CBS board. Lead CBS director Bruce Gordon asked the investment banking boutique Centerview Partners, which was also involved in the Fox-Disney deal, to make a presentation for CBS.

On December 14, after Moonves led the board through CBS's latest results (including a revenue gain in its most recent quarter), he said he was turning to a strategic analysis of the industry and potential merger partners for CBS. Shari looked over at Klieger in surprise: even though Gordon had told her something about a discussion of "the industry," such a strategic review wasn't on the agenda.

Centerview's list of potential partners included the usual suspects: MGM, Sony Entertainment, and Lionsgate were companies CBS might acquire; Verizon, Amazon, Apple—perhaps even Warren Buffett's Berkshire Hathaway—were among the larger companies that might want to acquire CBS.

There was a glaring omission. Viacom was barely mentioned, dismissed as largely irrelevant, even though it had just surprised Wall Street with better earnings than expected, suggesting that Bakish's strategy was yielding results.

One of Centerview's slides compared the relative fortunes of the Murdoch and Redstone families, with the Murdochs having fared far better financially.

Shari felt her temperature rising. To overlook Viacom, after she had formally proposed and supported such a merger, was insulting, the ultimate in being ignored.

She also felt ambushed. Shari wanted to walk out but resisted the impulse. The instant the presentation ended she stood up, grabbed her belongings, and stalked out without further comment. Klieger followed close behind.

A car was waiting downstairs. Once inside, Shari vented to Klieger. What was she doing on the board if no one listened to her or cared what she said? She felt like she was being goaded into another board fight like the one she'd just had at Viacom. But she didn't feel she had the energy. Maybe she should just bow out and let CBS do whatever it wanted.

Klieger seized the opening. "Rather than try to figure out if it makes sense to merge CBS and Viacom, and then deal with the inevitable litigation, why not let someone else figure that out?" The Redstones could sell National Amusements, the controlling shareholder of both Viacom and CBS. Shari could focus on Advancit Capital and her family.

The idea was bold, but to Klieger it made sense. National Amusements' assets—the controlling stakes in CBS and Viacom and the theater chain—would probably never be more valuable to a buyer looking for scale in the entertainment business than they were at that moment. Shari had said she was tired of fighting.

Shari said she'd think about it. She had her bankers at Evercore look into a range of options, even though it was unlikely she could ever persuade her father to sell National Amusements, given his hostility to a sale of even a stake in Paramount.

Whatever she decided, one thing was now clear to Klieger: some kind of showdown between Shari and Moonves was brewing.

———

On December 19, June Seley Kimmel, a former actress and aspiring screenwriter, weighed in on a Twitter discussion about how Hollywood tended to blame women victims for the sexual assaults coming to light post-Weinstein.

"Good time to say I had a pitch meeting w Les Moonves who was then head of development at 20th Century Fox," Kimmel tweeted. "Went great, said we'd do it, then he stuck his tongue down my throat . . ."

The tweet went unnoticed by journalists, but Shari saw it and forwarded it to Martha Minow, referring to "certain rumors" that were "now on Twitter." The two women spoke the next day. "We may have to deal with something that goes beyond Charlie Rose," Shari said.

Minow wondered aloud if they needed to alert the board to the tweet about Moonves, but Shari said she'd leave the decision up to her. Shari felt she already had enough issues with the board and didn't want to be seen as the one stirring up trouble for Moonves. Still, she told Minow she was hearing a lot of "noise" about Moonves and assumed Minow would pass on the tweet to other board members. Minow, however, had the impression they should be discreet, so she didn't say anything further.

Shari also forwarded the tweet to Klieger. The alleged incident was old—Moonves was at Fox before he joined Lorimar in 1985, so it had happened decades ago. Still, coming just days after the board meeting that so upset Shari, a #MeToo problem for Moonves would dramatically change the balance of power.

This could get interesting, Klieger thought.

———

Moonves gave no hint to other board members of the mounting pressure he faced. But to Dauer he showed a flash of despair, at one point suggesting he might retire early. But Moonves being stripped of his power as CBS chief executive would render him of little value to Dauer and his clients. Dauer weighed in on December 19: "You said you might retire early—because of the 'situation.' Then the bad people win. Too many people rely on you—your goal should be to go out on your own terms.—there I said my piece. Stay warm."

"I was a good guy. I still am," Moonves asserted.

"No one doubts that," Dauer assured him.

At a party Dauer ran into Elisabeth Sereda, a member of the Hollywood Foreign Press Association, which hosts the Golden Globes. She came up to him and said, "We're going to get Moonves."

"Why?" Dauer asked.

"There are so many," was all she said.

Dauer immediately reported the incident to Moonves. "Beware of a publicist named Elisabeth Sereda," he said. "I am hoping she was drunk because she was saying things about you. . . . Very creepy."

"What was she saying?" Moonves asked.

"This lady was so aggressive," Dauer said. "Said stupid things about you. . . . More women power crap."

"Did she know we know each other or she was just talking in general about me?" Moonves asked.

"I don't know." Dauer added, "I was really getting pissed—but stayed cool. She was the type of woman that makes me very happy I'm single."

Moonves wanted to know if she'd named anyone.

"There are really no names," Dauer said. "The publicist is a nobody gossip. . . . There really is nothing."

He added, "I don't want to ruin your holiday."

Though of course he just had.

EPISODE 4

"I Feel Sick All the Time"

Moonves spent Christmas with his wife and son in New York but was back in California for New Year's, staying at his $28 million beach house in Malibu with "too much family," as he lamented in a text to Dauer. Still, on New Year's Eve Moonves found the time to drive into Los Angeles and have breakfast with Dauer at Art's Delicatessen in Studio City, an industry hangout not far from the CBS studios.

Dauer still didn't know exactly what had happened between Moonves and Bobbie Phillips, but Moonves flatly denied ever assaulting the actress. He acknowledged they'd engaged in oral sex in his office, but he insisted it was "consensual." Dauer reassured him again that neither he nor Phillips was talking.

Dauer briefed Phillips on the meeting soon after and made the mistake of saying Moonves claimed their encounter was consensual. That set her off. It certainly didn't sound to her like Moonves was trying to make amends or gain her forgiveness.

Later that day Moonves texted Dauer his gratitude: "I enjoyed seeing you. Happy New Year to you. I know you have my back. You are a good guy. Thank you."

Still, Dauer, having gone to some lengths to get the autographed baseball to Charlie in time for Christmas, was disappointed that Moonves hadn't even mentioned it.

"Did Charlie like the ball?" Dauer prodded.

"Sorry. He Loved it," Moonves replied.

———

Shari was still angry about the December board meeting, but at least her fellow CBS directors seemed to recognize that something had to be done in the face of growing competitive threats. Maybe they could be persuaded to support a CBS-Viacom merger. Still, she was feeling drained from the Viacom battle, and she didn't have the appetite for another boardroom fight. She wasn't going to push a merger if Moonves opposed her.

Shari felt Moonves might be more candid with Rob Klieger rather than telling her what he thought she wanted to hear, so she asked Klieger to meet with Moonves and take his pulse. At the same time, Klieger felt maybe he could help close the widening gulf between Shari and the CBS chief executive.

Klieger showed up at Moonves's office in Studio City on January 5. Moonves was wearing jeans and didn't look at all pleased to see him. It probably didn't help that Klieger had mistakenly shown up a week early—their meeting was on Moonves's calendar for January 12. But now that he was there, they settled into a small conference room near Moonves's office. Moonves folded his arms across his chest.

"Maybe it's not my place to tell you this," Klieger began, for he realized he was just a lawyer trying to advise one of the most successful executives in entertainment. He genuinely thought Moonves was a business genius. He could understand that he'd be wary of someone he thought of as Shari's person, but he plunged ahead.

"Look, I know Shari has lots of ideas and thoughts about the business," he said. "I have no idea whether some of them are good or bad. Perhaps some are bad." He said he wasn't there to tell Moonves to do whatever Shari wanted. "If you don't think something's a good idea, don't do it. But why not make her feel like you care? Like you're considering her views and you're interested? Is that so hard?"

Klieger gave Moonves a few examples: If you're going to appoint someone to a high-level position, ask her opinion. A new show? Tell her you'd value her input. Then do what you think is right.

"If she feels she's part of the thinking and you're not keeping her at arm's length, you'll have a much better relationship. You won't have this constant fighting. It really does matter if you want to do the combination."

Which led to the topic of the merger. Klieger said he didn't know at this point if it was the right thing or not, but did Moonves support it?

"I'm not going to stand in the way," he said.

"That's not what she wants to hear," Klieger responded.

Moonves said he hadn't liked the way Shari stormed out of the last board meeting. And now she was complaining about his loyal and long-serving board member Gifford, even trying to get him off the board, over some minor incident at the Super Bowl.

Klieger stressed that he and Shari needed to get along. Shari didn't want the merger unless Moonves was enthusiastically behind it. "If you're reluctant, it won't work," he said. "Shari is becoming closer with Bob," Klieger warned, referring to Viacom's Bakish, who was proving a master at relationship management. Shari had an office at Viacom and Bakish was consulting her regularly. But Bakish wouldn't be the one figuring how best to fit the companies together—Moonves would. "I have to have faith you can bring this together," Klieger said. "Are you supportive?"

Moonves said he was. He'd get behind it.

His body language suggested otherwise. He looked glum. He clearly didn't seem to appreciate any guidance from Klieger.

Klieger reported to Shari that Moonves said he wanted to move forward with the merger but didn't seem all that enthusiastic.

Nonetheless, with Moonves seemingly on board, news leaked to *The Wrap*, and was quickly confirmed by CNBC, that "Viacom and CBS vice-chairwoman Shari Redstone are pursuing a merger of the two media companies that split more than a decade ago."

———

In Toronto, Phillips couldn't get Moonves off her mind. The more she thought about what Dauer had told her—that Moonves said their encounter was "consensual"—the angrier she got. She finally sent a Facebook message to Dauer on January 6:

> I did not sleep as I am feeling anger that Moonves is not sorry— and is calling me a liar basically. He is not allowed to play the victim card here. I did not bring this up as you know. I simply responded that I believe in forgiveness and moving forward in life. But, I will not be made a victim again. . . . I am doing my best to be a positive, forgiving person in my life. None of us are perfect. However, this does not sit well. I will go meditate and try to find my peace.

The next day, Phillips watched the Golden Globe Awards on TV as Oprah Winfrey became the first black woman to receive the Cecil B. DeMille lifetime achievement award. Winfrey delivered a stirring acceptance speech that addressed the burgeoning #MeToo movement.

"What I know for sure is that speaking your truth is the most powerful tool we all have," Winfrey said. "And I'm especially proud and inspired by all the women who have felt strong enough and empowered enough to speak up and share their personal stories." She continued, "I want tonight to express gratitude to all the women who have endured years of abuse and assault, because they—like my mother— had children to feed and bills to pay and dreams to pursue. They're the women whose names we'll never know."

"My God, this is me," Phillips thought.

A few days later Dauer texted Moonves that Winfrey's speech had "made the natives restless." He added: "My hope is when she is working all this will go far far away."

In London, the writer Janet Dulin Jones had lunch with a friend, a writer who was in town from Los Angeles. Naturally, Weinstein figured prominently in the conversation. Jones had been brooding about Moonves, who in some respects bothered her more than Weinstein. Weinstein had never pretended to be anything but a bully. The handsome and charming Moonves was still Hollywood's golden boy.

Jones's friend reminded her that years ago, when she had a meeting with Moonves, Jones had warned her to be sure to take her agent along with her. Back then the friend had wondered why. Jones hadn't felt like telling the real story—she was still afraid of Moonves and his blunt warning not to talk. But now she told her friend the real story.

Back in 1985 Jones, then a recent graduate of Long Beach State working as a writer's assistant, had just written her first treatment for a TV show. She'd taken her screenplay to a mentor, the writer Mike Marvin, who'd just scored with *Six Pack*, a movie starring country music star Kenny Rogers in his film debut.

Marvin and Moonves were close; both belonged to a men's support group that met every Wednesday. So Marvin called Moonves, who agreed to meet Jones.

Jones rehearsed her pitch for her boyfriend. She bought a navy pants suit at Bullock's department store even though she couldn't afford it. She wore her best Italian leather loafers. She arrived at Moonves's office at 4:30 p.m. carrying a stylish leather briefcase given to her by her writer friend Ann Marcus. ("Every writer needs a bag," Marcus had told her.)

Jones noticed Moonves's desk was filled with photos of his wife and children. Moonves offered her a glass of wine, which she declined—she wanted to be fully alert for the pitch. She and Moonves made small talk; she mentioned she'd interned at the Sundance Film Festival. She finally started talking about her story. About halfway through the pitch, Moonves stood up and moved toward the sofa where she was sitting. Was she speaking too softly? Jones wondered, so she raised her voice. Suddenly Moonves jumped on her, pushed her down, and tried to kiss her. It all happened with dizzying speed.

Jones cried out, struggled, and managed to push him away. Moonves moved to the other end of the sofa. "What do you think you're doing?" she asked, flabbergasted.

"I was hitting on you. I wanted a kiss," he said matter-of-factly.

She got up, shoved her papers into her bag, and headed for the door.

"Oh, come on, it's nothing," he said. "We're friends here. Sit down."

When she reached the door, it was locked. She started to panic. She said she'd scream if he didn't open it.

Moonves pushed a button behind his desk and the door opened.

Jones was so shaken she wasn't sure she could drive, but she made it to a friend's house in West Hollywood. She explained what had happened. It took her thirty minutes to calm down. She and her friend called her boyfriend and told him the story. They all agreed she was lucky she hadn't been raped. Should she report what had happened? Her friend and boyfriend both warned her that would end her career.

The next day Jones called Marvin, who'd set up the meeting. She didn't get into the details but told him Moonves had been "way out of line" and had done something inappropriate.

"I'm so sorry," Marvin told her. "He said he wasn't doing that anymore."

"What?" Jones asked, startled.

"He has a bit of a reputation for coming on to women." Marvin said he'd talk to Moonves about it.

When Jones finished the story, her friend hardly knew what to say. "God, what a jerk," she finally said.

But what could Jones do? Moonves was far more powerful than Harvey Weinstein had ever been. It was one thing for stars like Angelina Jolie or Gwyneth Paltrow to accuse Weinstein. Who would be interested in hearing from a little-known writer like Janet Jones?

———

The 2018 Consumer Electronics Show opened in Las Vegas on January 9, and Shari Redstone was one of the few prominent women in attendance for the annual tech showcase. All the keynote speakers were men. That didn't stop the buzz about sexual harassment in both Silicon Valley and Hollywood. Shari got asked about it at every turn, and one name kept coming up: Les Moonves. Specifically, that Ronan Farrow was on his trail, working on a big *New Yorker* exposé.

Shari again reached out to Minow, who was teaching at the University of Hawaii that week. Shari emailed her that "there is a lot of noise here at CES," specifically that Farrow was doing a #MeToo story on Moonves for *The New Yorker*. She said she didn't know anything more specific and hadn't heard any names of alleged victims.

Shari had also heard something about Moonves and Joe Ianniello at a meeting in Las Vegas, where both were wearing bathrobes—now a potent symbol of the #MeToo movement given both Weinstein's and Charlie Rose's propensity to confront women while wearing an open bathrobe. Again, Shari had few details.

This time Minow called another board member, Charles Gifford. He was skeptical. He told Minow that Shari was once again trying to undermine Moonves. For all he knew, Shari herself might be behind the rumors—or even planting a story with Farrow.

But Minow said it didn't matter. Whatever was happening, the board had a "duty" to investigate, she insisted. Gifford said he'd consult with Gordon.

Board member Linda Griego had also heard that something about

Moonves was about to break. Gil Schwartz, too, had heard that Farrow was working on a big piece. One reporter told him Shari had all but handed Farrow what he needed. Schwartz told Moonves, who was eager to blame Shari.

Schwartz continued to aggressively defend his boss. When he learned a reporter had been making calls about the #MeToo rumors, he pre-emptively attacked, writing on January 24: "You guys are fucking despicable," and later: "All you're doing is flailing around and digging up worthless trash. It's pathetic. This is a human being you're dealing with. I hope in the craven rush to not be beaten you don't forget that you ostensibly have standards to publish. There have never been ANY settlements or complaints. No NDAs to find. Have some fucking ethics. Find a real story."

Meanwhile Dauer was keeping the heat on Moonves, reporting more calls from the media—even one from the *Times* to Phillips's husband's hair salon in Toronto.

"I feel sick all the time," Moonves texted Dauer.

The rumors came to a head at a special meeting of the nominating and governance committee that month. Shari couldn't believe CBS wasn't preparing for a potential public relations catastrophe for CBS and its leadership. Moreover, the renewed plan to merge CBS and Viacom assumed that Moonves would be chief executive of the new, much larger company. Anything that put Moonves's viability in question threatened the merger.

The committee agreed to enlist Michael Aiello, the lawyer for the independent directors, and the head of the corporate department at the large New York firm Weil, Gotshal & Manges. Aiello would investigate the rumors and report back.

Shari assumed her dealings with the committee were confidential. But that wasn't explicit, and Gifford and Gordon shared everything with Moonves in a flurry of emails and conversations.

In response, Moonves alerted them "at a high level" that there were "decades-old incidents that were consensual, but that women might point to," which he wasn't comfortable discussing. Gifford and Gordon assured Moonves that they didn't need or want to hear the details themselves but advised him to tell Aiello everything.

Faced with the prospect of a formal board interview, Moonves hired Dan Petrocelli, who gained national fame after successfully representing the father of O. J. Simpson victim Ron Goldman. He also called on Ron Olson, one of Los Angeles's most prominent trial lawyers and a longtime lawyer for Moonves who had negotiated his lucrative contracts.

Aiello interviewed Moonves on January 16—the first time he'd been formally questioned about any #MeToo allegations. Aiello and Olson both took notes. Other lawyers from Weil Gotshal also listened to the call.

"If there are any stories out there, we need to know," Aiello began.

Moonves said there were two instances of possible concern, both now decades in the past, long before his employment by CBS.

In the first incident, a young actress had come in for a meeting when he was at Warner Bros. He didn't know her. He said he had exposed himself and she "ran out of room," according to a lawyer's notes of the interview. "Victim didn't say anything," Aiello wrote, meaning she hadn't complained.

"Let me take a step back," Aiello said. "What does 'exposed' mean?"

This time Moonves said they'd engaged in oral sex and that it was consensual. Afterward he heard from her manager that the actress was "upset." *The New York Times* had been making calls, and there was "buzz" about what had happened. "Friends were saying she wasn't happy about it," Aiello noted. Moonves hadn't spoken to the actress herself, although he knew her name. The actress "has never been heard from since" and has "shut down," according to another lawyer's notes of Moonves's comments.

There had been no threats of litigation, "no complaint ever made," and "no payments ever made either public or private," according to Aiello's notes.

This was obviously a description of Bobbie Phillips.

The second incident, Moonves said, involved a female television executive who had recently filed a police complaint against him for sexual assault. But the incident dated to the 1980s, and the statute of limitations had expired long ago, which would prevent any charges being filed. In any event, the sex had been consensual.

The highly abbreviated account was clearly about Golden-Gottlieb. Despite the gaping holes in Moonves's versions, Aiello was curiously uninquisitive. He didn't ask for the names of the women, even though Moonves had said he knew them. He didn't ask for the name of the actress's manager or any other witness who could corroborate Moonves's story. He didn't follow up on an obvious inconsistency: How could the actress have fled after Moonves "exposed" himself—but also stayed to have consensual oral sex?

Nothing in Aiello's notes suggests that Moonves volunteered anything about Dauer's requests for work for Phillips and other clients or any efforts Moonves was making to accommodate him.

———

The same day as the Aiello interview, Shari Redstone had lunch alone with Moonves at his office in Los Angeles. She laid out her long-term plans—CBS and Viacom would merge and then be in a stronger position to be acquired by another company. If necessary, National Amusements would give up its controlling interest once a deal was negotiated. As she'd said before, she didn't want to be a media mogul—she was looking forward to focusing on her family and her other ventures. Was Moonves on board?

He said he was.

Moonves, she said, was essential to the strategy. What were his future plans, given that he was nearing seventy?

Moonves told her he was looking forward to the "next stage" of life and would probably leave in two years' time. He said he understood she'd need to start thinking about a successor.

Shari also mentioned that some board changes would be necessary. After his offensive behavior toward her, Gifford was unacceptable. And she wanted to nominate Richard Parsons to the board. The grandson of a groundskeeper on the Rockefeller estate in Tarrytown, New York, the sixty-nine-year-old Parsons had retired as chief executive of Time Warner a decade earlier, served as chair of Citigroup for a few years, and then become a trusted adviser to many chief executives, as well as to Shari.

The choice of Parsons could hardly be faulted, but Gifford remained a sore spot with Moonves. Gifford was among his most loyal directors. An unusual provision in Moonves's contract provided that he could resign for "good reason" and collect an enormous golden parachute if a current or former chief executive of a rival company was nominated to the board. He pointed out that naming Parsons would trigger that option.

Finally, there was the delicate issue of the #MeToo rumors, now the subject of Aiello's investigation. Shari asked Moonves if there was any truth to them.

"Look me in the eyes," Moonves told Shari. "There is nothing there."

———

After the interview with Moonves that day, Aiello briefed Gifford and Gordon. He assured them he hadn't found anything they needed to be concerned about. He said nothing about any police report.

Aiello briefed the full committee on January 29, saying pretty much the same thing he'd told Gordon and Gifford: the board had nothing to worry about. Aiello said Moonves had brought up two incidents that were decades old, that occurred long before Moonves came to

CBS. Moonves may have been "clumsy" and made some "unwanted advances," but only before his marriage to Chen. Moonves was now happily married and by all accounts a model husband.

Minow asked for more detail about the two incidents. Aiello assured the committee members they "didn't want to know" and he "didn't want to go there," reflecting a squeamishness about discussing sex that seems to have pervaded the investigation. There was a brief discussion of whether CBS needed to beef up its human resources operation, but the consensus was that it was already adequate. When someone asked about the rumored *New Yorker* article, Aiello assured them that Schwartz was "monitoring it" and "had his finger on the pulse" but wasn't aware of anything concrete.

Minow questioned whether they'd done enough to get to the bottom of the rumors. Aiello assured her there was nothing left to investigate. (Further steps should have been obvious to anyone who'd watched an episode of *CSI*: interview the victims and get their version of the story, as well as potential witnesses. Aiello hasn't publicly explained why he didn't pursue anyone for corroboration, but he may have been concerned any inquiries would become public.)

Aiello cautioned the committee members to say nothing to other members of the CBS board, especially the nonindependent directors aligned with Shari. Given the suspicions about Shari, the committee members were afraid of leaks. In the current environment, news that the board had even looked into sexual allegations about Moonves could be devastating.

Shari subsequently asked Gordon what, if anything, Aiello had uncovered, but he told her only that Moonves had denied the allegations and so there was nothing to worry about. She was dubious. "Are you telling me a denial from Les is sufficient investigation that would pass legal review?" He insisted it was.

Shari went to Minow, who told her Aiello had said there was nothing more to investigate.

"Are you kidding me?" Shari replied. "I hope you got good legal advice," she said.

Gordon told Shari she could talk to Aiello herself if she wanted more information, but she didn't bother. She felt she'd get nowhere and had already done what she could.

That was basically the end of Aiello's investigation. The full board never got a briefing, and most seemed only too happy to rely on Aiello's conclusion and move on.

EPISODE 5

"This Is Insanity"

Despite her skepticism about Aiello's investigation, Shari, too, was happy to leave the Moonves rumors behind and concentrate on the merger. Two years earlier, she had believed it was Viacom that needed CBS to rescue it. But now she felt the tables had turned. Under Bakish's energetic leadership, she believed Viacom had a viable strategic plan. It had gone from virtually no digital presence to ambitious plans for its nascent streaming service. CBS, meanwhile, seemed stuck in a vanishing media world where all that mattered were Nielsen ratings. Its CBS All Access streaming platform seemed an afterthought.

On February 1, both CBS and Viacom announced they had appointed special committees of independent directors to "evaluate a potential combination." As before, Shari and her nonindependent board allies were excluded, though there was no doubt about what they wanted. National Amusements, the Redstone-owned controlling shareholder of both companies, issued a statement that a combination "has the potential to drive significant, long-term shareholder value."

A few days later Moonves and Shari showed their solidarity by sitting together in the CBS box at Super Bowl LII in Minneapolis, both cheering for Shari's Patriots over the Philadelphia Eagles, who nonetheless won, 41–33.

But the merger news was quickly overshadowed by renewed speculation about Moonves, as rumors intensified that the long-awaited

New Yorker story was about to drop. Even Dauer heard them, texting Moonves: "Have you heard of Ronan Farrow?"

The New Yorker typically came out on a Monday, with media copies circulating Sunday night. On Saturday, February 10, Klieger raised the issue with Shari: It seemed incredible that the topic of Moonves and a potential #MeToo problem hadn't even been mentioned to the full board. The concern wasn't so much whether any published allegations were true, but how would the board respond? Would the board put Moonves on leave? What statement would the board make? Klieger suggested he take up the issue with Bruce Gordon.

Shari texted Klieger: "I don't have a problem calling Bruce, but if I raise the issue they won't even speak to me or invite me to any meeting. What a waste of my time."

"This is a board responsibility and I have no qualms about raising the issue myself," Klieger responded. "It puts us in an awful position and creates massive exposure for the whole board."

Klieger scheduled a call with Gordon about a "sensitive matter" for Sunday morning. "This is insanity that we haven't met to consider this," he said. Gordon hardly seemed enthusiastic but conceded the board should meet by telephone later that day given *The New Yorker*'s publication schedule.

At 2:00 p.m. Klieger got a curt email from Gordon: "There will not be a board call today."

Klieger called him for an explanation. Gil Schwartz had found out that the much-anticipated *New Yorker* article wasn't about Moonves, Gordon said, so there was no need for any emergency meeting. The board could take the matter up in the regular course of business.

On February 16 Farrow's latest *New Yorker* exposé hit newsstands. Schwartz had been correct: the story had nothing to do with Moonves. It was about Donald Trump, his long-ago affair with the *Playboy* centerfold Karen McDougal, and her more recent dealings with the *National Enquirer*.

All the air went out of the Moonves rumors.

The reprieve did curiously little to buoy Moonves's spirits. He was still seething over his conviction that Shari was spreading rumors as part of a campaign to destroy him. He called Klieger to complain about it. Afterward Klieger texted Shari: "Just got a call from Les. He is genuinely concerned (paranoid) that you're behind the false rumors being spread against him and this is a less-than-direct way to get him out of the company. I assured him you were also upset about the rumors and had nothing to do with them. . . . I think he felt better after talking to me but is being worn down."

Shari and Moonves spoke later by phone. He was upset that Shari had gone to the nominating and governance committee about the rumors. Why hadn't she come to him with her concerns rather than raising them with a board committee? Why was she doing this to him?

Shari said it wasn't that she believed the allegations, but the board had to be prepared. Afterward she reported to Klieger that Moonves was "upset, but I think we're fine."

She also said it was obvious someone on the nominating and governance committee had leaked what she thought were confidential discussions to Moonves, likely either Gordon or Gifford.

"I actually think Bruce [Gordon] did me in," she wrote to Klieger. "Talk soon but I will never call anyone on the board again except you."

———

There was more good news for Moonves that month when the Los Angeles County district attorney declined to bring any charges with respect to Golden-Gottlieb because of the statute of limitations. That seemed to be the end of the police complaint, but Moonves knew he wasn't out of the woods yet—not with Dauer still nipping at his heels.

Dauer was finally getting some traction with CBS. Peter Golden, the head of casting, contacted Dauer to schedule an audition for

Phillips for a new CW crime drama series, *In the Dark*. LaRue read for a part on the CW series *Charmed*. And Moonves scheduled meetings with two more Dauer clients, Joshua Morrow and Philip Boyd.

Dauer reciprocated by offering Moonves one of his prized possessions: an autographed photo of Babe Ruth. "I'm pretty sure it will be in safekeeping with your family for a long time," he texted. "Let's get the Babe to you."

Moonves tried to beg off, but Dauer wouldn't take no for an answer—he said the photo was already off his wall and in his car, and Moonves should hang it in his office.

Moonves gave in.

Dauer even offered Moonves "a home on Catalina Island for two years free. If you are interested, I can do that." He added, "It's in a gated community."

Moonves ignored that.

Despite the promising auditions and readings, by late March none of Dauer's clients had landed a role at CBS, and Dauer was getting impatient. He texted Moonves to say Bobbie Phillips was nagging him, asking, "Is there anything at CBS?"

"Tell her I am looking," Moonves answered. "It's pilot time and most things are shooting. When series begin she will get some guest star jobs and hopefully it gets bigger from there. Ok?"

Dauer reminded him that he'd been struggling financially because his clients' submissions were getting blocked, and he'd nearly lost his house to foreclosure.

"That sucks," Moonves replied (on March 27, 2018). "About your clients. I will try to help. Let's set your guys up with Peter [Golden] and team. You need to make some money."

Moonves left the next week for Augusta, Georgia, and the Masters golf tournament, which aired live on CBS. Dauer texted him an emoji of a putting green.

———

A mid their rising tensions, Shari and Moonves met again that month to discuss the merger negotiations. The issue of control loomed large: Moonves said he wanted "his team" to manage the combined companies and he wanted "his people" on the board—specifically his allies Gordon, Cohen, Countryman, and Gifford. Gifford, of course, was a red flag. Shari agreed to the other three, but not him.

That still left open the question of Bakish. Moonves asked if she was going to insist that Bakish be his second-in-command or be named his successor.

Shari said no, she just wanted a "meaningful role" for Bakish that would be enough to "entice him to stay."

That wasn't what Moonves was hoping to hear, but he nonetheless agreed that he wanted "peace" with Shari and they should be "frank" with each other rather than fight publicly.

Shari came away reassured that her relationship with Moonves—and the merger—was back on track.

On March 29 CBS submitted to the Viacom board its long-awaited bid to acquire Viacom, an all-stock offer that valued Viacom at about $1 billion less than its then-market value of $12.5 billion. Nearly all takeover bids are made at a premium to the current market price, and usually a substantial one. But CBS could argue that Viacom's value had been artificially and unrealistically inflated by speculation that CBS would buy it.

The offer was also contingent on Moonves and his number two, Ianniello, running the merged companies as chief executive and president.

Dauer quickly picked up on the news. With Moonves in charge of Paramount and Viacom's cable channels, there might be even more opportunities for his clients, even in feature films. He texted Moonves, "Congratulations on the Viacom 'deal,'" and added, a week later, "Got a text from Bobbie saying congrats to you re: Viacom. I'm also congratulating you."

Moonves cautioned, "Viacom is far from being done. But thank her. And thank you."

The deal was, indeed, far from being done. Shari had told Moonves she wouldn't insist that Bakish be his successor, but neither he nor anyone else at CBS had consulted her about naming Ianniello president. In her view, Ianniello may have been a competent chief operating or chief financial officer, but he had no creativity, no vision, and no business running CBS, let alone the combined companies. She felt she'd been blindsided once again.

The issue of Bakish was put in stark relief the next week when Viacom's board said it wanted $14.7 billion. Bakish—not Ianniello—would be the combined companies' president and chief operating officer and Moonves's designated successor.

For Moonves, replacing his trusted ally Ianniello with Bakish, whom he saw as little more than a puppet being manipulated by Shari, was a nonstarter. Not only that, but under Ianniello's contract, if Ianniello was not named as Moonves's successor as chief executive, or if someone else was named president, Ianniello could resign "for good reason" and receive an enormous payout and benefits. Moonves had a similar contract that all but locked him in as chief executive.

The contracts had been negotiated by the CBS board's compensation committee, which included Gordon and Gifford, who defended them as necessary to ensure continuity in management. But recent board members—Klieger and Minow included—were shocked to discover that it was only the directors of the compensation committee who had weighed in and negotiated the "good reason" provisions in Moonves's and Ianniello's contracts. Though committee members said the contracts were disclosed to the full board at the time they were signed, Shari didn't recall being briefed about any such provisions. But the payout in the event Ianniello was not named as Moonves's successor was so enormous that it all but decided who the next chief executive would be—usually the most important responsibility exercised by the full board. Nor was that all.

On March 29, Anthony Ambrosio, the head of human relations for CBS, had sent a proposed term sheet for Moonves's new employment agreement to Moonves's lawyer for review. This agreement included a significant change from his previous ones regarding termination for "cause." This issue was critically important, because if CBS fired Moonves for "cause" pursuant to his contract, it wouldn't have to pay him over $100 million in severance and other benefits.

In high-level executive contracts like Moonves's, *cause* is a term of art with only a tenuous connection to its commonsense meaning. Not showing up for work, for example, wouldn't constitute "cause" for firing him. In Moonves's prior agreements, "cause" had been limited to "your willful malfeasance having a material adverse effect on the company." But the new contract further limited "malfeasance" by adding the words "during the employment defined term." In practical terms, that meant if Moonves committed any malfeasance before the start of the new contract, no matter what it was, he couldn't be terminated for cause.

That included any instance of sexual assault—misconduct serious enough to qualify as malfeasance. Ross Zimmerman, a compensation consultant hired to advise the board, spotted the change. He warned Bruce Gordon in a "heads-up" email in April that Moonves couldn't be fired for cause for anything he'd done before the beginning of the new contract, which was to take effect when the merger was consummated. "It struck me in these days of #MeToo this limitation could be an issue. In a worst case scenario, if embarrassing things came out," Zimmerman continued, "it could be controversial to exempt these."

That Ambrosio, CBS's head of human resources, who reported to Moonves, was trying to change the new contract to Moonves's advantage at the very time rumors of sexual harassment issues were swirling should have been an obvious red flag. But when the term sheet for Moonves's new contract was circulated to other board members, the revised definition of *cause* remained intact.

———

April 28, 2018, was Dauer's seventy-fifth birthday, and he'd planned the biggest blowout he could muster given his now-constrained financial resources. Prior to this, he'd reserved big parties for decade milestones like the last one, when he turned seventy. But at this point Dauer didn't know how many more years he had left. He didn't want to wait until he turned eighty. Thanks to his new relationship with Moonves, this party promised to be his best ever.

After Dauer badgered Moonves for weeks, Moonves texted Dauer on April 10 to say he and his wife would be "honored" to attend. In the Hollywood social firmament, the presence of Moonves at Dauer's party was of incalculable value. With Moonves there, Dauer could get any casting director he wanted to show up. His clients would be bowled over. The message would be clear: after his recent years of struggle, Dauer was back on top of his game.

Until the last minute Dauer worried that Moonves might not show up, and he fretted over every detail. He hadn't planned on assigned seating, but with Moonves expected, he set up a VIP table for Moonves and his wife, along with the biggest celebrities or near celebrities he could muster. The headliners were the actor James Woods; former Minnesota senator Norman Coleman; and Bruce McNall, the former movie producer (*Weekend at Bernie's*) and Los Angeles Kings owner who had served jail time for fraud. Dauer had kept up a friendly correspondence with McNall during his thirteen months in prison, and McNall and his ex-wife were hosting the party for Dauer at their sprawling home in Tarzana.

Dauer had even thought through the parking. He instructed Moonves: "When you get to the valet tell him that Marv Dauer said you are a

VIP so your car will be parked very close and you can get out of there." (Dauer didn't seem to mind that Moonves had double-booked that night, and he and his wife were headed to another party after dropping in on Dauer's.)

Moonves and Julie Chen made their entrance at about 8:00 p.m. Moonves brought Dauer a gift—a green-and-yellow Augusta National tie from the Masters tournament he'd recently attended. Moonves chatted with Eva LaRue. "It's been way too long since you've worked for CBS," he said.

There were over a hundred guests, including a contingent of Dauer's elementary-school classmates from Minnesota, a handful of professional hockey players, and an impressive array of casting agents. Woods delivered a funny tribute, steering clear of the right-wing politics he'd embraced. One of Dauer's ex-girlfriends, the stylish jazz singer Jan Daley, performed a medley of "Memories" and "Will You Still Love Me Tomorrow." LaRue, who'd gotten her start in show business as a singer in commercial jingles, delivered a rendition of the plaintive Shirley Horn ballad "Here's to Life." LaRue added, "When Marv wants something, he really does not give up, whether it's that cute twenty-year-old or that new career he pursued so many years ago to become an amazing manager."

Dauer texted Moonves the next day. "Last night (for me) was truly monumental—it could not have been any better—to be surrounded by friends from first grade—Hall of Fame hockey players—ex girlfriends—studio executives—actors. Etc etc.," Dauer wrote. "It was great to finally meet Julie—Thank you again so much for attending—I don't know if there's any way to express how grateful I am."

As for the tie, "The next time I see you I promise I will wear it—that's so cool—now if I can putt. !!"

Moonves was similarly effusive.

"What a great night last night. I sent a long text but I don't know if it went through. Anyway, we had a ball. Sorry we couldn't stay much longer. Eva was moving. Jimmy was his usual brilliant and funny self and Jan was a terrific singer. But the spirit of the party was phenomenal. There are a lot of people who love you. You should feel really good today. I am glad I was part of it."

Two days later, Dauer wrote to Moonves, "I just spoke to Eva and she is very excited—that you would like her back working on your network! After they announce the new pilots I will start looking for things and bother you."

"I will help," Moonves promised.

EPISODE 6

"Pencils Down"

Since failing to persuade Kopelson to come forward about Moonves, Dr. Anne Peters had been trying to figure out a way to disclose the incident on her own without violating any doctor-patient privilege. On May 1, she published an essay in the *Annals of Internal Medicine*: "I am a bit different from the others who have come forward in the #MeToo movement because, as a physician, I am legally unable to name the patient who harassed me," Peters began.

After describing her harrowing encounter with the unnamed patient, she wrote, "I had no idea what to do. I felt ashamed, I hadn't screamed—I was supposed to be offering 'extra-special' service to this man because he was rich and powerful and good for my institution (a place I no longer work)."

The next day, Peters continued, "the patient called and apologized. He said that he had a terrible problem and that he had done the same thing with many other women. That he basically couldn't control himself when alone with a woman. I told him that he needed to get counseling immediately and to never allow himself to be alone with a woman in a room."

Peters said she never heard from him again, but "he has become ever more powerful and venerated in his professional world."

The essay in the specialized medical journal went unnoticed by anyone at CBS or Viacom.

———

The CBS board's special committee deliberations on the proposed merger with Viacom were not going well, at least from Shari Redstone's point of view. The last time a Viacom merger had been mooted, the committee had never made any serious attempt to assess it, so hostile were Moonves's allies to the idea, or so Shari believed. This time, with Minow and Griego on the committee counterbalancing some of the old guard, the committee had heard from several investment banks and weighed the advantages and disadvantages. The committee met many times—eventually it held more than thirty meetings.

Shari fervently believed Bakish was turning Viacom around, but to the CBS committee, the results didn't show it. She kept pleading for more time. The committee believed Viacom was a hopelessly failing company, but it agreed with Shari that size mattered, and that CBS could benefit from adding Paramount and at least a few of Viacom's cable channels, as long as it didn't overpay. But this time price wasn't the major obstacle.

The issue was control. Bakish had said he had no problem working for Moonves. He'd known him for years and respected what he'd achieved. But what role would Bakish (and by extension Shari) have in the combined company? From Moonves's point of view, there was only one acceptable answer: none. Moonves didn't need Klieger to tell him that Bakish had warmly welcomed Shari into his inner circle at Viacom, a prospect that appalled Moonves. Moonves wanted to get along with Shari and keep her happy. He was willing to have dinner with her periodically and keep her informed. But that didn't extend to consulting her. Far from heeding Klieger's advice to consult with her, Moonves had pushed her even further to the margins, as the proposal to make Ianniello president and his designated successor had made all too clear. At one point Moonves implored Minow to "help me here. Shari is driving me crazy."

There seems to have been curiously little consideration by any of the factions of the possibility that Moonves might simply retire. After all, he was sixty-eight years old, youthful compared with Sumner, perhaps, but a respectable age at which to step down. He'd be going out at the apex of his career with a sterling reputation, young enough to embark on another chapter, as a producer, perhaps. His retirement was discussed, at least briefly, but Moonves insisted his job as chief executive wasn't finished, especially since he was shepherding CBS into the streaming era. In a few years Moonves would be willing to step down, one reason the issue of succession was so important.

From the board's point of view, a CBS without Moonves seemed unthinkable. Despite having locked in Ianniello as his successor, most directors didn't believe Ianniello was qualified. Shari and her allies recognized that the merger would cause enough turmoil without trying to change chief executives at the same time. Wall Street loved Moonves. Any hint he might leave could send the stock plunging.

As for Moonves himself, retiring would largely eliminate the #MeToo threat, as he'd suggested to Dauer. Few publications would be interested in decades-old allegations about someone no longer in power. In any event, the *New Yorker* article had come and gone.

Then there were the lavish trappings that went with his status as CBS chief executive—above and beyond the hundreds of millions in compensation he'd earned. It fell to Schwartz to make sure Moonves was treated like royalty. In foreign capitals like Paris, one of Schwartz's staff lavishly tipped hotel concierges and restaurant maître d's, showing them Moonves's photo in advance of his arrival to guarantee a warm welcome and ensure Moonves was treated like a VIP. As the chief executive's wife and a television star in her own right, Chen had access to the company plane and a retinue of hairdressers, makeup artists, stylists, and assistants who accompanied her, all paid for by CBS.

———

The special committees of both CBS and Viacom thought they'd reached a "handshake agreement" on the financial terms of a deal. But with Moonves and Shari at loggerheads over the future roles of Bakish and Gifford, the deal seemed in peril. So Shari called on Parsons, who had a famously genial personality and an ability to negotiate. She and Parsons met with Moonves and Bruce Gordon on May 1 at Moonves's sprawling Park Avenue apartment to propose a compromise: Bakish wouldn't be part of the management team and would instead join the board.

Moonves complained that Shari "likes Bakish more than me."

On the contrary, Shari insisted—she was much closer to Moonves on a personal level. She reminded him that on a recent trip to Los Angeles, she had joined Moonves and Julie Chen for dinner at La Dolce Vita in Beverly Hills, Moonves's favorite restaurant. They had had a great time laughing and talking. The next day Moonves had called Shari to say it was the best dinner they'd ever had. "Julie loves you," he'd said. "It was so nice."

Moonves also lamented that Shari didn't like Ianniello. Shari said she "barely knew him" and thought he was a great chief operating officer. But she didn't think he was cut out to be chief executive.

On the issue of Gifford, Shari wasn't backing down. She felt his exit from the board could be handled "privately and discreetly," but he had to go.

The bottom line was Shari wanted Moonves, not Bakish, to run the company. She wanted Moonves to be happy. "I want your enthusiastic support, not just your support" for the merger, she told him. "I won't do the deal if you don't want to."

Moonves assured her he was on board.

Shari thought the meeting had gone incredibly well. Despite feverish speculation among CBS board members that she was plotting to replace them, she was in a conciliatory frame of mind. Much as she believed in the merits of a CBS-Viacom merger, she wasn't looking for a debilitating fight. Moonves was more important to her than the merger.

Moonves and Gordon didn't make any commitments at the meeting but said they'd get back to Shari and Parsons. But a few days later Gordon informed Parsons that the CBS board had decided to go "pencils down" on the merger for the time being—i.e., to table further discussions—due to the following week's busy schedule, which included the CBS annual meeting on May 17.

Moonves had no intention of allowing Bakish to join the board or Gifford to be removed. As he texted Ianniello on May 11, "Remember her father always said you can never give up your control. She will literally [do anything] to keep that. That was his first rule."

———

The first Martha Minow heard about the tactic that came to be known as the "nuclear option" was when Martin Lipton and a retinue of lawyers from his firm, Wachtell, Lipton, Rosen & Katz, briefed the CBS special committee considering the Viacom merger.

Initially floated years earlier, Lipton's proposal for a special dividend had since been refined to accommodate the extraordinary circumstance that CBS now found itself in: the majority independent directors had turned against Shari, the de facto controlling shareholder who had put them in their positions as directors (and could still remove them at any time). Lipton's bold, potentially precedent-setting plan could well be the capstone of what was, for Lipton, already a legendary career as a corporate lawyer and strategist.

The plan was brilliant in its simplicity. Under the dual classes of stock at CBS (and Viacom), National Amusements—firmly controlled by the Redstones—owned class B shares, which represented just 10 percent of the value of the company but had 80 percent of the voting power. Other shareholders owned class A shares giving them roughly 20 percent of the votes. Most stock dividends consist of money. But Lipton's proposed dividend, which was explicitly authorized by the CBS charter, would be additional votes—enough to give class A shareholders roughly 83 percent of the total, reducing National Amusements to a 17 percent voting share. The move, if successful, would strip the Redstone family of its voting control.

Minow, for one, initially thought the idea was preposterous. Investors paid enormous premiums for control of a corporation. How could a board simply vote that away without compensation? And how would the dividend pass muster with the Delaware courts? CBS would need immediate help from the court system; otherwise the Redstones would just fire the directors and replace them—as they'd already done at Viacom.

But Moonves, without being explicit, had made it clear that he'd quit if Bakish gained a foothold in management or on the board. If that happened, the stock would likely plunge and chaos would ensue. That was indisputably not in the interest of CBS shareholders, and the directors had a duty to act in their interests, not Shari Redstone's. If that meant the nuclear option, so be it.

The independent board members were sworn to secrecy—there could obviously be no hint of this line of thinking to Shari and her allies. Klieger reached out to Gordon on May 11 to see if he'd made any progress getting Gifford to step down.

Gordon responded that he thought it would be a mistake to make any board changes while a merger was being discussed.

Had Gordon even brought up the resignation issue with Gifford? Klieger asked.

"I don't want to even think about that conversation," Gordon said. He bristled at the idea that Shari had the right to purge a board member. That should be a decision for the entire board.

Klieger concluded Gordon had no intention of replacing his longtime boardroom ally. Klieger said he'd talk to Shari but that she wouldn't be "comfortable" with the idea of keeping Gifford.

He and Gordon scheduled a follow-up call for Monday.

———

To the CBS special committee Moonves had initially portrayed unwavering confidence in the plan to dilute the Redstones' voting control. But now he vacillated. On May 11, the same day he texted Ianniello about the importance of control, he revealed a far different and more troubled state of mind to his longtime confidant and spokesman Gil Schwartz.

"I am not up for this," Moonves texted. "I know I had no choice. No options. But this will be more hell."

"You have the support and admiration of everyone," Schwartz assured him. "Uneasy lies the head that wears the crown," he added, quoting from Shakespeare's *Henry IV, Part 2*. "But you wear it very well."

Of course, Moonves knew what Schwartz did not—the persistent Dauer was a constant reminder.

"Admiration doesn't make me sleep better when there will be mortal enemies trying to destroy me," Moonves replied. Sinking further into despair, he added, "This will be torture. Every way was torture. I feel bad. I would have felt bad every other way too."

Schwartz worried about Moonves's mental state. "You're all alone there? Drinking and getting yourself into a blue funk."

Moonves admitted he was indeed drinking. "Scared of the attacks coming my way. I really want peace," he texted.

Moonves turned to the subject of Shari Redstone. "She can't get along with anybody," he maintained. "Always in court." He worried she "will come after me."

An hour later he added, "This is going to be hell."

"All Out War"

Schwartz wasn't the only member of Moonves's inner circle worried about his state of mind. "How you holding up?" Ianniello texted Moonves the next day, May 12. "We really don't have a choice and if we lose, we are leaving anyway. She caused this, not us."

Moonves wasn't feeling any better. "I feel like shit," he said. "I know she caused this. But it will be all out war."

Moonves described Shari as a "crazy person" and warned, "You are taking away her whole life."

"Viacom is her life," Ianniello countered. "She has nothing to do with our company. BTW—for her troubles we will make her an extra billion. She still has a toy in Viacom. [She] has her board and her guy to run it."

Though he was not a member of the special committee, Moonves's allies kept him informed every step of the way, and vice versa. The next day, on Sunday, May 13, Moonves wrote to Gordon: "This is NUCLEAR. The last meeting we had with them was not." He realized there would be no turning back. "After filing there can't be a deal." Referring to Shari: "She won't be manageable."

"She's not manageable now," Gordon responded.

Moonves hinted again at the unspoken threat from his past.

"She's going to bring up reasons why she mentioned firing me."

Ten minutes later, Moonves reversed course yet again, texting

Schwartz, "I can't do this. I do not want to file. It will be a public war for 6 months. I am not emotionally prepared for this. I would rather leave. Sorry."

Schwartz said only, "I get it."

Moonves conveyed his decision to Gordon. "Sorry Bruce. I'm not in for filing. We should try one more time to negotiate. I am out. Can't do this. Will be a horrible fight."

It fell to Gordon to coax Moonves back on board. He wasn't entirely surprised that Moonves was wavering. He knew Moonves didn't like conflict and was worried about what Shari and her PR advisers would dredge up about him (though it never crossed his mind those worries might involve #MeToo allegations). But Gordon felt his duty was to shareholders, not to make life easier for Moonves. And he was convinced a merger was not in the interest of CBS shareholders.

The board convened by phone that day to consider the special dividend and the attack on the Redstone family. With the meeting in progress, Gordon texted Moonves: "I really don't think you want to do this. You are destroying your credibility."

"I am not ready for the fight," Moonves replied. "I can't do it. 6 months of attacks. No."

"You will lose the board, your exec team, your employees and the market," Gordon countered. "You are worried about your reputation. This will ruin it." He added, "Chad [Gifford] will leave. Others will follow. Then what?"

Gordon continued. "You are making a huge mistake that you will regret. Are you going to call in and tell the group on the call of your decision? How do you expect this call to end?"

Moonves didn't immediately answer. Seven minutes later, Gordon took another tack.

"I feel I am not helping you deal with this. What can I do?"

"Nothing," Moonves responded. He agonized that if he supported the vote to dilute the Redstones and the ensuing lawsuit, Shari would attack him with all the ammunition she could muster. If he didn't, he'd lose the support of Gordon, Gifford, and other directors loyal to him.

"I am sick either way," Moonves added. "I have never felt worse." He continued, "A public spectacle." Shari "wants to run it. Let's let her."

Other members of the committee were well aware of Moonves's vacillations. In various conversations he'd reversed himself or given inconsistent answers when asked if he supported the decision to reject the merger and unleash the lawsuits to strip Shari of control. The committee had now resolved to go through with the nuclear option, but with a formal vote at hand, its members wanted to hear directly from Moonves. They wanted to go forward only with Moonves's full support.

Minutes later Gordon texted Moonves that it was time for him to join the board call.

"I think we will add you on momentarily. You ready?"

Somehow Gordon had talked him back from the brink. Moonves had done another about-face and was ready to go ahead.

"Less is more," Gordon advised him. "Leave us the flexibility to work details this week."

"Headline news," Moonves responded.

Moonves joined the board call in progress just after 3:00 p.m. He said the committee had his full support in its decision to block the merger and sue National Amusements. He was terse, and some board members could tell he was anguished. He showed no energy or enthusiasm. But he said he could see no other path forward. There was no way he could work with Shari.

The committee essentially had to choose between Shari and Moonves and believed Moonves to be essential to the health of the enterprise. It voted unanimously that a merger with Viacom was not in the interest of CBS shareholders except for National Amusements and the Redstones.

The committee could have stopped there, made its vote public, and let Shari and her lawyers take the next step. But, convinced that Shari would move swiftly to change the bylaws and replace them with directors who'd support a merger, the committee voted unanimously to file suit in Delaware the next day for a restraining order to prevent the Redstones from exercising their controlling power, and to convene a full board meeting later that week to vote on the special dividend to permanently dilute their voting power.

After the vote, Gordon checked in with Moonves.

"You ok?"

"Yes," Moonves answered. It was only about 5:40 p.m., but he was already drinking again. "On my third vodka and second egg roll. Go time."

"Hope you felt the commitment and support. 10 for 10," Gordon wrote, referring to the unanimous vote.

"I did. The ladies seemed nervous," Moonves observed, referring to Minow and Griego.

Moonves sounded far less confident when he wrote to Schwartz. "I'm back to doing it," he reported. "If we don't Chad gets fired. 3 people quit and we lose the company. it will be over. I am at great personal risk here."

"I know that," Schwartz replied. "I'm with you. We all are."

Ianniello was just as loyal and supportive: "I have your back to the end!" he texted.

"Well, I'm counting on you to stop me from dying here," Moonves replied.

"We are stronger together," Ianniello assured him. "Everyone feels the same way. We have no choice. There are only worse alternatives."

Moonves was still worrying about Shari. "She will come after me big time. I know you have my back!!! She threw us under the bus when not under pressure. Now??? Wow . . . She will be enraged."

An hour and a half later, Moonves threw down the gauntlet.

"Mattresses tomorrow am," he texted Ianniello. "And take the gun. We need it."

"We won't forget the cannoli too!" Ianniello answered.

In another *Godfather* reference, Moonves wrote to Schwartz: "Buckle up. Mattresses tomorrow."

By now Moonves must have been far beyond his third vodka of the evening. In his last text of the day, to Schwartz at 10:36 p.m., he was all but incoherent: "We need to lay their clowns think early on we are no hardship Barr no and will ill them handcuffs off. If they want to bring it n watch out. We will decimate. Old Sara we haven't done any-thing but party with you. Now we will kill Scarw her big. All of them scare them. I am going to prevent this public bulls hit rightbaway. And let's go after them head on NOW."

————

The next morning, May 14, Shari Redstone was at her apartment high in the tower of the Pierre Hotel in New York. Central Park sprawled outside her windows, its landscape now a vivid green with spring foliage.

At 9:30 a.m. she received an email saying that there would be a special CBS board meeting that Thursday. That was the first Shari had heard about any special board meeting.

She called one of her lawyers, Christopher Austin at Cleary Gott-lieb Steen & Hamilton in New York.

"What's this about a board meeting?"

"I'm afraid it's worse than that," Austin replied. "You've been sued. In Delaware."

"What?"

Austin outlined the claims: Shari was plotting to replace the CBS directors. She'd violated her duty to shareholders. Her fellow board members wanted to strip her, her father, and her family of their con-trol. As she saw it, they wanted to steal the company her father had built.

Shari wandered through the apartment in a daze. Her feelings were a potent mix of shock, hurt, and betrayal. She'd just decided to drop the merger idea if Moonves didn't support it. For all their difficulties, she and Moonves were friends. At least that's what she'd thought.

The phone rang. It was Shari's daughter, Kimberlee. "Are you okay?"

She was not.

In Los Angeles it was just after 6:30 a.m., so Shari texted Rob Klieger:

"I've been sued in Delaware. Call me. They've declared war. They made up facts. . . . I'm shaking, shaking, shaking. . . . I'm in shock literally."

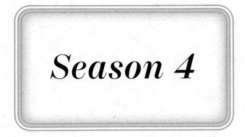

Season 4

A "Blatant Abuse of Power"

As Moonves had predicted, the CBS lawsuit to strip the Redstones of voting control was headline news, with many references to CBS having triggered a "nuclear option."

The CBS complaint couched the suit in noble terms of shareholder democracy rather than a clash of wills between Moonves and his board allies and Shari and hers. CBS argued that it held itself out to investors as a company managed by independent directors despite being controlled by the Redstones. CBS cited several ways Shari had undermined that premise: she'd put her own personal lawyer (Klieger) on the board; she'd talked about potential replacements for Moonves without board authority and had "disparaged" Ianniello; she'd rebuffed an overture from another company (Verizon) without even telling the board; and she was plotting to replace board members who didn't support the proposed merger with Viacom.

In a statement, National Amusements called the allegations "outrageous" and stressed that National Amusements "had absolutely no intention of replacing the CBS board or forcing a deal that was not supported by both companies. NAI's conduct throughout supports this, and reflects its commitment to a well-governed process."

Shari asked Klieger to break the news of the lawsuit to her father in person. She didn't want to tell him over the phone—it was too complicated and potentially too upsetting. When Klieger told him, Sumner was predictably livid. First Dauman, now Moonves had turned against him. But he took the news in stride. Litigation was in his DNA. This was a fight he expected to win.

Needless to say, Klieger's scheduled call with Gordon to resolve Gifford's fate never happened. Klieger was shocked that Gordon had made the argument that Gifford shouldn't be replaced during merger negotiations, when he knew the committee had already decided to reject it and file the suit. As for the further step to dilute the controlling shareholder, Klieger still couldn't believe his fellow board members had embraced such a drastic action, especially since Shari had no intention of trying to force through a merger.

It was probably a long shot, but maybe they could get the board to see reason and withdraw the suit. So he called Griego and Minow—the two independent directors he didn't consider to be part of the Moonves inner circle.

Griego was in London, so he ended up speaking only to Minow. "This is ridiculous," Klieger said. Shari "isn't doing anything, and even if she was, this isn't the answer." Minow said little but suggested further talks.

A larger group including Gordon convened by phone the next day. Gordon's mantra was that the directors were simply acting in accord with their fiduciary duties to shareholders other than Shari. There didn't seem to be anything else to discuss.

"Are you having fun?" Shari texted Klieger later that evening. "Anything productive?"

"That was a long ass call and a waste of time," he answered.

Klieger wondered if the real issue wasn't the proposed merger at all but Shari's effort to remove Gifford.

Texts and emails suggest Gifford was, indeed, a critical element.

"Without Chad [Gifford] we lose N and G," Moonves texted Ianniello that same day, referring to the all-important nominating and governance committee. "Then we will be dead."

"We can't cave on this piece," Ianniello responded.

"No way," Moonves affirmed.

Gordon, too, weighed in that morning, urging Moonves, "Call Chad. He's taking one for the team. He'd appreciate your support."

Moonves did call Gifford and reported back: "Just spoke to Chad. I think he felt better."

But by late that evening, Moonves's confidence had faded. "I still feel like shit," he texted his confidant Gil Schwartz. "I don't like conflict. Especially with people like these." Shari "wants to run the company. Period. End of story."

"Yup," Schwartz agreed.

A "blatant abuse of power," Moonves went on, seeming to make the case to himself, "at the expense of employees and shareholders."

Several hours later Schwartz urged Moonves to "sleep well." Schwartz's next texts suggest he knew more than he had let on about the real reasons for Moonves's anguish: there was "nothing we were worried about" in Shari's legal filings, which were "tedious. Nothing personal about you."

———

With talks aborted, Shari unleashed Austin and a team of lawyers from Cleary Gottlieb. They'd been in the background representing National Amusements since 2015, when the Redstones had replaced the Viacom directors. Austin and his colleagues were as surprised by the lawsuit as she was. They worked all night on a counterattack. Shari's "instructions to us were clear," said partner Victor Hou. National Amusements "did not start this war, but we are going to finish it."

To that end, National Amusements quickly took the same step it had taken to secure control of Viacom: its Redstone-dominated directors changed the CBS bylaws to require a 90 percent majority vote of the CBS board to issue a dividend. With fourteen board members, any two—Shari and Klieger, for example—could effectively veto the proposed dividend to dilute Redstone control scheduled to be voted on Thursday.

With the two sides at an impasse, the Delaware court hearing began, and at 4:00 p.m. Chancellor Andre Bouchard issued a ruling. "I've never seen anything quite like what transpired here," he said, before granting CBS's request for a temporary restraining order while he considered the merits. He promised a definitive ruling the next day.

It was a round-one victory for the CBS board.

———

Minutes after Bouchard issued his decision, the curtain rose at New York's Carnegie Hall for CBS's annual "upfront" presentation for advertisers, in which the network introduced its 2018 fall season—including a revived *Murphy Brown* with Candice Bergen and a new drama from *Law & Order* producer Dick Wolf. The upfronts were in many ways a throwback to the golden age of network television. Moonves had always choreographed them down to the smallest details.

With CBS director Bruce Gordon in the audience, the actor John Malkovich took center stage. His opening monologue was interrupted by a phone call in which the audience heard the disembodied voice of Moonves.

"Did you read the script?" Malkovich asked him.

"I've been reading that shit for twenty years. Now it's your turn," Moonves responded, metaphorically suggesting this might be his last upfront appearance. Everyone in the room knew what was happening in Delaware.

"Do you really expect me to say this crap?" Malkovich asked.

"John, please don't be a pain in the ass this time," Moonves begged.

"Fucking executive," Malkovich said under his breath as he hung up.

"Fucking talent," Moonves muttered in return.

Then Moonves made his entrance, triggering wild applause.

"So, how's your week been?" Moonves began, breaking the tension. A wave of laughter turned into a roar of applause and then a standing ovation—something never before witnessed at an upfront.

"For years I told you I'm only out here for a few minutes," Moonves said when the audience members took their seats. "And this year, perhaps for the first time, I actually mean it," he continued—another not-so-veiled reference to what might be his imminent departure.

Still, being onstage and soaking in the applause seemed to have buoyed Moonves's spirits. That evening he texted Gordon, "Enjoy the show? A good day for us."

"Show was great!" Gordon responded. "Specially the warm reception you received. It was a very good day. Let's see what tomorrow bring[s]. Starting to imagine what dinner might be." (He added various emojis including a wineglass.)

"Hope you are feeling good about your decision to move forward. The court of public opinion is cheering for you."

"Definitely we made the right call. You were my strength when I needed you. I will never forget that," Moonves said.

"That's what friends are for," Gordon responded.

CBS's court victory was short-lived. On Thursday morning Chancellor Bouchard denied its request for a restraining order against National Amusements, in theory leaving Shari and National Amusements free to make the bylaw change and to pursue other actions, like removing directors. But it was hardly a vindication for National Amusements. The chancellor ruled that CBS had made a "colorable claim" that Shari and National Amusements had breached their fiduciary duty to other CBS shareholders. But he found no "irreparable harm" (the threshold for a temporary restraining order) in letting events take their course, given that the court could later invalidate any bylaw change and, should Shari remove any directors for reasons the court deemed improper, the court could reverse those actions. So the court saw no need for any immediate order limiting what National Amusements could do.

The decision set the stage for that afternoon's board meeting, and for what would likely be years of litigation.

Late that afternoon, Shari, Klieger, and their lawyers from Cleary Gottlieb met at the bar of the Hilton Hotel in midtown Manhattan and then got into Lincoln Town Cars for the short trip to Black Rock. Traffic was terrible; at one point Shari worried that they'd be late for the crucial board meeting and the vote might be taken without them. As it was, they were the last to arrive: the other board members had already gathered in a large CBS conference room, with three—William Cohen, Leonard Goldberg, and Arnold Kopelson—participating by phone.

Ianniello and Schwartz were there from Moonves's inner circle on the management team. The room was also packed with lawyers: Weil Gotshal's Aiello, representing the special committee; Austin and a team from Cleary Gottlieb, representing Shari and National Amusements; even the venerable Marty Lipton himself, representing CBS. All told there were twelve outside lawyers crowded in, as well as Lawrence Tu, the CBS general counsel.

Conspicuously absent, even by phone, was the actual controlling shareholder himself: Sumner. He was no longer a board member and in any event was in no condition to participate. But there could be no doubt where Sumner stood on the one item on the agenda: the dividend to dilute the Redstones' voting power.

Moonves called the meeting to order just after 5:00 p.m. After a few preliminaries Gordon began by saying the committee was "disappointed" to be in this awkward position, which was "not what they set out to do," according to minutes of the meeting. But having concluded that the Viacom merger was "not in the best interest of all stockholders," he said it had recommended the special dividend because the committee was "concerned" about how National Amusements might react given its "past actions," a clear reference to what had happened at Viacom. He also cited the committee's belief that Shari had "engaged in conversations" with potential replacements for Moonves and that "at least one potential bidder had been discouraged" by Shari from making an offer for CBS, a reference to Verizon. There was a "very real threat" that National Amusements would continue to use its voting power to "thwart" the independent directors from exercising their fiduciary duties to all shareholders, and so the committee had recommended the special dividend.

Gordon stressed that the committee's motives had nothing to do with protecting their own positions on the board, and to underline that, he said that all five committee members had offered to resign once the special dividend was approved by the Delaware courts.

Moonves gave no hint of the ambivalence that had tortured him just days earlier and was surprisingly blunt, given that Shari was sitting at the same table. As the minutes put it, Moonves "described for the Board his view of the negative impact from what he claimed was interference by Ms. Redstone and NAI, including what he described as disparagement of CBS management and negative statements regarding the Company's strategic and succession plans and the independence of directors, on employee morale and the ability of CBS management successfully to oversee the operation of the business." He added that her statements were "extraordinarily insulting." And while he stopped short of threatening to quit, he made his intentions clear, saying he "did not believe he could continue to successfully lead the Company under these circumstances."

For Shari, such comments to the assembled directors of a company she and her father controlled—from someone she had until three days ago trusted and considered a friend—were extraordinarily painful. She had to struggle to contain her emotions, which were a mix of both hurt and anger. It was probably just as well that she was able to read a prepared statement. As the minutes put it, "Ms. Redstone read a statement that NAI did not have, and had never had, any intention to force through the Potential Transaction were a transaction not supported by the two special committees and that, prior to the recent actions taken by the Special Committee, it had no intention to remove any directors, other than a director previously identified in connection with the Pending Litigation," a reference to Gifford.

Shari couldn't resist adding, "Although there is a lot more that I would like to say, on the advice of counsel I will not say anything further."

When Klieger's turn came, he said he was speaking as a CBS director, not a Redstone lawyer, and felt the "terrible situation" at hand could have been avoided with better communication between the two camps. He said he had tried to be "constructive" notwithstanding his status as Shari's and Sumner's personal lawyer. He said he was especially troubled by the statement that the Redstones had injured "the best interests and welfare of the Corporation and its stockholders" and had been "detrimental to the Corporation's long-term effectiveness." In his view, the resolution was based on "conjecture and unsourced media reports." Klieger said the committee seemed to justify the stock dividend based on a concern that National Amusements would force through the merger, but given Shari's statement at the meeting that she had no intention of doing so, as well as his sincere belief that she'd act only in the best interests of all shareholders, no such threat actually existed.

The "real cause," Klieger continued, was that "management would prefer not to have a controlling stockholder." But he pointed out the fiduciary obligation of directors to all shareholders, including a controlling shareholder like National Amusements. Moreover, the proposed solution was far too broad. If the board feared National Amusements would force the merger, it could always seek an injunction against it rather than dilute the controlling stockholder "forever and for all purposes."

Klieger, for one, would accordingly vote against the dividend and accompanying resolutions.

Gordon promptly said he disagreed, and by this point, Klieger didn't really expect to change any minds or votes. But his tempered remarks prompted a response from Minow, whose views seemed to carry considerable weight given her status as the former dean of Harvard Law School. She, too, said no one on the special committee was happy about the circumstances that led to the meeting being called and that she hoped that discussions with National Amusements could continue and that the matter could still be resolved outside the courts. She also elaborated on the committee's reasoning, making even more clear how important Moonves was to the outcome. She talked about Shari's adverse impact on the "A+" management at CBS and "emphasized the importance to the special committee of Mr. Moonves having informed them that he could not continue to successfully manage the business under the present circumstances," according to the minutes.

The discussion lasted just over an hour. A little after 6:00 p.m. the board voted. Eleven, including all the independent directors, voted in favor of the proposal to issue the dividend, and three—Shari, Klieger, and David Andelman, Sumner's longtime lawyer—voted against it.

The resolution was "duly passed," the minutes reflected, but only if the National Amusements bylaw change requiring a 90 percent supermajority vote was struck down by a court.

The outcome thus remained in limbo. But in a sense, exercising the nuclear option had accomplished much of what Moonves and his allies had hoped for. With lawyers (and judges) now scrutinizing every move, Shari would have to be cautious about replacing directors, especially those who had revolted against her, and there was no way the existing board would approve a merger or remove Moonves. With so much litigation already underway, Shari's hands were effectively tied.

———

Despite the turmoil at the board level, the work of the network went on. Pilot season was over, but CBS was still casting that spring for *Blood & Treasure*, a possible midsummer replacement. The thriller featured an art thief, an antiquities expert, a terrorist, assorted Nazis, and Cleopatra's grave.

The same day as the pivotal board meeting, May 17, Moonves somehow found time to email the network's casting director, Peter Golden, about possible actors for *Blood & Treasure*—"Eva LaRue for 'Doctor Ana' and Philip Boyd for 'priest,'" Moonves suggested, mentioning two of Dauer's clients. "See if you can get them in for a reading."

"Will do," Golden answered.

"Both Philip & Eva felt their auditions went very well," Dauer reported. "We will see. Thanks for helping."

Moonves texted Dauer that he was also "looking into Blood and Treasure" for Bobbie Phillips.

"Still in NY," Moonves added. "Hell."

"I Was Never a Predator"

National Amusements and the Redstones launched their counter-attack on May 29 by asking the Delaware court to block CBS's attempt to dilute the Redstones' voting control. The suit argued that the purported threats from Shari—to force a merger with Viacom and interfere with CBS management—were "based entirely on unsourced media reports and conjecture." The suit stressed that "there was no truth to these imagined threats, which in any event do not remotely approach the requisite egregious, extreme conduct and compelling justification for a board to intentionally act to dilute the controlling stockholder."

The suit took specific aim at Moonves, who "has tired of having to deal with a stockholder with voting control and has taken particular umbrage that the exercise of such stockholder's control has migrated from Sumner Redstone to his daughter," the suit maintained. Moonves "has been a successful CEO and has richly benefitted under CBS's dual-class share structure, to the tune of nearly $700 million over his tenure as CEO (making him one of the highest paid CEOs in America, and the highest paid in the media industry)." The suit added that Moonves "apparently gave the Director Defendants an ultimatum: Either you remove NAI's voting control, or I resign."

Nonetheless, in many respects the complaint was restrained. It hardly burned bridges with Moonves—it was sprinkled with praise for him as an "extremely capable television executive"—or mounted the kind of personal counterattack that had so worried him in his text exchanges with Schwartz.

There was nothing about any rumors or incidents involving women.

———

That same month the screenwriter Janet Dulin Jones got a WhatsApp message that the veteran TV writer Nell Scovell, the creator of *Sabrina, the Teenage Witch*, was scouting around for Moonves victims and had heard about Jones. Scovell was on the front lines of the #MeToo movement—she'd recently published a book, *Just the Funny Parts . . . and a Few Hard Truths about Sneaking into the Hollywood Boys' Club*, and had famously blown the whistle on rampant sexism on *Late Night with David Letterman*, where she worked for just five months before quitting. She'd contributed to *The New Yorker* and was trying to help Ronan Farrow with his reporting.

Jones stared at the message. Just seeing Moonves's name made her feel ill. She still felt insignificant but agreed to talk to Farrow as long as she could be anonymous. When Farrow called, they spoke for some time about other subjects, and Jones warmed up to him. They spoke a second time, and that's when Moonves finally came up. Jones still wanted anonymity, and Farrow agreed. So she told him her story, how Moonves had jumped on her and the door was locked when she tried to flee. She mentioned her subsequent call to screenwriter Mike Marvin and said she'd heard something about a confrontation Marvin had subsequently had with Moonves. She didn't really remember but she thought they'd gotten into a shoving match at a barbecue.

But the call sent her into an emotional tailspin. It made her think of her late father, whom she idolized as a courageous man who'd always taught her to stand up to bullies. He'd always reminded her of Gregory Peck in *To Kill a Mockingbird*. Now she found herself thinking about Moonves and crying every morning.

Jones called a friend, the producer Gale Anne Hurd, anguishing over whether she should let Farrow use her name. Could Moonves still destroy her, even though she'd put an ocean between them? Hurd encouraged her to come forward, saying the environment had changed since Weinstein. "You'll regret not using your name," Hurd maintained.

Farrow suggested Jones speak to the actress Mira Sorvino, who'd been quoted by name in his Weinstein exposé and who'd volunteered to speak to other women worried about the consequences. Jones talked to her and came away thinking maybe it wouldn't be so bad.

Still, she wasn't ready to commit.

———

At CBS Gil Schwartz was again hearing rumors about a *New Yorker* article. Schwartz mentioned them to the *Vanity Fair* reporter William Cohan and assured him that Farrow's reporting would ultimately amount to nothing. He warned Cohan not to go down the same path. Periodically Moonves assured Schwartz there was nothing to be concerned about.

Now that Moonves and the independent directors had laid down the gauntlet with the lawsuit to strip Shari of control, any #MeToo issue with Moonves had naturally taken on new significance. On the one hand, Moonves's willingness to launch a lawsuit had seemed to confirm his innocence: What chief executive in his right mind would go to war with a controlling shareholder knowing there was a risk that inappropriate sexual behavior would emerge? On the other hand, since Moonves's continuation as chief executive was at the heart of the board's decision, anything that put his status in question would have an enormous impact on both the litigation and the company's future.

This wasn't lost on Shari and her allies. She and Klieger were hearing more rumors about Moonves and women, as well as incidents involving other CBS executives. Some came from former employees of

CBS itself, sources who asked to remain anonymous. They weren't very specific, but there was enough to convince Shari and Klieger that a more thorough and professional investigation than Aiello's half-hearted effort was needed.

On June 25, Shari and Klieger stepped up the pressure. They wrote to CBS's chief legal officer, Lawrence Tu, asking him to appoint outside counsel to conduct an independent investigation into "allegations of harassment, bullying, and favoritism involving senior CBS management and employees." The letter continued. "Although allegations and media reports of course do not constitute evidence that misconduct actually occurred, they also cannot lightly be dismissed. Yet, that appears to be what happened here." Even though Shari had raised concerns with board members Minow and Gordon and asked for a board meeting to discuss them,

> we understand that the only "investigation" undertaken with respect to those allegations was to ask Mr. Moonves, in substance, whether there was any truth to the allegations. Mr. Moonves's denial of the allegations apparently constituted the beginning and end of the inquiry.
>
> Our concerns regarding these matters have been heightened in light of additional alleged incidents of harassment by senior CBS executives, including Mr. Moonves, that have been reported to us in the weeks since CBS and the Special Committee filed suit. Because these incidents have been reported to us on a confidential basis, with obvious (and perhaps well founded) fear of reprisals, we are not comfortable disclosing specifics at this time. However, we are prepared to provide details subject to appropriate protections to independent outside counsel appointed by CBS so that counsel may follow up with the sources and otherwise investigate those and the other allegations that have been made.

We believe the concerns that we and others have raised must be addressed responsibly and fairly—especially at this watershed moment in time—and that a credible and thorough investigation is a fundamental issue of corporate governance and critical to restoring confidence in and preserving the culture of CBS going forward.

Tu responded a week later that outside investigations were already underway. The Proskauer law firm was examining Charlie Rose's behavior and the news division more generally, and Weil Gotshal had interviewed senior management and the head of human resources and concluded no further investigation was warranted.

Tu ended by chastising Klieger and Shari for even raising the issue: "It should be uncontroversial that surfacing unsubstantiated allegations making insinuations of this sort can be extremely unfair to individuals and cause serious damage to CBS and its stockholders. The differences that currently exist between you and the non-NAI affiliated members of the Board cannot justify or excuse such unfairness or other actions inconsistent with the responsibilities of CBS Board Members."

That prompted a blistering reply from Klieger on July 9:

At the outset, Ms. Redstone and I reject your thinly-veiled suggestion that we raised the concerns set forth in our letter as a reaction to the decision by CBS management and certain of its directors to sue its controlling stockholder. Both Ms. Redstone and I have been raising concerns about alleged harassment and bullying for more than six months, long before we had any idea that CBS management or members of its Board viewed themselves as "adverse" to the controlling stockholder and its representatives. We raised those concerns then, as we do now, out of our unwavering commitment to fulfill our obligations as fiduciaries and to act in the best interests of the company and its shareholders. The timing of our request for an independent investigation stems from the company's regrettable failure to act on those concerns.

It had come as news to Klieger that there even was a Proskauer-led investigation, and he asked to speak to the lawyers involved. As for Weil Gotshal's investigation, Klieger said that simply asking Moonves and accepting his denial "does not even qualify as an investigation, much less the type of independent investigation that any company, public or private, would be expected to undertake in response to alleged misconduct by senior executives. It is truly astounding that the members of the Nominating and Governance Committee believe they adequately discharged their fiduciary obligations through such an obviously perfunctory inquiry."

Tu didn't respond.

———

Shari and Klieger's letter pushing for a more thorough investigation of Moonves obviously made Bobbie Phillips's ongoing silence all the more important. Since the previous December, when Dauer had first contacted him, nearly all their interactions had been initiated by Dauer. But now Moonves reached out to Dauer, suggesting they meet again at Art's Delicatessen in Studio City on Friday, July 13. "See you then," Dauer responded.

At their lunch Moonves reiterated that his sexual encounter with Phillips had been consensual—"I was never a predator, I was a player" was how he put it. But he again poured on the remorse, saying he wanted to make amends and was still looking for a part for Phillips.

"Well, it's been eight months and you haven't gotten her anything," Dauer responded. "She's been very patient, and she'd like something to happen." He added, "She's getting angry."

The following week Moonves called Peter Golden, the head of

casting, to see if there was anything shooting in Toronto, because there was an actress there he wanted Golden to consider. At first Golden said no, but then he realized *Blood & Treasure* was casting in Toronto and much of it was being shot in Montreal. "Who's the actress?" Golden asked Moonves.

"Bobbie Phillips," Moonves answered, a name that, so far as Golden was concerned, came out of the blue. Moonves confided in Golden that he was facing a #MeToo situation. (Moonves said that Golden "understood this was a woman who was potentially making an accusation," although "I didn't get into specifics.")

Golden looked into *Blood & Treasure* and spotted the role of Erica—"a big, friendly woman clad in overalls," the casting breakdown specified. It was a relatively small part that paid $1,500 for a day's shooting. Golden thought it might be perfect for Phillips and called Taylor Elmore, the show's executive producer.

———

Just six days later, on July 19, CBS communications vice president Chris Ender, a twenty-two-year veteran at the company who worked for Gil Schwartz, returned from a meeting to find a message from Sean Lavery, a fact-checker at *The New Yorker*.

The long-rumored—and dreaded—call had come.

"What the Hell Are You Doing?"

Sean Lavery initially didn't tell Ender a whole lot, just that *The New Yorker* was reporting six incidents involving Moonves and women. He identified by name four of the women in the story—the actress Illeana Douglas, "J.D. Jones" (for fact-checking purposes, Jones had agreed to be identified by her first initials), Christine Peters (Sumner Redstone's old flame), and a television writer, Dinah Kirgo.

One of the purported victims, a former child star, was identified only by her first name, "Kimberly." The other was an actress who had played a police officer on a long-running CBS show.

Ender went to his boss, Schwartz, who called in Dana McClintock, the head of corporate communications in New York. Ender lived in California and handled the entertainment side of the company; an exposé involving the chief executive was way above his pay grade and would ordinarily have been handled by Schwartz himself or McClintock. But who would want to handle such a hot potato? Schwartz told Ender to do it, since he'd already started dealing with Lavery.

When Ender called Lavery back, it was evening on the East Coast. Farrow joined the call. He and Lavery went over the story in detail, working from a rough draft. Ender took copious notes. The call lasted about two hours. By the end Ender was dazed.

He duly reported everything to Schwartz, who immediately called Moonves.

Moonves's initial reaction was shock—he didn't remember any of the purported encounters. He was still convinced Shari was behind the accounts—a theory he pushed on anyone who would listen, although he cited no evidence to back it up. Moonves and CBS began a frantic effort to find out more. As Moonves recalled, "We were scrambling."

Schwartz swung into action. He notified a few board members and enlisted Tu. CBS hired an outside lawyer, James W. Quinn, the former head of litigation at Weil Gotshal, to oversee the effort. They brought in Matthew Hiltzik, a lawyer and crisis public-relations consultant. Schwartz put together an elaborate spreadsheet with the names, dates, places, and other facts as they emerged, along with a mounting list of errors in *The New Yorker*'s account.

Using the incomplete facts supplied by *The New Yorker*, Moonves tried to identify the unnamed women in the story, though he turned out to be wrong about "Kimberly"—he thought she was the former child star Kim Richards, one of the "Real Housewives of Beverly Hills," but it was a different Kimberly altogether. So of course he had no memory of ever meeting her.

He guessed right about the actress on the police series—she was someone he thought of as an old friend. She'd attended a big CBS gala in 2003, so Moonves thought she could hardly argue he'd retaliated against her for an incident that supposedly happened in 1995.

———

The next day Dauer sent Golden, the casting director, copies of Bobbie Phillips's résumé and demo reel. Golden forwarded them to the producer, Taylor, with the message: "Love for you to consider her for Erica, let me know."

Golden briefed Moonves, who responded, "Good."

Later that day Dauer got a text from a number he didn't recognize: "Marv: this is Billy [Bowers], Les Moonves' assistant. You can text this phone if need be. Les is going to call you now from this number."

Dauer figured Moonves was calling about a role for Phillips, which finally seemed to be happening. Dauer was watching his hometown baseball team, the Minnesota Twins, on TV when Moonves reached him. But Moonves wasn't calling him with good news about Phillips. Instead, he was terse and sounded stressed. Moonves asked Dauer to delete all their text messages, adding that he was asking all his friends to do the same thing. (A spokesman for Moonves denied he asked him to delete messages.)

Dauer wondered what that was all about. He hung up and went back to watching the game. He never deleted the messages.

When Dauer used the new number to text Moonves the next day, it was Bowers who answered: "Just tell me the message and I'll pass it along to him"—the kind of brush-off generations of Hollywood assistants have been trained to deliver. "Why can't I talk to him?" Dauer pleaded. "If Leslie is free—I'd like to talk to him," Dauer texted.

There was no response.

That week Moonves promoted Bowers to a new job—with a raise—as a director in CBS's unscripted department.

———

On July 24, five days after *The New Yorker* approached CBS, Mike Marvin's publicists got an email from Sean Lavery, asking if he'd talk to Farrow. He didn't say what about, except that it "occurred while he worked at Fox in the 80s," the email said.

The prospect made Marvin nervous. Back when he and Moonves were close friends and participating in the men's support group, Marvin was the successful screenwriter with a hit movie, and Moonves was a struggling young executive. Since then Marvin had never had another film as big as *Six Pack*. His writing career had withered, while Moonves ascended to the top echelon of Hollywood's most powerful executives.

Marvin was now touring as a singer and an acoustic guitar player in the Kingston Trio, the group that helped ignite the folk music craze with its 1958 hit "Tom Dooley" and, after being revived with new members, was playing to audiences of aging baby boomers. Marvin was the only member of the reconstituted group with any tie to an original member: he was a cousin to founder Nick Reynolds.

Like so many people, Marvin could still use a favor from Moonves: he was hoping to arrange an appearance for the trio on *CBS This Morning.* He knew an unflattering comment about Moonves in *The New Yorker* would be the end of that.

At the same time, Marvin harbored considerable resentment toward Moonves. Years earlier, Marvin had helped the television writer Anthony Zuiker, then working as a tram driver in Las Vegas, polish a movie script Zuiker had written, which became the 1999 crime thriller *The Runner.* After that Marvin had encouraged Zuiker to create and produce the CBS megahit *CSI,* for which Marvin had never gotten so much as a thank-you from Moonves, let alone any writing assignments. Moonves had pretty much dropped Marvin after the men's group broke up.

So Marvin called Lavery. One of the first things Marvin said was "As soon as I read about Weinstein, I knew I'd get this call about Leslie." Still, he wasn't exactly an enthusiastic source. Marvin seemed skeptical of the whole #MeToo movement. He wanted to know if there were other women in the story. Lavery told him there were six. Finally Marvin agreed to go on the record. He confirmed that Jones had been upset when she called him after the meeting with Moonves; *hysterical* was the word he used. But Marvin couldn't remember what she'd told him about the meeting.

Marvin thought there were also some troubling errors in Lavery's account. The fact-checker said Marvin had confronted Moonves by pushing him at a barbecue. He had confronted Moonves, but there was no pushing. It had happened during a meeting of the men's group, not a barbecue, when Marvin asked Moonves what the hell had happened and Moonves had started yelling at him.

And Jones's timing was wrong. If Jones was wrong about those things, she might be wrong about other things, too. Marvin figured Moonves had come on to Jones, but he had trouble believing Moonves would have actually assaulted her.

———

Moonves, too, was trying to fact-check what he'd learned about *The New Yorker* story. He was especially baffled by the Janet Dulin Jones incident. He had no memory of her. Nor did he remember Mike Marvin. He didn't remember any meeting Marvin had set up or an instance where Marvin had confronted him.

Moonves looked up a photograph of Marvin, and it jogged his memory—they'd both been in the men's support group organized by Dick Rosetti, a producer who'd hired Moonves at Fox. Moonves still had Rosetti's cell number but hadn't used it in years.

Rosetti, now working in real estate after a stint at Playboy Enterprises, was at his desk in Pacific Palisades when Moonves called.

"Hi, Dick," Moonves said. No one had called Rosetti "Dick" in ages. He now went by "Richard."

Like Marvin, Rosetti resented that Moonves had dropped him once he was powerful. He'd never asked him to lunch or offered to help when he could have used it.

"How you been?" Moonves asked casually. Rosetti wondered why he was calling.

"Can you tell me something?" Moonves went on. "Who's Mike Marvin?"

Rosetti laughed in disbelief. "Mike Marvin was in our support group," Rosetti said. "Mike was in pictures with us. You know Mike."

"Oh, yeah, Mike Marvin, yeah, yeah," Moonves replied unconvincingly.

Rosetti had a hunch this call from out of the blue had something to do with #MeToo. He had heard the rumors about Moonves. "What's the matter?" Rosetti asked.

Moonves explained that Marvin had told Ronan Farrow that he'd introduced Moonves to a woman and Moonves had sexually assaulted her. Marvin had confronted him afterward and there'd supposedly been some kind of shoving match at a social event.

Rosetti was shocked. He and Marvin had remained friends since the support-group days, but he didn't remember anything like this.

"Jeez, I'm sorry, Les. What do you want me to do?" he asked.

"I need Mike's number," Moonves replied. Rosetti offered to call Marvin first.

"Well, get back to me," Moonves said.

Rosetti immediately called Marvin. He couldn't believe his old friend had talked to a reporter, let alone accused Moonves of sexual assault, something that was at best hearsay. Rosetti might no longer have been close friends with Moonves, but the last thing he wanted was to have one of the most powerful men in Hollywood angry at him.

"Les just called me and he's really upset," Rosetti said. "He said this girl has just come out of the woodwork."

"Don't you remember?" Marvin asked. "That night he was screaming at me?"

"I don't remember at all, Mike," Rosetti replied. "We all did that." Rosetti was annoyed with his old friend. "Why would you do an interview and put your name on it? What the hell are you doing, man?" he asked in exasperation.

"What do you mean why?" Marvin snapped. "I don't have any reason to hold back."

"Well, Les says he doesn't remember you," Rosetti told him.

"Les Moonves says he doesn't remember me?" Marvin asked, incredulous. That was so insulting.

"Call Les back, give him my number, and tell him to call me directly," Marvin instructed.

"Okay," Rosetti said, "but keep me out of this. I don't want to get involved."

About two hours later, Moonves called Marvin. He started to talk but Marvin cut him off after a few seconds.

"Les, I can't believe you just told Rosetti you don't remember me," he said.

Moonves seemed defensive. "I told Dick I didn't remember the incident," he said.

"I don't understand how you could forget me," Marvin said.

"I didn't forget you," Moonves repeated, although Marvin didn't believe him. "Mike, I don't remember this woman," Moonves continued. "I don't remember anything about her."

Marvin told Moonves he remembered setting up a meeting between Moonves and Jones but didn't recall what happened after that. Moonves sounded satisfied and they hung up.

But when CBS relayed that to *The New Yorker*, Lavery, the fact-checker, said, "That's not what he told us," and provided more details of Marvin's earlier account.

Moonves called Marvin back. "Listen, just tell me the truth," Moonves said. "I promise, I'm not mad at you. I just want to know what you said."

So Marvin went over in more detail what he'd said to Lavery. The incident had happened while Moonves was at Fox, and Marvin had confronted Moonves at their men's group meeting, where Moonves had yelled at him. Marvin had stuck to the facts and hadn't embellished anything for *The New Yorker*. Jones had never told him Moonves had assaulted her.

Moonves said he still had no memory of Jones.

"Janet Jones, you don't remember me sending her?" Marvin asked. Moonves said he didn't.

"Well, it happened, Les," Marvin said.

The men chatted for a bit longer. Moonves asked about the Kingston Trio. Marvin told him the band was selling out nearly every show.

Moonves's tone softened, and suddenly he sounded like the friend and confidant he'd once been. "You know, Mike, they're really trying to take me down here."

The next day CBS's Ender asked Lavery if he'd interviewed Marvin. He said he had. "You'd better go back to him," Ender cautioned. "He had a lot of problems with your story."

So Lavery called Marvin again. It was as though he'd reached a different person. Marvin was angry. "I don't want to have anything to do with this," Marvin said. Lavery read back some of his notes of their earlier conversation. "I never said any of that," Marvin insisted. "You have it all wrong. I'm not going to talk to you."

He hung up.

———

Shari, Klieger, and most other board members knew nothing of the *New Yorker* calls or the resulting turmoil underway within the CBS communications operation. On July 24, an increasingly frustrated Klieger again wrote to CBS chief legal counsel Tu: "Despite the obvious importance of these matters, two weeks have passed without any response. That delay is unacceptable. Please provide the requested information before the end of this week."

He also called for an executive session without Moonves at the next board meeting scheduled for July 30, to discuss the mounting rumors about Moonves and the need for further investigation.

Tu finally replied on Thursday, July 26, firmly shutting the door on Klieger's demands while saying nothing about the imminent *New Yorker* article: "As you no doubt recognize, we do not agree with your characterization of how the matters are being and have been handled and with your accounts of prior events. We did not feel it would be productive to engage in further written debate about those factual disagreements, as we've already stated our views as to those matters."

———

As *The New Yorker*'s publication date loomed, Moonves said he'd talk to Farrow himself, albeit on background. No one thought that at this late juncture CBS could derail the story entirely. But Moonves was armed with notes of a long list of supposed factual errors—mostly dates, times, and details—and he thought that, coupled with his charm and candor, might lead to a softening of the piece.

When Farrow got on the phone, he asked if the fact-checker could join them. Moonves said no, he wanted it to be one on one. They spoke for a little more than an hour. Moonves went over his notes. He stressed that the Peters allegation was absurd, given that she was Sumner's ex-girlfriend (and ongoing companion). The only reason Moonves had met with Peters was because Sumner was pushing him to hire her. If Moonves had been crazy enough to try anything with Peters, Sumner would have destroyed him in retaliation.

Farrow mostly listened politely.

Farrow said he'd call Moonves again before the piece ran, and Moonves thought he might want to put some things on the record. But when Farrow called Moonves the day before the piece was slated to run, all he did was thank him for being cooperative.

On Thursday, Farrow was at the venerable *New Yorker* writer Roger Angell's desk, working frantically to close the Moonves piece, when Kim Masters called from *The Hollywood Reporter*, saying she was breaking the news about his Moonves exposé, and asked if he wanted to comment.

"Don't run this," Farrow asked. "I'm still reporting."

"I hear you're almost done," she said.

"You're not in the newsroom," Farrow said, annoyed.

Her piece would run early the next morning. She'd already called CBS for comment.

That gave Farrow less than twenty-four hours.

———

D auer was in Minnesota that week for his annual fishing trip, staying at his friend Clayton Reed's house. While in Austin he'd visited the Spam Museum, where he picked up matching T-shirts as gifts for Moonves and his son Charlie.

While he was there, Ashley Gray, a casting director in Toronto, emailed Dauer to say CBS wanted Phillips for a guest role on *Blood & Treasure* and asked for an audition tape, which was standard network practice. Dauer said no; Phillips was above that. Gray soon emailed that "we just got word the network doesn't need to see Bobbie self-tape" and formally offered Phillips the role of Erica.

Finally, Dauer thought.

But then he looked more closely at the breakdown for the part: "a big, friendly woman clad in overalls." He didn't have to read past "big," which in casting terms meant fat. Then he saw the money: a measly $1,500.

Dauer dutifully called Phillips with the offer. Predictably, she was insulted and dismissed it out of hand.

At the same time, she was baffled. Dauer told her Golden and Moonves himself had called urging her to take the role. Why was CBS top brass so interested in her taking such an insignificant part?

Dauer called Golden. "What do you know," he said. "She doesn't want to do it." Golden was surprised. He thought it was a good part for Phillips.

Moonves called Dauer that evening. "They're coming out with an article in *The New Yorker*," Moonves said, with Reed listening in the background (Dauer had put the call on speaker because he was using both hands to make a sandwich). "Bobbie has got to take this job. You have to keep her quiet or I'm done."

Golden called him with the same message, yelling at Dauer that Phillips had to take the part. Golden sweetened the offer to $5,000.

Dauer got off the call, and Reed asked him what that was all about. After Dauer explained, Reed told him he'd better keep quiet about it.

———

The night before the *New Yorker* story was set to close, on July 26, Lavery again reached out to Mike Marvin. Marvin seemed to have calmed down. Lavery asked Marvin if he'd speak to Farrow himself. "He can try me," Marvin said, sounding wary.

But when Farrow called, Marvin picked up. Farrow stressed that it would mean the world to Jones for Marvin to support her. It was time for everyone involved to be brave. He listened patiently as Marvin responded. Then he turned to Lavery, who was sitting next to him during the call, and gave him a thumbs-up.

Marvin was back on the record.

Farrow called Jones just before midnight. He said time had run out. The story was going to run online the next day, and she had to decide now whether he could use her name.

Jones thought about a call she'd just had with an ex-boyfriend. "If it was your daughter, what would you do?" she'd asked him.

"I'd tell her to use her name," he'd said. "But what's more important is that your father would tell you to use your name, and to not be afraid."

He was right. She thought about what her father would say to her: "You just have to do it," she imagined him saying.

She took a deep breath. "Yes, go ahead," she told Farrow.

"Let's Not Get Ahead of Ourselves"

At 8:45 a.m. on Friday, July 27, *The Hollywood Reporter* broke the news that "*The New Yorker* is poised to publish an article by Ronan Farrow that includes allegations of sexual misconduct on the part of embattled CBS chairman and CEO Leslie Moonves."

By midday, CBS shares had dropped nearly 7 percent in a heavy sell-off as Wall Street absorbed news that might threaten Moonves's tenure. Farrow realized that billions of dollars in market value rested on his story.

The article finally appeared on *The New Yorker*'s website at 5:38 p.m. Farrow wrote:

Six women who had professional dealings with him told me that, between the nineteen-eighties and the late aughts, Moonves sexually harassed them. Four described forcible touching or kissing during business meetings, in what they said appeared to be a practiced routine. Two told me that Moonves physically intimidated them or threatened to derail their careers. All said that he became cold or hostile after they rejected his advances, and that they believed their careers suffered as a result. "What happened to me was a sexual assault, and then I was fired for not participating," the actress and writer Illeana Douglas told me. All the women said that they still feared that speaking out would lead to retaliation from Moonves, who is known in the industry for his ability to make or break careers. "He has gotten away with it for decades," the writer Janet Jones, who alleges that she had to shove Moonves off her after he forcibly kissed her at a work meeting, told me. "And it's just not O.K."

Marvin was indeed quoted, despite Rosetti's admonition. "Mike Marvin told me that he remembers introducing Jones to Moonves, and that she was troubled by the meeting," Farrow reported. "He said that he confronted Moonves about it at a gathering, saying, 'Whatever happened, that girl was upset.' Moonves, Marvin said, became furious. 'We definitely had a screaming match over this,' Marvin told me."

Moonves himself, though not otherwise quoted, provided a statement: "Throughout my time at CBS, we have promoted a culture of respect and opportunity for all employees, and have consistently found success elevating women to top executive positions across our company. I recognize that there were times decades ago when I may have made some women uncomfortable by making advances. Those were mistakes, and I regret them immensely. But I always understood and respected—and abided by the principle—that 'no' means 'no,' and I have never misused my position to harm or hinder anyone's career."

The New Yorker reported that, according to CBS, there had been no misconduct claims and no settlements against Moonves during his twenty-four years at the network.

The article more broadly reported that sexual misconduct was pervasive at CBS, especially at its crown-jewel news program, *60 Minutes*: "Nineteen current and former employees told me that Jeff Fager, the former chairman of CBS News and the current executive producer of '60 Minutes,' allowed harassment in the division. 'It's top down, this culture of older men who have all this power and you are nothing,' one veteran producer told me. 'The company is shielding lots of bad behavior.'"

Moonves was dismayed that more of his denials and explanations hadn't made it into the article. *The New Yorker* had made all the corrections but took nothing of substance out.

But with the #MeToo movement in full hue and cry, Moonves was missing the forest for the trees: Four women were on the record accusing him of various degrees of grossly inappropriate sexual behavior as well as retaliation for rebuffing him. While strongly denying any retaliation, he himself admitted to "advances" that had made women "uncomfortable." For most readers, that was an admission of guilt.

CBS did what it could to blunt the impact. Moonves's loyalists on the board felt he was entitled to due process. They didn't trust the media and didn't want to appear to be bowing to a public frenzy. Bruce Gordon spoke to three of CBS's largest shareholders and reported that none wanted to see Moonves suspended while an investigation was underway.

In sharp contrast to Harvey Weinstein, who was immediately put on leave, CBS's independent directors said only that they would look into the allegations and immediately put them in the context of "the Company's very public legal dispute," as a statement from the directors put it. "While that litigation process continues, the CBS management team has the full support of the independent board members."

Two of CBS's highest-ranking women executives—chief advertising revenue officer Jo Ann Ross and head of daytime programming Angelica McDaniel—rallied behind Moonves with public statements praising his respect for and support of women at CBS. They were, of course, hardly objective observers, given that Moonves was their boss.

No one was stauncher in her support of Moonves than his wife, Julie Chen. With the exception of Christine Peters, none of the alleged incidents had happened during their marriage. She posted a statement on Twitter late that Friday: "I have known my husband, Leslie Moonves, since the late '90s, and I have been married to him for almost 14 years. Leslie is a good man and a loving father, devoted husband

and inspiring corporate leader. He has always been a kind, decent and moral human being. I fully support my husband."

Still, it was an awkward moment for Chen on Monday morning's episode of *The Talk*. "Some of you may be aware of what's been going on in my life for the past few days," Chen said at the show's opening. "I issued the one and only statement I will ever make on this topic on Twitter. I will stand by that statement today, tomorrow, forever." The audience broke into applause.

But the *New Yorker* exposé generated nearly as much negative publicity as had the Harvey Weinstein piece, and there were public calls for Moonves to step down or be suspended. Moonves's college alma mater, Bucknell, stripped him from its website and issued a statement that "Bucknell will not stand for sexual misconduct—on campus or beyond." The University of Southern California followed suit, suspending Moonves from the board of its School of Cinematic Arts. Moonves quietly resigned from the Hollywood sexual harassment commission led by Anita Hill.

In Toronto, Bobbie Phillips was stunned by all the publicity and the *New Yorker* article itself. There was, mercifully, no mention of her. But suddenly everything about the saga of finding her work made sense. Perhaps she'd been naive, but ever since that first call from Dauer, she'd believed she'd been the only victim of a Moonves assault, and that he was genuinely sorry and hoping to atone and gain her forgiveness. The article had unmasked all that. All Moonves had been doing was trying to buy her silence—even though she hadn't been planning to say anything. She felt manipulated and like a victim all over again. All the trauma of their long-ago encounter came back. She was so upset she developed physical symptoms and twice had to visit the emergency room.

Furious, she told Dauer that not only did she not want the *Blood &
Treasure* role, but she wouldn't accept anything else connected to CBS.
She also said she was calling a lawyer.

———

W hen the *Hollywood Reporter* item first appeared, Shari Redstone and Rob Klieger had been at the Cleary Gottlieb offices in New York, preparing for a round of depositions in the Delaware
lawsuits. After that, they had trouble concentrating and eventually
gave up.

Klieger texted Shari at 3:32 p.m. that he'd read the article. They
were both stunned and outraged by the allegations—both the alleged
assaults and Moonves's efforts to retaliate against the victims. It seemed
obvious to them that Moonves would have to be suspended pending a
thorough investigation.

But apparently it wasn't obvious to others on the board. Shari and
Klieger were astonished that no one from the board or CBS called
them after the article came out. Yet the independent directors had
gone ahead and issued a public statement that Moonves had their "full
support."

Klieger was furious, even more so than Shari. Early Saturday morning he fired off an email to the independent directors as well as chief
counsel Larry Tu.

"I am stunned that neither I nor any other NAI-affiliated director
has been contacted by any of you regarding yesterday's reporting or
any deliberations or decisions regarding appropriate next steps," he
wrote. "These are issues for the full Board, not the 'independent' directors or any other subset of the Board. This has nothing to do with
the pending litigation, and there is no conflict between the NAI-
affiliated directors and the company or full Board that could possibly
justify our exclusion."

"These will obviously be important topics for discussion at Monday's board meeting, and considerable time should be allotted for that purpose," he added.

Bruce Gordon called him later that morning, as Klieger was standing in Shari's driveway at her house in Connecticut. Gordon said the situation was "complicated." The independent directors now agreed there needed to be an outside investigation.

"We need to be a part of this," Klieger emphasized.

Gordon seemed genuinely befuddled. "We brought in Aiello," Gordon reminded him. "He said there was nothing there. Les said there was nothing there. What more were we supposed to do?"

There was plenty he could have done, Klieger thought, but kept that to himself. He felt passionately that Moonves couldn't stay and told Gordon he needed to be suspended while the investigation proceeded.

"Let's not get ahead of ourselves," Gordon said.

———

After reading the article, Shari Redstone could barely contain her anger and frustration. All of it had come as a shock, notwithstanding the months of rumors. She fired off a letter to her fellow directors.

I am frankly ashamed to sit on a Board with independent directors who have demonstrated such blind allegiance to senior management and repeatedly failed to act in the best interests of the company, its employees, and its shareholders. In December 2017, when rumors concerning allegations of personal misconduct by Les Moonves began circulating, I raised this matter with Martha Minow so that it could be addressed by the independent directors on the Nominations and Governance Committee. Martha told me that the committee or its representative had asked Les about the allegations and rumors, that Les had stated they were untrue, and that there was therefore no investigation necessary. Both Rob Klieger and I subsequently raised this matter with Bruce Gordon, who delivered the same message. Additionally, Les assured me at a lunch we had in January that there was absolutely no truth to these allegations, something he acknowledged to be untrue in his statement yesterday.

While rumors and allegations are not fact, they do require Board action, particularly given the intensity with which they were circulating. The Board does not discharge its obligations by asking the CEO if he engaged in any misconduct and taking his word for it when he says he did not. This Board has consistently refused to exercise any oversight over senior management and has repeatedly shut down my attempts to discharge my own obligations to the company and its shareholders.

I would have hoped that yesterday's events would have united us in an effort to do the right thing notwithstanding the animosity and litigation against NAI and me. Regrettably, that is not what happened. Instead, the independent directors double-downed on their allegiance to the company's CEO, publicly expressing their full support for Les before undertaking an investigation, and before the article raising these allegations was even published. Worse yet, they chose to ignore the critical issues *The New Yorker* article raises with respect to the company's culture as a whole and instead suggested that I am somehow behind these allegations or Ronan Farrow's investigation, which the article itself makes clear has been underway for more than eight months. To be clear, I had absolutely nothing to do with Ronan Farrow's investigation, the article, or any other press reports regarding alleged misconduct by Les. I have never spoken to Ronan Farrow, nor have I spoken with any of the women who have leveled accusations against Les. Indeed, I raised these issues only with my fellow directors.

That should have been enough, and much to my regret today, I did nothing further in the face of their refusal to act.

I will not accept any further suggestions that I am behind *The New Yorker* article or any allegations regarding Les. The false statements concerning my supposed involvement in the allegations or reporting are nothing short of defamatory.

She demanded that CBS "immediately retract" statements made on the CBS Evening News, as well as any other statements from CBS insinuating that she or anyone at National Amusements had been involved in the article.

Shari ended with a plea to the board to "finally come together to engage in a constructive conversation and take decisive action in the best interests of the company, its employees, and its shareholders."

———

Moonves himself spent the weekend calling the independent directors to gauge his support. A few—Minow, for one—wouldn't talk to him, deeming it improper. To those who listened, Moonves argued that the allegations in *The New Yorker* were false or grossly hyped. For the most part his arguments fell on receptive ears, especially among the aging cohort of male directors that made up his inner circle.

The board convened by phone on Monday morning in executive session, which meant Moonves was excluded. Klieger and Shari participated from offices at Cleary Gottlieb. From the outset of the meeting, it was clear that a cadre of directors had no interest in discussion and had already made up their minds. William Cohen, the former defense secretary, immediately rose to Moonves's defense. "We are going to stay in this meeting until midnight if we need to until we get an agreement that we stand 100 percent behind our C.E.O., and there will be no change in his status," Cohen stated emphatically.

While Cohen was making his pronouncement, Klieger looked over at Shari. She nodded for Klieger to go ahead and speak. He said he understood from Gordon that the board was interviewing law firms to conduct an investigation, and he was willing to wait a few days for their advice about how to proceed, including whether to suspend Moonves. But if Cohen was going to insist they stay there that day until they reached a unanimous consensus, then "I have a very different view from Bill about what that outcome should be, and I'm happy to have that discussion," he said.

Arnold Kopelson was especially ardent in his support for Moonves, dismissing the *New Yorker* incidents as ancient history and irrelevant to Moonves's tenure at CBS. He kept repeating that it was "pilot season," which was when CBS most needed Moonves's golden touch.

There was also considerable talk about the likely negative reaction on Wall Street if Moonves were suspended, given that Moonves was synonymous with the company's success.

The directors didn't have to stay until midnight to resolve their differences. They seemed only too happy to embrace Klieger's suggestion to wait until they heard from the outside lawyers hired for the investigation—anything to delay removing Moonves. The meeting adjourned in less than an hour.

Amid intense speculation about Moonves's fate, CBS issued a statement that the board was "in the process of selecting outside counsel to conduct an independent investigation" and "no other action was taken on this matter at today's board meeting."

Few were satisfied, either on Wall Street or beyond.

"It's shortsighted and cowardly of the board," Jeffrey Sonnenfeld, a professor at the Yale School of Management, told *The New York Times.* "They think they're showing courage on behalf of the C.E.O., but they're just circling the wagons right now."

But unlike Weinstein, Matt Lauer, or Charlie Rose, Moonves had survived.

The board named a three-person special committee to oversee the Moonves investigation rather than leave it to the now-discredited nominating and governance committee. Two members would be independent; the third would come from the Shari Redstone faction. Gordon and Klieger had agreed in advance that the members would be the two of them plus Linda Griego—one of the few board members both sides could agree on, who had the added benefit of being a woman.

"He Wants to Destroy Me"

Despite Shari Redstone's plea for the CBS board to come together, the board and the special committee couldn't even agree on an outside law firm for the investigation. During a board call Martha Minow said she'd resign if CBS didn't name a firm and announce an investigation that day. She finally broke the impasse by suggesting the board hire two firms.

The Shari-NAI faction settled on Debevoise & Plimpton and partner Mary Jo White, whose distinguished career in public service included stints as a former U.S. attorney for the Southern District of New York and chair of the Securities and Exchange Commission; Gordon and the independent directors went with Covington & Burling partner Nancy Kestenbaum, a former prosecutor who was cochair of the firm's white-collar crime practice.

The newly hired lawyers told the special committee members that it was customary to suspend an employee like Moonves while an investigation was underway, in part because someone still in power could influence potential witnesses. But given Moonves's importance to the company, they suggested keeping him in place while they made some preliminary inquiries.

Moonves himself would be the critical witness, but his lawyers said he wasn't available until the Monday after next, August 13 (in part because they were worried about board leaks and wanted to work out a strict confidentiality agreement before then). That bought Moonves at least another week's time.

CBS made the announcement about the law firms on Wednesday. On Thursday Moonves appeared at a meeting with Wall Street analysts to announce better-than-expected earnings for the quarter and acted as though nothing out of the ordinary had happened. Analysts were told ahead of time that Moonves wouldn't comment on the *New Yorker* article or the battle with Shari Redstone and National Amusements because of legal constraints. Still, "it was astonishing to hear these investment analysts go through questions about possible revenues from sports gambling, about their over-the-top streaming items, everything and ignoring the elephants in the room," NPR correspondent David Folkenflik reported. "The investment analysts were there to ask questions, and it's hard to understand the fortunes and future of CBS Corporation without understanding the fate of its CEO—Moonves has led them to so much financial success—and also whether they have any succession plans in place should he be displaced."

———

With events unfolding so rapidly, Klieger flew to New York, where Dick Parsons was mediating between Shari and Bruce Gordon. Parsons thought it might be a good idea for Shari and Moonves to meet to clear the air. They hadn't had any contact since the lawsuit was filed on May 14.

On July 31 Shari, accompanied by Klieger, met with Moonves and Tu in a conference room at Cleary Gottlieb. Shari wondered what Tu was doing there. As chief legal counsel he worked for and represented CBS and its shareholders—not Moonves. Nonetheless, she went ahead and did nearly all the talking. She was angry and hurt. She reminded Moonves how much she'd relied on and trusted him during the battle with Holland and Herzer and then Dauman. She had thought they were friends. Now he'd both lied to her, about the #MeToo issues, and betrayed her, with the lawsuit to strip her control. How could he?

Klieger was impressed that Moonves mostly listened patiently. He never got angry or raised his voice. He didn't contest any facts or argue. Pretty much all Moonves said was a vague "I'm sorry you feel that way."

On the other hand, Moonves didn't seem to recognize that his career at CBS was in peril. When Shari brought up the subject of transition, asking how Moonves wanted to handle his departure, he seemed surprised, as if the possibility, let alone the likelihood, of his leaving CBS hadn't occurred to him.

Afterward Shari worried that she'd been too hard on Moonves. Should she send him a text? She wanted to tell him that she still really valued what he'd done for the company and wished to find a way to get through this.

Klieger advised against it.

The three members of the special committee investigating Moonves met several times by phone that week. Klieger wasn't happy that Moonves wasn't going to be interviewed until August 13, which he considered little more than a delaying tactic. Both he and Shari remained convinced that Moonves needed to be suspended immediately while the investigation continued. Two weeks had passed since the *New Yorker* article.

A full board meeting was scheduled for Friday, August 10, when the hard choices about Moonves's future would be made. But Gordon and Griego balked, arguing that a vote then would be premature. The committee voted two to one to postpone the Friday board meeting.

Shari was indignant. So she called a special board meeting for Friday anyway, which she had the power to do as vice chair. "I know you're available," she emailed her fellow directors.

One by one they responded saying that suddenly they weren't. It was soon obvious that the only participants would be Shari, Klieger, and Andelman, the Redstone faction.

Shari spent that weekend with Sumner at the Montage Hotel in Laguna Beach. Klieger joined them there. Even though they lacked a quorum, they went ahead with the largely ceremonial meeting. Shari read a statement, noting that "each and every member of this Board had said they were available for a meeting that had previously been requested by Bruce Gordon." But "most of our colleagues suddenly became unavailable or have simply opted not to join this call. I am disappointed that those not in attendance were unwilling to address Mr. Moonves' status with the alacrity and level of deliberation that it deserves. However, given that we do not have a quorum, I have no choice but to adjourn this meeting."

That same Friday, William Cohan, the *Vanity Fair* reporter who'd written about Holland and Herzer and the drama at the Redstone mansion, called Gil Schwartz about another story.

Initially all Cohan had to go on was a tip from a source that Moonves had instigated a #MeToo incident with his diabetes doctor. Cohan hadn't known Moonves was diabetic (few people did). The source said he wouldn't name the doctor but would confirm the name if Cohan could figure it out.

When Cohan Googled the best female diabetes doctors in Los Angeles, Anne Peters's name was first on the list. His source confirmed he was right about the name and added she'd written about the incident. He didn't name the publication, but more research led Cohan to her essay in the medical journal. Peters wouldn't talk to him, but other sources confirmed that the patient she described was Moonves. Cohan drafted a story.

Cohan didn't tell Schwartz all that much, but said he was writing that Moonves had assaulted a doctor. Moonves had grabbed her, rubbed his crotch against her, and, when rebuffed, retreated to a corner and masturbated. He added that he had written confirmation from the victim herself. Cohan believed the incident had happened in 2011. He asked Schwartz if Moonves had any comment.

Schwartz was stunned. "This doesn't sound like Les," he told Cohan—Moonves was a "blow job guy," not a "masturbation guy."

Schwartz said he'd get back to him.

Schwartz briefed Moonves, saying there was something in writing, maybe on social media. Moonves admitted there was some truth to the account. He had consulted Peters. He had made a "pass" at her, as he described it, by putting his hand on her arm and trying to kiss her. But that had been all. It was definitely not as recent as 2011—Cohan was way off on that.

Still, it was too much for Schwartz. Coming on top of Farrow's story—which was still triggering calls for Moonves's suspension as chief executive—he didn't think Moonves could survive.

Schwartz also felt personally betrayed. He thought back to that first call from the Los Angeles police and Moonves's staunch denials that there was a problem. Now Schwartz understood why Moonves had agonized over the decision to file the lawsuit against the Redstones. "Heavy lies the head," Schwartz had told him. Little had he known.

Schwartz drafted a resignation letter for Moonves.

After talking to Schwartz, Moonves asked his daughter to do some internet research on Peters, focusing on Facebook and Twitter. She didn't find anything on social media, but she came across Peters's essay in the medical journal. Moonves told her to pay the $35 fee to gain access, and she read the article to him.

Moonves had an assistant review his calendars until he found the appointment: 7:00 a.m. on September 17, 1999. He told Schwartz that Cohan had the date wrong.

Schwartz called Cohan back. He said if *Vanity Fair* ran the story,

Moonves would resign. Schwartz told Cohan he had Moonves's resignation letter in his hand. "Whoa," Cohan thought. Schwartz didn't explicitly say so, but he was clearly putting the burden of Moonves's fate on Cohan's shoulders.

"Your date is off by a dozen years," Schwartz added, evidently hoping to sow doubts about the entire account.

"How do you know it was 1999?" Cohan asked. "Prove it."

Schwartz sent Cohan a screenshot of Moonves's handwritten calendar entry.

That, of course, confirmed that Moonves had met with Peters at an early hour, crucial elements of the story.

But much to Cohan's frustration, *Vanity Fair*'s lawyers balked at running the story. They raised doubts about the sourcing. Cohan obviously didn't have confirmation from Peters, since she wouldn't talk to him, but she had told other people, who confirmed to Cohan that Moonves was the patient described in Peters's article. Cohan was angry and told Schwartz the story wasn't running anytime soon, if ever.

Moonves had dodged another bullet. Schwartz put the resignation letter back in his drawer.

———

All that week Dauer had been trying to get through to Moonves, who for obvious reasons was preoccupied. But Moonves knew that keeping Phillips quiet was more important than ever. He and Dauer finally spoke on Saturday, August 11, and Dauer told him Phillips had both rejected the part and hired a lawyer. The news couldn't have come at a worse time. Moonves all but begged Dauer to keep Phillips quiet. "If Bobbie talks, I'm finished," Moonves said, much as he'd said before. "She's the one who could destroy me." He pleaded with Dauer to tell her to "wait until Wednesday until speaking to anyone" about him.

The significance of Wednesday wasn't clear to Dauer. Maybe Moonves would come up with a better part than "Erica." He hoped so.

Dauer briefed Phillips on his conversation with Moonves and managed to make matters worse. After he repeated Moonves's comments—that if she talked, "I'm finished," and that she was the only one who could bring him down—she started to panic. She wondered: Would Moonves consider other ways to keep her quiet once he realized that getting her a part hadn't worked? She wouldn't put it past him, given what he'd already done to her. She no longer felt safe.

Moonves brooded over the latest developments. He called Peter Golden, who confirmed Phillips had declined the offer. There was little more Moonves could do given the pending investigation and the fact that Phillips had hired a lawyer. Finally, at 6:00 p.m. he called one of his lawyers, Ron Olson, and disclosed that the actress's manager from all those years ago had been pressuring him to find her a part and that the actress herself—the one who had given him a blow job in his office at Warner Bros.—had hired a lawyer.

At 9:45 p.m. Olson, joined by Moonves's lawyer Dan Petrocelli, reached Aiello, who had conducted the interview with Moonves in January and advised the board it had nothing to worry about. Petrocelli told him a few things were going to emerge during Moonves's interview on Monday. First was an incident involving a doctor: he'd made a "pass" at her years ago, which she rejected.

Then Petrocelli turned to the subject of the actress, still not disclosing any names. Moonves had had a sexual encounter with her in his office. He'd said that in January. But now there was more: "Fast-forward to last December 2017," as Aiello described what Petrocelli told him. "This talent agent said this woman was making noises and maybe Les could get her some work so that she doesn't complain. Les, according to Dan, didn't do anything at the time and didn't hear anything more," according to Aiello's notes of the call.

Aiello continued, "Around the time of the Ronan Farrow article, the talent agent called and repeated the 2017 conversation, and [Moonves] said he'd find her something so she doesn't complain. According to Dan, Les asked his casting person if there was something for her. I didn't write it down—but I think she was Canadian, from Canada, and the production person called someone in Canada to see if there was anything for her. They offered her a small scene, $1,500 dollars, she passed on it, nothing happened." Then she had hired a lawyer.

Petrocelli gave a similar account to Tu, CBS's chief legal adviser.

This was such a drastically abbreviated account of what had actually happened—a version in which Moonves and the "agent" had had only three exchanges—that it suggests Moonves made the fundamental mistake of failing to tell his own lawyers the full truth about what had actually happened.

Aiello also briefed Bruce Gordon on the disclosures.

All of this set the stage for the pivotal interview of Moonves by the Debevoise and Covington lawyers, which took place in person at Debevoise's offices in New York at 8:51 a.m. on Monday, August 13.

"Moonves wants to fully cooperate," Petrocelli began. "He has a contractual duty to cooperate. He has an interest in a prompt and fair resolution of this. He is a supporter of this process." But "Klieger and Redstone have taken direct aim at Moonves. Klieger himself, who is a trial lawyer, is also a member of the committee that is liaising with you, which is totally inappropriate." As a result, he instructed Moonves to withhold some information, for fear that Klieger and Shari would use it against him.

The first incident Moonves discussed in any detail was the police report filed by Phyllis Golden-Gottlieb. Moonves said, "It was oral sex and it was consensual," and when asked for more detail, said, "We had a drink at a bar. In my car, we started kissing. Her claim was that it happened at lunch in a parking lot in broad daylight." He added, "We were friends. She was flirty. I knew her in previous jobs. One may have claimed she was chasing me more than I was chasing her. Maybe. It was thirty-two years ago."

Contrary to his assurances to Gil Schwartz that he'd told two board members about the police report, Moonves told the lawyers he hadn't told anyone on the board—or anyone else, except his wife—because he deemed it "personal."

Asked if there were other incidents, Moonves mentioned the "actress" and her "manager," but Petrocelli advised him to withhold their names. Moonves said the manager had called him in December.

"Do you remember so-and-so?" the manager had asked, according to Moonves.

"Yes," Moonves replied.

"She is making noises about you."

Moonves explained that "I had a meeting with her. She performed oral sex on me. Her claim was different than that. That's what he's telling me. He said, 'Remember when she came to see you? After she came to see you, she said she was unhappy, back then.'" The manager had added, "You know actresses."

"I don't know why. It was all fine," Moonves had told him. "But from her point of view, it wasn't. That was the end of it. I didn't hear from her again, until this past December. He said, 'She's making noises. Some of her friends are talking to her.'"

A lawyer asked how the encounter had ended.

"The oral sex was completed. I remember pleasantries. She left," he said.

As the questioning continued, Moonves speculated that Shari had triggered the investigation by Aiello based on a preposterous rumor that during a meeting in Las Vegas, he and Ianniello had come on to women while wearing bathrobes, the newly potent symbol of the #MeToo movement.

"Five years ago, we had a meeting in Vegas," Moonves explained. "Nothing happened." But Shari "called an emergency meeting to discuss me and Ianniello and sexual harassment. There were stories explained to us that made no sense about me and Joe being in bathrobes and beating up people." He added, "I was probably in shock when I heard it." He added, "Aiello said what Shari did was almost criminal."

Moonves told the lawyers the only incidents that concerned him were the two he had reported to Aiello—the police report and the actress whose manager had called. The "six stories in *The New Yorker* never entered my mind," he said.

The lawyers spent relatively little time on those incidents or the substance of the *New Yorker* article. They'd already pretty much decided that the incidents were too old to be relevant to whether Moonves needed to be immediately suspended.

Moonves did score a few points in his defense. Illeana Douglas had told *The New Yorker* that Moonves had retaliated by getting her agent at CAA to drop her. But Moonves explained that her agent had dropped her because Martin Scorsese, her then-boyfriend, had moved to another agency, and CAA was representing her only as a favor to Scorsese. It had nothing to do with any retaliation by Moonves. And the idea that he'd locked Janet Dulin Jones in his office was absurd— he said his office didn't have a lock or remote switch. Perhaps Jones had been confused. The door did have a magnetic catch that had to be released by pushing an adjacent button. But he hadn't been trying to lock anyone in.

Still, even if correct, these were relatively small details in a long article. As Moonves had acknowledged in his statement to the magazine, there had been incidents where his behavior had been inappropriate.

After nearly four hours, the interview started to wind down. Moonves again expressed his concerns about leaks and took a swipe at Klieger.

"Rob Klieger doesn't just want to win a lawsuit," he maintained. "He wants to destroy me. It's really bad. And he's capable of doing virtually anything. Any of this information can and will be used against me."

"Why?" White asked.

"He works with Shari. He's better able to do it than she is. I'm not a weak person. It's really worn me down. I don't trust him at all. It's not enough to win the game. You have to destroy your opponent."

EPISODE 6

"This Is a Deal Breaker"

The next day Dan Petrocelli spoke again to Aiello and reported that Moonves had been interviewed by the lawyers, and "we had a good conversation." Aiello asked if the issue of the actress and her manager had come up. Petrocelli answered in a way Aiello considered "odd": it had come up, but Moonves hadn't provided any "details" because "I have a real concern about confidentiality," Petrocelli told him.

Unsure about exactly what Petrocelli had or hadn't disclosed, Aiello decided he'd better tell White and Kestenbaum about his talks with Moonves's lawyers. He described their recent phone call and said Petrocelli had brought up the incident involving the doctor in a previous phone call. Moonves had tried to kiss her, but he "didn't remember any of the more salacious stuff," Petrocelli had said. "That was the extent of that."

Then he summarized the incident with the actress, adding crucial details about Moonves's interactions with her "agent": "This weekend, I don't know if it was Saturday or Sunday—the talent agent again called Les," Aiello told them. "He said the woman was very unhappy with the small part. She hired an attorney. No other details." He repeated that there were just three contacts between Moonves and the agent: one in December; the next about the time of the Farrow article; and the third the past weekend, when Moonves learned she was unhappy and had hired a lawyer.

This revelation about an "agent" came as a bombshell to the lawyers. A thirty-year-old allegation of a sexual assault was one thing. But this had just happened. It suggested Moonves had succumbed to pressure to cover up the incident, using company resources to silence a potential threat. And he hadn't told them about it. If Moonves was covering up this, what else might he be hiding?

The lawyers were shaken. They called for an immediate follow-up interview with Moonves, which was set for Wednesday afternoon.

At 4:00 p.m. White and Kestenbaum briefed the special committee: Gordon, Klieger, and Griego. They gave an account of the previous day's interview with Moonves, touching on the police report, the actress, and the incidents reported in *The New Yorker*. Kestenbaum summed up Moonves's response: "There were times when he would feel an attraction, think it was mutual, make an overture, and if he got rebuffed, he would leave it alone."

White continued, "Our sense is that whatever occurred, you don't see that after he gets married. Appears to have a fourteen-year period without this activity. We asked him what else might be out there. He said there was a time when I was dating, there could be something there, but all consensual. He mentioned an encounter with a female doctor, which was rebuffed. Wouldn't give the name or any details."

Then Kestenbaum mentioned the revelations from Aiello about the actress and her manager. "Petrocelli described this scenario as a shakedown," White said.

"In our view, this raises serious concerns both with respect to candor and forthrightness and the fact that Les took steps with human resources of CBS," Kestenbaum added.

White said that, "until we heard this example," the lawyers were inclined to leave Moonves in place as chief executive while the investigation continued "and speed up getting to the end line on ultimate findings of the investigation. We have a different view now."

Kestenbaum noted that given Moonves's tendency to act on a sexual attraction, "there could well be more" incidents.

White went on, the "other risk is what I would call naivete about what he needs to disclose and what is risk. No one heard about the actress and getting her a job. Petrocelli has recognized that Les needs to be disclosing here. He did disclose late to both Larry and Weil what happened here." She seemed especially concerned that while Moonves recognized the personal risk—"his stomach is churning"—he didn't recognize that there was a larger risk to the company that needed to be disclosed.

She paused, and Gordon urged her to "keep going. You concluded that for the reasons you just stated, you weren't going to recommend a change of status, but changed your mind."

Kestenbaum answered. "In light of recent events, with the casting director, we are recommending that there be a change in status. We now think there is something new. Troubling.

"This is a deal breaker," she concluded.

———

Moonves's follow-up interview with the Debevoise and Covington lawyers began at 4:28 p.m. on August 15, also by phone. It focused almost entirely on the Moonves-Phillips-Dauer saga. Moonves faced what must have been the agonizing challenge of reconciling what had actually happened; what he'd told his lawyers; what he'd told Aiello in January; and what he thought he could still conceal.

Moonves walked through the narrative, mentioning the first call from Dauer the previous December. "It didn't make me feel good," he acknowledged, in what was surely an understatement. "That was a time of great fear. I was concerned about it. He did mention she's an actress and always looking for work."

What did Dauer mean by that? Kestenbaum asked.

"See if you can find anything for her." He added, "I didn't respond. I left it there. Frankly, I didn't do anything about it for many months."

Moonves said there was unlikely to be any record of the call: "We don't log the telephone calls."

Moonves minimized his interactions with Dauer. "He would call me about various actors. One day he asked if I would meet two of his clients." As for the actress, he'd ask, "'Is there anything going on out there? Any potential roles for her?' These were all phone calls—there were a couple lunches thrown in. And that would basically be it. He'd call about her and some of the other clients. That would be it."

There was no mention of texts.

Pressed for more detail about his interactions with Dauer, Moonves responded, "Purely a guess, maybe five or six phone calls. He would generally call me. He called me about other things also. He was a big baseball fan. He sent over an autographed baseball for my son. We probably also communicated by email or text. It wasn't a lot of contact."

"We'd be interested in those," Kestenbaum said.

Moonves said he understood.

By the time of his second meal with Dauer, "there was more of a sense of urgency about 'You haven't gotten her anything,'" Moonves said. "I hadn't done a single thing during this whole time to attempt to get her a job."

"Did you think he was threatening you?" Kestenbaum asked.

"No. I thought her manager was just trying to relay what was going on," Moonves said.

But after his lunch with Dauer on July 13, "I called Peter Golden and told him to look for something for her. I felt increasing pressure. I told Peter there is this actress. I mentioned #MeToo and didn't give him specifics and said, 'Can you find something?'" Moonves continued, "He understood what I was talking about. He attempted to find her work. When you say #MeToo . . . He understood this was a woman who was potentially making an accusation."

White wondered why Moonves would have told Golden that.

"I told him because it was sort of true that after lunch with Marv, there was more pressure to find her something because I didn't want her to go public with the story."

The next Moonves heard was that the actress had rejected a part and hired a lawyer. He said he hadn't been involved, but "I heard the money was too low and part too small. No idea what the part was. It was a CBS program and it never happened. I didn't follow up on it."

"Did you wrestle with whether it was appropriate to find her a part?" White asked.

"Yes," Moonves answered. "However, I've done this a hundred times, not with accusers, I would call Golden a hundred times to look for something. Yes, this was somewhat unusual. I did think about whether this was appropriate."

"What was the thinking?" White asked.

"Is she going to come out with a bad story about me or try to get something done here?" Moonves said. "I realize the circumstances were not great. I thought it was relatively minor. I do this a lot, asking Golden for parts."

Moonves said he didn't remember if he'd told Aiello about the manager during their January interview, but he thought he would have, given that the call from Dauer had come just weeks earlier.

And Moonves addressed his curious failure to bring up the manager at Monday's session. The "reason I didn't bring it up on Monday is because we were going chronologically. Big events happened in July." He said he'd already told Aiello and Tu and assumed they would be passing along the information.

———

The next day Petrocelli told Aiello that he'd gotten a letter from Eric George, a trial lawyer in Los Angeles who was representing Bobbie Phillips. He had bad news: George was threatening to sue both CBS and Moonves.

White and Kestenbaum briefed the special committee on the second Moonves interview four days later, focusing on Moonves's effort to get work for Phillips. Kestenbaum said they were "willing to give Moonves the benefit of the doubt about the issue of his candor with us about this incident at Monday's interview, although neither he nor Petrocelli made sufficiently clear that Moonves was omitting important information related to the incident with the actress and her manager." But, she continued, "Moonves seemed to find it reasonable to seek work for the actress to keep her from coming out with a 'bad story.' As I previously mentioned during our meeting on Wednesday, his lack of judgment and awareness in this area is potentially a risk factor."

Afterward the lawyers briefed the full board. To at least some of the directors, including all of the Shari faction, the revelations of the police report, the incident with a doctor, and most of all, the saga of the actress and her manager, came as bombshells. Moonves's follow-up interview had only reinforced many of the points White and Kestenbaum had discussed the day before: Moonves's handling of the manager and his use of company resources to silence the actress had put the entire company at risk. That alone should be grounds to suspend him immediately.

Not only that, but Kestenbaum told them these were unlikely to be the last incidents the board learned about. Moonves had not been forthcoming. More women were likely to emerge.

Arnold Kopelson had already sent everyone on the board an email reminding them that "Les is innocent until proven guilty." Now he went even further. "I don't care if a hundred more women come forward," Kopelson said. "Les is our leader and we have to stand behind him."

The board took no further action that day.

EPISODE 7

"A Once-Unfathomable Outcome"

That same week Ronan Farrow was in Los Angeles, ringing the doorbell at the gated community where Phyllis Golden-Gottlieb lived. He'd emailed her on August 21, but she hadn't responded. He'd reached out to her son. Still nothing. So he'd finally just shown up on her doorstep.

It hadn't been easy finding her, though word of her police complaint had surfaced in the press. The *Los Angeles Times* had reported on August 2 that "an 81-year-old woman told detectives that Moonves sexually assaulted her three decades ago when they both worked at then-television powerhouse Lorimar Productions, the studio behind such shows as 'Dallas' and 'Knots Landing.'"

The story, by reporters Meg James and Richard Winton, noted that the alleged incidents were too old to prosecute. The woman wasn't named.

Farrow had read the item and reached out to Winton. "Good reporting," Farrow complimented him. Winton didn't know the woman's identity but offered to connect Farrow with one of his sources at the police department. "I couldn't get them to talk, but maybe you can," he told Farrow.

Farrow spoke to the detective, who refused to name the woman but said he'd contact her and see if she wanted to talk to Farrow. She didn't. The detective relayed the response to Farrow and in doing so inadvertently used the woman's first name: Phyllis.

Fortunately there weren't that many women executives at Lorimar at the time named Phyllis. An extensive internet search led to an old student newspaper profile: "Phyllis Golden-Gottlieb, Hollywood Door-buster," which described her career as a Lorimar executive. ("I had the feeling of having walked in the boys' locker room," she'd said.)

Since Farrow's first Moonves article a few weeks earlier, more women had reached out to him. He'd now uncovered five more credible incidents involving Moonves, not counting Golden-Gottlieb.

Golden-Gottlieb answered the bell and Farrow introduced himself. "I've been calling you," he said. "I just want to make sure you have the opportunity to hear me out."

To his surprise, she invited him in. She told him her lawyer, the well-known women's advocate Gloria Allred, had instructed her not to talk. But now that he was there, "I'm so glad you came," she said.

Farrow took out his tape recorder.

———

On August 26 Nancy Kestenbaum reached out to Bobbie Phillips's lawyer, Eric George, and Dauer. George was encouraging about arranging an interview with Phillips, but Dauer said he was on the golf course and couldn't talk then.

Dauer immediately reported the call to Moonves. "Don't talk to them," Moonves instructed—a blatant violation of his contractual obligation to cooperate in the investigation.

Kestenbaum sent Dauer two texts following up. He ignored them.

But that wasn't all Moonves did to conceal his relationship with Dauer. He deleted nearly all their text messages from his phone. When the lawyers later asked for his iPad, he produced his son's instead. When they finally got Moonves's iPad, the settings had been recently adjusted to delete all saved text messages older than thirty days.

The lawyers' forensic specialists eventually found four hundred texts between Moonves and Dauer over an eight-month period.

———

As the Debevoise and Covington investigation proceeded, board members were in nearly constant contact, either individually or in frequent board calls. Kopelson aside, Moonves's board support had all but evaporated with the revelation that Moonves was trying to get Phillips a job to keep her quiet. Clearly, Moonves had lied—in some cases, in one-on-one conversations with directors—when he assured them that he had no #MeToo issues and CBS had nothing to worry about.

The only issue was the terms on which Moonves would depart: "for cause," in which case he'd get no severance or benefits, or without cause, in which case CBS might owe him more than $100 million.

Shari was surprisingly willing to be generous, even asking Moonves if he wanted an ongoing consulting or producing role. As long as he was off the premises, she felt CBS might still benefit from his deep institutional and industry knowledge. He would resign and not be fired. While CBS didn't want to pay him his full exit package, it offered him a lucrative compromise: $70 million plus other benefits. Moonves accepted: $70 million was a windfall under any circumstances, and especially so given the context of his departure.

Ianniello would succeed Moonves on an interim basis, and CBS would announce a search for a new chief executive. (The board had never found anything to substantiate the "bathrobe" rumors, and no other complaints about Ianniello had surfaced.)

It wasn't lost on the independent directors, even those most suspicious of Shari and her intentions, that Moonves's exit pretty much pulled the rug out from under the lawsuit to strip her of control. As Minow had pointed out, a primary motive for filing the suit had been to retain Moonves as chief executive and keep him happy. Now that motive was gone. The directors would never have agreed to bring the suit had they known the issues lurking in Moonves's past. Now that they knew, there was collective disbelief that Moonves had permitted the suit to go forward. What had he been thinking? Various directors speculated, but all they could come up with was that his powers of denial must have been extraordinary.

So negotiations to settle the lawsuits got underway even as Moonves's fate was still being discussed. By the weekend, terms had been hammered out: Both sides would withdraw the suits. There would be no grand jurisprudence resolving the fundamental issues of shareholder democracy that the case had promised to resolve. CBS wouldn't try to strip the Redstones and National Amusements of control, and Shari agreed that she wouldn't propose another merger of CBS and Viacom for at least two years unless two thirds of the independent directors agreed. She'd also withdraw the bylaw requiring a supermajority vote to issue a dividend. And the board would undergo a thorough overhaul. Seven board members agreed to resign, including her nemesis Gifford, and Kopelson, Moonves's most vocal ally. Shari would propose six new members.

A board meeting was set for Sunday, September 9, to elect new board members and ratify the terms of the lawsuit settlements and Moonves's departure. The board would announce the results on Monday morning before markets opened.

And then Schwartz got another call from *The New Yorker*. Farrow had six more Moonves victims, all of them speaking on the record, including Golden-Gottlieb, for a story about to go online and in the magazine Monday.

Schwartz dutifully conveyed the details he was being asked to factcheck, and the Debevoise and Covington lawyers scheduled another interview with Moonves.

—

The lawyers interviewed Moonves by phone on Saturday afternoon. They began with Peters, the diabetes doctor. Moonves acknowledged, "I did make an attempt/pass at her," according to notes of the interview. She rejected it, and "I don't remember all the circumstances that followed it," Moonves said. "I know it was very uncomfortable/awkward and I got out soon thereafter." He added, "It happened, I'm not proud of it. I obviously misread signs and I was inappropriate. I got out as soon as I could. That's my recollection."

He denied that he'd masturbated in front of her: "Absolutely not true."

Mary Jo White asked about Moonves's apology the next day.

"It is possible that I did call to apologize for making the approach to her," Moonves acknowledged. But he emphatically denied ever saying he had a problem being alone in a room with a woman. "I've been with thousands of women alone during my career and that's a statement I would never make about being alone with women," he said. "It's something I never said and never would have."

"Have you ever received counseling for sexual addiction?" White asked.

"None whatsoever," Moonves said.

The lawyers turned to the subject of Dauer's client Eva LaRue. Moonves said her name had come up during Dauer's first call in December. After that, nothing—Moonves added that he didn't speak to Dauer again "for seven to eight months."

When Dauer requested work for Phillips, White asked, "did you think he was using the situation as leverage for his other clients?"

"Managers and agents are always hustling," Moonves said.

"You didn't feel pressure?" White asked.

"Not at all," Moonves said.

Nancy Kestenbaum asked if he'd ever tried to get LaRue a part in December 2017 or in 2018.

"Absolutely not," Moonves insisted.

Nearly all of this, the lawyers knew, was false.

———

Petrocelli had alerted the lawyers to six more sexual encounters between Moonves and women working at CBS, all supposedly consensual. None of these figured in the latest *New Yorker* account.

Moonves wasn't eager to discuss them. "These were people I had relationships with," he said. "A few of them I haven't seen in many years. Most of them I'm still friendly with. [A] few of them are in marriages and this could hurt their lives."

One in particular raised the lawyers' eyebrows: an assistant to Moonves, one of whose functions was apparently to be on call to give Moonves oral sex at the office. She had called Moonves recently, worried that someone might contact her. Others in the office knew about their relationship, Moonves said, which had gone on for perhaps two years.

Moonves said their encounters were "purely sexual, oral sex" and took place in his office late in the day, when everyone else had generally gone home. All were "1000% consensual," he insisted.

He also mentioned another woman, a relatively senior executive, with whom he had an affair that lasted nearly six years. "I think most people at CBS were aware of this," he said. "She's also someone who recently got married," he added. "We still remain close." She was "still a senior executive" at CBS.

He said the affair had ended when he started dating Julie Chen.

Then they went through the latest six allegations from *The New Yorker*. As before, he acknowledged having had many of the encounters, though he insisted all were consensual. Much of the discussion focused on Golden-Gottlieb and the police report.

"She says I threw her against the wall the next day," Moonves said. "I've never touched a woman in my life, physically like that," he said. "That absolutely did not happen. I didn't go to her office the day after. I didn't berate her. I don't know where this came from. Once again, she didn't say that in her police report. And this retribution stuff, that I moved her office, couldn't be further from the truth."

Moonves said he'd read (but no longer had in his possession) Golden-Gottlieb's police report and it was inconsistent with what she had told *The New Yorker*. The report "didn't claim that I forcibly sexually assaulted her orally. It did reference a second meeting in my office, where most of the recollection is quite a bit different from here. She said that I exposed myself and ran out—also not true. Once again, the entire Phyllis Gottlieb saga, from the first time I heard it in November, has been to me an entire lie. The whole thing. Consensual relationship that happened twice, nothing forced."

Moonves summed up, "The person described in this article isn't me. I realize I'm in potential peril here and I just wanted to let you know that." He continued, "Both these articles are full of people I wouldn't have thought of in a million years. I'm not perfect, but I'm pretty sure I've told you everything. And you've certainly grilled me on everything. I can't think of anything else. This has been very trying because most of the events never happened at all, or partial truths, or consensual. I find it a little bit coincidental that the latest article comes out the day before I do my settlement with CBS. I find that very curious. The whole thing has been quite upsetting and I'm trying to be as open with you as I can."

"I know you are," White reassured him. "It's agony to say the least."

———

Klieger was driving to Palm Springs for a meeting with a witness in another case when he got a call from a Connecticut area code. It was Farrow. Klieger had never talked to him before, but Farrow told him he was working on another Moonves article, and there were more women. He'd heard the board was about to do something. He wanted to get the story out before the board acted.

As usual, neither Schwartz nor anyone else had told Klieger or Shari that another *New Yorker* story was in the works. But Klieger was eager to see the story published. He had remained adamant that CBS shouldn't pay Moonves a dime. He already believed Moonves could be fired for cause and was frustrated he couldn't get the independent directors to agree. Maybe this latest article would be decisive.

Klieger told Farrow no board action was "imminent," but it might very well happen that weekend.

Farrow's *New Yorker* article went online Sunday morning, reporting that "six additional women are now accusing Moonves of sexual harassment or assault in incidents that took place between the nineteen-eighties and the early two-thousands. They include claims that Moonves forced them to perform oral sex on him, that he exposed himself to them without their consent, and that he used physical violence and intimidation against them."

Golden-Gottlieb was the first example. She'd added some new details when she spoke to Farrow. After the forced oral sex in the car, "she vomited. 'It was just sick,' she told me," Farrow wrote. "She didn't report the incident at the time because she was a single mother supporting two children and feared for her career. 'I realized he was the new golden boy,' she told me. 'I just kept quiet.' But the incident, she said, 'never left me.'"

The article also cited a "veteran showrunner" who recalled that Golden-Gottlieb, in a social setting about a decade earlier, recounted her claim that Moonves had exposed himself to her.

Moonves again provided a statement: "The appalling accusations in this article are untrue," he said. While he acknowledged that he had "consensual relations" with three of the women, "anyone who knows me knows that the person described in this article is not me." He added, "I can only surmise they are surfacing now for the first time, decades later, as part of a concerted effort by others to destroy my name, my reputation, and my career."

With the CBS board poised to decide his fate, it was conspicuously restrained, this time offering no support for Moonves. The board said only that it "is committed to a thorough and independent investigation of the allegations, and that investigation is actively underway."

As soon as the *New Yorker* story appeared, *Vanity Fair* decided that Cohan's article about Moonves and Peters was worthy of publication after all. Cohan felt the lawyers had been too timid until they had the cover of Farrow's article. Had the story run earlier, it might have been a blockbuster. Now Cohan figured it would be lost in the commotion over Farrow's piece. Still, at least it was running.

Cohan called Schwartz for comment. At this point Schwartz just threw up his hands.

The *Vanity Fair* article appeared online a few hours after *The New Yorker*'s. Cohan quoted extensively from Peters's essay, which "hadn't crossed over to a wider audience that often discusses #MeToo issues," he wrote. "Last month, however, I learned from a source familiar with the situation that Dr. Peters was referring to Moonves."

The implications were obvious.

"Moonves is finished," Cohan wrote, "a once-unfathomable outcome that will cap off a series of unprecedented events, giving Shari Redstone her long-sought triumph."

Cohan was wrong about his story going unnoticed. Shari, for one, found it dispositive. She knew people who knew Peters. They described her as a highly respected professional who wouldn't lie or embellish.

The CBS board rushed out the announcement it had planned for Monday. Klieger got his wish: Moonves wouldn't receive a penny. There would be no producing or consulting deal. CBS would pay $20 million to a women's charity designated by Moonves and would set aside

$120 million until Debevoise and Covington completed their investigation and decided whether Moonves could be terminated for cause.

Moonves's sixteen-year tenure as CBS's chief executive was unceremoniously over.

———

A little more than a month later, on October 18, White, Kestenbaum, and their colleagues interviewed Bobbie Phillips in Toronto. Whether Moonves would receive the $120 million turned in large part on her testimony. The lawyers had still heard only Moonves's version of his encounter with Phillips—that there had been consensual oral sex—and his relationship with Dauer, which in Moonves's telling was confined to just three contacts since December.

Phillips was understandably nervous. She'd been in emotional turmoil since Dauer had dredged up the incident almost a year ago, and now she had to relive it yet again for an audience of strangers. But she took a deep breath and plunged in.

Phillips mentioned her roles in *The Watcher* and *Showgirls* and said her manager, Dauer, had set up the meeting with Moonves, which took place in February or March of 1995. Then she got to the heart of the matter.

"Some things are very clear in my mind," Phillips said, according to the lawyers' notes of the interview. "He was standing by the desk. We exchanged pleasantries. We sat on either side of his desk. He immediately asked me about *Showgirls*. He said, 'I'm going to introduce you to the casting director John Levey.' He tried to get ahold of John but he wasn't there at the time. Then he said, 'I'll set you up with John Levey.' He said, 'Come see my boards of shows.' He had a board on this wall. He was showing me *ER* and different shows. I'm responding to that, saying something. When I'm turning back around, he has his penis out. I looked down, he said, 'See how hard you make me.' It's so shocking. He says, 'Be my girlfriend and I'll put you on any show.'

He pushes me down and puts his penis in my mouth. I can't believe it. Then the intercom thing comes on. He's got John Levey. He goes to the phone. I stood up and everything is—I'm trying to come back—I see a baseball bat and a picture of his wife."

The memory of the baseball bat prompted tears, and Phillips had trouble continuing. But she forged on: "He's on the phone saying, 'I have this great actress.' He's doing up his pants. I grab the baseball bat. My blood is boiling, I'm going to knock his head off. I'm trying to get my thoughts together. He's so casual. He says, 'John wants to meet you.' I put the bat down. I said, 'I have a meeting with Disney and I have to go.' I grabbed my purse and left. I had to get out of there."

Bobbie had talked.

Epilogue

The idea that Moonves could walk away from CBS with $120 million enraged many people. Protesters gathered outside the Museum of Modern Art the day of the annual shareholder meeting. Moonves's potential golden parachute became a lightning rod for the pent-up rage that was focused on corporate America, which had largely ignored the misconduct of so many rich and powerful men so long as they delivered profits and higher stock prices.

After the revelations about Moonves, CBS would have faced a public relations nightmare if the board gave in to his severance demands. And by the end of the investigation, he had lost all credibility with the board. Lawyers at Covington and Debevoise told the CBS directors in December they didn't believe his version of events and that he had repeatedly lied and misled them about his behavior.

As one of its first steps, the new CBS board voted unanimously to fire Moonves for cause.

With Moonves gone, the board resurrected the idea of merging with Viacom, notwithstanding the promise not to do so for at least two years. A deal was announced in August 2019 and the merger was completed in December. The new company was named ViacomCBS, with Bakish as chief executive and Shari as chair.

Rather than report to Bakish, Ianniello left with an exit package worth an astronomical $125 million, the amount due him under his contract since Bakish was named chief executive rather than him.

Moonves and his lawyers launched an effort to gain the $120 million CBS had placed in escrow, and not because he needed the money. He was one of the richest men ever to come out of the television industry—CBS paid him nearly $70 million during his last two years alone. Moonves believed he'd been unfairly railroaded out of the company, and the money would vindicate him.

His lawyers had uncovered some additional evidence to cast doubt on his accusers, especially Phyllis Golden-Gottlieb. After she became a teacher, Golden-Gottlieb had written a blog post in 2007 describing some of the abuse she'd experienced as a woman in the entertainment business: "The president of a studio I worked for picked me up and threw me against the wall for failing to include a favorite of his on a memo—and I didn't cry. A network department head threatened to throw me out the window for making a decision when he was out of town—and I didn't cry. Another studio head joined me at a meeting to share good news—without his pants—and I didn't cry."

Two of the incidents correspond to Golden-Gottlieb's allegations about Moonves: throwing her against a wall and exposing himself at a meeting. But in the blog post, Golden-Gottlieb described two different people: a "president of a studio" and "another studio head." At the time the incidents supposedly happened, while Golden-Gottlieb and Moonves were working together, Moonves was neither president of the studio where Golden-Gottlieb worked nor a "studio head." There was no mention of any incident in a car. Golden-Gottlieb had never mentioned the blog post to Farrow, *The New Yorker*'s fact-checkers, or other interviewers.

But the blog post was hardly conclusive. Perhaps Golden-Gottlieb had deliberately obscured Moonves's identity by making her assailants different people and inflating their job descriptions. There was now no way to find out, since Golden-Gottlieb was suffering from advanced dementia. (She died in 2022.)

Even if Moonves's lawyers could discredit Golden-Gottlieb, she was only one of many accusers. And to do so would thrust Moonves into the unsympathetic position of trying to undermine a purported victim who was both elderly and in no position to defend herself.

After more than two years of legal skirmishing, in May 2021 Moonves agreed to forfeit all of the $120 million. Still, he didn't walk away empty-handed. In a surprising twist, one of the CBS law firms, Covington & Burling, agreed to pay him a confidential amount (sources pegged it at more than $10 million), which Moonves said he would donate to charity. Little was heard from him after the settlement.

Sumner's ex-companions also receded from public view. In 2018 a judge dismissed Herzer's $100 million lawsuit against Shari and Tyler, ruling that since Sumner was still alive, Herzer had no standing to contest the disposition of his assets.

Meanwhile, Sumner's elder abuse case against Herzer and Holland had proceeded. But Shari had no appetite for more litigation, let alone further public attention on her father's sex life. And it was unclear how much more stress her father could endure.

Shari and her family begged Sumner to settle the cases, first with Holland, and then with Herzer. Sumner finally agreed. Holland withdrew her claims and paid $250,000 to the Sumner Redstone foundation. The foundation in turn agreed to donate that amount to autism causes. (Alexandra was autistic.) Holland also agreed to post $750,000 in escrow, to be returned to her over a three-year period provided she complied with the settlement's strict confidentiality provisions. The settlement had the added benefit for Holland that she no longer had to worry about Pilgrim's potentially explosive testimony. Herzer agreed to repay $3.25 million and drop all claims. A nondisclosure agreement was also part of her settlement.

The settlements were a victory for Sumner in the sense that both Holland and Herzer had to forfeit something. But it was largely symbolic: the money they repaid was a tiny fraction of the roughly

$150 million he'd bestowed upon them. Still, "S and M," as Shari had so often referred to them, were out of her life at last.

———

Many characters in this saga came to Hollywood and reinvented themselves in pursuit of a distinctly twenty-first-century, California version of the American dream: money, power, sex, and a trophy mansion, more or less in that order. Sumner Redstone from Boston; Les Moonves from Long Island; Marv Dauer from Austin, Minnesota; Sydney Holland from San Diego; Manuela Herzer from Argentina. In this latest iteration of "the ends justify the means," seemingly no gambit was too outrageous, deceitful, or immoral, as long as it worked.

The actor George Pilgrim may have taken this to an extreme by impersonating a Hearst heir, crossing the sometimes-porous line between reinvention and fraud. But even a stint in prison didn't set him back for long: when he wrote those fateful messages to Holland, he was already promoting a new reality-TV series. But for his epiphany at Wally's, Pilgrim would have walked away with at least $10 million. Even after that, he never seemed to run short of cash.

Still, Pilgrim could no longer rely on his good looks and charm to extricate himself from the contentious situations he continued to find himself in. Over the years he faced a litany of lawsuits, from small claims and breach of contract to failure to provide child support.

By 2021 Pilgrim was back living with his mother and stepfather in Sedona. He was single again and seemed to have no trouble lining up dates with attractive women. While his autobiography, *Citizen Pilgrim*, hadn't yet found a publisher, he was working with a writer to adapt it as a screenplay. Ever the optimist, Pilgrim seemed to think his next big score was just over the horizon—along with a romantic reunion with Holland.

That possibility seemed farfetched, given their years of hostility, court proceedings, and Holland's ongoing efforts to erase Pilgrim from her life. For several seasons after her ouster from Beverly Park, Holland was reported to be a leading candidate for *The Real Housewives of Beverly Hills*. But no TV appearances materialized. In the meantime she continued buying, redecorating, and flipping high-end real estate. Three years after selling a Mulholland Estates mansion for $10.2 million in 2017, she listed her 6,700-square-foot white clapboard colonial in Pacific Palisades for $11.5 million.

In 2021 Holland bought a secluded ranch-style house with pool and tennis court for $4 million in Rancho Santa Fe, a residential enclave within metropolitan San Diego. She cited rising crime in Los Angeles and a nearby homeless encampment as reasons for the move back to a community near her hometown. ("There were needles on the street" near Pacific Palisades, she told *The Hollywood Reporter.*)

There may well have been other reasons, too. After Pilgrim's Los Angeles restraining orders expired in early 2022, he learned that Holland was romantically involved with a rich, elderly doctor in the San Diego area—in his view, another Sumner. In March he emailed her: "I love you," he insisted. But he also warned she was reverting to her "old ways" by sleeping with a "90 plus dr.," "another dinosaur with a trust." "Don't go there," he pleaded.

(A friend of Holland's said her romance with the doctor was short-lived. Holland's profile subsequently showed up on Raya, a selective, members-only dating app favored by celebrities.)

Pilgrim also proposed a DNA test to determine the twins' paternity.

Pilgrim's renewed emails—not to mention his unsettling knowledge of her move to Rancho Santa Fe and her personal circumstances—prompted Holland to seek another restraining order, which was granted by a San Diego court in June 2022 pending a court hearing the following month. (That hearing was postponed while lawyers for Holland and Pilgrim attempted to negotiate a settlement.)

Holland continued to give interviews to glossy local magazines about being a female entrepreneur and art patron, and a couture fashion show she hosted in 2022 at her new home in Rancho Santa Fe made the local society pages.

Holland sat on a number of boards, including UCLA's Institute of the Environment and Sustainability. Her biography on the Institute's website described her as a "renowned philanthropist," movie producer, and fashion consultant, touting her work "on the establishment and expansion of some of the most well-known international brands." No one at UCLA independently verified those claims. There is no mention in her biography of Sumner Redstone.

Before their expulsion by Sumner, Herzer and Holland were often photographed together at museum galas, including the Hammer Museum's gala at UCLA. But afterward, Herzer appears to have supplanted Holland at the Hammer. Herzer, not Holland, joined the museum's board in 2015, and recent galas have featured Herzer posing in designer outfits on the red carpet accompanied by one or more of her children and, on at least one occasion, Matt Marciano.

In 2019 Herzer applied for an account at First Republic Bank, a private bank known for personalized service to wealthy individuals. She was turned down and promptly sued the bank for gender discrimination. In her complaint she said the bank told her it rejected her application because she represented a reputational risk as someone who the bank believed had engaged in elder abuse. First Republic denied the allegations.

First Republic might well have rejected Herzer as a serial litigator, a reputation borne out by her subsequent lawsuit. Not only was Herzer embroiled in court with the Redstones for years, but she had been in near-constant litigation with a host of other defendants. Among them were her former lawyer Pierce O'Donnell, Sumner's estate lawyer Leah Bishop, and the general contractor and various subcontractors working on the seemingly never-ending renovation of her nine-thousand-square-foot Mulholland Drive estate overlooking the city. (All denied her allegations and, in the case of the contractor, countersued for non-payment.)

What might have happened had Holland rebuffed Pilgrim's overtures and, in league with Herzer, maintained and even increased her sway over Sumner? Both Shari and Klieger believed there was every chance Holland and Herzer would have gained control over National Amusements, and through it CBS and Viacom. The pair would no doubt have made a colorful addition to the roster of moguls gathered at Sun Valley.

———

Malia Andelin, the flight attendant who so transfixed Sumner, never heard from him again after her email cutting off their relationship. Two years later she married the man she'd been dating in a ceremony in the Peruvian Andes and helped care for his three children. Though she'd hoped to put the relationship with Sumner behind her, she spent years in therapy trying to deal with the shame and embarrassment she still felt about it.

Bobbie Phillips settled her claims against CBS, Covington & Burling, and Les Moonves in 2021. Though the terms remain confidential, she was paid more than $10 million, in part because her identity and account of being assaulted by Moonves were leaked to the press. After rebuffing the role of Erica in *Blood & Treasure*, she had no more interest in resuming an acting career. She and her husband invested in a wellness resort in Costa Rica.

Phillips was furious when she learned that her manager had been using her to gain leverage over Moonves. For his part, Marv Dauer said he was baffled that anyone would think he had tried to extort Moonves. In his view he was simply acting in the time-honored tradition of a Hollywood manager, which was to seize every advantage to advance his clients' interests.

Although Dauer had believed he and Moonves were friends, Moonves showed no interest in the Spam T-shirts Dauer brought back from Minnesota and ignored Dauer's subsequent messages.

While everyone else seemed to be walking away with millions, Dauer felt he'd become persona non grata in Hollywood. Both Phillips and his biggest client, Eva LaRue, left him. Phillips stopped taking his calls. His client list never recovered. Dauer had to sell his condo and give up his membership at MountainGate Country Club. He moved to an apartment in the San Fernando Valley, where he still manages to golf and, because of the pandemic, play bridge online.

Like many departing studio heads, Moonves formed a new production company, Moon Rise Unlimited, with an office on Sunset Boulevard initially paid for by CBS. But there's no indication Moon Rise embarked on any significant development projects. After leaving CBS, Moonves spent nearly all his time in California with his son Charlie and his wife, who began using the name "Julie Chen Moonves" in a show of support for her husband. They divided their time between the beachfront property in Malibu and their Beverly Hills estate. Moonves kept a low profile, giving up golf at the Bel Air Country Club because of a bad shoulder and declining press interviews.

After leaving the cast of *The Talk*, Julie Chen Moonves continued hosting the CBS summer reality series *Big Brother*, which had its twenty-third season in 2021. A small group of Moonves's old friends—the entertainment lawyer Allen Grubman, the songwriter Carole Bayer Sager, and the billionaire David Geffen among them—continued to socialize with him and his wife.

Several friends have said the famously hard-charging Moonves adapted to a more leisurely role of husband and father and was especially glad to spend time with his son. They've predicted it's only a matter of time until Moonves, backed by his large fortune, his loyal and popular wife, and his vast network of Hollywood contacts, re-emerges as one of Hollywood's éminences grises.

Still, Moonves chafed at being lumped together with Harvey Weinstein in the pantheon of #MeToo offenders. Unlike Weinstein, Moonves was never charged with assault or any other crime (most of the alleged incidents were too old), nor was he sued civilly. Had any of the allegations been litigated, some would have been hard to prove. A few former CBS board members remained convinced that Moonves was swept up in a mass hysteria (Arnold Kopelson, who died soon after Moonves resigned, foremost among them). But most of them found his behavior inexcusable, then or now. Whether or not a crime, his conduct had grossly violated professional norms.

———

Having emerged on top after years of conflict, Shari Redstone appeared on the cover of the October 31, 2019, issue of the Forbes 400 richest people in America. And the magazine ranked her twenty-fourth on its list of the world's most powerful women, ahead of Queen Elizabeth II.

After long describing herself as a reluctant mogul, Shari told friends and advisers she loved her new role as chair of ViacomCBS. She felt her years at Advancit investing in new technologies had attuned her to the younger generation the company needed to attract. She was fascinated by the intersection of entertainment and technology. As one example, she pressed the company to jump on the nascent market for nonfungible tokens after the artist known as Beeple sold a token for $69 million. She enjoyed matching Viacom executives and entrepreneurs and thinkers in hopes of igniting creative sparks.

The chief executive she anointed, Bob Bakish, warmly welcomed Shari's ideas and involvement. Still, his tenure wasn't without its issues. A former Viacom employee alleged that Bakish fondled her at a holiday party in 2016, a claim reported by the website *The Information* in 2020. With the accusation coming so soon after the Moonves scandal, both Shari and Klieger insisted the board hire an outside law firm and conduct an investigation. The board subsequently issued a statement that the company took any such allegation seriously, but the results of the investigation "did not support the allegation." The company hasn't released any details of the probe.

Though Sumner was no doubt an exceptionally difficult client, the years of constant litigation left Shari with an understandably jaded view of the legal profession, or at least some members of it, and its supposedly sacred obligation to put the client's interest first. She found Leah Bishop's claims that she had only carried out Sumner's wishes to be especially galling. Whose interests had CBS's chief legal counsel Lawrence Tu been serving when he repeatedly blocked her efforts to investigate the Moonves allegations? What could possibly explain Michael Aiello's cursory investigation and subsequent exoneration of Moonves? Not to mention his support for the misguided lawsuit against the Redstones' interests cooked up by Wachtell Lipton.

Nor had her experience bolstered her confidence in shareholder democracy. The Viacom and CBS boards of directors were dominated by allies of her father who, when they had to choose, cast their lot with their respective (male) chief executives and went to war with a (female) controlling shareholder. Even without any element of sexism, Shari had confronted a pervasive problem in American corporations, which is the way chief executives dominate the boards charged with overseeing them. The CBS and Viacom directors all purported to be acting on behalf of all shareholders, but how had shareholders benefited?

By most objective measures, Shari was proven right about the merger and her choice of Bakish as chief executive. During the two years he'd presided at Viacom, Bakish had brought the company back from the brink. Adopting a posture of humility, he managed to coax back the big cable operators, and he concluded a multiyear renewal deal with the rebellious Charter Communications. Viacom acquired Pluto TV and laid plans for its Paramount+ streaming service, combining the CBS All Access platform and Viacom's streaming operations. In June 2021 Bakish announced that Pluto would reach $1 billion in revenue a year ahead of schedule. In February 2022 ViacomCBS indicated that a new era was at hand, renaming itself Paramount Global, with the studio's iconic mountain peak as its logo. Gone was Sumner's cherished but little-recognized Viacom name, not to mention CBS, a still-potent brand, but one dwindling in significance along with the other legacy networks.

That summer Paramount had a huge but distinctly old-media box office success in *Top Gun: Maverick*, the return of Tom Cruise in a sequel to his 1980s megahit *Top Gun*. The film opened exclusively in theaters, breathing new life into struggling theater chains (including National Amusements) before migrating midsummer to streaming (although it was available immediately on Paramount+ with a trial subscription).

Shari did her best to reform the male-centric culture she inherited, especially at CBS. In 2019 CBS named Susan Zirinsky president of CBS News, the first woman to lead the news division. (She stepped down in 2021 and was succeeded by coheads, one a woman.) Seven of thirteen ViacomCBS board members were women, including Shari and Linda Griego, the lone holdovers from the Moonves-era CBS board.

There's no question that combining CBS and Viacom allowed the company to gain greater scale. But was it enough? While its streaming services had a better-than-expected 36 million subscribers in mid-2021, that was only big enough to rank sixth. ViacomCBS was far behind the leaders: Netflix (213 million), Amazon Prime (175 million), Disney+ (118 million), and Peacock (54 million).

Wall Street analysts were skeptical. And by the measure Sumner cared most about—the stock price—the merger had failed to stem the company's decline. The combined market capitalization of Viacom and CBS was $30 billion when the merger was announced in 2019. By mid-June 2022 it was less than half that, just under $15 billion. It was up against competitors that were many times larger: Amazon (market capitalization of over $1 trillion), Netflix ($77 billion), and Walt Disney ($172 billion).

While its competitors seized the opportunities presented by the digital revolution, Viacom and CBS lost precious years to their internal struggles. It's safe to say that the intracompany warfare prior to 2018 delivered the worst possible outcome—neither a merger of CBS and Viacom nor a sale to someone else.

Since the merger, Shari has said she'd sell the company at the right price. Rumors swirled briefly after she was spotted at 2021's Sun Valley conference (where she no longer needed someone like Moonves to show her around) talking to possible suitor Brian Roberts, the chief executive of Comcast. But nothing immediately came of it. Rather than megadeals, she has said she would prefer to focus on joint ventures, expanding Paramount Global's reach while preserving Redstone family control.

Shari was also running the Sumner M. Redstone Charitable Foundation, focusing on education and efforts to combat anti-Semitism and other forms of discrimination by reaching children at an early age.

For most of the pandemic she worked from her house in Connecticut, located just steps from the beach on Long Island Sound. She sometimes found herself getting just three to four hours of sleep a night, but she managed to take her young grandchildren to the movies—they watched Paramount's *PAW Patrol* (which both streamed on Paramount+ and was a box office success in August 2021) at a National Amusements multiplex in Westchester County (where Shari checked out the candy display).

———

I t's not clear to what extent Sumner himself understood or was able to savor his daughter's success. Peter Bart, the former longtime editor of *Variety*, who was close to Sumner, was granted a rare visit in

2019. "His withered hand signaled a greeting, or the semblance of one," Bart reported in a column for *Deadline Hollywood*. "His eyes flickered weakly, but his effort at conversation was reduced to a grunt, mixed with an occasional scream of rage and frustration over his limitations." Sumner was bedridden, being fed intravenously, and "a team of nurses and conservators stand by for needed assistance," Bart observed.

On the morning of October 11, 2020, Sumner's nurse called Shari from Beverly Park to tell her she thought the end was near.

Shari told the nurse to put warmers on Sumner's hands and to hold him. She kept the phone line open so her father could hear her talk, even if he wasn't conscious. She imagined him saying, "What the fuck are you talking about? I'm not going anywhere." But "just in case," she said, "here's what you need to know."

Over the next several hours she reviewed his life's accomplishments. She promised to take care of the family and to nurture the business empire he'd created. "It will be here forever," she assured him. "I love you," she said over and over.

Finally the nurse told her that Sumner had quietly stopped breathing. Shari screamed.

Sumner was ninety-seven. National Amusements announced his death, describing him as "the self-made businessman, philanthropist and World War II veteran who built one of the largest collections of media assets in the world."

Despite their late-in-life reconciliation, Shari could never be certain she'd gained her father's approval given his impaired faculties. Just after Sumner died, she reached out to Tad Jankowski, her father's former teaching assistant, friend, and longtime business colleague, for reassurance. Had she done the right thing? she asked, citing Dauman's ouster and firing Moonves. Would her father have approved? Had he really loved her?

What could he say? Jankowski emphasized that Sumner had loved a fight and loved to win. Shari had never given up. She'd proven her mettle. Her father would have "loved and respected that," he assured her. He would be proud of her.

Sumner's remains were flown to Boston. Shari, Tyler, and Kimberlee accompanied the hearse to the family plot at Sharon Memorial Park that Holland and Herzer had tried to get their hands on. (Brandon was in Israel, but participated using FaceTime.) Sumner's son Brent and his family were absent. Due to the pandemic, no one else was present except for Shari's ex-husband, Rabbi Korff, who conducted the burial ceremony.

The gathering was so intimate Shari felt no need to restrain her emotions. She knelt so close to the grave her children worried she might fall in. Between bouts of crying, she told her father everything she'd ever wanted to say to him.

Finally she stopped. "Is there anything else?" she asked.

Her daughter reminded her that Sumner had asked that Frank Sinatra's recording of "My Way" be played at his funeral. Shari had always cringed on the many occasions Sumner had insisted on listening to it. But now she asked Kim to pull up the lyrics on her phone. Shari began singing:

And now the end is here
And so I face that final curtain

She struggled through the five verses, each ending with the refrain:

I did it my way.

ACKNOWLEDGMENTS

There were many people who made this book possible, including colleagues at *The New York Times* who contributed to the work that inspired it. David Enrich was our editor throughout our reporting on Les Moonves and CBS, including "'If Bobbie Talks, I'm Finished'" and other stories that ran in the paper in 2018. He's the perfect combination of exacting and fun. David was the first to suggest we had the makings of a book and acted as a sounding board throughout the process. We're extremely grateful for his time, perceptive feedback, and good judgment.

Our fellow *Times* reporter Ellen Gabler contributed invaluable reporting to "'If Bobbie Talks'" and was on the Moonves case from the earliest days of the #MeToo movement. Nick Summers, then-editor of the Sunday edition of *The New York Times*, came up with the "Bobbie" headline and steered the story into the paper.

The story would likely not have happened without Jim Windolf, then the *Times*'s media editor, whose direction early on led to a key source. David McCraw, the *Times*'s lawyer with an editor's eye, helped us navigate legal issues and bulletproofed our work. The intrepid *Times* researchers Alain Delaquérière, Doris Burke, and Susan Beachy contributed to our stories, and Susan Beachy also worked with us on our book, helping us to track down the most elusive of sources and court records.

Acknowledgments

We would also like to thank the *Times*'s business editor Ellen Pollock, who supported our reporting and was enthusiastic about the results. The top leadership of the *Times* backed our reporting over the years, helping to challenge and elevate it, and allowed us to take time off to write this book. Deputy Managing Editor Matthew Purdy was especially inspiring and encouraging. We are grateful to be part of the *Times*'s mission, and to be surrounded by such an array of thoughtful, talented, and committed journalists.

Our colleagues on the business desk, in the Styles section, and in other bureaus and parts of the paper were generous with their guidance when we had questions. They embody the spirit of collaboration we have enjoyed while working at the *Times*.

Our powerhouse agent, Amanda Urban, jumped on the idea for this book the moment we brought it up and supported us at every step of the reporting, writing, editing, and publishing process. Our agent in Hollywood, Ron Bernstein, was an early and perceptive reader.

At Penguin, our editor, Ann Godoff, was our north star. This will be James's fourth book with Ann, a staunch supporter of the highest standards of journalism and whose keen eye for a good story guided us throughout. Her assistant, Casey Denis, kept us on track. Yuki Hirose guided us through a thorough legal review, for which we're especially grateful.

We also owe an enormous debt of gratitude to our unbelievably careful, hardworking, and well-organized fact-checker and researcher, Gabriel Joseph Baumgaertner. We wouldn't want to think about what this process would have been like without him.

Lastly, we'd like to thank Bojan Vukadinovic, Mirza Feratovic, and the rest of the friendly staff of Wolfgang's Steakhouse on Forty-first Street, an unofficial gathering place in the *Times* building. It's where so many of us have gone over the years to celebrate, commiserate, and share the stories that we're excited to work on a few floors above.

Acknowledgments

From James:

Writing a book during a pandemic made the support of my friends and family all the more precious and valuable, especially on the rare occasions when we could actually spend time together in person. I'm grateful to my brother, Michael; his wife, Anna; and my nephews and niece Aidan, Blaine, and Cassie; my sister, Jane Holden; her husband, John; their children, Lindsey, Laura, Jack, and Margaret, and their growing families.

My longtime friend Steve Swartz was a valuable sounding board during our frequent lunches, as was James Cramer. My friend of many years and former editor Jane Berentson taught me the importance of the telling detail, which I hope is reflected in these pages. My friends and fellow authors Sylvia Nasar and Arthur Lubow were always available to commiserate and to encourage me.

Steve Coll, the former dean of the Columbia School of Journalism; Winnie O'Kelley, dean of academic affairs; and Bill Grueskin have been valuable and supportive colleagues of mine at the journalism school.

Over the years I've been lucky to work with and learn from some fantastic editors: Steven Brill, Jane Amsterdam, Norman Pearlstine, Paul Steiger, Tina Brown, David Remnick, and John Bennet, my longtime editor at *The New Yorker*, not to mention one of the best: Alice Mayhew, the legendary Simon & Schuster editor, who died in 2020 as I was working on this book. Alice gave me my start in book publishing and was always there for me.

This is the first book I've written with a coauthor. I barely knew Rachel Abrams when a chance encounter in the newsroom led to "'If Bobbie Talks'" and the beginnings of this book. Since then we've been in contact nearly every day. She was a dream collaborator: incredibly hardworking, resourceful, ethical, considerate, and brimming with enthusiasm for every discovery. Working with her was both inspiring and fun.

Finally, I have my husband, Benjamin Weil, to thank. Along with all the usual demands and tribulations of researching and writing a book, which alone would be more than enough, he got me (and us) through the illness, isolation, quarantines, and disruptions of the pandemic, his chicken soup always at the ready. There's no way to repay him or to express my gratitude.

From Rachel:

I'm very grateful to the many people who have supported me personally and professionally in three different newsrooms. Voice of America's Mike O'Sullivan gave me my first internship, and Shalini Dore gave me my first paid job at *Variety*. I owe a huge debt to *Variety*'s Cynthia Littleton, a mentor of seemingly endless patience from whom I learned so much about reporting on the entertainment industry.

At the *Times*, Susanne Craig has never been too busy to help me think through a tough story, despite working on Pulitzer Prize–winning reporting about Donald Trump's taxes. I am so thankful for Rebecca Ruiz, one of the most talented journalists I know, for her many years of friendship and wisdom. Bill Brink, Jim Windolf, David Enrich, Jason Stallman, and Kevin Flynn are the types of editors that every journalist should be lucky enough to work with.

Thank you to my friends Rachel and Adam Horne, Andrew Hearst, Bronwyn James, Mike Kellogg, Bjarni Sighvatsson, Michael Dreyfuss, Ashley Graf, Jon Spagnola, Kate Myers, Ali Mendes, and Tom Wilson for listening to me talk about this project far past the point any of you were actually interested. Thank you to Andrew Jacobs and Dan Levin for sheltering me during the height of the pandemic, and for the kindness and generosity that you have shown me and so many other people.

Jim Stewart may have ruined all future book projects for me, because I can't imagine having a better experience than this one. Jim is a

Acknowledgments

master storyteller whose reputation is belied by his grace and humility. Working with him has made me a better journalist, and I am very grateful to have had him as a partner.

Thank you to my loving family, Mike, Robyn, Carol, Erin, and Rebecca. And lastly, thank you to my wonderful parents, Ian and Alice. My father, who cocreated a television show that ran on CBS and steeped me in the media world, has basically pushed me to do a book since I learned to walk. He is a brilliant writer and has been an invaluable sounding board on this project. And to my extraordinary mother, who worked in a newsroom and elsewhere in a very different era, and who pushed and endured so that I might see more dignity and respect in my lifetime.

NOTES

Unscripted grew out of our November 28, 2018, *New York Times* story "'If Bobbie Talks, I'm Finished,'" which focused on the downfall of Leslie Moonves and his dealings with Bobbie Phillips and Marv Dauer. Much of this book comes from an additional three years of interviews and research.

We interviewed many people on a not-for-attribution basis. Sources had a variety of reasons for requesting anonymity, including settlement and severance agreements that stipulated promises not to talk; fear of being sued by wealthy and potentially litigious opponents; and the attorney-client privilege or pending litigation. In addition to the welter of lawsuits described in the text and noted below, several cases were ongoing at the end of 2021.

Many sources did speak on the record; supplied copies of texts, emails, and other documents; or agreed to be identified as sources.

George Pilgrim cooperated extensively, and everything he told us was on the record. We were mindful that Pilgrim is a convicted felon and has previously falsified aspects of his past, such as his purported biological connection to William Randolph Hearst. In our interviews he readily acknowledged his past misdeeds and fabrications. Much of what he told us was corroborated by other witnesses or documents, as indicated in the text and in the notes below. He also described many of the incidents to others at the time they occurred, who in turn corroborated his accounts. He also wrote much of his story in early drafts of his autobiography, which we reviewed, and they were consistent with his subsequent accounts.

In June 2022 Stanton L. Stein, a lawyer for Holland, sent us a letter "to put you on notice that Mr. Pilgrim is not a reliable source of information" and "has a history of making false and defamatory statements about Ms. Holland." In response we offered to go over any information we planned to use. We also sent Holland and Stein a detailed memo outlining matters to which we thought she might wish to respond.

Holland again declined. "I should be clear that her decision not to speak or to engage on a point-by-point rebuttal to your request is not an admission or acknowledgment of the truth of any of the items set forth in your memo," Stein wrote. "Ms. Holland has long ago moved on and there is nothing to be gained by a back-and-forth on any of these topics." He added, "I should reiterate that, to the extent you are relying on Mr. Pilgrim as a source, you are doing so at your own peril."

Of the women who accused Moonves of sexual misconduct, Janet Jones, Dinah Kirgo, Phyllis Golden-Gottlieb, and Bobbie Phillips were interviewed on the record. We were reminded again how painful it was for these women to relive such traumatic experiences and the courage that it took for them to share their stories.

Marv Dauer cooperated extensively and all of his interviews were on the record.

Patti Stanger was interviewed on the record and participated in fact-checking.

Shari Redstone responded to all our questions either directly or through a spokesperson, and participated in fact-checking, as did Tyler and Brandon Korff.

Everyone named in the book other than in passing was given the opportunity to comment. Many participated in fact-checking but asked not to be identified as sources. Some, notably Sydney Holland and Manuela Herzer, rebuffed multiple efforts to interview them.

Nevertheless, we were able to incorporate much of their version of events thanks to the numerous lawsuits they filed or participated in.

Terry Holbrook declined to be interviewed but offered this comment: "I adored and love Sumner and his family. I was there before Sydney and remained there until the end." She said some prior reporting about her was "not the truth" but declined to be specific.

Leslie Moonves provided his version of events in extensive interviews with lawyers from Covington & Burling and Debevoise & Plimpton representing CBS. Since we had access to those transcripts we were able to incorporate his version of events in the text. Michael Aiello was interviewed by the same lawyers. He otherwise declined to speak to us, as did Leah Bishop, Sumner's estate lawyer, citing attorney-client privilege. So did Sumner's longtime estate lawyer David Andelman, although we had access to his affidavit described in the text.

By 2018, when we began our reporting, Sumner Redstone was seriously incapacitated and no longer speaking to journalists (or hardly anyone else) other than close family members and caregivers, except for the journalist Peter Bart, whose 2019 visit is described in the text.

As discussed in the preface, we had the benefit of a trove of documents provided by confidential sources. Many of those documents are quoted in the text. A few text messages were edited to a minor degree, and a few were deleted within extended exchanges for reasons of clarity. Much of the dialogue comes from transcripts or recordings, as indicated in the text and notes. Some is based on participants' recollections.

Other reporters have written extensively about the extended saga of the Redstone family and the companies they controlled. While instances where we relied on their work are indicated in the notes below, several warrant special recognition.

Ronan Farrow of *The New Yorker* and William D. Cohan writing for *Vanity Fair* had a significant influence on the course of events and appear as characters in our story.

"The Disturbing Decline of Sumner Redstone" by Peter Elkind with Marty Jones, a three-part series published in *Fortune* on May 5, 2016, just before the trial of Manuela Herzer's health care proxy challenge, was the first article to reveal many of the bizarre goings-on inside Sumner's Beverly Park mansion, his relationship to his two companions, and Holland's clandestine relationship with Pilgrim.

The King of Content, a biography of Sumner Redstone by Keach Hagey, a reporter for *The Wall Street Journal*, was published by Harper Business in June 2018, when Sumner was still alive. For readers interested in the early history of National Amusements, the book contains much more detail on the contentious Redstone family history that resulted in Sumner's control.

The New York Times, *The Wall Street Journal*, *Deadline Hollywood*, *Variety*, and *The Hollywood Reporter* also had extensive and sometimes groundbreaking coverage.

Preface
xiv **"We all did that"**: "'Disaster for CBS Shareholders': Damning Report on Moonves Reveals Total Failure at Top," December 4, 2018, https://www.nytimes.com/2018/12/04/business/leslie-moonves-cbs-board.html.

Trailer
1 **"Sydney Holland, the 43-year-old"**: Matthew Belloni and Eriq Gardner, "Sumner Redstone Legal Turmoil: Fighting Women, Lie-Detector Tests, Stolen Laptop with 'Private' Photos," *Hollywood Reporter*, June 25, 2014.

1 **There was a photo**: Belloni and Gardner, "Sumner Redstone Legal Turmoil."

1 **"So glad you're taking"**: Peter Elkind and Marty Jones, "The Disturbing Decline of Sumner Redstone (Part 3 of 3)," *Fortune*, May 5, 2016, https://fortune.com/longform/sumner-redstone-part-3/.

2 **Pilgrim had starred in**: Kevin Harlin, "Hearst Impostor Admits to Fraud—Californian Sold Ads While Pretending to Be Times Union Executive," *Times Union* (Albany), April 26, 2001.

3 **Pilgrim pleaded guilty**: Harlin, "Hearst Impostor Admits to Fraud."

3 **"I know who has"**: Elkind and Jones, "Disturbing Decline of Sumner Redstone (Part 3 of 3)."

3 **In her lawsuit**: Complaint 2, Sydney Holland v. Heather Naylor (Superior Court of the State of California for the County of Los Angeles) (Case No. BC519989).

3 **"Congrats on your"**: Elkind and Jones, "Disturbing Decline of Sumner Redstone (Part 3 of 3)."

Season 1, Episode 1: *"I'm Going to Hell Anyway"*
9 **Herzer had complained**: William D. Cohan, "Endless Sumner," *Vanity Fair*, June 2015, 112.

10 **Sumner was soon calling**: Mark David, "In Other . . . ," *Variety*, March 30, 2009.

10 **He bought her a $3.85 million**: Complaint at page no. 5, para no. 21, Manuela Herzer v. Leah Bishop (Superior Court of the State of California for the County of Los Angeles, West Judicial District) (Case No. SC129651).

Notes

10 **After two years:** William D. Cohan, "Hostage to Fortune," *Vanity Fair*, April 2016, 124.

10 **While Herzer's house:** Redstone Elder Abuse Complaint at 7, Sumner M. Redstone v. Manuela Herzer and Sydney Holland (Superior Court of the State of California for the County of Los Angeles, Central District) (Case No. BC638054).

10 **They had hired a prominent:** Exhibit U at 445, April 25, 2016, In re: Advance Health Care Directive of Sumner M. Redstone (Superior Court of the State of California for the County of Los Angeles) (Case No. BP 168725).

10 **And Holland had already initiated:** Petition for Probate of Will and for Letters Testamentary at Item B, Attached Pages, Estate of Sumner M. Redstone (Superior Court of the State of California for the County of Los Angeles) (Case No. 20STPB08647).

10 **She owned 20 percent:** CBS Corp. et al. v. National Amusements Inc., Shari Redstone, Sumner Redstone et al., in RE: CBS Corporation Litigation, Consolidated, page 11 (In the Court of Chancery of the State of Delaware) (Civil Action No. 2018-0342-AGB).

11 **She and Holland maintained:** Holland's Answer to Complaint at 12–14, Redstone v. Herzer and Holland.

11 **Holland had skipped college:** Redstone Elder Abuse Complaint at 5, Redstone v. Herzer and Holland.

11 **"to bring the feuding family together":** Holland's answer to complaint at 11, Redstone v. Herzer and Holland.

11 **"I have come to the conclusion":** Plaintiff Sumner M. Redstone's Amended Separate Statement in Opposition to Defendant Manuela Herzer's Motion for Summary Judgment at 11, Redstone v. Herzer and Holland.

11 **"I am not going":** Keach Hagey, *The King of Content: Sumner Redstone's Battle for Viacom, CBS, and Everlasting Control of His Media Empire* (New York: Harper Business, 2018), 238.

11 **Holland and Herzer as "whores":** First Amended Complaint at 34, Manuela Herzer v. Shari Redstone and Tyler Korff (United States District Court Central District of California) (Case No. 2:17-cv-07545-PSG (KSx)).

11 **But he was surely one:** Cohan, "Hostage to Fortune," 124.

12 **The family lived briefly:** Sumner Redstone, *A Passion to Win* (New York: Simon & Schuster, 2001), 41.

12 **"My mother had one":** Redstone, *A Passion to Win*, 42.

13 **"I had no social life":** Redstone, *A Passion to Win*, 44.

13 **"studied all the time":** Redstone, *A Passion to Win*, 49.

13 **The next year, at twenty-four:** "Sumner Redstone to Wed Miss Raphael," *Boston Globe*, January 26, 1947.

13 **Sumner coined the word:** Larry Edelman, "Building a Fortune in Drive-ins to MTV," *Boston Globe*, September 13, 1993.

13 **When *Jaws* opened:** Letters, *Quad-City Times*, August 24, 1975.

14 **"The pain was excruciating":** Redstone, *A Passion to Win*, 16.

14 **Sumner required sixty hours:** Kathryn Harris, "Sumner Redstone Prevails by 'Force of Will,'" *Los Angeles Times*, November 11, 1989.

14 **"the will to win":** Redstone, *A Passion to Win*, 20.

14 **wearing a sports jacket:** Edmund Lee, "Sumner Redstone, Hollywood Brawler," *New York Times*, August 12, 2020.

14 **"I just want to beat Barry":** Cohan, "Endless Sumner," 117.

14 **In October 2000 *Forbes* estimated:** Peter Newcomb et al., "Content Kings," *Forbes*, October 9, 2000, 140–61.

15 **companion Delsa Winer:** William R. Cash, "List of Those Hospitalized after Fires," *Boston Globe*, March 30, 1979.

15 **who exited the hotel window:** Deborah Mitchell, "A Very Good Summer Read," *New York Daily News*, June 18, 2000.

15 **Twice she'd sued:** Johnnie Roberts, "Redstone's Wife Filed for Divorce but Dropped Suit," *Wall Street Journal*, December 22, 1993.

15 **But when accounts of an affair:** Jeane MacIntosh, "Viacom Mogul Could Be Sumner $quashed," *New York Post*, September 19, 1999.

15 **Soon after meeting, Sumner and Peters:** Mitchell Fink, "Chief's Sizzling Summer Vacation," *New York Daily News*, September 8, 1998.

15 **dining at the famed La Tour d'Argent:** Christine Peters, "My 18-Year Relationship with Sumner Redstone," *Hollywood Reporter*, August 19, 2020.

15 **After the Rupert Murdoch–owned:** Jeane MacIntosh, "Viacom Tycoon Confesses to Affair with H'Wood Exec," *New York Post*, September 22, 1999.

Notes

16 **Armed with evidence of:** MacIntosh, "Viacom Mogul Could Be Sumner $quashed."

16 **a share to which she was entitled:** James Cox, "Viacom: Divorce Rumors Unfounded," *USA Today*, December 23, 1993.

16 **She, too, felt betrayed:** George Rush and Joanna Molloy with Lola Ogunnaike, "Theme from a Sumner Place," *New York Daily News*, November 14, 2000.

16 **"I just didn't see myself":** Peters, "My 18-Year Relationship with Sumner Redstone."

16 **He dictated and faxed:** Peter Elkind, "The Disturbing Decline of Sumner Redstone (Part 1 of 3)," *Fortune*, May 5, 2016.

16 **"he had been banned":** Peters, "My 18-Year Relationship with Sumner Redstone."

16 **which included an incident in Hawaii:** Elkind, "Disturbing Decline of Sumner Redstone (Part 1 of 3)."

16 **"I'm going to hell anyway":** Elkind, "Disturbing Decline of Sumner Redstone (Part 1 of 3)."

17 **That hadn't deterred Herzer:** George Rush and Joanna Molloy with Kasia Anderson, "Tracy's Girls Stand by Their Man," *New York Daily News*, March 13, 2001.

17 **When she and Sumner met:** Cohan, "Hostage to Fortune."

17 **Herzer was born in Argentina:** Complaint at 4, Sumner M. Redstone v. Sydney Holland and Manuela Herzer (Superior Court of the State of California for the County of Los Angeles) (Case No. BC638054).

17 **she'd been educated:** Complaint at 4, Redstone v. Holland and Herzer.

17 **She'd already gone through:** Complaint at 4–5, Redstone v. Holland and Herzer.

17 **That relationship ended:** Complaint at 4–5, Redstone v. Holland and Herzer; James Rainey, "Sumner Redstone Sues Two Ex-companions for $150 Million," *Variety*, October 25, 2016.

18 **Sweetwood set Sumner up:** Bryan Burrough, "Sleeping with the Fishes," *Vanity Fair*, December 2006, 244.

18 **She'd never heard of:** Burrough, "Sleeping with the Fishes."

18 **After their first dinner:** Burrough, "Sleeping with the Fishes."

18 **After three years of intense:** "Pro Golfer Ponders Building Local Course; Media Mogul's Marriage Ends," *Boston Globe*, July 27, 2002.

19 **the shares themselves:** Elkind, "Disturbing Decline of Sumner Redstone (Part 1 of 3)."

19 **There were five nonfamily:** "The Sumner M. Redstone National Amusements Trust," May 20, 2016, "Sumner Redstone Plans to Add National Amusements Executive to Trust: Sources," Reuters, May 22, 2016.

19 **As part of the settlement:** Phyllis G. Redstone, Schedule 13D under the Securities Exchange Act of 1934: Midway Games Inc., July 30, 2002, www.sec.gov/Archives/edgar/data/0001179070/000095013 502003591/b43894mgsc13d.txt.

19 **seemed to think Midway:** "Redstone Snaps Up Huge Stake in Midway," *Mergers & Acquisitions*, December 16, 2002.

19 **Redstone and Fortunato were married:** "Fortune and Fortunato," *New York Daily News*, April 7, 2003.

19 **He paid close to $16 million:** Gayle Pollard-Terry, "Some Tips on That Redstone Gift," *Los Angeles Times*, February 10, 2003.

20 **still on eastern time:** Burrough, "Sleeping with the Fishes."

20 **Chief among them:** Amy Chozick, "The Man Who Would Be Redstone," *New York Times*, September 23, 2012.

20 **"We shed a lot of blood":** Chozick, "Man Who Would Be Redstone."

20 **"closest advisors and colleagues":** Philippe Dauman Complaint in Equity at 5, Philippe Dauman and George S. Abrams v. Shari Redstone et al. (Commonwealth of Massachusetts) (No. NO16E0020QC).

20 **"the smartest person":** Chozick, "Man Who Would Be Redstone."

21 **He rewarded his surrogate son:** Philippe Dauman Complaint in Equity at 5, Dauman and Abrams v. Redstone et al.

21 **He'd grown up in Valley Stream:** Iris Wiener, "Les Moonves Reflects on His Valley Stream Roots," *LI Herald*, August 18, 2010.

21 **"the man with the golden gut":** Josef Adalian, "How Will Leslie Moonves' Exit Affect CBS?" *New York*, September 9, 2018.

22 **Sumner largely left Moonves:** Laura Rich, "A Succession Plan. Well, Almost," *New York Times*, June 20, 2004.

22 **"There's no question":** Burrough, "Sleeping with the Fishes."

22 **Just months later, the Hollywood:** Nikki Finke, "Redstone Family Woes: Now His Marriage," *Deadline*, August 3, 2007.

23 **Soon Sumner was again squiring:** George Rush and Joanna Rush Molloy with Patrick Huguenin and Sean Evans, "Miller-Diddy? Kim-possible!" *New York Daily News*, August 8, 2007.

23 **who now had a production:** Kim Masters, "Sumner Redstone Gal Pal Says She Got Nothing," *Hollywood Reporter*, July 28, 2010.

23 **And Herzer was back:** Cohan, "Endless Sumner."

23 **Sumner confided in both women:** Elkind, "Disturbing Decline of Sumner Redstone (Part 1 of 3)."

23 **Much of the publicity:** Nikki Finke, "Who's Crazier: Viacom or Tom Cruise?," *Deadline*, August 22, 2006.

23 **Citing the usual:** Petition at 1, Dissolution of Marriage of Petitioner Sumner M. Redstone and Respondent Paula Fortunato Redstone (Los Angeles Superior Court) (Case No. 60494653), https://web.archive .org/web/20131231171917/; www.aolcdn.com/tmz_documents/1021_sumner_wm.pdf.

Season 1, Episode 2: "Sumner in a Skirt"

24 **But this didn't mean:** Complaint at 3, Brent D. Redstone v. National Amusements Inc. (Circuit Court of Maryland for Baltimore City) (Case No. 24-C-06-0014-93).

24 **Also, Shari's husband:** Mark Jurkowitz, "Transformed by Tradition," *Boston Globe*, April 1, 1999.

25 **But by the late 1980s:** Jurkowitz, "Transformed by Tradition."

25 **Korff bought the weekly:** Jurkowitz, "Transformed by Tradition."

25 **Brent had finally agreed:** Complaint at 1, Brent D. Redstone v. National Amusements.

25 **Even after leaving:** Dawn Chmielewski, "The Real-Life 'Succession,'" *Forbes*, October 31, 2019.

25 **He also offered her:** Chmielewski, "The Real-Life 'Succession.'"

25 **She expanded the chain:** Richard Verrier, Ben Fritz, and Sergei Loiko, "From Russia (and Brazil and China) with Love," *Los Angeles Times*, July 4, 2011.

26 **"Nobody in the entertainment industry":** Dyan Machan, "Redstone Rising," *Forbes*, May 13, 2002.

26 **Brent refused to sell:** Geraldine Fabrikant, "Inside a Media Mogul's Closet, a Son Sees Dirty Laundry," *New York Times*, February 15, 2006.

26 **Brent maintained that his father:** Complaint at 6–9, Brent D. Redstone v. National Amusements.

26 **He and his family:** Luke O'Brien, "Trouble in the House of Redstone," *Boston*, November 23, 2009.

27 **Two years after:** Laura Rich, "A Succession Plan. Well, Almost," *New York Times*, June 20, 2004.

28 **In 2005 Sumner told:** Sallie Hofmeister, "Viacom OKs Plan to Split, but One Man Will Still Run the Show," *Los Angeles Times*, June 15, 2005.

28 **"What is this":** Robert Lenzner and Devon Pendleton, "Family Feud," *Forbes*, November 12, 2007.

28 **"Sumner in a skirt":** Keach Hagey, *The King of Content: Sumner Redstone's Battle for Viacom, CBS, and Everlasting Control of His Media Empire* (New York: Harper Business, 2018).

30 **Sumner proposed splitting Viacom:** John M. Higgins, "ViaSlow vs. ViaGrow: Sumner Redstone Fine-Tunes His Plan to Split Viacom," *Broadcasting & Cable*, May 9, 2005.

30 **Viacom's stock had fallen:** Matthew Karnitschnig, "Viacom Lawsuit on Executive Pay Can Go Forward," *Wall Street Journal*, June 30, 2006.

30 **To address this:** Motion for a Temporary Restraining Order at 9, CBS Corp. et al. v. National Amusements Inc. et al. (In the Court of Chancery of the State of Delaware) (Civil Action No. 2018-0342-AGB).

31 **Judith A. Spreiser, a former:** "Viacom Inc. Names Independent Directors to the Boards of Post-separation Companies," PR Newswire, November 22, 2005.

31 **Sumner issued a press release:** Geraldine Fabrikant, "Redstone Takes a Cut in His Salary," *New York Times*, September 26, 2006.

31 **After their departure:** Tim Arango, "New Crack in the House of Redstone," *CNN Money*, July 19, 2007.

32 **In an October 2006:** Geraldine Fabrikant, "Family Laundry Redux," *New York Times*, November 21, 2006.

32 **In 2005 Sumner had:** Sumner M. Redstone, Schedule 13D under the Securities Exchange Act of 1934: Midway Games, December 28, 2005.

32 **given sole authority:** Sumner M. Redstone, Schedule 13D.

33 **She was outvoted:** Tim Arango, "A New Flashpoint for Dueling Redstones," *CNN Money/Forbes*, August 1, 2007.

33 **National Amusements sold its entire:** Wailin Wong, "Midway Games Faces Default," *Chicago Tribune*, December 6, 2008.

34 **Shari argued that:** Tim Arango, "Redstone and Daughter Said to Clash on Debt Plan," *CNN.com /Forbes*, December 19, 2008.

34 **In April, when Shari:** Luke O'Brien, "Trouble in the House of Redstone," *Boston*, November 23, 2009.

34 **They stopped speaking to and seeing:** Martin Peers, Matthew Karnitschnig, and Melissa Marr, "Shaken from the Family Tree: Sumner Redstone Looks to Oust Daughter and Heir-Apparent Shari from Viacom Empire," *Globe and Mail* (Toronto), July 20, 2007.

34 **In a 2007 letter:** First Amended Complaint at 29, Manuela Herzer v. Shari Redstone and Tyler Korff (United States District Court Central District of California) (Case No. 2:17-cv-07545-PSG (KSx)).

Notes

34 **"While my daughter"**: Robert Lenzner, "Redstone Blasts Daughter," *Forbes*, July 20, 2007.

34 **"If she insists on"**: Lenzner and Pendleton, "Family Feud."

35 **"It must be remembered"**: William Cohan, "It's the Story of a Person Who Was Mistreated by Her Father," *Vanity Fair*, April 25, 2018.

35 **It was forced to sell**: Melissa Marr, "Market Turmoil Pressures Redstone," *Wall Street Journal*, October 14, 2008.

35 *Forbes* **estimated that**: Georg Szalai, "Billionaire Club Takes Beating," *Hollywood Reporter*, March 12, 2009.

36 **She had her lawyers**: Hagey, *King of Content*, 215.

36 **She also got full**: Hagey, *King of Content*, 218.

Season 1, Episode 3: Sumner Will Live Forever

41 **At its annual global conference**: Joe Flint, "Sumner Redstone Vows Immortality, Hones Borscht Belt Act," *Company Town* (blog), *Los Angeles Times*, April 29, 2009.

41 **"I have the vital statistics"**: "A Conversation with Sumner Redstone: If You Could Live Forever, What Would Life Be Like?," https://milkeninstitute.org/videos/conversation-sumner-redstone-if-you-could-live-forever-what-would-life-be.

42 **"A lot of guys say"**: Dave Gardetta, "Valley Girl Interrupted," *Los Angeles Magazine*, October 2001, https://www.lamag.com/longform/valley-girl-interrupted-2.

42 **At Sumner's insistence, CBS's Showtime**: Peter Lauria, "Sumner Redstone Hires Another 'Friend,' Rohini Singh," *Daily Beast*, July 27, 2010.

42 **Herzer maintained that Sumner**: Keach Hagey, "'Waiting for a Man to Die!!!' Inside the Fall of Sumner Redstone's Girlfriends," *Hollywood Reporter*, July 10, 2018.

42 **Dauman, who as a cotrustee**: Philippe Dauman Complaint in Equity at 2, Philippe Dauman and George S. Abrams v. Shari Redstone, Tyler Korff et al. (Commonwealth of Massachusetts) (No. NO16E0020QC).

43 **"tall, tan, fembot-like"**: Peter Lauria, "Sumner Redstone and His All-Girl Band, the Electric Barbarellas," *Daily Beast*, June 2, 2010.

43 **"unwatchable" . . . "I won't be defied"**: Peter Lauria, "Sumner Redstone Offers Reward to Get the Electric Barbarellas Leak," *Daily Beast*, July 20, 2010.

43 **"young, male executive"**: Lauria, "Sumner Redstone Offers Reward."

43 *New York Times* **media columnist**: David Carr, "Sumner Redstone: The Spoken Word Performance," *New York Times*, July 20, 2010.

44 **But the show attracted**: Margaret Lyons, "*The Electric Barbarellas* Might Be the Phoniest Reality Show Ever," *New York*, May 6, 2011.

44 **Redstone stayed in touch**: Complaint at 5, Sydney Holland v. Heather Naylor (Superior Court of the State of California for the County of Los Angeles) (Case No. BC519989).

44 **Sumner also showered Naylor**: Holland's Answer to Complaint at 20, Sumner M. Redstone v. Manuela Herzer and Sydney Holland (Superior Court of the State of California for the County of Los Angeles) (Case No. BC638054).

44 **After** *The Hollywood Reporter* **revealed**: Kim Masters, "Sumner Redstone 'Thinks He's Paul Newman,'" *Hollywood Reporter*, July 25, 2010.

Season 1, Episode 4: The Inner Circle VIP Social Club

45 **In the fall of 2010**: Peter Elkind, "The Disturbing Decline of Sumner Redstone (Part 2 of 3)," *Fortune*, May 5, 2016.

46 **between grandfather and grandson**: Keach Hagey, *The King of Content: Sumner Redstone's Battle for Viacom, CBS, and Everlasting Control of His Media Empire* (New York: Harper Business, 2018).

46 **Stanger had moved**: Linda Childers, "Millionaire Matchmaker Patti Stanger: Create a Love Affair with the Consumer," *CNN Money*, August 5, 2011.

47 **Stanger's mother and grandmother**: Tamar Caspi, "Make Me a Match," *Jerusalem Post*, February 12, 2010.

47 **Brash, outspoken, earthy**: Joshua Gillin, "'Millionaire Matchmaker' Patti Stanger Offends Jews, Gays and Other Key Demographics," *Tampa Bay Times* blog, September 26, 2011.

48 **One of Sumner's first dates**: "This Day in Music," *St. Petersburg Times*, October 10, 1994.

49 **gentleman of the old school**: Danika Fears, "'Millionaire Matchmaker' Says Redstone Loves 'Busty Brunettes,'" *New York Post*, December 13, 2016.

Notes

49 **Holland's maiden name:** Complaint at 5, Sumner M. Redstone v. Manuela Herzer and Sydney Holland (Superior Court of the State of California for the County of Los Angeles) (Case No. BC638054).

49 **though they didn't know:** Complaint at 5, Redstone v. Herzer and Holland.

50 **Cecil Holland, a building contractor:** Hagey, *King of Content*, 227.

50 **the top sales executive:** "The Marketing 100: The Biggest Bertha: Bruce Parker," *Advertising Age*, June 29, 1998.

50 **But just months later:** Elkind, "Disturbing Decline of Sumner Redstone (Part 2 of 3)."

50 **Many of her bills went:** William D. Cohan, "Endless Sumner," *Vanity Fair*, June 2015, 112.

50 **Inner Circle VIP Social Club:** Complaint at 20, Redstone v. Herzer and Holland.

50 **Holland claimed Parker had promised:** Complaint at 19, Redstone v. Herzer and Holland.

51 **Holland described their courtship:** Holland Answer to Complaint at 1, Redstone v. Herzer and Holland.

51 **Soon after they met:** Hagey, *King of Content*, 236.

51 **Less than a year later:** Holland Answer to Complaint at 2, Redstone v. Herzer and Holland, December 12, 2015.

52 **Holland reached out:** Claire Atkinson, "The Explosive, Plotting Emails of Sumner Redstone's Girlfriend," *New York Post*, May 19, 2015.

52 **When Jensen first met her:** Tim Jensen, "Sumner Redstone's Driver: I Delivered $1 Million in Cash to Women," *Hollywood Reporter*, July 15, 2015.

52 **One of his primary duties:** Jensen, "Sumner Redstone's Driver."

52 **To keep track:** Jensen, "Sumner Redstone's Driver."

52 **His complaint went nowhere:** Jensen, "Sumner Redstone's Driver."

53 **She served at Sumner's:** Holland Answer to Complaint at 21, Redstone v. Herzer and Holland.

53 **When Sumner asked Holland to move in:** Holland Answer to Complaint at 5, Redstone v. Herzer and Holland.

53 **"could do whatever he wanted":** Holland Answer to Complaint at 21, Redstone v. Herzer and Holland.

Season 1, Episode 5: "What's Mine Is Yours"

54 **In June 2012:** Meg James, "Paramount Pictures Marks 100 Years," *Los Angeles Times*, June 1, 2012, www.latimes.com/entertainment/envelope/la-xpm-2012-jun-01-la-et-ct-paramount-pictures-marks-100-years-20120601-story.html.

54 **About a hundred guests:** "Paramount Gathers 116 of Its Greatest Stars for a Landmark Photo Shoot," *Vanity Fair*, June 13, 2012.

54 **strolled past the sound stages:** James, "Paramount Pictures Marks 100 Years."

54 **"Who's that?":** Amy Chozick, "The Man Who Would Be Redstone," *New York Times*, September 23, 2012.

54 **"Here's to us who won":** James, "Paramount Pictures Marks 100 Years."

54 **the same words:** Geraldine Fabrikant, "Viacom's Victory: Viacom Is Winner over QVC in Fight to Get Paramount," *New York Times*, February 16, 1994.

55 **"Usually buildings are named":** James, "Paramount Pictures Marks 100 Years."

55 **the $84.5 million he was paid in 2010:** "Viacom's Philippe Dauman Is Nation's Highest-Paid CEO (Report)," *Hollywood Reporter*, April 10, 2011.

55 **"Everyone understands, I think":** Chozick, "Man Who Would Be Redstone."

55 **"I've called Philippe my mentor":** Chozick, "Man Who Would Be Redstone."

55 **Folta was pressed:** Kim Masters, "The Men Who Would Be Redstone," *Hollywood Reporter*, October 23, 2012.

56 **While Herzer's house:** First Amended Complaint at 2–3, Manuela Herzer v. Shari Redstone, Tyler Korff et al. (United States District Court Central District of California) (Case No. 2:17-cv-07545-PSG (KSx)).

56 **Staff members viewed Herzer:** Declaration of Giovanni Paz at 1, Sumner M. Redstone v. Manuela Herzer and Sydney Holland (Superior Court of the State of California for the County of Los Angeles) (Case No. BC638054).

56 **She stayed on, more or less:** Holland Answer to Complaint at 21, Redstone v. Herzer and Holland.

56 **At Sumner's, Herzer had:** First Amended Complaint at 2–3, Herzer v. Redstone-Korff.

56 **In fact, neither woman:** Declaration of Jeremy Jagiello at 1, Redstone v. Herzer and Holland.

56 **Holland would reluctantly:** Redstone Elder Abuse Complaint at 10, Redstone v. Herzer and Holland.

56 **One of his nurses, Jeremy Jagiello:** Declaration of Jeremy Jagiello at 1, Redstone v. Herzer and Holland.

56 **Herzer was often traveling:** Declaration of Jeremy Jagiello at 1, Redstone v. Herzer and Holland.

57 **Herzer nonetheless complained:** Herzer Complaint at 15, Manuela Herzer v. Shari Redstone, Tyler Korff et al. (Superior Court of the State of California for the County of Los Angeles) (Case No. 17-CV-07545 PSG (KSx)).

57 **He attended Bryan Herzer's:** Complaint at 8, Herzer v. Redstone-Korff.

57 **Sumner escorted her to work:** Complaint at 8, Herzer v. Redstone-Korff.

57 **and had already interned:** Al Gore (@algore), "Congratulations to former @ClimateReality staffer @kathrineherzer on her breakout TV role!" Twitter, October 1, 2014, 8:45 a.m., https://twitter.com /algore/status/517339414922407937.

58 **Surveillance cameras were installed:** Declaration of Jeremy Jagiello at 6, Redstone v. Herzer and Holland.

58 **nurses and staff were subjected:** Declaration of Giovanni Paz at 1, Redstone v. Herzer and Holland.

58 **She ordered them to speak:** Declaration of Joseph Octaviano at 3, Redstone v. Herzer and Holland.

58 **Anyone deemed disloyal:** Declaration of Giovanni Paz at 1, Redstone v. Herzer and Holland.

58 **Holland or Herzer sat:** Declaration of Giovanni Paz at 2, Redstone v. Herzer and Holland.

58 **"When family members came":** Declaration of Giovanni Paz at 2, Redstone v. Herzer and Holland.

58 **Most of the family's calls:** Declaration of Joseph Octaviano at 3, Redstone v. Herzer and Holland.

58 **"Sydney and Manuela reacted":** Declaration of Jeremy Jagiello at 2, Redstone v. Herzer and Holland.

59 **In what Jagiello described:** Declaration of Jeremy Jagiello at 2, Redstone v. Herzer and Holland.

59 **At the same time, Keryn:** Declaration of Keryn Redstone at 1–2, In re: Advance Health Care Directive of Sumner M. Redstone (Superior Court of the State of California for the County of Los Angeles) (Case No. BP 168725).

64 **The guest list was a who's who:** "Photos: Sumner Redstone's 90th Birthday Party," *Variety*, June 6, 2013.

64 **former vice president's Climate Reality Project:** Kim Masters, "How Sumner Redstone's Lady Friends Scored Millions of Dollars," *Hollywood Reporter*, February 10, 2016.

64 **"Celebrating with you":** "Watch Sumner Redstone's 90th Birthday Celebration Video," *Fortune* video, May 5, 2016, 16:47, https://fortune.com/videos/watch/Watch-Sumner-Redstones-90th-Birthday-Cele bration-Video/95c353f7-f5f4-4435-b118-72c1bed0690e.

65 **A private detective—hired:** "Watch Sumner Redstone's 90th Birthday Celebration Video."

66 **"seduced and influenced [him]":** Redstone's Amended Opposition to Defendant Motion for Summary Judgment at 4, Redstone v. Herzer and Holland.

67 **Holland dutifully transcribed:** Redstone's Amended Opposition to Defendant Motion for Summary Judgment at 4, Redstone v. Herzer and Holland.

67 **Alexandra had Sumner's distinctive:** "Billionaire Sumner Redstone 'Spending Time with' the Baby That His Girlfriend Adopted," *Daily Mail* (online), September 13, 2013.

67 **The child's middle name:** "Rumors Surround Sumner Redstone's New Baby," *New York Post*, September 13, 2013.

68 **He added Alexandra:** Petition for Probate of Will and for Letters Testamentary at 19, (Superior Court of the State of California for the County of Los Angeles) (Case No. 20STPB08647).

68 **The same day Holland:** Second Amended Cross-Complaint at 4, Sydney Holland v. Heather Naylor (Superior Court of the State of California for the County of Los Angeles) (Case No. BC519989).

68 **Naylor had gotten back:** Mike Hale, "Girl Group Just Wants to Be Famous (Again)," *New York Times*, June 4, 2013.

68 **Naylor attributed Holland's campaign:** First Amended Cross-Complaint at 3–5, Holland v. Naylor.

68 **Despite Holland's efforts:** Second Amended Cross-Complaint at 4, Holland v. Naylor.

68 **She also showed:** Complaint at 2–3, Holland v. Naylor.

68 **They were interrupted:** Complaint at 2–3, Holland v. Naylor.

68 **Herzer breezily made light:** Peter Elkind, "The Disturbing Decline of Sumner Redstone (Part 2 of 3)," *Fortune*, May 5, 2016.

69 **Naylor must have stolen:** Complaint at 3, Holland v. Naylor.

69 **Holland called Naylor:** Second Amended Cross-Complaint at 4, Holland v. Naylor.

69 **She went ahead and scheduled:** Second Amended Cross-Complaint at 5, Holland v. Naylor.

68 **But to her increasing frustration:** Videotaped Deposition of Sumner M. Redstone at 12, In re: Advance Health Care Directive of Sumner M. Redstone.

69 **On July 24 Naylor:** Second Amended Cross-Complaint at 5, Holland v. Naylor.

69 **Not long after:** Second Amended Cross-Complaint at 5, Holland v. Naylor.

69 **Sumner and Martinez had become:** Declaration of David R. Andelman at 2, Redstone v. Herzer and Holland.

69 **The decision alarmed:** Declaration of David R. Andelman at 2, Redstone v. Herzer and Holland.

Notes

70 **"Sydney Holland's decision to sue":** Matthew Belloni and Eriq Gardner, "Sumner Redstone Embroiled in Girlfriend's Legal War," *Hollywood Reporter*, June 25, 2014.

70 **Jagiello observed that Sumner:** Declaration of Jeremy Jagiello at 3, Redstone v. Herzer and Holland.

70 **That year *Forbes* placed:** Robert Lenzner, "Sumner Redstone Still Passionate and Winning at 90," *Forbes*, May 28, 2013.

70 **Sumner assured Herzer:** Complaint at 10, Herzer v. Redstone, Korff et al.

71 **In an amendment:** Sumner M. Redstone's Amended Separate Statement in Opposition to Defendant Manuela Herzer's Motion for Summary Judgment at 4, Redstone v. Herzer and Holland.

71 **Holland and Herzer received:** Redstone Elder Abuse Complaint at 8, Redstone v. Herzer and Holland.

71 **Holland and Herzer would inherit:** Sumner M. Redstone's Amended Separate Statement in Opposition to Defendant Manuela Herzer's Motion for Summary Judgment at 10, Redstone v. Herzer and Holland.

71 **Holland would get custody:** Holland Complaint at 8, Redstone v. Herzer and Holland.

71 **Sumner also spent millions:** Sumner M. Redstone's Amended Separate Statement in Opposition to Defendant Manuela Herzer's Motion for Summary Judgment at 8, Redstone v. Herzer and Holland.

71 **With Sumner's financial backing:** Redstone Elder Abuse Complaint at 8, Redstone v. Herzer and Holland.

71 **She redecorated a Beverly Hills:** Ryan Gajewski, "Jennifer Lawrence Buys L.A. Home Previously Owned by Jessica Simpson," *Hollywood Reporter*, November 2, 2014.

71 **Sumner deleted Shari:** Sumner M. Redstone's Amended Separate Statement in Opposition to Defendant Manuela Herzer's Motion for Summary Judgment at 4, Redstone v. Herzer and Holland.

Season 1, Episode 6: "You Know How He Is about Women"

72 **By March of 2014:** Redstone Elder Abuse Complaint at 10–11, Sumner M. Redstone v. Manuela Herzer and Sydney Holland (Superior Court of the State of California for the County of Los Angeles, Central District) (Case No. BC638054).

72 **Unlike the billions in stock:** Redstone Elder Abuse Complaint at 10–11, Redstone v. Herzer and Holland.

72 **Holland and Herzer hired:** Notice of Filing of Documents Ordered Unsealed by the Court, exhibit 4, exhibit U, p. 446, In re: Advance Health Care Directive of Sumner M. Redstone (Superior Court of the State of California for the County of Los Angeles) (Case No. BP 168725).

72 **On March 21:** Redstone Elder Abuse Complaint at 11, Redstone v. Herzer and Holland.

72 **Getting Sumner to go along:** Declaration of Giovanni Paz at 2, Redstone v. Herzer and Holland.

72 **They told him that Shari:** Declaration of Joseph Octaviano at 2, Redstone v. Herzer and Holland.

73 **To Holland's frustration:** Redstone Elder Abuse Complaint at 11, Redstone v. Herzer and Holland.

73 **A few weeks later, in April:** Redstone Elder Abuse Complaint at 13, Redstone v. Herzer and Holland.

73 **Andelman, who found out:** Declaration of David R. Andelman at 2, Redstone v. Herzer and Holland.

73 **With Andelman sidelined:** Declaration of Giovanni Paz at 2, Redstone v. Herzer and Holland.

73 **That day he sold:** Sumner M. Redstone, SEC Form 4: Statement of Changes in Beneficial Ownership of Securities, May 16, 2014.

73 **The proceeds went:** Declaration of David R. Andelman at 3, Redstone v. Herzer and Holland.

73 **The next day Holland had:** Declaration of Jeremy Jagiello at 3, Redstone v. Herzer and Holland.

74 **Two days later, Andelman:** Declaration of David R. Andelman at 3, Redstone v. Herzer and Holland.

74 **Andelman pressed for an explanation:** Declaration of David R. Andelman at 3, Redstone v. Herzer and Holland.

74 **Andelman was alarmed:** Declaration of David R. Andelman at 3, Redstone v. Herzer and Holland.

74 **He would eventually:** Redstone Elder Abuse Complaint at 12, Redstone v. Herzer and Holland.

74 **Andelman confronted Sumner:** Declaration of David R. Andelman at 3, Redstone v. Herzer and Holland.

74 **Sumner wondered aloud:** Sumner M. Redstone's Amended Separate Statement in Opposition to Defendant Manuela Herzer's Motion for Summary Judgment at 32, Redstone v. Herzer and Holland.

75 **"Sometimes I would be surprised":** Sumner M. Redstone's Amended Separate Statement in Opposition to Defendant Manuela Herzer's Motion for Summary Judgment at 7, Redstone v. Herzer and Holland.

75 **In the midst of this:** Redstone Elder Abuse Complaint at 13, Redstone v. Herzer and Holland.

75 **The effort worked:** Sumner M. Redstone's Amended Separate Statement in Opposition to Defendant Manuela Herzer's Motion for Summary Judgment at 9, Redstone v. Herzer and Holland.

75 **"the testamentary decisions":** Sumner M. Redstone's Amended Separate Statement in Opposition to Defendant Manuela Herzer's Motion for Summary Judgment at 9, Redstone v. Herzer and Holland.

Notes

76 **"There needs to be a plan":** Sumner M. Redstone's Amended Separate Statement in Opposition to Defendant Manuela Herzer's Motion for Summary Judgment at 15, Redstone v. Herzer and Holland.

76 **And on May 26, 2014:** Sumner M. Redstone's Amended Separate Statement in Opposition to Defendant Manuela Herzer's Motion for Summary Judgment at 15, Redstone v. Herzer and Holland.

76 **Given his declining health:** Peter Elkind, "The Disturbing Decline of Sumner Redstone (Part 2 of 3)," *Fortune*, May 5, 2016.

76 **According to witnesses:** Declaration of Keryn Redstone at 3, In re: Advance Health Care Directive of Sumner M. Redstone.

76 **That summer Shari also:** Holland Complaint at 15, Redstone v. Herzer and Holland.

77 **"It's upsetting that this":** William D. Cohan, "Hostage to Fortune," *Vanity Fair*, April 2016.

77 **Bishop also reached out:** Elkind, "Disturbing Decline of Sumner Redstone (Part 2 of 3)."

77 **Bishop had him meet again:** Sumner M. Redstone's Amended Separate Statement in Opposition to Defendant Manuela Herzer's Motion for Summary Judgment at 10, Redstone v. Herzer and Holland.

78 **"My father delivered a message":** First Amended Complaint at 22, Manuela Herzer v. Shari Redstone and Tyler Korff (United States District Court Central District of California) (Case No. 2:17-cv-07545-PSG (KSx)).

Season 1, Episode 7: "I Want My $45 Million Back"

79 **But on June 25 the case:** Matthew Belloni and Eriq Gardner, "Sumner Redstone Legal Turmoil: Fighting Women, Lie-Detector Tests, Stolen Laptop with 'Private' Photos," *Hollywood Reporter*, June 25, 2014.

79 **"Holland has effectively taken over":** Second Amended Cross-Complaint at 7, Sydney Holland v. Heather Naylor (Superior Court of California, County of Los Angeles) (Case No. BC519989).

82 **five-bedroom house:** Peter Elkind, "The Disturbing Decline of Sumner Redstone (Part 3 of 3)," *Fortune*, May 5, 2016.

82 **Holland boasted she had:** Cohan, "Hostage to Fortune."

82 **sacks of hundred-dollar bills:** Declaration of Jeremy Jagiello at 2–3, Sumner M. Redstone v. Manuela Herzer and Sydney Holland (Superior Court of the State of California for the County of Los Angeles) (Case No. BC638054).

82 **Holland and Herzer charged virtually everything:** Redstone Elder Abuse Complaint at 9–10, Redstone v. Herzer and Holland.

84 **In late June Holland:** Declaration of Jeremy Jagiello at 3, Redstone v. Herzer and Holland.

84 **One of his nurses, Joseph Octaviano:** Declaration of Joseph Octaviano at 2, Redstone v. Herzer and Holland.

85 **In early September Herzer:** Declaration of Joseph Octaviano at 2, Redstone v. Herzer and Holland.

85 **Sumner was rushed:** Declaration of Giovanni Paz at 3, Redstone v. Herzer and Holland.

86 **As he was helping move:** Declaration of Giovanni Paz at 2, Redstone v. Herzer and Holland.

86 **"I will give you your money":** Declaration of Giovanni Paz at 2, Redstone v. Herzer and Holland.

86 **"We have to put him":** Declaration of Giovanni Paz at 2, Redstone v. Herzer and Holland.

86 **Holland and the other nurse:** Declaration of Giovanni Paz at 2, Redstone v. Herzer and Holland.

86 **Brandon arrived and passed Paz:** Declaration of Giovanni Paz at 2, Redstone v. Herzer and Holland.

87 **When Paz left the hospital:** Declaration of Giovanni Paz at 2, Redstone v. Herzer and Holland.

87 **When Brandon called:** Declaration of Giovanni Paz at 2, Redstone v. Herzer and Holland.

87 **Shari arrived later that day:** Declaration of Joseph Octaviano at 3, Redstone v. Herzer and Holland.

87 **He asked her to step outside:** Declaration of Joseph Octaviano at 3, Redstone v. Herzer and Holland.

87 **Worried that he might:** Declaration of Joseph Octaviano at 3, Redstone v. Herzer and Holland.

87 **"I am at your side":** First Amended Complaint at 30, Manuela Herzer v. Shari Redstone and Tyler Korff (United States District Court Central District of California) (Case No. 2:17-cv-07545-PSG (KSx)).

87 **Herzer described it:** Complaint at 9, Herzer v. Redstone, Korff et al.

88 **"Will you still marry me?":** Email from Joseph Octaviano to Shari Redstone, dated 9/9/2014, exhibit A, Herzer v. Redstone, Korff et al.

88 **The perils of communicating:** Declaration of Giovanni Paz at 3–4, Redstone v. Herzer and Holland.

88 **Two days later, a lawyer:** Declaration of Giovanni Paz at 4, Redstone v. Herzer and Holland.

88 **"the Sumner whisperer":** Keach Hagey, *The King of Content: Sumner Redstone's Battle for Viacom, CBS, and Everlasting Control of His Media Empire* (New York: Harper Business, 2018), 2.

89 **Nor did he seem aware:** Reporter's Transcript of Proceedings, May 6, 2016, at 84–86, In re: Advance Health Care Directive of Sumner M. Redstone Redstone (Superior Court of the State of California for the County of Los Angeles) (Case No. BP 168725).

89 **"We would not win":** First Amended Complaint at 23, Herzer v. Redstone, Korff et al.

Notes

89 **The next day Shari and Tyler:** Redstone Elder Abuse Complaint at 15, Redstone v. Herzer and Holland.

90 **"Are they upsetting you?":** Redstone Elder Abuse Complaint at 15, Redstone v. Herzer and Holland.

90 **"Today's incident is so unforgiving":** Redstone Elder Abuse Complaint at 16, Redstone v. Herzer and Holland.

90 **"Every move in that house":** Redstone Elder Abuse Complaint at 16, Redstone v. Herzer and Holland.

90 **She thanked Octaviano:** Redstone Elder Abuse Complaint at 16, Redstone v. Herzer and Holland.

Season 1, Episode 8: "This Is Your Family"

94 **Instead, she and Herzer:** Declaration of Joseph Octaviano at 6, Sumner M. Redstone v. Manuela Herzer and Sydney Holland (Superior Court of the State of California for the County of Los Angeles) (Case No. BC638054).

95 **Sumner "immediately began sobbing":** Declaration of Joseph Octaviano at 6, Redstone v. Herzer and Holland.

95 **After nearly a year's effort:** Keach Hagey, *The King of Content: Sumner Redstone's Battle for Viacom, CBS, and Everlasting Control of His Media Empire* (New York: Harper Business, 2018), 240.

95 **"Manuela and Sydney dictate":** First Amended Complaint at 25, Manuela Herzer v. Shari Redstone and Tyler Korff (United States District Court Central District of California) (Case No. 2:17-cv-07545-PSG (KSx)).

95 **Sumner insisted that Shari:** Redstone Elder Abuse Complaint at 16, Redstone v. Herzer and Holland.

95 **Octaviano was on duty:** Declaration of Joseph Octaviano at 5, Redstone v. Herzer and Holland.

95 **In Octaviano's account:** Declaration of Joseph Octaviano at 5, Redstone v. Herzer and Holland.

95 **Bishop arrived at 11:30 a.m.:** Declaration of Joseph Octaviano at 5, Redstone v. Herzer and Holland.

96 **When Kimberlee called:** Declaration of Joseph Octaviano at 5, Redstone v. Herzer and Holland.

96 **Later that afternoon:** Declaration of Joseph Octaviano at 5, Redstone v. Herzer and Holland.

96 **A letter sent:** Sumner M. Redstone's Amended Separate Statement in Opposition to Defendant Manuela Herzer's Motion for Summary Judgment at 11–13, Redstone v. Herzer and Holland.

96 **Shari was stunned:** Hagey, *King of Content*, 243.

96 **The next day Octaviano reported:** Redstone Elder Abuse Complaint at 18, Redstone v. Herzer and Holland.

96 **That evening Sumner's executive assistant:** Redstone Elder Abuse Complaint at 17, Redstone v. Herzer and Holland.

97 **"Sydney wrote a note":** Redstone Elder Abuse Complaint at 18, Redstone v. Herzer and Holland.

98 **That same day, January 12:** Redstone Elder Abuse Complaint at 18, Redstone v. Herzer and Holland.

98 **Holland told Sumner that Kimberlee:** Redstone Elder Abuse Complaint at 18, Redstone v. Herzer and Holland.

98 **Octaviano duly reported:** Hagey, *King of Content*, 251.

99 **"not banning anyone":** First Amended Complaint at 34, Herzer v. Redstone, Korff et al.

99 **Shari told her children:** First Amended Complaint at 34, Herzer v. Redstone, Korff et al.

99 **On January 29 he and several:** Redstone Elder Abuse Complaint at 19, Redstone v. Herzer and Holland.

99 **"From my personal observations":** Declaration of Jeremy Jagiello at 5, Redstone v. Herzer and Holland.

99 **"Based on the interactions":** Declaration of Jeremy Jagiello at 5, Redstone v. Herzer and Holland.

99 **His base pay was $1.75 million:** Emily Steel and Sydney Ember, "Sumner Redstone's Total Pay from CBS Plummeted Last Year," *New York Times*, April 15, 2016.

100 **The committee had clearly spelled:** Memorandum Opinion at 7, exhibit C, R. A. Feuer v. Sumner M. Redstone et al. (In the Court of Chancery of the State of Delaware) (Civil Action No. 12575-CB).

100 **At the CBS annual meeting:** Memorandum Opinion at 8, exhibit C, Feuer v. Redstone et al.

100 **Yet the minutes:** Settlement Doc at 4, exhibit G, Feuer v. Redstone et al.

100 **At Viacom, Dauman was presumably:** Memorandum Opinion at 1, Feuer v. Redstone et al.

100 **A few days after Jagiello:** Petition for Determinations re: Advance Health Care Directive of Sumner M. Redstone at 14, In re: Advance Health Care Directive of Sumner M. Redstone (Superior Court of the State of California for the County of Los Angeles) (Case No. BP 168725).

100 **She ordered the staff:** Redstone elder abuse complaint at p. 19, Herzer v. Redstone Korff et al.

100 **He was "upset":** Declaration of Jeremy Jagiello at 5–6, Redstone v. Herzer and Holland.

100 **"I'm in trouble":** Declaration of Jeremy Jagiello at 5–6, Redstone v. Herzer and Holland.

100 **Minutes later Robert Shapiro:** Declaration of Jeremy Jagiello at 5–6, Redstone v. Herzer and Holland.

101 **Jagiello reported that the investigators:** Declaration of Jeremy Jagiello at 5–6, Redstone v. Herzer and Holland.

Notes

101 **Nor did they reach out:** Redstone Elder Abuse Complaint at 19, Redstone v. Herzer and Holland.
101 **Octaviano warned Tyler in April:** First Amended Complaint at 31, Herzer v. Redstone, Korff et al.
101 **"These women and their":** Complaint at 17–18, Herzer v. Redstone, Korff et al.

Season 1, Episode 9, "You Want to Go to War?"
102 **each sat for on-the-record interviews:** William D. Cohan, "Endless Sumner," *Vanity Fair*, June 2015, 112.
102 **mogul as "clearly ailing":** Cohan, "Endless Sumner," 114.
102 **"I think he's pretty":** Cohan, "Endless Sumner," 116.
102 **Sumner's old friend Robert Evans:** Cohan, "Endless Sumner," 115.
102 **"A person who was visiting":** Cohan, "Endless Sumner," 116.
103 **where Sumner had "gifted" her:** Complaint at 2, Manuela Herzer v. Leah Bishop (Superior Court of the State of California for the County of Los Angeles, West Judicial District) (Case No. SC129651).
103 **Holland stayed dutifully on message:** Cohan, "Endless Sumner," 148.
103 **"It's such a fine line":** Cohan, "Endless Sumner," 149.
103 **"I was like":** Cohan, "Endless Sumner," 147.
103 **"It would be almost disgusting":** Cohan, "Endless Sumner," 149.
104 **"There is nothing more important":** Cohan, "Endless Sumner," 148.
104 **Shari had earlier written:** Keach Hagey, *The King of Content: Sumner Redstone's Battle for Viacom, CBS, and Everlasting Control of His Media Empire* (New York: Harper Business, 2018).
104 **The allegation that he had:** Cohan, "Endless Sumner," 148.
104 **That concern was only heightened:** Declaration of Joseph Octaviano at 7, Sumner M. Redstone v. Manuela Herzer and Sydney Holland (Superior Court of the State of California for the County of Los Angeles) (Case No. BC638054).
104 **In an email to Tyler:** First Amended Complaint at 31, Manuela Herzer v. Shari Redstone and Tyler Korff (United States District Court Central District of California) (Case No. 2:17-cv-07545-PSG (KSx)).
105 **An angry Pilgrim called Holland:** William D. Cohan, "Why Sumner Redstone Really Kicked Sydney Holland Out," *Vanity Fair*, September 21, 2015.
105 **Holland and Herzer hosted another:** Emmet McDermott, "Sumner Redstone Serenaded by Tony Bennett as Execs (and Girlfriends) Celebrate 92nd Birthday Bash," *Hollywood Reporter*, May 28, 2015.
106 **Guests included the usual suspects:** McDermott, "Sumner Redstone Serenaded."
106 **The ninety-two-year-old made his entrance:** Peter Elkind, "The Disturbing Decline of Sumner Redstone (Part 2 of 3)," *Fortune*, May 5, 2016.
106 **But his frail appearance:** "Inside Sumner Redstone's 92nd Birthday Party with Leslie Moonves, Tony Bennett and the Mogul's Girlfriends (Exclusive Photos)," *Hollywood Reporter*, June 3, 2015.
106 **He made no public remarks:** McDermott, "Sumner Redstone Serenaded."
106 **When the lights came up:** McDermott, "Sumner Redstone Serenaded."
106 **The next month:** Manuela Herzer Petition for Determination of Advance Health Care of Sumner Redstone at 5, In re: Advance Health Care Directive of Sumner M. Redstone (Superior Court of the State of California for the County of Los Angeles) (Case No. BP 168725).
107 **Sumner asked that Herzer's son:** Redstone Elder Abuse Complaint at 14, Redstone v. Herzer and Holland.
107 **When they returned:** Sumner M. Redstone's Amended Separate Statement in Opposition to Defendant Manuela Herzer's Motion for Summary Judgment at 12, Redstone v. Herzer and Holland.

Season 2, Episode 1: "I'd Better Not Tell Manuela"
114 **Holland withdrew her complaint:** Eriq Gardner, "Sumner Redstone's Girlfriend Must Pay Former MTV Star's $190,000 Legal Bill," *Hollywood Reporter*, July 8, 2015.
114 **The judge ruled that Holland:** Gardner, "Sumner Redstone's Girlfriend Must Pay."
120 **Holland described the affair:** Holland Answer to Redstone's Complaint at 21, Sumner M. Redstone v. Manuela Herzer and Sydney Holland (Superior Court of the State of California for the County of Los Angeles, Central District) (Case No. BC638054).
120 **Herzer cut the grace period:** Redstone Elder Abuse Complaint at 22, Redstone v. Herzer and Holland.

Season 2, Episode 2: "Operation Freedom"
121 **On September 2 estate lawyer:** Sumner M. Redstone's Amended Separate Statement in Opposition to Defendant Manuela Herzer's Motion for Summary Judgment at 13, Sumner M. Redstone v. Manuela

Notes

Herzer and Sydney Holland (Superior Court of the State of California for the County of Los Angeles, Central District) (Case No. BC638054).

121 **Herzer was designated:** Manuela Herzer Petition for Determination of Advance Health Care of Sumner Redstone at 1, In re: Advance Health Care Directive of Sumner M. Redstone (Superior Court of the State of California for the County of Los Angeles) (Case No. BP 168725).

121 **Sumner named Viacom chief Dauman:** Decision/Order at 2, Philippe Dauman v. Manuela Herzer (Supreme Court of the State of New York, In re: Advance Health Care Directive of Sumner M. Redstone, BP1678725).

121 **After Octaviano told her:** Declaration of Joseph Octaviano at 8, Redstone v. Herzer and Holland.

121 **A week later Shari:** Declaration of Joseph Octaviano at 8, Redstone v. Herzer and Holland.

121 **Herzer asked Sumner's doctor:** Declaration of Jeremy Jagiello at 6, Redstone v. Herzer and Holland.

121 **Octaviano overheard Herzer:** Declaration of Joseph Octaviano at 8, Redstone v. Herzer and Holland.

122 **hidden cameras throughout the house:** Declaration of Jeremy Jagiello at 6, Redstone v. Herzer and Holland.

122 **She tightened her grip:** Redstone Elder Abuse Complaint at 22, Redstone v. Herzer and Holland.

122 **The staff was barred:** Redstone Elder Abuse Complaint at 22, Redstone v. Herzer and Holland.

122 **Herzer asked Keryn to move:** Complaint at 15, Manuela Herzer v. Shari Redstone and Tyler Korff (United States District Court Central District of California) (Case No. 2:17-cv-07545-PSG (KSx)).

122 **She also had Sumner create:** Declaration of Keryn Redstone at 4–5; Declaration of Keryn Redstone at 3, In re: Advance Health Care Directive of Sumner M. Redstone.

122 **Herzer took off for Paris:** Redstone Elder Abuse Complaint at 22, Redstone v. Herzer and Holland.

122 **"giddily sadistic black comedy":** Glen Kenny, "Keanu Reeves, as a Cheating Husband, Endures a Come-uppance in 'Knock Knock,'" *New York Times*, October 8, 2015.

122 **While Herzer was away:** Declaration of Jeremy Jagiello at 6, Redstone v. Herzer and Holland.

122 **Herzer took Sumner to a Malibu:** Declaration of Jeremy Jagiello at 7, Redstone v. Herzer and Holland.

122 **"He appeared to care far less":** Declaration of Joseph Octaviano at 9, Redstone v. Herzer and Holland.

122 **Herzer complained that Sumner:** Manuela Herzer Petition for Determination of Advance Health Care of Sumner Redstone at 10, exhibit F, In re: Advance Health Care Directive of Sumner M. Redstone.

122 **He asked repeatedly to see:** Complaint at 13, Manuela Herzer v. Shari Redstone, Tyler Korff, Giovanni Paz et al. (Superior Court of the State of California for the County of Los Angeles) (Case No. BC619766).

123 **When Sumner asked for Holbrook:** Redstone Elder Abuse Complaint at 23, Redstone v. Herzer and Holland; Trial Brief of Respondent Sumner Redstone at 8, In re: Advance Health Care Directive of Sumner M. Redstone.

123 **After Sumner asked Jagiello:** Declaration of Jeremy Jagiello at 6, Redstone v. Herzer and Holland.

123 **Herzer instead dialed:** Redstone Elder Abuse Complaint at 23, Redstone v. Herzer and Holland; Declaration of Jeremy Jagiello at 6, Redstone v. Herzer and Holland.

123 **She'd been a character:** Peter Elkind, "The Disturbing Decline of Sumner Redstone (Part 3 of 3)," *Fortune*, May 5, 2016.

123 **In a sworn affidavit:** Declaration of Heidi MacKinney in Support of Petition for Determinations at 2, In re: Advance Health Care Directive of Sumner M. Redstone.

123 **Jagiello, his nurse:** Declaration of Heidi MacKinney in Support of Petition for Determinations at 2, In re: Advance Health Care Directive of Sumner M. Redstone.

124 **And Holland was by no means:** Declaration of Keryn Redstone at 5, In re: Advance Health Care Directive of Sumner M. Redstone.

124 **"tried her best to show":** Holland Answer to Redstone's Complaint at 21, Redstone v. Herzer and Holland.

124 **When she tried to phone:** Holland Answer to Redstone's Complaint at 21, Redstone v. Herzer and Holland.

124 **"I am beyond sorry":** Elkind, "Disturbing Decline of Sumner Redstone (Part 3 of 3)."

124 **Bishop brought the letter:** Declaration of Jeremy Jagiello at 7, Redstone v. Herzer and Holland.

124 **But after just a few words:** Declaration of Jeremy Jagiello at 7, Redstone v. Herzer and Holland.

124 **Later that day Herzer rejoined:** Redstone Elder Abuse Complaint at 24, Redstone v. Herzer and Holland.

125 **It was readily apparent:** Declaration of Jeremy Jagiello at 8, Redstone v. Herzer and Holland.

125 **When he entered:** Declaration of Jeremy Jagiello at 7, Redstone v. Herzer and Holland.

125 **By contrast, Herzer:** Declaration of Jeremy Jagiello at 6, Redstone v. Herzer and Holland.

125 **Octaviano acknowledged that:** Reporter's Transcript of Proceedings, May 6, 2016, at 196, In re: The Matter of Sumner M. Redstone, In re: Advance Health Care Directive of Sumner M. Redstone.

Notes

126 **"Thanks for talking":** Complaint at 21, Herzer v. Redstone, Korff et al.
126 **"Once he knows the truth":** Complaint at 21, Herzer v. Redstone, Korff et al.

Season 2, Episode 3: "I Never Thought I'd See You Again"

127 **That year, Netflix spent:** "Netflix and Amazon Outspend CBS, HBO and Turner on TV Programming, IHS Markit Says," Business Wire, October 17, 2016.
127 **Dauman, the consummate deal lawyer:** "Event Brief of Viacom Names Philippe Dauman President and CEO, Succeeding Tom Freston—Final," *FD (Fair Disclosure) Wire*, September 5, 2006.
127 **Instead, he spent $15 billion:** Paul Bond, "Viacom Controlling Company Slams CEO Philippe Dauman after Earnings," *Hollywood Reporter*, August 4, 2016.
128 **Years prior, Viacom had sued:** Viacom International Inc. et al. v. YouTube, YouTube LLC, and Google Inc. (United States District Court, Southern District of New York) (No. 07 Civ. 2103).
128 **Early in his tenure:** Bryan Burrough, "Showdown at Fort Sumner," *Vanity Fair*, December 2007.
128 **He had gotten rid:** Meg James, "MTV Pioneer Steps Down," *Los Angeles Times*, May 6, 2011.
128 **MTV's ratings had since plunged:** Christopher Zara, "At Viacom, Ratings Woes Soak Up 'SpongeBob' Profits," *International Business Times*, April 29, 2015.
128 **His tone-deaf comments:** William Cohan, "Inside the Viacom Brain Drain," *Vanity Fair*, April 12, 2016.
128 **Dauman's relations with cable operators:** cmarcucci, "NCTC Fires Off Letter to Viacom CEO Seeking Blackout Ban," *Radio and Television Business Report*, March 31, 2014.
129 **In October 2014:** Daniel Frankel, "Viacom Renews FiOS Deal, Blocks Suddenlink Broadband Subs from SpongeBob and Jon Stewart," *FierceCable*, October 1, 2014.
129 **Sixty small cable companies:** Shalini Ramachandran, "Viacom, 60 Cable Firms Part Ways in Rural U.S.," *Wall Street Journal*, June 17, 2004.
129 **"When you don't like":** Cohan, "Inside the Viacom Brain Drain."
130 **"Philippe is my long-time":** Matthew Garrahan, "An Ailing Titan of the Small Screen," *Financial Times*, October 10, 2015.
130 **Sumner was quoted:** Keach Hagey and Amol Sharma, "Battle Brews atop Media Giant Viacom," *Wall Street Journal*, October 7, 2015.
131 **Dauman met with Sumner:** Complaint in Equity at 15, Philippe Dauman and George S. Abrams, as Trustees of the Sumner M. Redstone National Amusements Trust v. Shari Redstone, Tyler Korff et al. (Commonwealth of Massachusetts) (No. NO16E0020QC).
131 **But Herzer, who was:** Declaration of Manuela Herzer in Support of Ex Parte Application for Discovery in Support of Response to Respondent's Request to Dismiss Petition at 3, In re: Advance Health Care Directive of Sumner M. Redstone (Superior Court of the State of California for the County of Los Angeles) (Case No. BP 168725).
131 **"was no two-way conversation":** Declaration of Manuela Herzer at 3, In re: Advance Health Care Directive of Sumner M. Redstone.
131 **"a monologue" by Dauman:** Declaration of Manuela Herzer at 4, In re: Advance Health Care Directive of Sumner M. Redstone.
131 **"Sumner did not say":** Declaration of Manuela Herzer at 7, In re: Advance Health Care Directive of Sumner M. Redstone.
131 **Two CBS directors:** Memorandum Opinion at 12, exhibit D, R. A. Feuer v. Sumner M. Redstone et al. (In the Court of Chancery of the State of Delaware) (Civil Action No. 12575-CB).
131 **Sumner was no longer:** Memorandum Opinion at 10, exhibit D, Feuer v. Redstone et al.
131 **CBS didn't pay him a bonus:** Memorandum Opinion at 11, exhibit D, Feuer v. Redstone et al.
131 **Viacom similarly paid:** Viacom Inc., SEC Form 8-K: Current Report Pursuant to Section 13 or 15(d) of the Securities Exchange Act of 1934, January 21, 2016.
131 **Both companies again:** Memorandum Opinion at 16, exhibit E, Feuer v. Redstone et al.
131 **Jagiello had hinted:** Declaration of Jeremy Jagiello at 8, Sumner Redstone vs. Manuela Herzer and Sydney Holland (Superior Court of the State of California for the County of Los Angeles, Central District) (Case No. BC638054).
132 **"become irate," as Herzer put it:** Manuela Herzer Petition for Determination of Advance Health Care of Sumner Redstone, In re: Advance Health Care Directive of Sumner M. Redstone.
132 **"He appeared even more":** Declaration of Heidi MacKinney in Support of Petition for Determinations at 2, In re: Advance Health Care Directive of Sumner M. Redstone.
132 **"especially cold and aloof":** Declaration of Jeremy Jagiello at 8, Redstone v. Herzer and Holland.
132 **Sumner complained to Jagiello:** Declaration of Jeremy Jagiello at 8, Redstone v. Herzer and Holland.

Notes

132 **But Sumner was insistent:** Declaration of Jeremy Jagiello at 8, Redstone v. Herzer and Holland.

132 **Though Jagiello was still:** Declaration of Jeremy Jagiello at 8, Redstone v. Herzer and Holland.

132 **Mazzeo told him Bishop:** Declaration of Jeremy Jagiello at 8, Redstone v. Herzer and Holland.

132 **They agreed Bishop:** Declaration of Manuela Herzer at 13, In re: Advance Health Care Directive of Sumner M. Redstone.

132 **"Since Mr. Redstone had articulated":** Declaration of Jeremy Jagiello at 8, Redstone v. Herzer and Holland.

133 **It was just as well:** First Amended Complaint at 13, Manuela Herzer v. Shari Redstone and Tyler Korff (United States District Court Central District of California) (Case No. 2:17-cv-07545-PSG (KSx)).

133 **In the few months since Holland:** Trial Brief of Respondent Sumner Redstone at 7, In re: Advance Health Care Directive of Sumner M. Redstone.

133 **Just over a week earlier:** Trial Brief of Respondent Sumner Redstone at 7, In re: Advance Health Care Directive of Sumner M. Redstone.

133 **That weekend Herzer:** Declaration of Jeremy Jagiello at 8, Redstone v. Herzer and Holland.

133 **Despite the growing tensions:** William D. Cohan, "Hostage to Fortune," *Vanity Fair*, April 2016.

133 **On tap was the new:** Declaration of Carlos A. Herzer in Support of Petition for Determinations at 3, In re: Advance Health Care Directive of Sumner M. Redstone.

133 **Sumner fell asleep:** Manuela Herzer Petition for Determination of Advance Health Care of Sumner Redstone at 15, exhibit F, In re: Advance Health Care Directive of Sumner M. Redstone; Declaration of Carlos A. Herzer in Support of Petition for Determinations at 3, In re: Advance Health Care Directive of Sumner M. Redstone.

133 **Later, after the guests left:** Manuela Herzer Petition for Determination of Advance Health Care of Sumner Redstone at 15, In re: Advance Health Care Directive of Sumner M. Redstone.

133 **The next morning, October 12:** Manuela Herzer Petition for Determination of Advance Health Care of Sumner Redstone at 15, In re: Advance Health Care Directive of Sumner M. Redstone.

133 **Jagiello, Octaviano, Tuanaki:** Declaration of Jeremy Jagiello at 8, Redstone v. Herzer and Holland.

133 **The group told Sumner:** Declaration of Jeremy Jagiello at 8, Redstone v. Herzer and Holland.

134 **They said they'd been afraid:** Complaint at 15–16, Manuela Herzer v. Shari Redstone, Tyler Korff, Giovanni Paz et al. (Superior Court of the State of California for the County of Los Angeles) (Case No. BC619766).

134 **Jagiello described Sumner as "shocked":** Declaration of Jeremy Jagiello at 8, Redstone v. Herzer and Holland.

134 **Bishop and another Loeb & Loeb:** Keach Hagey, *The King of Content: Sumner Redstone's Battle for Viacom, CBS, and Everlasting Control of His Media Empire* (New York: Harper Business, 2018).

134 **His other lawyer:** Declaration of Jeremy Jagiello at 8, Redstone v. Herzer and Holland.

134 **and then "stormed":** Declaration of Jeremy Jagiello at 8–9, Redstone v. Herzer and Holland.

134 **Tuanaki intercepted her:** Manuela Herzer Petition for Determination of Advance Health Care of Sumner Redstone at 15, In re: Advance Health Care Directive of Sumner M. Redstone.

134 **Bishop looked startled:** Manuela Herzer Petition for Determination of Advance Health Care of Sumner Redstone at 15–16, In re: Advance Health Care Directive of Sumner M. Redstone.

134 **Herzer went up to Sumner:** Manuela Herzer Petition for Determination of Advance Health Care of Sumner Redstone at 15–16, In re: Advance Health Care Directive of Sumner M. Redstone.

134 **"He wants you to leave":** Declaration of Jeremy Jagiello at 8–9, Redstone v. Herzer and Holland.

134 **"But where will I live?":** Reporter's Transcript of Proceedings, May 9, 2016, at 17–18, In re: Advance Health Care Directive of Sumner M. Redstone.

134 **Herzer turned to Bishop:** Hagey, *King of Content*, 264.

134 **But Bishop had turned cold:** Manuela Herzer Petition for Determination of Advance Health Care of Sumner Redstone at 16, In re: Advance Health Care Directive of Sumner M. Redstone.

135 **When Herzer left, the nurses:** First Amended Complaint at 22, Herzer v. Redstone, Korff et al.

135 **Herzer went to her daughter's:** Cohan, "Hostage to Fortune."

135 **She asked to see Sumner:** First Amended Complaint at 5, Herzer v. Redstone, Korff et al.

135 **Herzer tried frantically:** Complaint at 16, Herzer v. Redstone, Korff et al.

135 **In a measure of their close:** Manuela Herzer Petition for Determination of Advance Health Care of Sumner Redstone at 15–16, In re: Advance Health Care Directive of Sumner M. Redstone.

135 **Dauman apparently made no mention:** Manuela Herzer Petition for Determination of Advance Health Care of Sumner Redstone at 15–16, In re: Advance Health Care Directive of Sumner M. Redstone.

135 **"Manuela, now you have":** Cohan, "Hostage to Fortune."

136 **"Manuela evicted . . . her family":** First Amended Complaint at 42, Herzer v. Redstone, Korff et al.

Notes

136 **He excised Herzer:** Decision Order at 2, Philippe Dauman v. Manuela Herzer (Supreme Court of the State of New York, In re: Advance Health Care Directive of Sumner M. Redstone, BP1678725).

136 **He removed Herzer and her children:** Complaint at 15, Herzer v. Redstone, Korff et al.

136 **The $50 million and the proceeds:** Cohan, "Hostage to Fortune."

136 **"I threw Sydney out":** Reporter's Transcript of Proceedings, May 9, 2016, at 17–18, In re: Advance Health Care Directive of Sumner M. Redstone.

Season 2, Episode 4: "I'm Not Going to Fire Him"

137 **Shari quickly filled the void:** Shari Supplemental Declarations in Support of Motion to Dismiss Petition, exhibit A, In re: Advance Health Care Directive of Sumner M. Redstone (Superior Court of the State of California for the County of Los Angeles) (Case No. BP 168725).

137 **When father and daughter weren't:** Shari Supplemental Declarations in Support of Motion to Dismiss Petition, exhibit A, In re: Advance Health Care Directive of Sumner M. Redstone.

138 **On November 24:** Manuela Herzer Petition for Determination of Advance Health Care of Sumner Redstone, In re: Advance Health Care Directive of Sumner M. Redstone.

138 **Describing Sumner as "a tragic figure":** Manuela Herzer Petition for Determination of Advance Health Care of Sumner Redstone at 2, In re: Advance Health Care Directive of Sumner M. Redstone.

138 **"His choice was based":** Manuela Herzer Petition for Determination of Advance Health Care of Sumner Redstone at 2–3, In re: Advance Health Care Directive of Sumner M. Redstone.

138 **"a living ghost":** Manuela Herzer Petition for Determination of Advance Health Care of Sumner Redstone at 3, In re: Advance Health Care Directive of Sumner M. Redstone.

139 **O'Donnell had gained a national:** Kim Masters, "Holy Lawsuit, 'Batman'!," *Washington Post*, March 27, 1992.

139 **Herzer maintained her motive:** Manuela Herzer Petition for Determination of Advance Health Care of Sumner Redstone at 4, In re: Advance Health Care Directive of Sumner M. Redstone.

139 **It described Sumner:** Manuela Herzer Petition for Determination of Advance Health Care of Sumner Redstone at 9, In re: Advance Health Care Directive of Sumner M. Redstone.

140 **"sex-obsessed" sumner:** Page Six Team, "'Sex-Obsessed' Sumner Redstone Kept Beautiful Women on Retainer," *New York Post*, March 21, 2016.

140 *The New York Times* **described:** Michael Cieply and Brooks Barnes, "Court Filing Challenges Competence of Sumner Redstone," *New York Times*, November 26, 2015.

140 **Holland "is absolutely disgusted":** Peter Elkind, "The Disturbing Decline of Sumner Redstone (Part 3 of 3)," *Fortune*, May 5, 2016.

140 **"it was like a switch":** Manuela Herzer Petition for Determination of Advance Health Care of Sumner Redstone at 9, In re: Advance Health Care Directive of Sumner M. Redstone.

140 **one was from her paid:** Manuela Herzer Petition for Determination of Advance Health Care of Sumner Redstone at 12, In re: Advance Health Care Directive of Sumner M. Redstone.

140 **Her "claim that she filed":** "U.S. Lawsuit Raises New Questions about Redstone's Ability to Run Media Companies," Reuters, November 25, 2015.

140 **"Sumner's family members now":** Cieply and Barnes, "Court Filing Challenges Competence."

141 **"I wish to put our family":** William D. Cohan, "Hostage to Fortune," *Vanity Fair*, April 2016.

141 **"should be considered withdrawn":** Joe Flint and Amol Sharma, "Behind Shari Redstone's Rise at Her Father's $40 Billion Media Empire," *Wall Street Journal*, June 10, 2016.

141 **By now Sumner's signature:** First Amended Complaint at 49, Manuela Herzer v. Shari Redstone, Tyler Korff et al. (United States District Court Central District of California) (Case No. 2:17-cv-07545-PSG (KSx)).

141 **Shari, her children, and two great-grandchildren:** Emily Steel, "Power Struggle at Viacom as New Leader Is Named," *New York Times*, February 4, 2016.

141 **In a pretrial deposition:** Opposition of Sumner Redstone to Ex Parte Application Seeking Evidentiary Hearing at 11, In re: Advance Health Care Directive of Sumner M. Redstone.

141 **"to be engaged and attentive":** Declaration of Philippe Dauman at 1, In re: Advance Health Care Directive of Sumner M. Redstone.

141 **"Sumner asked me to send regards":** Declaration of Philippe Dauman at 1, In re: Advance Health Care Directive of Sumner M. Redstone.

142 **Dauman also said:** Declaration of Philippe Dauman at 1, In re: Advance Health Care Directive of Sumner M. Redstone.

142 **Dauman added that he cared:** Declaration of Philippe Dauman at 2, In re: Advance Health Care Directive of Sumner M. Redstone.

Notes

142 **In January he quietly hired:** Emily Steel, "Viacom Chief Must Testify on Sumner Redstone's Mental State," *New York Times*, February 25, 2016.

142 **"Is he or isn't he":** Jessica Toonkel, "Exclusive: Top Investors Question Whether Viacom's Redstone Should Step Down," Reuters, December 2, 2015.

143 **Jackson called Viacom "creatively bankrupt":** Eric Jackson, "How Many Photo Ops Does It Take to Cut a Stock in Half? Bringing Viacom Back," SpringOwl Asset Management, January 2016, 15.

143 **He compared the situation:** Jackson, "How Many Photo Ops," 39.

143 **Viacom stock had lost 46.9 percent:** Jackson, "How Many Photo Ops," 7.

143 **Over the past three years:** Jackson, "How Many Photo Ops," 8.

143 **CBS had gained 34.5 percent:** Jackson, "How Many Photo Ops," 10.

143 **Jackson criticized Sumner:** Jackson, "How Many Photo Ops," 39.

143 **faulted the lack of succession planning:** Jackson, "How Many Photo Ops," 13.

143 **bluntly called for "a new chair":** Jackson, "How Many Photo Ops," 14.

143 **paid a total of $432 million:** Jackson, "How Many Photo Ops," 14.

143 **"Viacom management has underperformed":** Jackson, "How Many Photo Ops," 13.

143 **"Mr. Redstone's physicians have publicly":** Emily Steel, "Shareholder Calls for Check of Sumner Redstone's Condition," *New York Times*, December 2, 2015.

144 **"take away Ms. Redstone's whole life":** Dawn C. Chmielewski and Dade Hayes, "Secret Messages Reveal Bond between Les Moonves and Joe Ianniello in CBS Battle with National Amusements," *Deadline*, August 21, 2018.

144 **"back to the end":** Chmielewski and Hayes, "Secret Messages Reveal Bond."

Season 2, Episode 5: "This Is Your Battle, Not Mine"

145 **Read administered a version:** Reporter's Transcript of Proceedings, May 6, 2016, p. 11, In re: Advance Health Care Directive of Sumner M. Redstone (Superior Court of the State of California for the County of Los Angeles) (Case No. BP 168725).

145 **In some respects Sumner performed:** Appeal from an Order of the Superior Court of Los Angeles County, David J. Cowan, Judge, at 7, Manuela Herzer v. Sumner Redstone (Superior Court of the State of California for the County of Los Angeles) (Case No. BP 168725).

145 **He understood that if:** Appeal from an Order of the Superior Court at 8, Herzer v. Redstone.

145 **He was able to repeat:** Appeal from an Order of the Superior Court at 7–8, Herzer v. Redstone.

145 **Asked to identify a picture:** Reporter's Transcript of Proceedings at 50, In re: The Matter of Sumner M. Redstone.

146 **Read asked him:** Reporter's Transcript of Proceedings at 50, In re: The Matter of Sumner M. Redstone.

146 **But as soon as Read mentioned:** Reporter's Transcript of Proceedings at 130, In re: The Matter of Sumner M. Redstone.

146 **Read tried again:** Reporter's Transcript of Proceedings at 131, In re: The Matter of Sumner M. Redstone.

146 **Sumner couldn't perform:** Reporter's Transcript of Proceedings at 129, In re: The Matter of Sumner M. Redstone.

146 **Asked to spell *world*:** Reporter's Transcript of Proceedings at 68, In re: The Matter of Sumner M. Redstone.

146 **Read asked Sumner about:** Reporter's Transcript of Proceedings at 84, In re: The Matter of Sumner M. Redstone.

146 **Sumner also insisted that Herzer:** Reporter's Transcript of Proceedings at 71, In re: The Matter of Sumner M. Redstone.

146 **Read found it improbable:** Reporter's Transcript of Proceedings at 72–73, In re: The Matter of Sumner M. Redstone.

146 **When frustrated, Sumner often:** Appeal from an Order of the Superior Court at 3, Herzer v. Redstone.

146 **"Redstone manifests features of dementia":** Appeal from an Order of the Superior Court at 8, Herzer v. Redstone.

147 **In a thirty-seven-page:** Appeal from an Order of the Superior Court at 7, Herzer v. Redstone.

147 **"It was a very sad event":** Reporter's Transcript of Proceedings at 44, In re: The Matter of Sumner M. Redstone.

147 **"very painful to see":** Reporter's Transcript of Proceedings at 44, In re: The Matter of Sumner M. Redstone.

147 **"Mr. Redstone was a phenomenal figure":** Reporter's Transcript of Proceedings at 44, In re: The Matter of Sumner M. Redstone.

147 **Just a few days after Read's:** "CBS Corporation Announces That Leslie Moonves Has Been Named Chairman of the Company," PR Newswire, February 3, 2016.

Notes

148 **Both boards named him:** R. A. Feuer v. Sumner M. Redstone et al. (In the Court of Chancery of the State of Delaware) (Civil Action No. 12575-CB).

148 **and $1.75 million at Viacom:** Joann S. Lublin and Keach Hagey, "Viacom Board Weighs Further Cut in Sumner Redstone's Pay," *Wall Street Journal*, May 9, 2016.

148 **The board voted unanimously:** Emily Steel, "Sumner Redstone Steps Down as CBS Chairman, Replaced by Leslie Moonves," *New York Times*, May 3, 2016.

148 **"It is my firm belief":** Brian Stelter, "Philippe Dauman Succeeds Sumner Redstone in Viacom Board Battle," *CNN*, February 4, 2016.

148 **"Shari is going to continue":** Stelter, "Philippe Dauman Succeeds Sumner Redstone."

148 **As the roll call proceeded:** Paul Bond, "Inside Viacom's Board Meeting: Dauman Calls from St. Barths, Redstone in L.A.," *Hollywood Reporter*, February 4, 2016.

148 **"In choosing a successor":** Emily Steel, "Power Struggle at Viacom as New Leader Is Named," *New York Times*, February 4, 2016.

149 **Paramount had ended 2015:** Emily Steel, "Viacom Says It Will Sell a Stake in Paramount," *New York Times*, February 23, 2016.

149 **Viacom's stock plunged 21 percent:** Emily Steel, "Viacom Chief Is Defensive on Its Weak Earnings," *New York Times*, February 9, 2016.

149 **He lashed out at an analyst:** "Viacom (VIAB) Earnings Report: Q4 2015 Conference Call Transcript," *TheStreet.com*, February 9, 2016.

149 **"I think it's obvious to everybody":** "Viacom (VIAB) Earnings Report."

149 **And even *Rogue Nation*:** Simon Thompson, "Why Viacom Should Up Film Production at Paramount Pictures Rather Than Sell It Off," *Forbes*, February 18, 2016.

149 **Paramount had lost over $100 million:** Viacom Inc., SEC Form 10-Q: Quarterly Report Pursuant to Section 13 or 15(d) of the Securities Exchange Act of 1934, February 9, 2016, 18.

149 **Dauman told analysts:** "Viacom (VIAB) Earnings Report."

150 **including SpringOwl's Jackson:** Eric Jackson, "How Many Photo Ops Does It Take to Cut a Stock in Half? Bringing Viacom Back," SpringOwl Asset Management, January 2016, 83.

151 **Dauman asked Jagiello and other nurses:** Keach Hagey, *The King of Content: Sumner Redstone's Battle for Viacom, CBS, and Everlasting Control of His Media Empire* (New York: Harper Business, 2018).

151 **Sumner was sitting in his chair:** Hagey, *King of Content*, 3.

151 **In Dauman's account:** Hagey, *King of Content*, 3–4.

151 **In a telephone meeting:** Hagey, *King of Content*, 4.

151 **The next day:** "Viacom Seeks Minority Investor for Paramount Film Studio," Dow Jones Institutional News Service, February 23, 2016.

151 **In a company-wide memo:** Emily Steel, "Viacom Says It Will Sell a Stake in Paramount," *New York Times*, February 23, 2016.

152 **"almost totally non-responsive":** Cynthia Littleton, "Sumner Redstone Fight: Philippe Dauman Slams Shari Redstone as Hearing Approaches," *Variety*, June 27, 2016.

152 **In later discussions:** Eriq Gardner, "Philippe Dauman Says Redstone Battles Have Slowed, but Not Killed Plan to Sell Paramount Stake," *Hollywood Reporter*, June 9, 2016.

Season 2, Episode 6: "A Public Spectacle"

154 **But Judge Cowan, after digesting:** Emily Steel, "Sumner Redstone Competency Case Will Go Forward," *New York Times*, March 1, 2016.

154 **Sumner was suffering from:** Tentative Ruling on Motions to Dismiss Petition, February 29, 2016, at 12, In re: Advance Health Care Directive of Sumner M. Redstone (Superior Court of the State of California for the County of Los Angeles) (Case No. BP 168725).

154 **He also found it odd:** Tentative Ruling on Motions to Dismiss Petition at 16, In re: Advance Health Care Directive of Sumner M. Redstone.

155 **a partner at the litigation firm:** "Star Entertainment Attorney Robert Klieger Joins Partnership," Hueston Hennigan, July 6, 2015; www.hueston.com/star-entertainment-attorney-robert-klieger-joins-partnership/.

156 **former chief financial officer of Verizon:** "Frederic Salerno," New Mountain Capital, www.newmountaincapital.com/team/frederic-salerno/.

156 **Boston lawyer who had long represented:** "Viacom Drama's Cast of Lawyers," *Bloomberg Law*, August 3, 2016.

158 **Herzer's claims that Shari:** Complaint at 14–15, Manuela Herzer v. Shari Redstone, Tyler Korff et al. (United States District Court Central District of California) (Case No.: 2:17-cv-07545-PSG (KSx)).

Notes

160 **In an ominous sign for Dauman:** Motion for Expedited Discovery and Trial at 18, Philippe Dauman and George Abrams v. Sumner Redstone et al. (Commonwealth of Massachusetts) (Civil Action No. 16E002QC).

160 **The tape could be played:** Tentative Ruling on Motion to Dismiss Petition, May 9, 2016, at 14, In re: Advance Health Care Directive of Sumner M. Redstone.

160 **"Nobody deserves to have a career":** Ruling on Motion to Quash Notice to Appear, May 9, 2016, at 7, In re: Advance Health Care Directive of Sumner M. Redstone.

161 **To keep the crowd:** Ruling on Motion to Quash Notice to Appear at 5–6, In re: Advance Health Care Directive of Sumner M. Redstone.

161 **"She is . . . ," Sumner began:** Videotaped Deposition of Sumner M. Redstone at 7, In re: Advance Health Care Directive of Sumner M. Redstone.

161 **The much-anticipated deposition:** Videotaped Deposition of Sumner M. Redstone, In re: Advance Health Care Directive of Sumner M. Redstone.

Season 2, Episode 7: "A Modern-Day Love Story"

162 **Pierce O'Donnell began:** Reporter's Transcript of Proceedings, May 6, 2016, at 3, In re: The Matter of Sumner M. Redstone (Superior Court of the State of California for the County of Los Angeles) (Case No. BP 168725).

162 **"This is a modern-day":** Reporter's Transcript of Proceedings at 5, In re: The Matter of Sumner M. Redstone.

163 **"The only individuals who were":** Reporter's Transcript of Proceedings at 28, In re: The Matter of Sumner M. Redstone.

163 **"Ms. Herzer and Ms. Holland were emotionally":** Reporter's Transcript of Proceedings at 26, In re: The Matter of Sumner M. Redstone.

163 **"They told him they were":** Reporter's Transcript of Proceedings at 27, In re: The Matter of Sumner M. Redstone.

163 **"his family is back in his life":** Reporter's Transcript of Proceedings at 29, In re: The Matter of Sumner M. Redstone.

163 **"someone who does not":** Reporter's Transcript of Proceedings at 29, In re: The Matter of Sumner M. Redstone.

163 **"How long have you known":** Videotaped Deposition of Sumner M. Redstone at 7, In re: Advance Health Care Directive of Sumner M. Redstone (Superior Court of the State of California for the County of Los Angeles) (Case No. BP 168725).

164 **O'Donnell asked the question again:** Videotaped Deposition of Sumner M. Redstone at 11, In re: Advance Health Care Directive of Sumner M. Redstone.

164 **"When was the photo taken":** Videotaped Deposition of Sumner M. Redstone at 11, In re: Advance Health Care Directive of Sumner M. Redstone.

164 **O'Donnell changed subjects:** Videotaped Deposition of Sumner M. Redstone at 13, In re: Advance Health Care Directive of Sumner M. Redstone.

164 **"When Manuela was leaving":** Videotaped Deposition of Sumner M. Redstone at 14, In re: Advance Health Care Directive of Sumner M. Redstone.

165 **"Mr. Redstone, why did you":** Videotaped Deposition of Sumner M. Redstone at 15–16, In re: Advance Health Care Directive of Sumner M. Redstone.

165 **Sumner's testimony made an immediate:** Videotaped Deposition of Sumner M. Redstone at 131, In re: Advance Health Care Directive of Sumner M. Redstone.

166 **Read conceded there was:** Reporter's Transcript of Proceedings at 146, In re: The Matter of Sumner M. Redstone.

166 **"The court has heard":** Tentative Ruling on Motion to Dismiss Petition, May 9, 2016, at 5, In re: Advance Health Care Directive of Sumner M. Redstone.

166 **"Even if Redstone and Shari":** Tentative Ruling on Motion to Dismiss Petition at 14, In re: Advance Health Care Directive of Sumner M. Redstone.

166 **"I am grateful to the court":** Matt Reynolds, "Judge Dismisses Sumner Redstone Case," *Courthouse News*, May 9, 2016.

166 **"I was thinking back":** Emily Steel, "Sumner Redstone Competency Case Abruptly Dismissed by Judge," *New York Times*, May 9, 2016.

167 **that same day he filed:** Complaint at 18, Manuela Herzer v. Shari Redstone, Tyler Korff et al. (United States District Court Central District of California) (Case No. 2:17-cv-07545-PSG (KSx)).

167 **Herzer's complaint accused Shari:** Complaint at 4, Herzer v. Redstone, Korff et al.

167 **The Redstone family made only one:** Complaint at 12, Herzer v. Redstone, Korff et al.
167 **"baseless attack":** Lisa Richwine, "New Lawsuit Alleges Paid Informants, Pricey Escort at Redstone Mansion," Reuters, May 9, 2016.
168 **Dauman had defiantly continued:** Keach Hagey, "Viacom Draws Interest for Minority Stake in Paramount Pictures Studio," *Wall Street Journal*, March 17, 2016.
168 **Dauman appeared to have:** Verified Complaint at 5, Frederic V. Salerno v. National Amusements Inc., NAI Entertainment Holdings LLC et al. (In the Court of Chancery of the State of Delaware) (No. 12473-CB).
169 **On Sumner's behalf Tu sent:** Emily Steel, "Paramount Stars in War at Viacom," *New York Times*, May 25, 2016.
169 **Salerno's lawyers called Tu:** Verified Complaint at 33, Salerno v. National Amusements International, NAI Entertainment Holdings LLC et al.
170 **The next day the Viacom board:** Verified Complaint at 33, Salerno v. National Amusements International, NAI Entertainment Holdings LLC et al.
170 **So Dauman and Abrams:** Motion for Expedited Discovery and Trial at 5, Philippe Dauman and George S. Abrams v. Shari Redstone, Tyler Korff et al. (Commonwealth of Massachusetts) (Civil Action No. 16E0020QC).
170 **Tad Jankowski, Sumner's longtime employee:** Complaint in Equity at 8, Dauman and Abrams v. Redstone, Korff et al.
171 **In a press statement, he called:** Complaint at 25, Herzer v. Redstone, Korff et al.
171 **The timing of the ouster:** Complaint in Equity at 2, Dauman and Abrams v. Redstone, Korff et al.
171 **Herzer's lawyer O'Donnell submitted:** Joe Flint, "Massachusetts Court to Hear Next Chapter in Redstone Saga," *Wall Street Journal*, June 29, 2016.
172 **Dauman attempted to argue:** Complaint in Equity at 15, Dauman and Abrams v. Redstone, Korff et al.
172 **"Mr. Redstone's health has rapidly declined":** Complaint in Equity at 15, Dauman and Abrams v. Redstone, Korff, et al.
172 **Dauman now said he'd visited Sumner:** Complaint in Equity at 15, Dauman and Abrams v. Redstone, Korff et al.
172 **In total, Sumner:** Complaint in Equity at 3, Dauman and Abrams v. Redstone, Korff et al.

Season 2, Episode 8: "No One Likes Drama"
173 **"Mr. Redstone seems much happier":** Declaration of Jeremy Jagiello at 9, Sumner M. Redstone v. Manuela Herzer and Sydney Holland (Superior Court of the State of California for the County of Los Angeles, Central District) (Case No. BC638054).
173 **On Friday, June 10, Sumner:** Kim Masters, "Sumner Redstone Visits Paramount Lot amid Viacom Drama (Exclusive)," *Hollywood Reporter*, June 14, 2016.
173 **The following Tuesday:** Joe Flint, "Sumner Redstone Makes Rare Appearances at CBS, Paramount," *Wall Street Journal*, June 14, 2016.
174 **"You and I have worked together":** David Lieberman, "Viacom Open Letter to Sumner Redstone Raises Fear He Is 'Not Being Heard,'" *Deadline*, June 14, 2016.
175 **Folta denounced the move:** Emily Steel, "New Questions Arise over Viacom Mogul's Competency After He Alters Trust," *New York Times*, May 23, 2016.
175 **The bylaw change pretty much:** Michael J. de la Merced and Emily Steel, "National Amusements Alters Viacom Bylaws to Stymie Sale of Paramount," *New York Times*, June 6, 2016.
175 **Nonetheless *The Wall Street Journal* reported:** Rick Carew, Amol Sharma, and Ben Fritz, "Viacom in Talks to Sell Paramount Pictures to Chinese Group," *Wall Street Journal*, July 13, 2016.
176 **On June 16 the long-expected:** Joe Flint, Amol Sharma, and Joann S. Lublin, "Sumner Redstone's National Amusements Moves to Oust Five Viacom Directors," *Wall Street Journal*, June 16, 2016.
176 **"It will be the responsibility":** "National Amusements, Inc. Elects Five Independent Directors to Viacom Board; Five Existing Directors Removed," PR Newswire, June 16, 2016.
176 **That same day Shari:** Joe Flint, "Viacom Detente Yields Promotion for New Interim CEO," *Wall Street Journal*, August 21, 2016.
176 **"A stock price at any given":** Alan Murray, "Philippe Dauman's Last Stand," *Fortune*, April 20, 2016.
177 **With participants Justin Trudeau:** Paul Bond, "Sun Valley: Shari Redstone Takes Center Stage as Media Moguls Gather," *Hollywood Reporter*, July 6, 2016.
177 **both Moonves and Dauman:** Georg Szalai, "Viacom's Philippe Dauman Skipping Sun Valley Mogul Gathering," *Hollywood Reporter*, July 7, 2016.

Notes

177 **It came as something:** Szalai, "Viacom's Philippe Dauman Skipping."

177 **"a terrific board member":** Meg James, "Viacom Struggle Ends: Shari Redstone at Helm," *Los Angeles Times*, August 20, 2016.

177 ***Vanity Fair* reported Shari:** Emily Jane Fox, "Shari Redstone Goes Shoe Shopping in Sun Valley," *Vanity Fair*, July 8, 2016.

177 **Tyler was deep in negotiations:** Keach Hagey, "Redstone Family's Next Generation Takes On Bigger Roles, Influence in National Amusements," *Wall Street Journal*, November 15, 2016.

177 **Without initially telling Shari:** Joe Flint, "Can CBS and Viacom Merge? It Depends on the Redstone-Moonves Dance," *Wall Street Journal*, September 30, 2016.

178 **Dauman would withdraw:** Confidential Settlement and Release Agreement between Sumner M. Redstone et al. and Philippe P. Dauman et al., August 18, 2016, 64.

178 **and step down as Viacom's:** Confidential Settlement and Release Agreement, August 18, 2016, p. 5.

178 **Dooley would replace him:** "Viacom and National Amusements Announce Resolution of Governance Dispute and Transition to New Leadership," BusinessWire, August 20, 2016.

178 **In return, Dauman would get:** Confidential Settlement and Release Agreement, August 18, 2016, 28.

178 **It fell to Dauman:** Keach Hagey, *The King of Content: Sumner Redstone's Battle for Viacom, CBS, and Everlasting Control of His Media Empire* (New York: Harper Business, 2018).

179 **Dauman gave no hint:** "Viacom's (VIAB) CEO Philippe Dauman on Q3 2016 Results—Earnings Call Transcript," August 4, 2016.

179 **They were another disaster:** Emily Steel, "Viacom's Profit Slumps 29%, Providing a Lens into a Business in Turmoil," *New York Times*, August 4, 2016.

179 **Those were just the most:** "Viacom (VIAB) Beats Earnings and Revenue Estimates in Q3," Zacks Equity Research, August 4, 2016.

179 **"Dauman is focused on stocks":** Brian Price, "Former Viacom CEO Tom Freston Speaks Out on Company's 'Serious Errors,'" *CNBC*, June 15, 2016.

179 **After a weekend meeting:** Hagey, *King of Content*.

179 **in addition to Dauman's $72 million:** Confidential Settlement and Release Agreement, August 18, 2016, 14.

179 **and provide an office:** Confidential Settlement and Release Agreement, August 18, 2016, 27.

179 **One face-saving provision:** Confidential Settlement and Release Agreement, August 18, 2016, 8.

179 **Dooley, the newly minted:** Confidential Settlement and Release Agreement, August 18, 2016, 1.

180 **He proceeded to buy:** Gene Maddaus, "One Year after Exec Shakeup, Viacom Sees Stability but Faces Stock Struggles," *Variety*, August 30, 2017.

180 **nor did he name the buyer:** Claire Atkinson, "Bon Voyage, Philippe! We Hardly Knew You," *New York Post*, September 14, 2016.

180 **"I can't say it was":** Anita Balakrishnan, "Shari Redstone Said CBS, Viacom Are Right to Explore Merger," *CNBC*, November 10, 2016.

Season 2, Episode 9: "An Overwhelming Stench of Greed"

182 **Shari had always opposed:** Keach Hagey and Joe Flint, "Sumner Redstone's National Amusements to Call on Viacom and CBS to Explore Merger," *Wall Street Journal*, September 28, 2016.

182 **On September 29, just two:** "Press Release: Viacom Announces Receipt of Letter from National Amusements," Dow Jones Institutional News, September 29, 2016.

182 **But their holding company:** "Press Release: Viacom Announces Receipt."

182 **Both Sumner and Shari signed:** "Press Release: Viacom Announces Receipt."

182 **The next day the boards:** Joe Flint, Keach Hagey, and Joann S. Lublin, "Viacom and CBS Boards Name Special Committees to Review Merger," *Wall Street Journal*, September 30, 2016.

183 **In 2016 Shari met with:** Joe Flint and Drew FitzGerald, "AT&T Expressed Interest in CBS to Shari Redstone before Time Warner Deal," *Wall Street Journal*, June 24, 2018.

183 **Verizon chief executive Lowell McAdam:** Kim Masters, "Shari Redstone's Viacom-CBS Merger Plans Take Shape amid Tension," *Hollywood Reporter*, January 25, 2018.

183 **As Dauman's longtime ally:** Paul Bond, "Viacom Interim CEO Tom Dooley to Depart, Company to Consider 'All Options,'" *Hollywood Reporter*, September 21, 2016.

184 **"Viacom is tanking":** Memorandum Opinion, September 17, 2020, p. 22, In re: CBS Corporation Stockholder Class Action and Derivative Litigation (In the Court of Chancery of the State of Delaware) (Civil Action No. 2020-0111-JRS).

184 **"Now you'll realize":** David Lieberman, "Viacom Names Bob Bakish Acting CEO When Tom Dooley Steps Down," *Deadline*, October 31, 2016.

Notes

184 **"We have a great CEO":** Anita Balakrishnan, "Shari Redstone Said CBS, Viacom Are Right to Explore Merger," *CNBC*, November 10, 2016.

186 **The Redstones hired Bennett Blum:** Declaration of Bennett Blum M.D. at 1, Sumner M. Redstone v. Manuela Herzer and Sydney Holland (Superior Court of the State of California for the County of Los Angeles, Central District) (Case No. BC638054).

186 **Blum acknowledged that Sumner:** Declaration of Bennett Blum M.D. at 3, Redstone v. Herzer and Holland.

186 **But due to the long:** Declaration of Bennett Blum M.D. at 2, Redstone v. Herzer and Holland.

186 **Blum stressed that even:** Declaration of Bennett Blum M.D. at 2, Redstone v. Herzer and Holland.

186 **As Blum explained in his:** Declaration of Bennett Blum M.D. at 2–3, Redstone v. Herzer and Holland.

186 **Both Holland and Herzer "engaged":** Declaration of Bennett Blum M.D. at 4, Redstone v. Herzer and Holland.

186 **Sumner hired a retired:** Peter Elkind, "The Disturbing Decline of Sumner Redstone (Part 2 of 3)," *Fortune*, May 5, 2016.

186 **Citing Sumner's "near complete dependence":** Redstone Elder Abuse Complaint at 1–2, Redstone v. Herzer and Holland.

187 **For good measure, Sumner also:** Opinion, Sumner Redstone v. Manuela Herzer and Hotel Carlyle (Appellate Division of the Supreme Court: First Judicial Department in the County of New York) (February 15, 2018) (Case No. 6987-6988N).

187 **But faced with the elder abuse:** Holland Cross-Complaint at 20, Redstone v. Herzer and Holland.

187 **"Sydney may be forced":** Holland Cross-Complaint at 20, Redstone v. Herzer and Holland.

187 **"knew about Redstone's largest":** Holland Cross-Complaint at 20, Redstone v. Herzer and Holland.

187 **Klieger responded that Holland's:** Ashley Cullins, "Sumner Redstone Ex Asks Court to Order Independent Medical Evaluation," *Hollywood Reporter*, January 18, 2017.

188 **restraining order against him:** *Sydney Holland v. George M. Pilgrim*, case no. SQ007229, order dated January 8, 2016.

188 **three years' probation:** Criminal Case Summary, Los Angeles Superior Court, Van Nuys Courthouse West, sentencing date April 13, 2016.

189 **"Knowing that her father's":** Complaint at 1, Manuela Herzer v. Shari Redstone, Tyler Korff et al. (United States District Court Central District of California) (Case No. 2:17-cv-07545-PSG (KSx)).

189 **Herzer's complaint alleged:** Complaint at 6, Herzer v. Redstone, Korff et al.

Season 2, Episode 10: "Don't Go Near This"

191 **With CBS the most-watched:** Lisa de Moraes, "NBC Wins 2016–17 Season in Ratings Demo; CBS Takes Total Viewers," *Deadline*, May 23, 2017.

191 **More fundamentally, Moonves was willing:** Keach Hagey and Joe Flint, "Redstone Daughter Seeks a Viacom Reunion," *Wall Street Journal*, September 29, 2016.

191 **essentially requiring the Redstones:** Verified Complaint at 21, CBS et al. v. NAI, Shari Redstone et al. (In the Court of Chancery of the State of Delaware) (Civil Action No. 2018-0342-AGB).

192 **The Redstones' initial letter:** Joe Flint, "Two Wary Moguls Hold Key to CBS Deal," *Wall Street Journal*, September 30, 2016.

192 **On December 12, the companies:** Keach Hagey, Joe Flint, and Joshua Jamerson, "Redstones Abandon Plan to Merge Viacom and CBS," *Wall Street Journal*, December 13, 2016.

192 **"We know Viacom has":** "National Amusements, Inc. Asks Boards of CBS and Viacom to Discontinue Exploration of a Potential Combination," PR Newswire, December 12, 2016.

193 **She proposed meeting for coffee:** Memorandum Opinion, December 29, 2020, at 61, In re: Viacom Inc. Stockholders Litigation (In the Court of Chancery of the State of Delaware) (Civil Action No. 2020-0111-JRS).

193 **was often rumored:** Glenn Thrush, "Obama Consults on SCOTUS Choice," *Politico*, April 21, 2010.

193 **Newton Minow, had been chair:** "'Wasteland' Revisited: Newton Minow Looks Back at His FCC Tempest and Forward to the Future of Televised Debates," *Broadcasting & Cable*, February 29, 2016.

193 **as a "vast wasteland":** "'Wasteland' Revisited."

193 **Shari had maintained:** Kim Masters and Paul Bond, "Shari Redstone Explores Plan to Launch Fox News Competitor (Exclusive)," *Hollywood Reporter*, October 15, 2019.

193 **"tremendous supporter of me personally":** Kim Masters, "Shari Redstone Named THR's Women in Entertainment Executive of the Year," *Hollywood Reporter*, December 6, 2016.

Notes

194 **They'd served together:** "2012 JFK Profile in Courage Award Winners Announced," Targeted News Service, March 12, 2012.

194 **She'd made the pilgrimage:** "Sumner Redstone Makes Donation to Harvard Law School in Support of Public Service," Professional Services Close-Up Business Insights, January 24, 2014.

194 **"It galls me to this day":** Sumner Redstone, *A Passion to Win* (New York: Simon & Schuster, 2001).

195 **When she went over:** Irin Carmon, "Last Woman Standing," *New York*, July 8, 2019.

195 **"I hear you're upset":** Carmon, "Last Woman Standing."

197 **"Everyone at CBS":** Jessica Toonkel, "CBS' CEO Moonves Says Viacom Undervalued," Reuters, May 19, 2017.

197 **Ianniello also got:** Keach Hagey and Joe Flint, "Shari Redstone Alleges CBS CEO Threatened to Quit If Board Didn't Strip Redstones of Control," *Wall Street Journal*, May 29, 2018, www.wsj.com/articles /shari-redstone-alleges-cbs-ceo-threatened-to-quit-if-board-didnt-strip-redstones-of-control -1527608926.

197 **Minow was the top vote getter:** CBS Corporation, SEC Form 8-K: Current Report Pursuant to Section 13 or 15(d) of the Securities Exchange Act of 1934, May 9, 2017.

198 **Klieger assumed Sumner's:** "Robert Klieger Elected to CBS Board of Directors," Hueston Hennigan, July 28, 2017.

199 **"Is *The New York Times* about":** Kim Masters and Chris Gardner, "Harvey Weinstein Lawyers Battling N.Y. Times, New Yorker over Potentially Explosive Stories," *Hollywood Reporter*, October 4, 2017.

199 **over three hundred Oscar nominations:** Neda Ulaby, "Harvey Weinstein Expelled from the Academy of Motion Pictures Arts and Sciences," *NPR*, October 14, 2017.

199 **The *Times* article, by reporters:** Jodi Kantor and Megan Twohey, "Harvey Weinstein Paid Off Sexual Harassment Accusers for Decades," *New York Times*, October 5, 2017.

199 **Weinstein conceded he had:** Kantor and Twohey, "Harvey Weinstein Paid Off."

199 **The Weinstein Company board:** Andrew Limbong, "Weinstein Company Fires Co-founder Harvey Weinstein," *NPR Morning Edition*, October 9, 2017.

199 **The *New Yorker* article by Ronan:** Ronan Farrow, "From Aggressive Overtures to Sexual Assault: Harvey Weinstein's Accusers Tell Their Stories," *New Yorker*, October 10, 2017.

200 **"You can do anything":** David A. Farenthold, "Trump Recorded Having Extremely Lewd Conversation about Women in 2005," *Washington Post*, October 8, 2016, https://www.washingtonpost.com/politics/ trump-recorded-having-extremely-lewd-conversation-about-women-in-2005/2016/10/07/3b9ce776 -8cb4-11e6-bf8a-3d26847eeed4_story.html.

200 **Bill O'Reilly, the star:** Manuel Roig-Franzia and Ben Terris, "'The Mission Was to Bring Down Bill O'Reilly': The Final Days of a Fox News Superstar," *Washington Post*, April 21, 2017.

200 **Roger Ailes, the head:** Paul Farhi, "Roger Ailes Resigns as CEO of Fox News; Rupert Murdoch Will Be Acting CEO," *Washington Post*, July 21, 2016.

200 **he was eventually convicted:** Mamta Balkar, "Bill Cosby Convicted of Sexual Assault," *Financial Times*, April 26, 2018.

200 **the conviction was later overturned:** "Bill Cosby's Accusers React to His Overturned Conviction," *NBC Nightly News*, June 30, 2021.

200 **coined by sexual abuse awareness activist:** Mary Pflum, "A Year Ago, Alyssa Milano Started a Conversation about #MeToo. These Women Replied," *NBC News*, October 15, 2018.

200 **"If you've been sexually harassed":** Alyssa Milano (@Alyssa_Milano), "If you've been sexually harassed or assaulted write 'me too' as a reply to this," Twitter, October 15, 2017, 1:21 p.m., https://twitter.com /alyssa_milano/status/919659438700670976?lang=en.

200 **"the patron saint of actresses":** David Remnick, "Illeana Douglas Steps Forward, and Rachel Carson at Sea," *New Yorker Radio Hour*, September 14, 2018.

201 **"son and his brother-in-law":** Michael Schulman, "Ronan Farrow: The Youngest Old Guy in the Room," *New York Times*, October 25, 2013.

201 **And Farrow had backed his sister:** Ronan Farrow, *Catch and Kill: Lies, Spies, and a Conspiracy to Protect Predators* (New York: Little Brown, 2019).

201 **Farrow had graduated:** Schulman, "Ronan Farrow: The Youngest Old Guy."

201 **As a journalist, he'd looked:** Erik Wemple, "Here's the Cosby-Oriented Interview That Ronan Farrow Laments," *Washington Post*, May 11, 2016.

201 **and sexual abuse on campus:** Matt Lauer and Ronan Farrow, "It's Also a Dangerous Time Right Now at This Moment When It Comes to This Issue, Sexual Assault on Campus," *Today*, October 12, 2016.

Notes

201 **had initially been researching Weinstein:** Farrow, *Catch and Kill*, 403–5.

201 **her grandfather was:** "Illeana Douglas," *Contemporary Theatre, Film and Television*, vol. 70 (Farmington Hills, MI: Gale, 2006).

201 **Douglas met Moonves in 1996:** Ronan Farrow, "Les Moonves and CBS Face Allegations of Sexual Misconduct," *New Yorker*, July 27, 2018.

201 **After appearing in his films:** Remnick, "Illeana Douglas Steps Forward."

201 **In 1997 CBS had cast her:** Farrow, "Les Moonves and CBS Face Allegations."

202 **When she and Moonves met:** Farrow, "Les Moonves and CBS Face Allegations."

202 **"In a millisecond":** Farrow, "Les Moonves and CBS Face Allegations."

202 **disheveled and crying:** Farrow, "Les Moonves and CBS Face Allegations."

202 **who became tabloid fodder:** Chris Gardner, "Jeff Bezos Battle Begins to Rattle National Enquirer Insiders," *Hollywood Reporter*, February 13, 2019.

Season 3, Episode 1: "We All Did That"

205 **As Bing he'd published:** Richard Sandomir, "Gil Schwartz, CBS Spokesman with Alter Ego Who Mocked Corporate Misdeeds, Dies at 68," *New York Times*, May 8, 2020.

205 **"The ability to feel deep":** Stanley Bing, "If Tonya Did Business," *Esquire*, June 1, 1994.

205 **Moonves responded with a high:** Stephen Battaglio, "Gil Schwartz, Longtime CBS Communications Executive and Author, Dies," *Los Angeles Times*, May 3, 2020.

206 **He'd had to bat down:** George Rush and Joanna Molloy with Suzanne Rozdeba and Ben Widdicombe, "Moonves' Marriage May Get an Airing," *New York Daily News*, April 23, 2003.

206 **a veteran television producer:** Meg James and Richard Winton, "'This Has Been with Me the Whole Time': Accuser Talks to CBS Investigators in Moonves Inquiry," *Los Angeles Times*, September 13, 2018.

206 **"For those of you tuning in":** Ty Duffy, Ryan Glasspiegel, and Dan Reilly, "How Late-Night Hosts Discussed Louis C.K.," *Vulture*, November 10, 2017, https://variety.com/2017/tv/news/stephen-colbert-louis-ck-1202611764/.

206 **For Golden-Gottlieb, the revelation:** James and Winton, "'This Has Been with Me.'"

207 **There he parked:** Ronan Farrow, "As Leslie Moonves Negotiates His Exit from CBS, Six Women Raise New Assault and Harassment Claims," *New Yorker*, September 9, 2018.

207 **Two years later she was in:** Farrow, "As Leslie Moonves Negotiates."

207 **The next day he berated her:** Farrow, "As Leslie Moonves Negotiates."

209 **Berk preferred to work:** Ann O'Neill, "Blair Berk Makes Stars' Legal Scrapes Disappear," *CNN*, October 4, 2010.

209 **"The applicable statutes of limitation":** "L.A. Prosecutors Decline to Pursue Sex Abuse Charges against CBS CEO Moonves," *Reuters*, July 31, 2018.

210 **at Kopelson's urging:** Rachel Abrams and Edmund Lee, "Les Moonves Obstructed Investigation into Misconduct Claims, Report Says," *New York Times*, December 4, 2018.

210 **"the early-morning light filtering":** Anne L. Peters, "A Physician's Place in the #MeToo Movement," *Annals of Internal Medicine* 168, no. 9 (May 1, 2018): 676–77.

210 **Moonves grabbed her:** Peters, "A Physician's Place."

210 **that of a "monster":** Peters, "A Physician's Place."

210 **He left the room:** Abrams and Lee, "Les Moonves Obstructed Investigation."

210 **When Peters reported the incident:** Peters, "A Physician's Place."

211 **Kopelson had brushed aside:** James B. Stewart, "'Disaster for CBS Shareholders': Damning Report on Moonves Reveals Total Failure at Top," *New York Times*, December 4, 2018.

211 **"we all did that":** Stewart, "'Disaster for CBS Shareholders.'"

211 **The little-known Zimmerman:** John Koblin and Prashant S. Rao, "Hoda Kotb Named to Replace Matt Lauer as Co-anchor of NBC's 'Today,'" *New York Times*, January 2, 2018.

211 **Longtime director Linda Griego:** Amended Verified Complaint at 9, CBS Corporation, Gary L. Countryman et al. v. National Amusements Inc., Shari Redstone et al. (In the Court of Chancery of the State of Delaware) (Civil Action No. 2018-0342-AGB).

211 **Just two days later:** Irin Carmon and Amy Brittain, "Eight Women Say Charlie Rose Sexually Harassed Them—with Nudity, Groping and Lewd Calls," *Washington Post*, November 20, 2017.

212 **The behavior identified by the *Post*:** Carmon and Brittain, "Eight Women Say Charlie Rose."

212 **Rose conceded he "had behaved":** Carmon and Brittain, "Eight Women Say Charlie Rose."

212 **both CBS and PBS fired:** "CBS Fires Charlie Rose After Sexual Misconduct Allegations," *CBS News*, November 21, 2017.

212 **"I've enjoyed a friendship"**: Erik Wemple, "CBS News Makes Quick Work of Charlie Rose," *Washington Post*, November 21, 2017.

212 **Moonves was the keynote speaker**: Leslie Moonves, "Photos from Variety's 2017 Innovate Summit."

212 **NBC finally fired Matt Lauer**: David Folkenflik, "NBC Fires 'Today' Host Matt Lauer Following Complaint of 'Inappropriate Sexual Behavior,'" *All Things Considered*, NPR, November 29, 2017.

212 **Moonves said there was "no question"**: Tara Bitran, "Leslie Moonves Recently Called Sexual Harassment Revelations a 'Watershed Moment,'" *Variety*, July 27, 2018.

212 **He called it a "watershed moment"**: Tara Bitran, "Leslie Moonves Recently Called."

212 **A few weeks later, Moonves**: Cara Buckley, "Anita Hill to Lead Hollywood Commission on Sexual Harassment," *New York Times*, December 15, 2017.

Season 3, Episode 2: "If Bobbie Talks"

213 **With a perpetual tan**: James B. Stewart, Rachel Abrams, and Ellen Gabler, "'If Bobbie Talks, I'm Finished': How Les Moonves Tried to Silence an Accuser," *New York Times*, November 28, 2018.

213 **birthplace of the canned meat Spam**: Pamela Selbert, "Spam Turns 80," *Trailer Life*, July 2017, 9.

213 **He lived in a West Hollywood**: Meg James, "Talent Manager Marv Dauer Defends His Role in Dealings with Ex-CBS Boss Leslie Moonves," *Los Angeles Times*, December 5, 2018.

213 **Only thanks to a winning**: Stewart, Abrams, and Gabler, "If Bobbie Talks, I'm Finished.'"

214 **On November 28, 2017**: Stewart, Abrams, and Gabler, "If Bobbie Talks, I'm Finished.'"

214 **Moonves had just been named**: "The THR 100: Hollywood Reporter's Most Powerful People in Entertainment," *Hollywood Reporter*, June 21, 2017.

215 **Dauer's client LaRue**: David Robb, "'CSI: Miami' Co-star Eva LaRue Alleges Steven Seagal Sexually Harassed Her," *Deadline*, November 10, 2017.

216 **By then Lorimar and Warner**: Steve Coe, "Lorimar, WBTV Melded Under Moonves," *Broadcasting & Cable*, July 19, 1993.

217 **Dauer called Phillips**: Stewart, Abrams, and Gabler, "If Bobbie Talks, I'm Finished.'"

217 **"Absolutely not. Keep him away"**: Stewart, Abrams, and Gabler, "If Bobbie Talks, I'm Finished.'"

217 **She told Dauer she never**: Stewart, Abrams, and Gabler, "If Bobbie Talks, I'm Finished.'"

217 **Once, before a movie screening**: Stewart, Abrams, and Gabler, "If Bobbie Talks, I'm Finished.'"

217 **more time in a bathing suit**: Bruce Fretts, "Bobbie Phillips on 'The Cape,'" *Entertainment Weekly*, December 13, 1996.

218 **And recently she'd put a toe**: "Solar Eclipse Teaser Release at Dubai Film Festival on 8th," PR Newswire, December 24, 2016.

218 **Dauer said no one would believe**: Stewart, Abrams, and Gabler, "If Bobbie Talks, I'm Finished.'"

218 **"I think I'll be okay"**: Stewart, Abrams, and Gabler, "If Bobbie Talks, I'm Finished.'"

Season 3, Episode 3: "I Was a Good Guy"

219 **"always looking for work"**: James B. Stewart, Rachel Abrams, and Ellen Gabler, "'If Bobbie Talks, I'm Finished': How Les Moonves Tried to Silence an Accuser," *New York Times*, November 28, 2018.

219 **California governor Jerry Brown**: "As California Governor Declares State of Emergency, Experts Are Available to Discuss Insurance Implications of Wildfire," States News Service, December 6, 2017.

223 **CNBC had reported**: David Faber, "21st Century Fox Has Been Holding Talks to Sell Most of the Company to Disney: Sources," *CNBC*, November 6, 2017.

223 **including a revenue gain**: Trefis Team, "Key Takeaways from CBS' Q3 Earnings," *Forbes*, November 3, 2017.

224 **just surprised Wall Street**: Alexia Quadrani, "Viacom: Raise F2018 Estimates with Lower Expenses Offsetting Softer Advertising/Affiliate," JPMorgan Chase, November 16, 2017.

225 **The next day, December 19**: Alex Johnson and Stephanie Giambruno, "New Accuser Says She Confronted Leslie Moonves in Public after 'Gross' Encounter," *NBC News*, December 5, 2018.

225 **The tweet went unnoticed**: June Seley Kimmel as told to Kim Masters, "New Leslie Moonves Accuser Speaks Out: What I Told CBS Investigators," *Hollywood Reporter*, December 5, 2018.

Season 3, Episode 4: "I Feel Sick All the Time"

228 **Klieger showed up at Moonves's office**: Verified Complaint at 30, National Amusements Inc., NAI Entertainment Holdings LLC, and Shari Redstone v. Leslie "Les" Moonves, CBS Corporation et al. (In the Court of Chancery of the State of Delaware) (Civil Action No. 2018-0374).

229 **"That's not what she wants to hear"**: Verified Complaint at 30, National Amusements Inc., NAI Entertainment Holdings, and Redstone v. Moonves, CBS Corp. et al.

230 **Nonetheless, with Moonves seemingly:** Sharon Waxman and Matt Donnelly, "Viacom and CBS Are Seeking to Merge, Insiders Say (Exclusive)," *Wrap*, January 12, 2018.

230 **Oprah Winfrey became the first:** "Oprah's Light: Rocking the Golden Globes," ABC News transcript, January 8, 2018.

231 **She'd taken her screenplay:** Ronan Farrow, "Les Moonves and CBS Face Allegations of Sexual Misconduct," *New Yorker*, July 27, 2018.

232 **"What do you think you're doing?":** Farrow, "Les Moonves and CBS Face Allegations."

232 **She said she'd scream:** Farrow, "Les Moonves and CBS Face Allegations."

233 **All the keynote speakers:** Jessica Guynn, "CES Fail: No Women Keynote Addresses Triggers Backlash," *USA Today*, January 5, 2018.

235 **who gained national fame:** Dan Petrocelli, "O.J. Simpson 20th Anniversary: A Lawyer's Never-Revealed Details of a Sister's Tears, $33M Win," *Hollywood Reporter*, June 18, 2014.

235 **one of Los Angeles's most prominent:** "25 Attorneys Who Bring Big Business to Their Firms," *Los Angeles Business Journal*, March 4, 2002.

235 **Other lawyers from Weil Gotshal:** James B. Stewart, "Why CBS's Board Turned Against Leslie Moonves," *New York Times*, September 12, 2018.

236 **He said he understood she'd need:** Verified Complaint at 31, National Amusements Inc., NAI Entertainment Holdings, and Redstone v. Moonves, CBS Corp. et al.

237 **The grandson of a groundskeeper:** Nicholas Jasinski and Brian Price, "Richard Parsons Tried to Save Time Warner and AOL. Here's What He Thinks of Today's Deals," *Barron's*, July 30, 2021.

237 **then become a trusted adviser:** Irin Carmon, "Last Woman Standing," *New York*, July 8, 2019.

237 **He pointed out that naming:** Verified Complaint at 32, National Amusements Inc., NAI Entertainment Holdings, and Redstone v. Moonves, CBS Corp. et al.

237 **the board had nothing:** James B. Stewart, Rachel Abrams, and Ellen Gabler, "'If Bobbie Talks, I'm Finished': How Les Moonves Tried to Silence an Accuser," *New York Times*, November 28, 2018.

Season 3, Episode 5: "This Is Insanity"

240 **"evaluate a potential combination":** Shannon Bond, "Viacom Forms Committee to Explore CBS Merger," *Financial Times*, February 1, 2018.

240 **"has the potential to drive":** Emily Steel and Sydney Ember, "Reunited? CBS and Viacom Are Talking about It," *New York Times*, February 1, 2018.

240 **Moonves and Shari showed:** Michael J. de la Merced and John Koblin, "Two Moguls Vie for Power in CBS Fight," *New York Times*, May 18, 2018.

241 **It was about Donald Trump:** Ronan Farrow, "Donald Trump, a Playboy Model, and a System for Concealing Infidelity," *New Yorker*, February 16, 2018.

242 **There was more good news:** Meg James and Richard Winton, "CBS Investigators Interview Phyllis Golden-Gottlieb, Who Accused Leslie Moonves of Sexual Assault," *Los Angeles Times*, September 12, 2018.

242 **Peter Golden, the head of casting:** Daniel Holloway, "CBS Casting Chief Peter Golden Exits Following Allegations of Inappropriate Behavior (Exclusive)," *Variety*, May 3, 2019.

244 **Shari agreed to the other three:** Verified Complaint at 33, National Amusements Inc., NAI Entertainment Holdings LLC, and Shari Redstone v. Leslie "Les" Moonves, CBS Corporation et al. (In the Court of Chancery of the State of Delaware) (Civil Action No. 2018-0374).

244 **Moonves asked if she was:** Verified Complaint at 34, National Amusements Inc., NAI Entertainment Holdings, and Redstone v. Moonves, CBS Corp. et al.

244 **about $1 billion less:** Ali Haseeb, "Viacom Seeks Higher Valuation from CBS," SNL Kagan Media & Communications Report, April 9, 2018.

244 **But CBS could argue:** Joe Flint, "CBS Submits Initial Bid for Viacom at Price Below Market Value," *Wall Street Journal*, April 3, 2018.

244 **The offer was also contingent:** Verified Complaint at 34, National Amusements Inc., NAI Entertainment Holdings, and Redstone v. Moonves, CBS Corp. et al.

245 **She felt she'd been blindsided:** Verified Complaint at 36, National Amusements Inc., NAI Entertainment Holdings, and Redstone v. Moonves, CBS Corp. et al.

245 **Not only that, but under:** Trey Williams and Sean Burch, "Shari Redstone v. Les Moonves: A Timeline of the Battle for CBS," *Wrap*, May 29, 2018.

245 **But the payout in the event:** Exhibit 10(a), Execution Copy, CBS Corporation to Joseph Ianniello, July 1, 2017, www.sec.gov/Archives/edgar/data/813828/000081382817000048/cbs_ex10a-093017.htm.

246 **On March 29, Anthony Ambrosio:** Verified Complaint at 34, National Amusements Inc., NAI Entertainment Holdings, and Redstone v. Moonves, CBS Corp. et al.

246 **This issue was critically important:** Verified Complaint at 19–20, National Amusements Inc., NAI Entertainment Holdings, and Redstone v. Moonves, CBS Corp. et al.

246 **In practical terms, that meant:** Exhibit 10(a), Execution Copy, CBS Corporation to Leslie Moonves, May 19, 2017, 22, www.sec.gov/Archives/edgar/data/813828/000081382817000048/cbs_ex10a-09 3017.htm.

Season 3, Episode 6: "Pencils Down"

250 **"I am a bit different":** Anne L. Peters, "A Physician's Place in the #MeToo Movement," *Annals of Internal Medicine* 168, no. 9 (May 1, 2018): 676–77.

250 **"I had no idea":** Peters, "A Physician's Place."

250 **The next day, Peters continued:** Peters, "A Physician's Place."

250 **Peters said she never:** Peters, "A Physician's Place."

251 **The committee met many times:** Verified Complaint at 21, National Amusements Inc., NAI Entertainment Holdings LLC, and Shari Redstone v. Leslie "Les" Moonves, CBS Corporation et al. (In the Court of Chancery of the State of Delaware) (Civil Action No. 2018-0342-AGB).

252 **Moonves insisted his job:** Keach Hagey and Joe Flint, "Once Allies, Two Media Chiefs Go to War over the Future of CBS," *Wall Street Journal*, May 28, 2018.

253 **The special committees of both:** Verified Complaint at 38, NAI v. CBS (In the Court of Chancery of the State of Delaware) (Civil Action No. 2018-0374).

253 **She and Parsons met:** Verified Complaint at 35, NAI v. CBS.

253 **But she didn't think:** Verified Complaint at 36, NAI v. CBS.

253 **She felt his exit:** Verified Complaint at 36, NAI v. CBS.

253 **The bottom line was Shari:** Verified Complaint at 35, NAI v. CBS.

254 **But a few days later:** Verified Complaint at 5, NAI v. CBS.

254 **Moonves had no intention of allowing:** First Amended Verified Class Action Complaint at 3–4, In re: Viacom Inc. Stockholders C.A. (In the Court of Chancery of the State of Delaware) (Civil Action No. 2019-0948-JRS).

254 **The first Martha Minow:** First Amended Verified Class Action Complaint at 34, In re: Viacom Inc. Stockholders C.A.

254 **Lipton's proposal for a special dividend:** Meg James and Samantha Masunaga, "CBS Chooses 'Nuclear Option' against Shari Redstone: It Sues to Thwart Viacom Merger," *Los Angeles Times*, May 14, 2018.

255 **enough to give class A shareholders:** First Amended Verified Class Action Complaint at 34, In re: Viacom Inc. Stockholders C.A.

255 **The move, if successful:** James and Masunaga, "CBS Chooses 'Nuclear Option.'"

255 **Klieger reached out to Gordon:** Hagey and Flint, "Once Allies, Two Media Chiefs."

Season 3, Episode 7: "All Out War"

259 **It voted unanimously:** "CBS Board of Directors Declares Dividend to Protect and Give Voting Power to Stockholders," PR Newswire, May 17, 2018.

259 **But, convinced that Shari:** "CBS Board of Directors Declares."

260 **"Mattresses tomorrow am":** Gene Maddaus, "Leslie Moonves Quoted 'The Godfather' to Prepare for Redstone Battle," *Variety*, August 21, 2018.

Season 4, Episode 1: A "Blatant Abuse of Power"

265 **with many references to CBS:** James Fontanella-Khan and Sujeet Indap, "CBS Sues Redstones in Attempt to Block Merger with Viacom," *Financial Times*, May 14, 2018.

265 **CBS cited several ways:** Oral Argument on Plaintiffs' Motion for a Temporary Restraining Order at 2, NAI v. CBS (In the Court of Chancery of the State of Delaware) (Civil Action No. 2018-0342-AGB).

265 **she was plotting to replace:** Oral Argument on Plaintiffs' Motion for a Temporary Restraining Order at 21, NAI v. CBS.

265 **In a statement, National Amusements:** Chris Ariens, "CBS Is Suing Majority Owners Sumner and Shari Redstone," *Adweek* (online), May 14, 2018.

267 **Shari's "instructions to us were clear":** Jenna Greene, "Litigators of the Week: In 'Nuclear' Showdown over CBS, Cleary's Kotler and Hou on Top," *American Lawyer*, September 14, 2018.

267 **With fourteen board members:** Keach Hagey and Joe Flint, "Shari Redstone Moves to Defend Family's Voting Power over CBS," *Wall Street Journal*, May 16, 2018.

268 **"I've never seen anything quite like":** Oral Argument on Plaintiffs' Motion for a Temporary Restraining Order at 89, NAI v. CBS.

268 **the curtain rose at New York's:** Lisa de Moraes, "CBS Upfront Presentation: Live Blog," *Deadline*, May 16, 2018.

269 **A wave of laughter:** John Koblin and Sapna Maheshwari, "CBS Puts on a Happy Face for Ad Buyers amid Off-Stage Tensions," *New York Times*, May 17, 2018.

269 **"For years I told you":** de Moraes, "CBS Upfront Presentation."

269 **The chancellor ruled that CBS:** Court's Ruling at 2, CBS Corporation et al. v. NAI et al.

270 **The room was also packed:** Minutes of a Special Meeting of the Board of Directors of CBS Corporation, May 17, 2018, 1.

270 **After a few preliminaries:** Minutes of a Special Meeting, 2.

270 **"not in the best interest":** Minutes of a Special Meeting, 2.

271 **"concerned" about how:** Minutes of a Special Meeting, 3.

271 **He also cited:** Minutes of a Special Meeting, 3.

271 **"described for the Board":** Minutes of a Special Meeting, 3–4.

272 **"Ms. Redstone read a statement":** Minutes of a Special Meeting, 5.

272 **"Although there is a lot more":** Minutes of a Special Meeting, 5.

272 **When Klieger's turn came:** Minutes of a Special Meeting, 6–7.

273 **Gordon promptly said:** Minutes of a Special Meeting, 7.

273 **She talked about Shari's adverse:** Minutes of a Special Meeting, 7.

273 **The resolution was "duly passed":** Minutes of a Special Meeting, 7.

Season 4, Episode 2: "I Was Never a Predator"

275 **The suit argued that:** Verified Complaint at 4, National Amusements Inc., NAI Entertainment Holdings LLC, and Shari Redstone v. Leslie "Les" Moonves, CBS Corporation et al. (In the Court of Chancery of the State of Delaware) (Civil Action No. 2018-0374).

275 **The suit stressed that:** Verified Complaint at 4, National Amusements Inc., NAI Entertainment Holdings, and Redstone v. Moonves, CBS Corp. et al.

275 **The suit took specific aim:** Verified Complaint at 8, National Amusements Inc., NAI Entertainment Holdings, and Redstone v. Moonves, CBS Corp. et al.

276 **the creator of *Sabrina, the Teenage Witch:*** Lisa de Moraes, "UTA Casts Its Spell on Scovell," *Hollywood Reporter*, July 31, 1997.

276 **she'd recently published a book:** Melena Ryzik, "Not-So-Funny Business," *New York Times Book Review*, March 25, 2018.

276 **had famously blown the whistle:** Nell Scovell, "Letterman and Me," *Vanity Fair*, October 27, 2009.

276 **She'd contributed to *The New Yorker:*** Nell Scovell, "Robert Benchley's Legacy in an Era of Fraught Comedy," *New Yorker*, December 26, 2019.

278 **They wrote to CBS's chief:** EX-10 (A): Settlement and Release Agreement in the Case of Moonves, by His Execution and Delivery of the Moonves Settlement at 34.

279 **The Proskauer law firm was examining:** "CBS Board of Directors Takes Over Investigation into CBS News That Was to Conclude This Month," *CBS News*, August 7, 2018.

280 **"I was never a predator":** James B. Stewart, Rachel Abrams, and Ellen Gabler, "'If Bobbie Talks, I'm Finished': How Les Moonves Tried to Silence an Accuser," *New York Times*, November 28, 2018.

281 **It was a relatively small part:** Stewart, Abrams, and Gabler, "'If Bobbie Talks, I'm Finished'"

Season 4, Episode 3: "What the Hell Are You Doing?"

285 **Marvin was now touring:** Steve Aaronson, "Interview: Mike Marvin of the Kingston Trio," *WDIY*, October 29, 2021.

285 **he was a cousin:** Aaronson, "Interview: Mike Marvin."

286 **Rosetti, now working:** Hannah Miet, "Brokerage Founder Credits Star for Guiding Career," *Los Angeles Business Journal*, December 7, 2015.

291 **While in Austin:** James B. Stewart, Rachel Abrams, and Ellen Gabler, "'If Bobbie Talks, I'm Finished': How Les Moonves Tried to Silence an Accuser," *New York Times*, November 28, 2018.

291 **"They're coming out with":** Stewart, Abrams, and Gabler, "'If Bobbie Talks, I'm Finished.'"

292 **Golden sweetened the offer:** Stewart, Abrams, and Gabler, "'If Bobbie Talks, I'm Finished.'"

Notes

Season 4, Episode 4: "Let's Not Get Ahead of Ourselves"

293 **At 8:45 a.m. on Friday:** Kim Masters, "Leslie Moonves Accused of Sexual Misconduct in Ronan Farrow Exposé," *Hollywood Reporter*, July 27, 2018.

293 **"Six women who had professional dealings":** Ronan Farrow, "Les Moonves and CBS Face Allegations of Sexual Misconduct," *New Yorker*, July 27, 2018.

295 **"the Company's very public":** "CBS Independent Directors Respond to Report of Misconduct by CEO Les Moonves," *CBS News*, July 27, 2018.

295 **Two of CBS's highest-ranking:** Nellie Andreeva, "CBS' Ad Sales Chief Jo Ann Ross & Head of Daytime Angelica McDaniel Speak in Support of Les Moonves after Allegations," *Deadline*, July 27, 2018.

295 **"I have known my husband":** Julie Chen Moonves (@JCMoonves), "I have known my husband, Leslie Moonves, since the late '90s, and I have been married to him for almost 14 years. Leslie is a good man and a loving father, devoted husband and inspiring corporate . . . ," Twitter, July 27, 2018, 3:14 p.m., https://twitter.com/JCMoonves/status/1022968567728427012.

296 **"Some of you may be aware":** Rebecca Rubin, "Julie Chen Says She 'Stands By' Statement Supporting Leslie Moonves on 'The Talk,'" *Variety*, July 30, 2018.

296 **Moonves's college alma mater:** "Bucknell Drops Alum Les Moonves from Website in Wake of Allegations," Associated Press, July 30, 2018.

296 **The University of Southern California followed:** Tara Bitran, "USC School of Cinematic Arts Suspends Leslie Moonves from Board," *Variety*, August 1, 2018.

296 **Moonves quietly resigned:** Katie Kilkenny, "Leslie Moonves Steps Down from Board of Anita Hill–Led Anti–Sexual Harassment Commission," *Hollywood Reporter*, August 1, 2018.

300 **"We are going to stay":** James B. Stewart, "Revelation of Moonves's Deceit Was Last Straw for CBS Board," *New York Times*, September 13, 2018.

301 **Arnold Kopelson was especially ardent:** Stewart, "Revelation of Moonves's Deceit."

301 **CBS issued a statement:** Bill Hutchinson, "CBS Board Takes No Immediate Action on Les Moonves as Network Launches Investigation of Sexual Misconduct," *ABC News*, July 30, 2018.

301 **"It's shortsighted and cowardly":** Edmund Lee, "Les Moonves Stays as CBS C.E.O. While Its Board Plans an Investigation," *New York Times*, July 30, 2018.

301 **But unlike Weinstein, Matt Lauer:** Edmund Lee, "Leslie Moonves Speaks on CBS Earnings Call but Not about Harassment Allegations," *New York Times*, August 2, 2018.

302 **The board named:** Joe Flint and Keach Hagey, "CBS to Appoint Outside Law Firm to Handle Probe into Moonves Allegations," *Wall Street Journal*, July 30, 2018.

302 **Two members would be independent:** Katie Kilkenny, "CBS Hires Multiple Law Firms to Investigate Claims against Leslie Moonves," *Hollywood Reporter*, August 1, 2018.

Season 4, Episode 5: "He Wants to Destroy Me"

303 **The Shari-NAI faction settled:** Eriq Gardner, "Leslie Moonves Probe 'May Prove to Be a Tame Investigation,'" *Hollywood Reporter*, August 8, 2018.

304 **CBS made the announcement:** Edmund Lee, "Leslie Moonves Speaks on CBS Earnings Call but Not about Harassment Allegations," *New York Times*, August 2, 2018.

304 **On Thursday Moonves appeared:** Lee, "Leslie Moonves Speaks."

304 **Still, "it was astonishing":** David Folkenflik, "CEO Les Moonves Speaks during First CBS Earnings Call Since Allegations Broke," *NPR*, August 2, 2018.

308 **He pleaded with Dauer:** James B. Stewart, Rachel Abrams, and Ellen Gabler, "'If Bobbie Talks, I'm Finished': How Les Moonves Tried to Silence an Accuser," *New York Times*, November 28, 2018.

Season 4, Episode 7: "A Once-Unfathomable Outcome"

320 **The *Los Angeles Times* had reported:** Meg James and Richard Winton, "CBS Chief Talks Finances, Is Silent on Assault Claims," *Los Angeles Times*, August 3, 2018.

320 **The story, by reporters:** James and Winton, "CBS Chief Talks Finances."

323 **CBS wouldn't try:** CBS Corporation, SEC Form 8-K: Current Report Pursuant to Section 13 or 15(d) of the Securities Exchange Act of 1934, September 9, 2018, 2.

323 **Shari agreed that she wouldn't:** CBS Corporation, SEC Form 8-K, 3.

323 **She'd also withdraw:** CBS Corporation, SEC Form 8-K, 3.

327 **Farrow's *New Yorker* article went:** Ronan Farrow, "As Leslie Moonves Negotiates His Exit from CBS, Six Women Raise New Assault and Harassment Claims," *New Yorker*, September 9, 2018.

Notes

327 **"The appalling accusations":** Farrow, "As Leslie Moonves Negotiates."

328 **Cohan quoted extensively:** William D. Cohan, "Les Moonves Admits to Unwanted Kissing of His Doctor 19 Years Ago," *Vanity Fair*, September 9, 2018.

328 **"Moonves is finished":** Cohan, "Les Moonves Admits."

328 **CBS would pay $20 million:** CBS Corporation, SEC Form 8-K, 3.

Epilogue

331 **Protesters gathered outside:** Dade Hayes and Dawn C. Chmielewski, "CBS Shareholders Elect Strauss Zelnick, 10 Other Board Members in Drama-Free Annual Meeting," *Deadline*, December 11, 2018.

331 **As one of its first steps:** James B. Stewart, "Threats and Deception: Why CBS's Board Turned Against Leslie Moonves," *New York Times*, September 12, 2018.

331 **A deal was announced:** Mike Reynolds, "CBS, Viacom to Merge in All-Stock Deal," SNL Kagan Media and Communications Report, August 21, 2019.

331 **The new company was named:** Meg James, "CBS and Viacom Are Together Again," *Los Angeles Times*, December 4, 2019.

331 **Rather than report to Bakish:** Memorandum Opinion, September 17, 2020, at 55, In re: CBS Corporation Stockholder Class Action and Derivative Litigation (In the Court of Chancery of the State of Delaware) (Civil Action No. 2020-0111-JRS).

332 **CBS paid him nearly:** CBS Corporation, Schedule 14A: Proxy Statement Pursuant to Section 14(a) of the Securities Exchange Act of 1934, April 2019; ViacomCBS Inc., SEC Form 10-Q: Quarterly Report Pursuant to Section 13 or 15(d) of the Securities Exchange Act of 1934, June 2020.

332 **"The president of a studio":** Phyllis Gottlieb, "Tears for the Teacher," *Inner City Blues*, June 2007.

333 **After more than two years:** Alex Weprin, "Les Moonves Settles with ViacomCBS over Departure," *Hollywood Reporter*, May 14, 2021.

333 **In a surprising twist:** Kathryn Rubino, "Covington Reportedly Paying Settlement over Leak of Les Moonves Sexual Misconduct Report," *Above the Law*, May 18, 2021.

333 **In 2018 a judge dismissed:** Civil Minutes—General at 1, Manuela Herzer v. Shari Redstone, Tyler Korff et al. (United States District Court Central District of California) (Case No. 17-CV-07545 PSG(KSx)).

333 **Herzer agreed to repay:** Meg James, "Sumner Redstone and Family Settle Legal Dispute with His Ex-companion Manuela Herzer," *Los Angeles Times*, January 8, 2019.

334 **litany of lawsuits:** Los Angeles Superior Court docket, George M. Pilgrim.

335 **For several seasons after:** Joe Flint, "Sydney Holland, Ex-girlfriend of Sumner Redstone, May Join Cast of 'Real Housewives,'" *Wall Street Journal*, May 31, 2016.

335 **after selling a Mulholland Estates:** James McClain, "Sydney Holland Lists West Hollywood Contemporary," *Dirt*, October 24, 2019.

335 **she listed her 6,700-square-foot:** Lily Tinoco, "Philanthropist, Entrepreneur Sydney Holland Lists Riviera Home," *Palisadian-Post*, September 10, 2020.

335 **"There were needles":** Gary Baum, "The Hollywood Publicist," *The Hollywood Reporter*, February 7, 2022.

335 **home in Rancho Santa Fe:** "Julie de Libran Paris Showing and Dinner Held in Rancho Santa Fe," *Rancho Santa Fe Review*, January 15, 2022.

336 **"renowned philanthropist":** Institute of the Environment and Sustainability, UCLA, board of advisors biography page, https://www.ioes.ucla.edu/person/sydney-holland.

336 **She was turned down:** Complaint at 3, Manuela Herzer v. First Republic Bank and Jared Barnes (Superior Court of the State of California for the County of Los Angeles–Santa Monica Courthouse) (West District) (Case No. 20SMCV01997).

337 **Although Dauer had believed:** James B. Stewart, Rachel Abrams, and Ellen Gabler, "'If Bobbie Talks, I'm Finished': How Les Moonves Tried to Silence an Accuser," *New York Times*, November 28, 2018.

338 **Like many departing studio heads:** Rachel Abrams and Edmund Lee, "Les Moonves, Fired by CBS, Sets Up Shop in Hollywood," *New York Times*, August 2, 2019.

339 **Having emerged on top:** "Forbes Releases 38th Annual Forbes 400 Ranking of the Richest Americans," *Forbes*, October 2, 2019.

339 **A former Viacom employee:** Jessica Toonkel, "ViacomCBS Probed Sexual Misconduct Allegation against CEO Bob Bakish," *The Information*, September 24, 2020.

339 **The board subsequently issued:** Phoebe Magdirila, "ViacomCBS Clears CEO in Sexual Misconduct Probe," SNL Kagan Media & Communications Report, September 25, 2020.

340 **In June 2021 Bakish announced:** Georg Szalai, "Pluto TV Ad Revenue to Exceed $1B in 2022, Says ViacomCBS CEO," *Hollywood Reporter*, June 7, 2021.

382

Notes

341 **In 2019 CBS named:** David Folkenflik, "CBS Names Legendary Producer Susan Zirinsky as Head of News," *NPR*, January 7, 2019.

341 **She stepped down in 2021:** "CBS Names Two New Presidents of Unified News and Television Division," *CBS News*, May 3, 2021.

341 **ViacomCBS was far behind:** The market capitalization of Paramount Global was $14.75 billion on June 16, 2022, as reported on CNBC.com. The market caps of its rivals Amazon, Netflix, and Disney are also from CNBC.com as of June 16, 2022.

341 **The combined market capitalization:** Irina Ivanova, "CBS and Viacom Agree to $30 Billion Media Merger," *CBS News*, August 13, 2019.

342 **Since the merger:** Josh Kosman and Alexandra Steigrad, "ViacomCBS Waiting for Other Suitors," *New York Post*, August 10, 2021.

342 **Rather than megadeals:** Kosman and Steigrad, "ViacomCBS Waiting for Other Suitors."

343 **"His withered hand":** Peter Bart, "Viacom and CBS Teeter toward Merger with Their Master Dealmaker on the Sidelines," *Deadline*, July 11, 2019.

343 **National Amusements announced his death:** "Statement from National Amusements," BusinessWire, August 12, 2020.

INDEX

Index

Index

Index

Index